Palgrave Studies in Prisons and Penolo

This is a unique and innovative series,
to prison scholarship. At a historical pc
reached an all-time high, the series see.
sequences of incarceration and related forms of punishment. Palgrave Studies
in Prisons and Penology provides an important forum for burgeoning prison research across the world.

Series Editors:

YVONNE JEWKES is Professor of Criminology, Leicester University, UK. He
has authored numerous papers on the subject and is editor of the *Handbook on
Prisons*.

BEN CREWE is Deputy Director of the Prisons Research Centre at the Institute of
Criminology, University of Cambridge, UK and editor of *The Prisoner*.

THOMAS UGELVIK is Senior Research Fellow in the Department of Criminology
at the University of Oslo, Norway and editor of *Penal Exceptionalism? Nordic Prison
Policy and Practice*.

Advisory Board:

Anna Eriksson, Monash University, Australia
Andrew M. Jefferson, Rehabilitation and Research Centre for Torture Victims,
Denmark
Shadd Maruna, Queen's University Belfast, UK
Jonathan Simon, UC Berkeley, California, US
Michael Welch, Rutgers University, New Jersey, US

Titles include

Vincenzo Ruggiero, Mick Ryan
PUNISHMENT IN EUROPE
A Critical Anatomy of Penal Systems

Palgrave Studies in Prisons and Penology
Series Standing Order ISBN 978–1–137–27090–0 (hardback)

You can receive future titles in this series as they are published by placing a standing order.
Please contact your bookseller or, in case of difficulty, write to us at the address below with
your name and address, the title of the series and the ISBNs quoted above.

Customer Services Department, Macmillan Distribution Ltd, Houndmills, Basingstoke,
Hampshire RG21 6XS, England

Also by Vincenzo Ruggiero

EURODRUGS (*with N. South*)

WESTERN EUROPEAN PENAL SYSTEMS: A Critical Anatomy (*co-edited with Mick Ryan and Joe Sim*)

ORGANISED AND CORPORATE CRIME IN EUROPE

THE NEW EUROPEAN CRIMINOLOGY (*with N. South and I. Taylor*)

CRIME AND MARKETS

MOVEMENTS IN THE CITY

CRIME IN LITERATURE: Sociology of Deviance and Fiction

UNDERSTANDING POLITICAL VIOLENCE

SOCIAL MOVEMENTS: A Reader (*with N. Montagna*)

PENAL ABOLITIONISM

CORRUPTION AND ORGANISED CRIME IN EUROPE (*with P. Gounev*)

THE CRIMES OF THE ECONOMY

Also by Mick Ryan

LOBBYING FROM BELOW: Inquest in Defence of Civil Liberties

POLICY NETWORKS IN CRIMINAL JUSTICE (*co-edited with S. Savage and D. S. Wall*)

PRIVATISATION AND THE PENAL SYSTEM: The American Experience and the Debate in Britain (*with Tony Ward*)

PENAL POLICY AND POLITICAL CULTURE IN ENGLAND AND WALES

THE ACCEPTABLE PRESSURE GROUP: A Case Study of the Howard League and Radical Alternatives to Prison

THE POLITICS OF PENAL REFORM

WESTERN EUROPEAN PENAL SYSTEMS: A Critical Anatomy (*co-edited with Vincenzo Ruggiero and Joe Sim*)

Punishment in Europe

A Critical Anatomy of Penal Systems

Edited by

Vincenzo Ruggiero
Professor of Sociology, University of Middlesex

and

Mick Ryan
Emeritus Professor, Law and Criminology, University of Greenwich

palgrave
macmillan

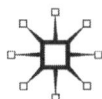

First published 2013 by
PALGRAVE MACMILLAN

Palgrave Macmillan in the UK is an imprint of Macmillan Publishers Limited,
registered in England, company number 785998, of Houndmills, Basingstoke,
Hampshire RG21 6XS.

Palgrave Macmillan in the US is a division of St Martin's Press LLC,
175 Fifth Avenue, New York, NY 10010.

Palgrave Macmillan is the global academic imprint of the above companies
and has companies and representatives throughout the world.

Palgrave® and Macmillan® are registered trademarks in the United States,
the United Kingdom, Europe and other countries.

ISBN 978-1-349-43996-6   ISBN 978-1-137-02821-1 (eBook)
DOI 10.1057/9781137028211

A catalogue record for this book is available from the British Library.

A catalog record for this book is available from the Library of Congress.

Contents

List of Tables   vii

List of Figures   ix

Preface   x

Acknowledgements   xii

Notes on Contributors   xiii

1   Introduction   1
        Mick Ryan

2   Regression to the Mean: Punishment in the Netherlands   9
        Miranda Boone and René van Swaaningen

3   Punishment in Sweden: A Changing Penal Landscape   33
        Hanns von Hofer and Henrik Tham

4   Punishment as Politics: The Penal System in England
        and Wales   58
        Emma Bell

5   The Irish Penal System: Pragmatism, Neglect and the
        Effects of Austerity   86
        Mary Rogan

6   The French Criminal Justice System   111
        Philippe Robert

7   Contradictions in German Penal Practices: The Long Goodbye
        from the Rehabilitation Principle   132
        Bernd Dollinger and Andrea Kretschmann

8   The Russian Penal System   157
        Laura Piacentini

9   Poland: The Political Legacy and Penal Practice   183
        Monika Płatek

10 Soft and Harsh Penalties in Bulgaria   206
    Philip Gounev

11 Italy: Between Amnesties and Emergencies   226
    Patrizio Gonnella

12 The Spanish Penal and Penitentiary System: From the
    Re-Socialising Objective to the Internal Governance of
    Prison   245
    Mónica Aranda Ocaña and Iñaki Rivera Beiras

13 Greece: Prisons Are Bad but Necessary (and Expanding),
    Policies Are Necessary but Bad (and Declining)   263
    Vassilis Karydis and Nikolaos K. Koulouris

14 Conclusion   287
    Vincenzo Ruggiero

Index   297

COOK WITH THE UK'S
#1 RECIPE BOX

QUICK & EASY

CALORIE SMART

FAMILY FRIENDLY

PREMIUM

VEGGIE

DESSERT

60% OFF 1ST BOX
+ 25% OFF FOR 2 MONTHS

Scan the QR code to receive your
free dessert for life!

OR

1. Go to hellofresh.co.uk/freeforlife
2. Apply your voucher code
3. Select your recipes and free dessert!

HF8601887

HF940507

The offer above is for 12 months+ lapsed users only, alternatively
use the following code to get 30% off your next 2 boxes:

ENJOY FREE GÜ DESSERTS
EVERY WEEK FOR LIFE

HELLO FRESH

HELLO EASY DINNERS!

We deliver simple recipes and fresh ingredients, so you don't have to spend valuable time shopping and planning.

60% OFF YOUR FIRST BOX
+ 25% OFF FOR 2 MONTHS

+ FREE DESSERT FOR LIFE!

Free next day delivery when you order before noon

First box ~~£3.25~~ **£1.30** per serving*

Flexible subscription: pause, skip or cancel anytime

Cook in as little as 15 minutes

DISCOVER MORE NOW!

GET STARTED OR TRY US AGAIN

HELLO FRESH

List of Tables

3.1 Number of prison inmates in Sweden, 1 October 1997, 2004 and 2011 respectively, by offence type   34

3.2 Social and economic backgrounds of prisoners and general population, 1997   40

3.3 Expansion and contraction of penal law 1968–2012 and type of government   47

6.1 Sanctions (minor offences excluded)   111

6.2 Distribution of different sanctions and measures according to country   112

6.3 Detention rate per 100,000 of the total population on 1 September   112

6.4 Classification of criminal cases by the public prosecutor, 2010   113

6.5 Prisoners on 1 January, according to offence, 1980–2010   114

6.6 Recorded crime and people charged, European France, 2011   116

6.7 Sentenced prisoners (final sentence) on 1 September 2010 by main offence   118

6.8 The French criminal justice system compared to that of the rest of Europe   125

8.1 Types of penal facilities in Russia   163

8.2 Russia's prison population, 1993–2009   165

10.1 Types of penal sanctions imposed, 2007–2011   211

10.2 Organised crime related offences and penalties   215

10.3 Number and types of prosecuted high profile cases in 2011   217

10.4 Crime suspects and homicide rate per 100,000 population   219

12.1 General secretariat of penitentiary institutions (Spain)   253

12.2 General direction of penitentiary services (Catalonia)   254

12.3 Distribution of imprisoned population by sex   256

12.4 Distribution of non-national imprisoned population   256

12.5 Imprisoned population by age groups   257

12.6 Criminal typology   257

12.7 Number of inmates, number of prison officers, that of other prison staff, and the staff–prisoner ratio, 2001–2010   258

13.1 Imprisonment rate per 100,000 inhabitants   272

13.2 Total number of inmates   273

13.3   Crimes recorded by the police in Greece, 2002–2008
       (figures include penal code offences)   279
13.4   General statistical table for inmates and
       sentences, 2003–2012   280

List of Figures

3.1   Number of prisoners, including remand prisoners,
per 100,000 population, 1921–2011   33

3.2   Sum of years meted out by the courts of first instance in
drug cases, 1973–2011   35

3.3   Aggregate number of years of imprisonment meted out
by courts of first instance in cases involving violence and
sex crimes, 1973–2011   36

4.1   Average annual prison population   60

4.2   Sentences handed down by all Criminal Courts in
England and Wales in 2011   61

5.1   Average daily prison population, 1922–2012   87

5.2   Committal rate, 2000–2011   87

5.3   Types of crimes for which sentences were given in 2011   88

5.4   Offences with sentences in the five to ten-year range   89

5.5   Offences with sentences in the ten years and more range   90

6.1   Police statistics of cases handed over to the public
prosecutor, 1950–2009   115

10.1   Number of inmates in prisons and pre-trial
detention facilities   209

10.2   Duration and frequency of custodial sentences   210

12.1   Imprisoned population per 100,000 inhabitants   252

12.2   Annual crime rates   255

Preface

It was over 20 years ago that we began working, with Joe Sim, to put together a collection on European penal systems (*European Penal Systems: A Critical Anatomy*, 1995). We were all aware, in the aftermath of the collapse of the Berlin Wall, of the great political change that we were living through, and were therefore tempted to include some of the newly independent Eastern Bloc states in our collection. However, it soon became clear that the transition period to even what President Putin has recently called "managed democracies" was going to be a long and difficult one, and so we went ahead, limiting our collection to western European systems, and even more narrowly, to those in the European Union.

We have always regretted this – how shall we put it? – confirmation of the brutal division of Europe with which we had all grown up since 1945. This collection enables us to make a timid start in overcoming this omission – a chance to catch up with history, so to speak. However, our readers will find that there is still a long way to go before a comparison between west and east Europe can be constructively made, and that differences between eastern countries themselves are, if anything, greater than between themselves and countries further west.

We believed such a collection, albeit a limited one, was needed in 1995 because evidence at the time suggested that both academic criminologists and criminal practitioners in the UK were ill-informed about penal regimes in neighbouring western European countries, including the more exclusive European Union. Instead, their reference point was more likely to be the USA than Europe, so inviting us to consider, for example, the advantages of private prisons or the potential of electronic tagging. As a result, we knew more about punishment in America than in Germany, France, Sweden, Italy or Spain.

This Anglo-Saxon bias is still with us, but perhaps it has diminished in stature. Explaining this change is far from easy. The fact that over 20 years later we now pay more attention to penal practice in other countries is partly due to the growing number of academic courses in comparative penal systems. While we see some virtues in this comparative work, and discuss our position in this respect in our introduction and conclusion, we have encouraged our contributors, instead, to conduct their enquiries into national penal systems. We hope this volume will ultimately persuade the public to engage with different ways of thinking about delivering punishment in European societies, inside or outside the European Union, which challenge taken-for-granted categories and create new alliances in defence of the excluded and the socially disadvantaged, caught up in Europe's expanding penal networks. We invited contributors who were sympathetic to this wider political purpose.

We are extremely grateful to Emma Bell for her perceptive translation of Philippe Robert's chapter on France. Philippe came to this project late and, using his considerable expertise, chose to interpret the brief we gave him in a highly individual way. We thank him for generously coming to our rescue.

Acknowledgements

Vincenzo Ruggiero would like to thank all those who, over the years, have discussed with him issues relating to penal systems, particularly the regular and occasional scholars, colleagues, comrades and friends who attend the annual conference of the European Group for the Study of Deviance and Social Control. Special thanks go to Mick Ryan, whose original idea it was to engage me in this joint effort after a similar effort resulted in the publication of a book on the same topic in 1995. Finally, Lucia Ruggiero, from her European observatory located in Madrid, gave me invaluable advice as to how to bring the project to fruition.

Mick Ryan would like to thank the University of Greenwich (London) for extending his role as Emeritus Professor in Greenwich Law School, and for the support and interest of his criminology colleagues in this project, particularly Dr Richard Wild and Dr Maria Kaspersson. The former contributed his considerable language skills, and straightened out several technical hitches.

More directly, the work of Rebecca Roberts and Helen Mills at the Centre for Criminal Justice Studies in London into how penal policy is made, and how such research might be used to facilitate the creation of more progressive penal policies, has reinforced my views about the limited value of chasing a fully developed comparative criminology.

Joan Ryan's eye for an inconsistent argument is as sharp as ever and this collection could not have been put together without her strong support when the going got tough.

The editors are particularly grateful to Emma Bell for her rapid translation of Chapter 5. Finally, this project was conceived at a conference in France in September 2011, where the editors first met with Palgrave Macmillan. They wish to express their thanks to Julia Willan for her editorial patience, and to all our contributors for their independent, critical contributions.

Notes on Contributors

Mónica Aranda Ocaña holds a PhD in Penal Law from the University of Barcelona, Spain. She is the coordinator of the area of Deprivation Liberty and Human Rights at the Research Centre "Observatory of Penal System and Human Rights" and the coordinator of the Penitentiary Legal Clinic at the Faculty of Law at the University of Barcelona. She has authored several publications relating to criminal matters and prison in Spain, Portugal and Latin America.

Emma Bell is Senior Lecturer in British Studies at the Université de Savoie, Chambéry, France. Her research focuses on contemporary penal policy in Britain and attempts to situate it in its wider social and political context. She is the author of *Criminal Justice and Neoliberalism* (2011).

Miranda Boone is Associate Professor at the Utrecht Willem Pompe Institute of Criminology and Criminal Law, The Netherlands. She is also Professor of Penology and Penitentiary Law at the University of Groningen. A member of the European Society for Criminology, she has co-edited a book questioning the progressive credentials of Dutch prison policy, and has also researched and published extensively on the use of alternative punishments, such as community service and probation in several European states.

Bernd Dollinger is Professor of Social Work at the University of Siegen, Germany. His current research focuses on professionalism in penal systems, punitiveness and attitudes towards delinquency. His first book, on drug use and social control (*Drogen im sozialen Kontext*), was published in 2002; his most recent monograph, *Jugendkriminalität als Kulturkonflikt* (2010), deals with cultural theories of delinquency. He has also co-edited, with Henning Schmidt-Semisch, a handbook on juvenile delinquency (*Handbuch Jugendkriminalität*, 2010).

Patrizio Gonnella is the President of Antigone, an Italian NGO involved in penal issues and human rights protection within penitentiary systems. A former postgraduate student of Human Rights at Padua University, Italy, he has published extensively on prison matters and is the co-author of *Patrie Galere* (2005) and *Il carcere spiegato ai ragazzi* (2010). Since

1998 he has been writing for daily papers *Italia Oggi* and *Il Manifesto*. He contributes to the teaching of Philosophy of Law at the University of Roma 3 and conducts a weekly radio programme.

Philip Gounev works at the Centre for the Study of Democracy in Sofia, Bulgaria. He has conducted numerous research studies on organised crime, including EU studies on the abuse of the non-profit organisation by terrorists and organised crime; criminal asset confiscation; the links between corruption and organised crime and cooperation between border guards and customs. He has published in major criminological journals and edited volumes, and has co-authored several studies on organised crime in Bulgaria.

Vassilis Karydis studied at the Athens Law School (BA), University College London (LL.M) and University of Thrace (Law School, PhD), where he taught criminological courses from 1993 to 2005. He is currently Professor at the Department of Social and Educational Policy, University of Peloponnese, Greece and Visiting Professor at the Department of Political Science and Public Administration, University of Athens. He has been Deputy Greek Ombudsman for human rights since 2010. He has worked extensively in the fields of immigrant integration and crime, youth cultures and violence, hidden criminality, prison systems, justice system and delivery of criminal justice. His most recent books include *Visions of Social Control in Greece: Moral Panics, Criminal Justice* (2010) and (with E. Fytrakis) *Imprisonment and Rights: The Perspective of the Greek Ombudsman* (2011). He is a member of *ad hoc* law-making committees at the Ministry of Public Order and Ministry of Justice as well as a staff member of the academic network "Critical Criminology and Criminal Justice Systems in Europe" and of the steering committee of the Greek National Committee for Human Rights.

Nikolaos K. Koulouris is Assistant Professor in Penology and Penal Policy at the Social Administration Department, Democritus University of Thrace, Greece, and a teaching staff member in the International Intensive Common Study Program Criminal Justice and Critical Criminology. He has been a postgraduate scholar in Criminology and Penology at the Law School, Sector of Penal Sciences, University of Athens. Formerly working as a criminologist at Korydallos Judicial Prison, Piraeus, and being a member and secretary of the Central Scientific Council of Prisons, an advisory policy body, he has research experience in the fields of criminal justice, prison policy and human rights issues, authoring and editing books, reports and articles on deviance, penal and prison reform, community sentences and the dispersal of social control.

Andrea Kretschmann is a doctoral candidate at Bielefeld University, Germany, and an associate at the Institut für Rechts-& Kriminalsoziologie in Vienna. Her research interests include the sociology of law, critical security studies, policing, and migration studies. She has published in a variety of criminological and sociological areas.

Laura Piacentini is Reader in Criminology at Strathclyde Law School, University of Strathclyde, UK. She has conducted empirical research in Russian penal colonies since 1997 and interviewed over 300 prisoners and staff over four separate research projects. She has published in the areas of contemporary Russian penal theory, geographies of confinement, women's imprisonment and the relationship between culture, transition and imprisonment. How Russia 'responds' to new crime dynamics is another focus of her research. Her publications include *Surviving Russian Prisons: Punishment, Politics and Economy in Transition* in 2004, which won the British Society of Criminology Book of the Year in 2005. Her latest book, *Gender, Geography, and Punishment: The Experience of Women in Carceral Russia*, was co-authored with Judith Pallot and published in 2012.

Monika Platek is Professor of Law and Head of the Criminology Department at the Law Faculty of Warsaw University, Poland. She also serves as the Adviser to the Polish Prosecutor General and is the Honorary Chairwoman of the Polish Association for Legal Education [PSEP] that she co-founded and chaired from 1994 to 2009. A legal and human rights expert of the Human Rights Commission at the Polish Parliament and a member of International Advisory Board of *The British Journal of Criminology*, she teaches comparative criminology, criminal justice, correction, comparative criminal law and gender studies.

Iñaki Rivera Beiras completed his PhD in Penal Law from the University of Barcelona in 1991. He teaches penal law, criminology and penal policy at the University of Barcelona, Spain. He is the Director of the Observatory of the Penal System and Human Rights of the University of Barcelona and Coordinator of the master's and PhD programmes in Criminology and Sociology of Law. He is the author of 20 books and more than 100 articles published in Spain, Italy, the UK, Portugal and many countries of Latin America. He is also a visiting professor in several Latin American univeristies.

Philippe Robert was trained in sociology, law and political science at Bordeaux University, France where he received his PhD in 1967. A Director of Research at the CNRS, he founded CESDIP which he headed until 1990. He was also the head of a European network on norms and deviance, the GERN, a federation of some 40 research centres from Germany, Belgium, United Kingdom, Spain, Italy, Poland, Portugal, The Netherlands, Slovenia and Switzerland. His fields of interest are victimisation and fear of crime, criminal policy, crime index, pre-trial detention, history and sociology of law and criminal justice, sociology of norms and deviance, youth gangs, and sentencing. He has been teaching as an invited professor at the Universities of Montreal, Ottawa, Liège, Geneva, Sarrebrücken, Hamburg, Porto, Bologna, Padua, Louvain, Leuven, and at the Facultés universitaires Saint-Louis in Brussels. A former president of the Council of Europe's Criminological Scientific Council, he is doctor *honoris causa* at the UU of Liège and Macerata and Chevalier of the Légion d'honneur as well as of the Ordre national du mérite.

Mary Rogan is Lecturer in Socio-Legal Studies at Dublin Institute of Technology, Ireland. She is a graduate of Trinity College Dublin and the University of Oxford. She is the author of *Prison Policy in Ireland: Politics, Penal-Welfarism and Political Imprisonment* (2011). Mary is a barrister and the current chairperson of the Irish Penal Reform Trust.

Vincenzo Ruggiero is Professor of Sociology at Middlesex University in London. He has conducted research on behalf of many national and international bodies, including the Home Office, the ESRC, the European Commission and the United Nations. He has published extensively in a variety of criminological and sociological areas, and his previous books include: *European Penal Systems* (1995, co-edited); *Eurodrugs* (1995, co-authored); *Organised and Corporate Crime in Europe* (1996); *The New European Criminology* (1998, co-edited); *Crime and Markets* (2000); *Movements in the City* (2001), *Economic and Financial Crime* (2002, co-edited); *Crime in Literature* (2003); *Understanding Political Violence* (2006); *Social Movements: A Reader* (2008, co-edited); *Potere e Violenza* (2009, co-edited); *Penal Abolitionism* (2010); *Il delitto, la legge e la pena* (2011); *Corruption and Organised Crime in Europe* (2012, co-edited) and *The Crimes of the Economy* (2013)

Mick Ryan is Emeritus Professor of Penal Politics at the University of Greenwich, London. His first book, *The Acceptable Pressure Group* (1978), on the Howard League and Radical Alternatives to Prison was distributed in the USA as a Praeger special study. He contributed *The Politics of Penal Reform* (1983) to the Politics Today series edited by Bernard Crick, and with Tony Ward he co-authored *Privatisation and the Penal System* (1989). He invited Vincenzo Ruggiero and Joe Sim to join him in editing Western European Penal Systems (1995). With David Wall and Steve Savage he co-edited *Policy Networks in Criminal Justice* (2001). His most recent full monograph is *Penal Policy and Political Culture* (2003).

Enrik Tham is Emeritus Professor of Criminology at Stockholm University, Sweden. His research has mainly focused on living conditions and social exclusion, crime trends and historical studies, drug and crime policy and victimology. He is currently engaged in a Scandinavian project on the general sense of justice. He was President of the European Society of Criminology, 2011–2012. Articles in English include 'The Swedish drug policy and the vision of the good society' (2005), 'Individual prediction and crime trends' (2009), and 'The emergence of the crime victim: Sweden in Scandinavian context' (2011).

Rene van Swanningen is Professor of International and Comparative Criminology at the Erasmus University, Rotterdam, Academic Director of the Erasmus Graduate School of Law and President of the Netherlands' Society of Criminology (NVK). He has written extensively on Dutch penal policy in recent years, and his theoretical contribution to European criminology was marked by his earlier work, *Critical Criminology: Visions from Europe* (1997).

Hanns von Hofer is Emeritus Professor of Criminology, Stockholm University, Sweden. His research interests include criminal statistics, international comparisons and historical analyses of crime and punishment. He was a founding member of the European Sourcebook of Crime and Criminal Justice Statistics project and of the *European Journal of Criminology*.

1
Introduction
Mick Ryan

In this short introduction we outline three ways of looking at penal systems, the purpose of which is to locate our own perspective, and to better illustrate the brief that we have invited our contributors to follow.

The common sense approach

Let us begin with some basic ideas about punishment which are usually *taken for granted* by members of the public, our first year law students and many criminal justice professionals.

In most societies there are rules, and it is anticipated that those who break these rules, who come up against the criminal law, will be identified, charged and then taken before the courts. If found guilty by the criminal courts, offenders will then be sentenced to a punishment in proportion to the harm or injury they are judged to have caused. The punishment (and the tariff) ordered by the criminal courts will have been codified by politicians in Parliament, either in the form of a comprehensive penal code, or as a cumulative series of separate criminal justice statutes.

We take it that this way of thinking about punishment is *fairly routine*, as is the understanding that in most western societies the penal apparatus in place for delivering these punishments extends from deep end capital punishment or imprisonment, to supervision in the community, or a fine for less serious offences.

To suggest that thinking about punishment in this way is *taken for granted*, or is *fairly routine*, is not to suggest that there are no areas of difference or disagreement. That would be clearly wrong.

For example, people disagree about what the rules are and what behaviour should be designated criminal. And, even where they do agree about these things, they frequently quarrel over what punishments are appropriate for those who break the rules. These quarrels sometimes arise because of differences of opinion over what the penal apparatus in any society can be expected to deliver: punishment or reform of the offender, or both. Such disagreements, within the banal sociological observation that all societies have rules which people expect to be enforced through the application of sanctions or punishments, should therefore hardly surprise us. In mature democracies they constitute the legitimate *politics of punishment*.

Nor should we be surprised to learn that such disagreements have different outcomes in different societies, something that many thoughtful members of the public are aware of in our increasingly inter-connected world. So, many German, Italian and French people will be aware that the rules governing the public purchase and use of certain so-called 'recreational' drugs in the Netherlands differ from their own national practices; while the use of imprisonment in the USA as a whole, and in California in particular, is far greater than in most European countries.

To emphasise different penal practices or structures within and across continents is hardly, therefore, a provocative insight. So, we are back again in the world of the sociologically banal.

A comparative approach

However, there are those who suggest that we should go beyond what is superficially obvious and pay more attention to analysing penal systems in order to understand why some are more punitive than others.

Michael Cavadino and James Dignan (2006), for example, claim that the severity of different penal systems, as measured by rates of imprisonment, is related to the type of political economy in which they operate.[1] This is a bold claim. It is one thing cheerfully to argue, as we have done, that there are rules and those who break those rules are likely to be punished; it is quite another to claim that the relative severity of the punishment they are likely to receive is somehow related to the organisation of the wider political economy.

Briefly, Cavadino and Dignan present a typology drawn from several sources (e.g. Esping-Anderson 1990; Lash and Urry 1987) that divides modern capitalist societies into four broad categories: neo-liberal, free market capitalist states (e.g. America and the UK); conservative, corporatist states (e.g. France and Germany); social democratic, corporatist states (e.g. Sweden); and then finally oriental corporatist states such as Japan. It is claimed that countries *within* each of these categories are in most cases closely matched in terms of their imprisonment rates with neo-liberal states having the highest rates, conservative corporatist states the next highest, and so on, in descending order. Liberal states are characterised as favouring low welfare expenditure and *exclusive* penal policies, while social democratic states are more likely to implement more *inclusive* penal policies and spend generously on welfare.[2]

Liberal states are further defined by their reliance on informal mechanisms of social control and support, such as the family, which acts as a break on their prison sanctions.

It is very important to register that these categories can be contested, as can the allocation of countries to this or that category. These definitions and boundaries are thus far from certain. But this should not surprise us unduly, most heuristic devices can be challenged in this way. And such exercises are rarely without a teleological bias. The time frame is also relatively short to sustain a general theory. Nor, as Cavadino and Dignan freely admit, are imprisonment rates necessarily the most reliable guide to the overall severity of any penal system (Pease 1994).

These are highly significant qualifications, nonetheless, as are the consequences of raising, albeit somewhat casually, the question of whether or not punishment is a single 'entity' (Cavadino and Dignan 2006), a question which immediately raises for us, albeit at a tangent, a whole raft of other philosophical problems (Ruggiero 2010). Finally, Cavadino and Dignan's pioneering work is arguably stronger in establishing correlations than identifying causal links, a point well made by Nicola Lacey (2007) who, although highly appreciative of their work, as we are, prefers instead the greater explanatory power offered by the typologies of western economies put forward by Hall and Soskice (2003).

However, in our view what is really significant for our present purpose is that, when it comes to making sense of penal policy in any specific country, the wider material framework – corporatist, liberal market or whatever – interfaces with a whole range of other ideological, historical and administrative inputs that will likely produce very individual results, even within one category. Hence the different rates of imprisonment between America and several key European countries, including the UK. In other words, the shape and direction of a national penal system is significantly influenced by the wider political economy, but is far from being *determined* by it. Cavadino and Dignan characterise this complex, not to say messy, interaction in the following way:

> The precise nature of the relationship between politics and economics, ideological and material factors, and the interplay between them,

is likely to vary within different kinds of societies. A society's *penal* ideology and culture will be greatly shaped by (and to some extent will also shape) the more general ideology and culture of the society, as well as by its material conditions. Finally, penal practices will be influenced by both general and penal ideology and the culture and the material realm in which they operate, and will also have some reciprocal effect on these forces and factors. (Cavadino and Dignan 2006: 12–3)

In their search for ways of reducing the overall level of the UK's prison population, Mills and Roberts appear to endorse this interpretation, recently observing that:

For [Cavadino and Dignan], therefore, the use of imprisonment is embedded in wider political economy, economic, social structural, cultural and ideological factors are all part of this. They argue that these factors can best be interpreted as a complex whole for any one nation rather than being reduced to straightforward fixed variables that can be applied universally. (Mills and Roberts 2012: 15–6)

This conclusion, one which in our view relies heavily on the lesson we all learnt many years ago from David Garland (1985), mercifully takes us well beyond relying on single variables to explain levels of imprisonment, the state of the labour market, for example, which can be applied across the board. (Rusche and Kirhchemier 1939).

However, at the same time it does make the task that Mills and Roberts[3] have set themselves, of discovering ways of reducing the prison population, that much more difficult because, while connection has been made by Cavadino and Dignan between wide social and economic circumstances and imprisonment:

it is not clear from these accounts that a more specific set of interventions can be identified that could be straightforwardly adopted by those seeking to significantly reduce imprisonment. (Roberts and Mills: 17)

So there can be no 'cherry picking', no simple cross-national transplants to ease the delivery of pain. Indeed, such accounts are said to raise as many problems as they solve (Mills and Roberts: 17). This position is largely consistent with the one taken by Nicola Lacey who has suggested that, while policy transfers cannot be ruled out, these are always problematic and 'contingent on the dynamics of the local environment' (Lacey 2007: 31). Of course, even if policy transfers do not accrue, we can at least agree that comparative work is likely to contribute towards a better general understanding of how penal cultures are formed, differ and operate (Lacey 2007). But this is a relatively modest gain when set against what is often the implied promise of comparative penology, namely, that it will provide us with the knowledge to secure progressive penal practice.

Penal systems in their national contexts

In the context of our present investigation of 12 European penal systems, this encounter with comparative penology, while providing useful suggestions about the relationship between welfare expenditure and levels of imprisonment (Beckett and Western 2001, Downes and Hansen 2006), has nonetheless reinforced our view: that in order to prepare the ground for effective strategic interventions, penal systems need to be first and foremost interrogated in their own terms; that we should focus more on national *particularities* rather than across the board *commonalities*, even though we are likely to find that countries at similar stages of economic development will share some trends in common (see below).

We acknowledge that this preference for emphasising the particular is perhaps reinforced by having lived and worked in the UK, where levels of welfare expenditure, for example, are mediated through the lens of a highly distinctive, not to say unique, penal culture which has been routinely mobilised at strategic moments (e.g. Hall 1978; Downes 1988) by ruling elites to discipline those at the margins who challenge 'the rule of law'. The harsh political and judicial response to the English city riots of 2011 is just the most recent example (*The Guardian*, 4 July 2012 *Analysis*).

But the UK is not alone in displaying its own *particularities*.

So we have encouraged our authors to interpret in a critical spirit the dynamics of individual national penal systems, without paying overdue attention to any anxiety that their accounts might be massaged to fit into a pre-ordained descriptive (or comparative) box – whether it be classified neo-liberal, corporatist or adjusted to account for post-communist countries, such as Bulgaria, Poland or Russia, as *transitional*. (And history alone suggests that this particular classification would quickly divide into component, national parts.)

Mobilising a more critical and accessible public criminology

We would repeat that, while we have encouraged our contributors to concentrate on the particular, to focus on interpreting penal systems within their national contexts, it is highly likely that their investigations will reveal common features.

For example, the liberalisation of western markets during the last two decades, facilitated by globalisation, has destabilised labour markets. This has swollen the number of un- or under-employed, who are targeted through increasingly harsh social policies aimed more at *exclusion* and control than *inclusion* and integration. Europe's porous borders exacerbate this problem, mobilising public opinion against incoming 'Others' who, shunted from one form of detention to another, are portrayed as the cause of current instability, rather than its victims (Young 1999; Garland 2001). Those living on low pay or benefits see their living standards reduced as many European states struggle to reduce spiralling fiscal deficits. Some states even hope that newly created markets within the penal system, from prison to probation, will help to balance the books in a new age of austerity.

A full understanding of the processes at work here will require, first and foremost, the development of a more critical and accessible *public criminology* that goes beyond the academy to embrace wider social movements (Ruggiero 2012). This wider connection is needed to heighten public awareness and ensure that the public debate goes beyond the parameters of conventional penal discourse, the *taken for granted* categories that hide so many inequalities, injustices and prejudices, and which invite the suspicion that it is mostly the poor and the underprivileged who end up being punished while those who do the most damage go largely unpunished (Barbara Hudson 1993; Hillyard and Tombs 2007).

Only when this general level of awareness has been raised can we hope to build (and sustain) public support for progressive penal change – a consent that is informed by an understanding of the political, material and ideological forces that help to shape individual national systems. We hope these essays will contribute towards building up this awareness in the countries they cover.

Achieving this ambitious goal is not entirely at odds with Loader and Spark's (2011) promotion of a more cautious and interlocutory public criminology. However, working in the slipstream of neo-liberalism we are not inclined to see academic criminology cast in such a *passive* trajectory. In such troubled times some of the 'under labourers' identified by Loader and Sparks are more relevant than others when it comes to standing up for the disadvantaged and the dispossessed.

We feel there is no choice but to engage in a critical way with social movements against imprisoning the poor and the disadvantaged, against racism and sexism in the criminal justice system (Ruggiero 2010). Interlocutors *take sides by standing aside*, and when they do, albeit under the commendable guise of modesty and (very properly) in the name of *objectivity*, their case for building such a broadly based *public criminology* can be interpreted as a very conservative one.

Finally, we will later raise more critical questions about how those *taken for granted* views of punishment we began with might be contested by excavating an alternative, critical discourse that is deeply rooted in European culture.

Notes

1. Nicola Lacey (2007) explores this thesis in some detail, though overlays it with the suggestive cultural historical perspective of James Q. Whitman.
2. Leon Radzinowicz recognised this convergence in his autobiography when he wrote about Labour's post 1945 consolidation of the Welfare State: The continued advancement of social policy, in the widest sense of the term, was increasingly being recognised as one of the more sensitive tasks of the state. This evolution inevitably exercised a profound influence on the evolution of criminal policy. A state which recognises, as one of the basic aims of its domestic policy, improvements in the condition of the population especially of its poor and underprivileged strata of society, cannot maintain a merely formal, passive attitude towards penal repression...Under such a political climate social policy and criminal policy come closer to each other...at certain sensitive crossings (Radzinowicz 1999: 115).
3. Mick Ryan made a contribution to part one of the Esmee Fairbairn Foundations 2012 investigation into *Reducing the numbers in custody: Looking beyond criminal justice solutions* (London: Centre for Criminal Justice Studies).

References

Beckett K. and Western B. (2001) 'Governing Social Marginality: Welfare, Incarceration and the Transformation of State Policy, Punishment and Society', 3 (1): 43–95.

Cavadino M. and Dignan J. (2006) *Penal Systems: A Comparative Approach* (London: Sage).

Downes D. (1988) *Contrasts in Tolerance* (Oxford: Clarendon).

Downes D. and Hansen K. (2006) *Welfare and Punishment: The Relationship between Welfare Spending and Imprisonment* (London: Crime and Society Foundation).

Esping-Anderson G. (1990) *The Three Worlds of Welfare Capitalism* (Cambridge: Polity Press).

Garland D. (2001) *The Culture of Control* (Oxford: Oxford University Press).

Garland D.(1985) *Punishment and Welfare* (Aldershot: Gower).

Hillyard P. and Tombs S. (2007) *From "Crime" to Social Harm, Crime, Law and Social Change*, 48 (1 and 2): 9–25.

Hall P. and D. Soskice D . (2003) 'An Invitation to the Varieties of Capitalism', in Hall P. and Soskice D., *Varieties of Capitalism* (Oxford: Oxford University Press).

Hall S. Crichter C. Jefferson T. Clarke J. and Roberts B (1978) *Policing the Crisis* (Basingstoke: Macmillan).

Hudson B. (1993) *Penal Policy and Social Justice* (Basingstoke: Palgrave Macmillan).

Lacey N. (2007) *Criminal Justice and Democratic Systems: Inclusionary and Exclusionary Dynamics in the Institutional Structure of Late Modern Societies Center for European Studies*, Working Paper, 148.

Lash S. and Urry J. (1987) *The End of Organised Capitalism* (Cambridge: Polity Press).

Loader I. and Sparks R. (2011) *Public Criminology* (London: Routledge).

Mills H. and Roberts R. (2012) *Reducing the Numbers in Custody: Looking beyond Criminal Justice Solutions* (London: Centre for Criminal Justice Studies).

Pease K. (1994) 'Cross National Imprisonment Rates; Limitations of Method and Possible Conclusions', *British Journal of Criminology*, 34(Special Issue): 116–30.

Radzinowicz L. (1999) *Adventures in Criminology* (London: Routledge).

Ruggiero V. (2012) 'How Public is Public Criminology?', *Crime, Media, Culture*, 8 (2): 151–60.

Ruggiero V. (2010) *Penal Abolitionism* (Oxford: Oxford University Press).

Rusche G. and Kircheimer O. (1939) *Punishment a Social Structure* (Russell and Russell: New York).

Young J. (1999) *The Exclusive Society* (London: Sage).

Whitman J.Q. (2003) *Hard Justice* (Oxford: Oxford University Press).

2

Regression to the Mean: Punishment in the Netherlands

Miranda Boone and René van Swaaningen

Introduction

When René van Swaaningen and Gerard de Jonge (1995) wrote their chapter on the Netherlands in the previous volume of critical anatomies of European penal systems nearly 20 years ago, they observed a trend, from humanitarian paternalism in the 1960s and 70s to a rather bleak penal business management in the 1980s and 90s. Their key conclusions then were that policymakers no longer considered rehabilitation to be the main goal of punishment, but the protection of society; that non-custodial sanctions were no longer intended as alternatives to custody, but as relatively cheap remedies to ease the capacity problem in prisons; that the sharp distinctions between custodial and non-custodial, repression and prevention were blurring; and that penal policy has become increasingly motivated by an alleged public sentiment against leniency in law enforcement. All of these conclusions can be reiterated in this chapter.

Yet, it would be wrong to conclude that there has been a standstill in the last 20 years. If we are to choose two new phrases to characterise today's penal policy it would be 'risk-assessment' and 'evidence-based best practice': two aspects that were not yet central in the mid-1990s. The prefix 'pre-' would cover a lot of what has happened since: the focus is increasingly on 'pre-crime', to be countered by 'precautionary' measures which lead to a politics of 'prepression' – that is the complete merger of prevention and repression. The change of emphasis is now embodied in new multi-disciplinary and multi-agency approaches to tackling crime which are accepted as preferred policy options among politicians and their advisors, who need to be seen to be doing something to combat the public's growing sense of insecurity.

The political and cultural context

Since the mid-1980s, playing the 'tough on crime' card has become an important tactic in Dutch electoral campaigns. Before that, crime was hardly an issue in the Netherlands. Yet, by 2002 every single political party, from the far right to the radical left, had an elaborate paragraph on crime and insecurity in its electoral manifesto. Moreover, these paragraphs also became rather similar in their orientation: more punitive responses, more prevention and early intervention – though obviously within the limits of due process. In this period the number of parliamentary debates on crime and insecurity has risen from 15 in 1995 to almost 60 in 2003: that is a fourfold increase in less than a decade (Keijzers 2005: 90). From the late 1990s onwards there is strong support for the 'governance through crime (and insecurity)' thesis in the Netherlands (Tonry 2001: 524; van Swaaningen 2005). This policy shift, in which crime and insecurity are central themes in the political debate, is accompanied by a shift from a rather general disbelief in the effectiveness of prison sentences up to the 1990s, to a renewed belief in prison as the obvious, sound reaction to crime from the 90s on. 'Prison works' is the new slogan, albeit mainly as a symbol of collective condemnation and not so much because of its actual effects in reducing crime. Similarly, community safety gains another dimension too. It is no longer linked to positive ideals, such as a social policy guaranteeing everyone full participation in society. From the mid-1990s on, community safety is merely interpreted as taking action against those who threaten the citizen's feelings of security. Apart from people who really menace or rob, here it is also a question of beggars, streetwalkers and 'addicts avoiding treatment': in short, all those who the law-abiding citizen finds an 'antisocial' irritant (van Swaaningen 2005).

The political debate on crime and insecurity largely focuses on mischief in the public domain. Little distinction is made between crime and nuisance. Moreover, politicians often display unwarrantedly high, if not naive, expectations of 'strong intervention'. Not only are general nuisances, incivilities and disorder all too easily treated as crime, but also the boundaries between policing and intelligence are often blurred – especially with respect to the fight against jihadi terrorism. Compared to David Garland (2001), who discerns a process in which crime is on the one hand 'defined up' and on the other hand 'defined down' – depending on the political context – we argue that, in the Netherlands a process of defining crime down took place in the early 1980s (notably with respect to petty criminality), but in the 1990s and 2000s we witness a continual tendency to define crime up. Examples of this tendency in the public domain are the increased criminalisation of begging, of alcohol or cannabis consumption, of gatherings of the homeless or the young in certain urban areas, of urinating in the street and of swearing at police officers. Also, the more recent plans to criminalise wearing a burka or undocumented stays in the Netherlands are highly symbolic of the immanent belief that criminal law serves to make a statement to the general public.

The current tendency to govern through crime and insecurity is to be understood in the context of a process by which crime is increasingly situated amongst the 'other'; that is people who are not like 'us'. Through this process of othering, punitive responses become far more obvious than if you see an offender as a person who is just like yourself. Because ethnic minorities are the most prone to such othering, we need to focus on the changed attitude towards immigrants in the Netherlands. By the turn of the millennium, the multicultural ideal was seen to have resulted in a multicultural tragedy. It was thought that ethnic minorities were not sufficiently integrated into Dutch society, undermined social cohesion and just caused trouble. In this context, the public debate on crime control became increasingly defined in terms of 'us' – the white Dutch – against 'them' – the foreigners who make our society increasingly unpleasant. So, crime is implicitly portrayed as a problem outside 'our' society, rather than as a problem rooted in social and economic relations, as was hitherto the common vision.

Three events in particular have contributed to what we could call a social climate of fear and rancour in the Netherlands that reached its highest level in 2004. These are the 2001 attack on the Twin Towers in New York, the murder of the populist political leader Pim Fortuyn by a radical environmentalist in 2002, and the murder, in 2004, of film director Theo van Gogh – who had made a film about the allegedly misogynous nature of Islam – by a Dutch-Moroccan Muslim fundamentalist. The subsequent fear and moral panic about Muslims as a whole resulted in an Islamophobia that varied from attempts to refuse girls with headscarves into schools, a proposal for a so-called 'stop to immigration' in 'Muslim' neighbourhoods, cultural pleas to punish immigrant youths who commit misdemeanours differently (because they would not understand the 'soft' Dutch language of corrections), stiffening regulations for asylum-seekers and other immigrants after a number of – rather shadowy – terrorist trials and, last but not least, new anti-terrorist legislation that allowed very far-reaching infringements of civil liberties.

Ultimately, these events of the early 2000s marked the end of the Dutch self-image as a beacon of tolerance and enlightenment in a generally savage and uncivilised world. The mental consequences of this national identity crisis have been quite disturbing. It seemed as if the Dutch wanted to 'close the curtains' and keep the door closed to the evil world outside. Despite this, despite the long history of the Netherlands as a trading nation, and indeed despite the political process of European unification and economic globalisation, it seemed as if the mental horizon of the Dutch suddenly stopped at their own doorstep. Nearly forgotten words such as 'community spirit' and 'decency' gained importance again, albeit with narrow-minded, provincial connotations. The implicit message was: our communities were safe and the people were decent in the pre-globalised world of the 1950s, when we could still understand the world around us, so we should get back to that situation. The political naivety implied in this message is rather alarming. Despite being a country of commerce, with a long colonial history that now embraces the neo-liberal politics of globalisation and has supported military interventions in countries such as Afghanistan and Iraq, we did not expect 'the bad world out there' to disrupt our peaceful country. In this context, immigration is increasingly treated as a security risk and thus, argue criminologists Joanne van der Leun and Maartje van der Woude (2012), the Netherlands has witnessed a process of 'crimmigration' – the intertwinement of crime control and migration control.

Till the 1990s it was politically incorrect to address social problems along ethnic lines. However, this 'taboo' gradually disappeared. By the early 2000s newspaper articles about street nuisances, gangs or terrorism seldom lacked reference to the cultural background of the offenders. In post-1990 Dutch criminology, we also find many studies that demonstrate a far larger involvement of various ethnic minority groups – mainly Moroccans and Antilleans – in crime, even when corrected for demographic and socio-economic differences. After 2010 a similar xenophobia was oriented increasingly against Poles, Bulgarians and Rumanians.

Politics and penal policy

The demise of tolerance as a key characteristic of Dutch society also marks a significant shift in penal policy. In penology, the 'Dutch model' traditionally referred to the period of sustained reduction of imprisonment rates between 1947 and 1974. David Downes and René van Swaaningen (2007) have shown how the Netherlands moved away from being a 'beacon of tolerance' in the penal sphere to a very average European country with a rather bleak penal politics. In this section we will summarise some main lines from the latter period which Downes and van Swaaningen (2007) distinguished: 1990 to 2005.

Around 1990, 'acting out' against crime and insecurity accompanied the earlier 'adaptive strategies' of crime management (Garland 2001: 113–27). The 'glue' between these two strategies is provided by a third kind of discourse: that of actuarialism and its 'new penology' (Feeley and Simon 1992). The so-called 'old' penology is rooted in a concern for individuals and is preoccupied with concepts such as guilt, responsibility and obligation, as well as diagnoses, intervention and treatment of the individual offender. In the 'new' penology crime is seen to be a normal phenomenon, and the key problem is how to manage it most efficiently. The answer to this question is a risk-assessment concerned with techniques for identifying, classifying and managing groups according to their levels of dangerousness. Most criminal justice agencies, including the probation service, nowadays employ elaborate risk-assessment techniques to determine the kind of intervention that is 'needed'.

Today, we may well know quite a lot more about risk factors and the effectiveness of certain sanctions than 20 years ago, but it is questionable whether the current orientation toward 'evidence-based best practice' will actually bring recidivism rates down – as is the firm belief of present-day penal policymakers. Critics argue that we have ended up in an evidence maze (Nelen 2008), with rigid, positivist ideas on effect measurement and that the 'belief ' in certain measures that have been 'proven' to 'work' is probably larger than their actual effect (Rovers 2008). Moreover, knowing that something 'works' does not mean that we also know *how* it works. Moreover, the old problems of selectivity and stigmatisation labelling scholars have pointed at acquired a completely different complexion in a system dominated by risk management. There is a danger that these negative effects of criminal justice become even more structural if they are rationalised and institutionalised.

The politics of 'acting out' against crime and insecurity has resulted in numerous punitive measures with a highly symbolic value. This has included proposals to introduce minimum sentences for every offence, to exclude the possibility of non-custodial sanctions for violent offences, and to have persons sentenced to non-custodial sanctions wear fluorescent smocks bearing the text 'I am working for the community'. Furthermore, the maximum duration of temporary prison sentences has been increased, regulations with respect to immigration have been stiffened, custodial consequences have been connected to a breach of parole and a non-fulfilment of non-custodial sanctions; a so-called 'long stay' department has been established in penal-psychiatric TBS-clinics (where dangerous 'incurable' mentally ill offenders will stay till they die); various kinds of Anti-Social Behaviour Orders have been introduced, as well as very intrusive anti-terrorist legislation, that not only focuses on actual acts of terrorism but predominantly on early signs of radicalisation. The new Dutch punitiveness is also shown in: the selective incapacitation of specific 'problematic groups' (most notably habitual offenders); austere, cheaply built cells far away from the larger cities where most of the prisoners and their families come from; a shift of focus in penal policy, from rehabilitation to the protection of society and 'expressive sanctioning'; violations of penal principles (including EU anti-torture paragraphs); and penal crises with respect to fire hazards and prison staff that have been silenced because they criticised the official policy-line of the Minister of Justice (Downes and van Swaaningen 2007).

In a discussion for this chapter with us, David Downes argued: 'once a punitive turn is taken, there is hardly ever a way back.' With 134 prisoners per 100,000 inhabitants in 2005, the Netherlands indeed approached the West European peak – after Britain and Spain. But, after 2005 the Dutch prison population started to *decrease*: the rather grim portrayal we had drawn was written exactly at the turning point of a thirty-year period of penal expansionism that was followed by a sustained decrease. With an imprisonment rate of 87 in 2011, the Netherlands is back at the level of 2001. In a recent trend analysis the Dutch Ministry of Security and Justice's research department WODC expects imprisonment rates to go down even further, albeit not at the same pace as between 2005 and 2010 (Sonnenschein et al. 2011). Eight prisons are closed; one has been rented out to Belgium, the neighbouring country that suffers structural overcrowding. The closure of six more juvenile institutions and of nearly all small prisons is proposed.

No penal expert had predicted this. There have been no remarkable changes in the socio-cultural fabric of the country that would explain it. There has definitely been no revival of a reductionist agenda or any clear decriminalisations or other policy initiatives that could have any depenalising effect. In fact, the political developments of the early 2000s, with a strong rise of the neo-nationalist populist right – for whom 'get tough' in the fight against crime was a key-issue in the electoral campaigns – plead completely against it. In the next section we will go a bit deeper into the reasons for this decline, although that has been done more elaborately elsewhere (Boone and Moerings 2008; van Swaaningen 2013). The key question here is whether we can argue that the Netherlands has actually become any less punitive since imprisonment rates went down after 2005.

Decreasing prison population: reversing a punitive turn?

Despite the declining imprisonment rates, the percentage of offenders who get a custodial sentence in the Netherlands is, in comparison with other European countries, still quite high (Kalidien and de Heer 2011). On the political right there is, moreover, a continuous pressure to use the present excess of prison capacity to 'finally start punishing properly'. Successive governments have, as mentioned above, proposed very punitive measures; quite a number have already been introduced some time ago – such as the super-max EBI prison or the watered down 'three strikes and you're out' ISD measure for habitual offenders. And, if we put together custodial sanctions and non-custodial sanctions, the quantum of pain being delivered has arguably risen.

Moreover, there is little political or intellectual counter-weight to this punitive drift. At the political level, nearly all parties seem to agree that we are still too lenient and need more repressive sanctions. The once rather influential Dutch League for Penal Reform, the Coornhert Liga, has even ceased to exist. So, a coherent penal philosophy to replace the old, progressive reductionist agenda has been notably absent for quite some time, not least amongst senior officials whose task it is to shape Dutch penal policy. When studying policy documents from the last 25 years in order to find out what reasons officials gave for not contesting the continuous expansion of the penal system, Miranda Boone and Martin Moerings (2007) were struck by the absence of compelling arguments. They came across only two official storylines: the alleged public outcry over penal leniency (that functions as a mantra that is not supposed to be studied seriously); and the alleged rising crime rates (which have actually been rather stable since the 1990s and dropping since 2002).

So, in order to discover the reasons for the sharp drop in the prison population we must look elsewhere. For example, one of the most direct causes for the decrease can be found in sentencing practices. Both the absolute number and relative share of unconditional prison sentences have decreased since 2003 (Kalidien and de Heer-de Lange 2011, Tables 6 and 7). This phenomenon is (partly) explained by the 'production agreements' and 'output financing' of the police in 2003. Police officers are encouraged to focus on (large numbers of) minor cases instead of (fewer) more serious and complicated ones. As a consequence,

less severe sentences were imposed by the courts, resulting in a reduction of the prison population. Criminal law scholar Ybo Buruma had
already warned, in 2004, of a 'miniaturisation' of criminal law as a result
of these developments. His argument was endorsed by a member of the
Supreme Court and the chair of the Council for the Administration of
Law. Maybe these warnings have had some effect; since 2009 there has
been a slight increase in the length of prison sentences, which could
mean that more serious cases are being brought to court again.

Miranda Boone and Martin Moerings, who studied fluctuations in the
rates of six different categories of prisoners, concluded in 2007 that,
while the category of convicted offenders in prison had already started
to stabilise, or even fall, from 1995 there had been an impressive increase
of the other categories of prisoners: prisoners on remand, mentally ill
offenders in penal-psychiatric TBS-clinics, irregular immigrants awaiting
deportation (i.e. not for any offence!) and youngsters detained for private
law reasons (i.e. not for any offence either!). The development of these
categories is most influential in explaining the recent fall of imprisonment rates, but does not really relate to a (reverse of a) punitive turn. To
give just two examples. The number of irregular immigrants awaiting
deportation in detention halved, partly as a result of a stricter immigration policy, but mainly because of the entry of Bulgaria and Rumania
into the EU, that led to a spectacular decrease in the number of asylum-
seekers – from 45,000 in 1998 to 10,000 in 2007, and rising again to
18,000 today. A general pardon involving about 27,000 people also
influenced the number of irregular migrants in prison, as did the acceptance of the European Union's guideline on Forced Return. According to
this guideline, the maximum term of administrative detention awaiting
deportation is six months. Because the Netherlands used to detain
deportees for much longer, this EU guideline has resulted in a large
number of releases. Also, the separation of juveniles detained for private
law reasons from juveniles detained because they have committed an
offence has influenced the general detention rate. Before 2008, these
two categories of juveniles were detained in the same penal institutions.
Since their separate detention the total number of juveniles in *prison* has
more than halved.

In criminology, the phenomenon that former prisoners are detained
in another type of (more or less) closed institution is called transcarceration. It is debatable whether this can be interpreted as a sign of decreasing
punitiveness.

The introduction of the Prosecution Service's discretion to impose
so-called 'Punishment Orders' (*strafbeschikkingen*) may also have contributed

to a decrease in the number of prisoners. This new possibility gives the Prosecutor the power to decide on a case without further intervention by a judge. The difference with an out-of-court settlement (*transactie*) is that the offender does not have to agree with the sanction. Although this enactment must definitely be seen as another effort to react more firmly on punishable behaviour in a more efficient way, a side effect could be fewer prison sentences, since it is only the judge who has the power to impose them.

Alternatives to custody

Alternatives to custody were applied for the first time in the Netherlands in 1971 when three steel benders, who had committed a violent offence, were ordered to undertake 'unpaid labour in the public interest' instead of being sentenced to prison. Subsequently, the rather open Dutch penal procedure allowed judges to use their discretionary powers in this way. However, in 1979 a governmental committee on 'alternative' sanctions advised that a start be made with community service orders on a more systematic (but experimental) basis. In the 1980s, various social work organisations operated probation-established bureaus for the supervision of community service orders (Boone 2010; uit Beijerse and van Swaaningen 2007). With hindsight, this was the beginning of the transformation of the probation service from a social work institution to a field organisation of the Ministry of Justice (van Swaaningen 2000). In 2001, non-custodial sanctions were introduced as a primary punishment in the Criminal Code as 'assignment penalties' (*taakstraffen*). From then onwards it was no longer necessary that a labour penalty be substituted with an unconditional prison sentence of up to six months – as the law had previously prescribed. At this point the 'alternative to custody' culture, in which non-custodial sanctions had been developed, was left behind. Former 'alternatives' – such as community service orders, educational schemes or electronic monitoring – thus became integral parts of the penal system and were reshaped in accordance with the expansionist penal discourse. One of the changes under the 2001 bill was the power given to the Prosecution Service to impose a community service order as a pre-condition for an out-of-court settlement with the offender – a possibility that was still unthinkable under the 1989 Act because of the supposed punitive character of a community sentence order (Boone 2010).

In 1993, Peter van der Laan could still be confident that community sanctions had the support of the Dutch people. Even in more recent research much support was found for the community service order (Ruiter et al. 2011). Despite this kind of evidence, every now and then the imposition of a community service order has led to a great deal of media attention and political and public disapproval. The television programme *Zembla* of 14 October 2007 had an extremely negative impact on the public's perception of the community service order. This renowned current affairs programme argued that non-custodial sanctions were also imposed for serious offences such as murder and rape. Fierce debates followed on the internet and in the media. Members of Parliament asked the Minister of Justice to exclude this possibility by law. A later study demonstrated, however, that the programme makers had used unreliable data, for example formal definitions of crimes that did not correspond to the seriousness of the actual offences: 'rape' turned out to be an enforced French kiss, 'attempted homicide' a traffic offence and 'attempted murder' a rather wild threat. Moreover, the fact that non-custodial sanctions were in these cases often combined with prison sentences was not mentioned (Klijn et al. 2008). Yet the image of a 'soft' judiciary had been created. The result of this debate was that recidivists and offenders of (serious) violent and sexual offences are by now legally excluded from non-custodial sanctions. Another effect of the now-assumed lack of public acceptance is that efforts are continually made to stress the punitive nature of community sentences.

The number of non-custodial sanctions has increased dramatically since the 1980s. From 217 non-custodial sanctions for adults in 1981, the number grew to 20,949 in 2002, reaching an all-time high of 38,500 in 2008. Since 2008 the number of non-custodial sanctions has decreased, but only by a fraction.

The steepest expansion in the use of non-custodial sentences took place at the same time as the prison system also expanded dramatically.[1] This analysis makes us suspicious of the often-heard thesis that imprisonment rates dropped after 2005 because so many more non-custodial sentences were imposed (van Swaaningen 2013). The last systematic study on this topic was published in 1995. Based on the criminal records of offenders, Eric Spaans (1995) compared the seriousness scores of 600 offenders who had received a community service order with similar scores of 600 offenders who had been subjected to a short prison sentence. He came to the conclusion that an estimated 45–50 per cent of the community service orders substituted short-term unconditional sentences. Looking at prison sentences of under six months, which should have been replaced by community service orders, one sees an *increase* – from 19,000 in 1995 to 23,000 in 2003 – and a *decrease* since then. Combined with the continuing increase in non-custodial sanctions since 2002, one could imagine that short prison sentences have indeed been replaced by non-custodial sanctions – a conclusion that is supported by interviews with judges (van der Heide et al. 2007). This development probably came to an end with the acceptance of the bill that prohibits judges from imposing community sanctions in cases of serious violence and sex offences, or in cases of recidivism, for comparable cases in a period of five years. The continuing decrease of the average length of community service orders seems to suggest that they are being imposed for less serious offences (Boone 2010). Statistics show a sharp decline in community sanctions consisting of 180 hours or more (a decrease of 32% compared to 2005) and a continuing increase in the number of community service orders consisting of less than 40 hours (Kalidien and de Heer-de Lange 2011: Table 6.12).

In 2005, electronic detention was also codified as a principal punishment – that is not as substitution for another penalty. It is meant to be less intensive and less 'total' than detention, and it can be imposed in cases where fines or non-custodial sanctions are felt to be insufficient. Electronic monitoring can also be used for offenders who are a nuisance at a particular place – that is shopping malls, soccer stadiums, discotheques, swimming pools, etc. – or for offenders with a physical handicap which makes a stay in prison more difficult – for example someone in a wheelchair. It can also be used for fine defaulters, but only if the judge explicitly mentions this possibility in the verdict (van Swaaningen and uit Beijerse 2013).

The growth and expansion in the use of non-custodial sanctions has probably not influenced imprisonment rates. As in other countries, for example – England and Wales – Dutch offenders caught up in what used to be thought of as the shallow end of the penal apparatus are now subjected to higher levels of control and surveillance than the progressive advocates of alternatives to prison from the 1960s or 1970s would ever have supported.

The social composition of the people sanctioned

Just as in the rest of Europe, the vast majority of prisoners in the Netherlands are male; the percentage of female prisoners has even decreased in recent years – to 5.6 per cent in 2010, although this percentage does not include women in aliens detention (Dienst Justitiële Inrichtingen 2012: 28). The ethnic composition of the prison population in the Netherlands is probably more divergent than in most other EU countries. Almost half the inmates serving their sentence under an ordinary prison regime were also born outside the Netherlands, although their share of the entire Dutch population is only 12 per cent (Verhagen 2011: 22; Dienst Justitiële Inrichtingen 2011: 29). The fact that this percentage has actually remained rather stable for the last two decades is seldom mentioned. It remains, however, a very high percentage that, moreover, does not tell us very much about the actual ethnic mix of the prison population. The over-whelming complexion of detainees in the Netherlands is dark, although you will not find that reflected in any statistics, since people are only registered on the basis of their country of birth, not their race. The ethnic composition has slightly changed; there are more Eastern European and sub-Saharan African prisoners, and of the traditional migrant groups the percentage of Antilleans has risen, the number of Surinamese remains high at the same level, whereas that of Moroccans and Turks is slightly decreasing – if only because a higher percentage of them are now Dutch born and have Dutch nationality. The most significant change is that, in all likelihood, in the 1980s the over-representation of various ethnic minorities in the criminal justice system would have been explained by a selective criminal justice system along with the underprivileged position of these migrant groups. Today, however, it is more readily accepted that it is a true reflection of a real over-representation in criminal behaviour by these groups (Bovenkerk 2009).

The prison population deviates from the average Dutch population in a number of other ways. Jos Verhagen (2011) has listed a number of features of prison inmates based on the Recidivism Assessment Scales (RISc) which the Dutch Probation Office and Prison Department use for screening offenders. Approximately half of the prisoners are character-ised as problematic drug users (Verhagen 2011: 96). Only a quarter of the prisoners were gainfully employed shortly before their detention, and a third have never been employed at any time in their life. Half the prisoners have more debts than they would be able to pay back with the income they have. In the past, the Health Council and other agencies have observed that approximately six per cent of the prison population suffer from psychotic disorders, 14–35 per cent have depressions and approximately half of them some anti-social personality disorder. These percentages are much higher than the normal prevalence in society (Raad voor Strafrechtstoepassing en Jeugdbescherming 2007). More recently it has even been acknowledged that many offenders are mentally handicapped: up to 20–5 per cent (Raad voor Strafrechtstoepassing en Jeugdbescherming 2008). Recent research makes clear that the chance of receiving a community sentence is much higher for women, Dutch nationals, white offenders and offenders who were employed during the offence (Boone 2012).

Specific penal regimes

In his seminal book *Contrasts in Tolerance* David Downes (1988) argued that the Dutch penal regime was in many aspects superior to the English one. Downes's findings were confirmed in a replication of his study by Candace Kruttschnitt and Anja Dirkzwager (2011). English prisoners are *still* more positive about the Dutch penal regime than Dutch prisoners about the English one; in particular about security measures and inmate–staff relations. Also, in other comparative studies some extraordinary aspects of the Dutch prison regime have been emphasised; such as the comparably strong legal position of detainees, a comprehensive complaint procedure and an, until recently, more or less sustained principle of one prisoner per cell (Ruggiero et al. 1995; Van Zyl Smit and Dünkel 1991). During the last decade, the Dutch prison system has, however, undergone far-reaching changes. The principle of one prisoner per cell has been abandoned and due to drastic financial cut-backs the regime has become much more austere. In a certain sense, rehabilitation (in the limited sense of reducing recidivism) *did* return as a central goal of sentencing. All inmates who have more than a four-month non-suspended prison sentence are subjected to an analysis of their recidivism risk, their causes of offending and their so-called 'learning styles'. The outcome of this test can lead to behavioural interventions designed to reduce their risk of recidivism and to facilitate their safe return to society. These opportunities are, however, only available to a limited part of the prison population (Fischer et al. 2012). Regardless of that fact, specific penal regimes were also introduced for several categories of prisoners who were almost totally excluded from the regular rehabilitation programmes.

Michael Cavadino and James Dignan (2006: 126) call the EBI maximum security prison in the town of Vught a typical example of the Dutch bifurcation strategy. This prison was originally designed for convicts who are classified as an escape risk. To prevent them from escaping, an unprecedentedly strict regime has been created. No activities are allowed in groups of more than two, inmates can only see their visitors from behind glass, and they are handcuffed and searched all over – including anally – on a regular basis.

This regime also applies to inmates suspected – and convicted – of terrorist crimes. The 'terrorist wing' of the EBI prison at Vught was opened in 2005 to keep this category of prisoners away from other inmates to whom they could spread their radical ideas. They are not only isolated from prisoners who are not doing time for terrorist acts, but they are also subjected to an extremely limited regime and can usually only take part in a limited number of activities specially organised for them. After a number of highly critical evaluations, the terrorist wing is no longer used (Van Veldhuis et al. 2010, Sackers 2011).

It would be possible to defend the lengthy sentences and severe regimes described above by arguing that they are designed for offenders who have committed the most heinous crimes, but this certainly does not hold true for some other regimes that are just as well character- ised by extreme austerity and an absence of activities oriented toward a return into society. It is not true, for example, that the detention centres opened in a rush in 2002 can cope with the great number of drug couriers at Schiphol Amsterdam Airport. Although cell-sharing remained rare in the Netherlands, it was introduced on a large scale for this particular category of offenders. Moreover, there were no facilities for these offenders to engage in sport, attend courses or even visit a library, let alone attend courses to reintegrate into society. These deten- tion centres have since become mainly populated by foreigners who are about to be deported and by foreign offenders who will be deported after serving their sentences.

Post-custodial measures

One of the principles of the Dutch penal system has always been that prisoners were gradually prepared for their return into society. When the new Penitentiary Principles Act was passed in 1999, so-called 'peniten- tiary programmes' were introduced in order to enable inmates to spend the last phase of their detention outside the prison walls and take part in activities under a probation order. These penitentiary programmes start a year ahead of the date of conditional release and aim at a smooth transition from prison into society. Those sentenced no longer have to do time inside prison walls, but can work, or conduct educational activi- ties, during the day and stay at their own home at night – under the supervision of the probation service. Electronic monitoring is almost always used to control prisoners during their penitentiary programme. A penitentiary programme is seen as (the final) part of a prison sentence. Convicts who participate in a penitentiary programme are still consid- ered to be detainees, despite the fact that they spend their time outside the prison walls. This aspect distinguishes penitentiary programmes from the regular conditional release system.

In 2006 and 2008, the Inspection for Sanction Implementation (*Inspectie voor de sanctietoepassing*) completed a study on how penitentiary programmes are put into practice. The inspection noted that in 2005 only one third of the 5,000 inmates eligible for a penitentiary programme actually ended their incarceration period outside the prison walls. Moreover, they were mainly prisoners with relatively few psychological or social problems, who did not require any special interventions and represented only a limited risk of recidivism. Inmates who exhibit more problematic behaviour during their incarceration, use drugs or need special care, are not selected for the extra-mural penitentiary programme.

Conditional release

Up to 2008 prison sentences ended with automatic early release after two thirds of the term. Since 2008, however, only a *conditional* release is available for offenders with a prison sentence of one year or more. Exceptions are made for prisoners who misbehave during their prison sentence and for those with a high risk of recidivism. The probation service supervises this conditional release. If the offender breaches the conditions of their parole, the probation service informs the public prosecutor who decides whether the conditional release should be ended and the offender sent back to prison. As a result of the fact that 93 per cent of unconditional prison sentences are shorter than one year, only 2.1 per cent of the prisoners released in 2009 and 2010 were released under conditions (Flight et al. 2011).

It is noteworthy that irregular migrants are only eligible for conditional release if they leave the country and never return. If they cannot fulfil these conditions they have to serve their full sentence. Should the irregular migrant return to the Netherlands, he would have to serve the remainder of his custodial sentence. This policy was introduced in April 2012 (Boone and Kox 2012).

Private sector involvement

Compared to, in particular, the United Kingdom and the United States, the level of private sector involvement in maintaining public security has remained very moderate in the Netherlands. Privatisation, in the sense of private organisations executing originally public sector duties, is actually only visible in the form of private security and investigation services. Their scale is comparable to that of neighbouring countries, but one has to keep in mind that their powers do not exceed those of regular citizens. In addition to this first form of privatisation – the offloading of public tasks to the private sector – Henk van de Bunt and René van Swaaningen (2005) distinguish a second form of privatisation, namely the tendency to run criminal justice agencies as if they were private companies. Contrary to the first, this second form of privatisation fits very well with current Dutch politics: it keeps management in the hands of the State, but allows the claim that the institutions are being dealt with more efficiently.

Until recently, privatisation has remained limited to services: for example, the provision of supplies to the prison kitchen. Yet, private security staff *have* been assigned to some detention centres for foreign prisoners. In 2010, the first detention centre for foreigners awaiting deportation was opened as a public-private partnership (*publiek-private samenwerking*). The 2010 coalition agreement of the first Cabinet of the neo-liberal Prime-Minister Marc Rutte – this minority coalition with the Christian Democrats, condoned by the populist right, dissolved in 2012 – pronounced that 'The Cabinet would prepare a privatisation of relevant tasks of the prison system in order to economise.' These ambitions to privatise have been left by the second Cabinet Rutte – a coalition between neo-Liberals and Labour. A study of the Ministry of Justice's research department WODC was rather negative about the possibility of arriving at a cost reduction without a loss of detention quality (Wilms et al. 2011). They see a strong call for harsher sentencing as one of the possible dangers of continuing privatisation, which is purely inspired by a desire to economise. Yet, in 2013 the pressure to economise has increased. Solutions are now sought in closing relatively expensive, smaller prisons and constructing two new very large ones, leaving the penitentiary programme (as described above) and replacing short term prison sentences with electronic monitoring. Critics fear a further decline of rehabilitative programmes.

Preventative programmes

Crime prevention has been on the Dutch penal policy agenda since the early 1980s. Since then, a whole range of crime prevention initiatives at a structural, situational and an individual level has been set up (van Swaaningen 2002). Every town of a certain size currently has its own community safety plan, albeit within the framework of national guidelines. Most of these plans are not so much directed at crime in the strictly legal sense of the word, but at fighting a much wider range of activities called 'anti-social behaviour', 'nuisance' or 'incivilities', and indeed at tackling insecurity and fear of (street) crime in very general terms. From the early 1990s on, an 'integral' approach of community safety has been the political buzz. This means that an increasing number of actors – police, social work, local authorities, housing corporations, private security firms and the citizenry alike – are now 'responsibilised' to contribute their share.

The Dutch politics of community safety cannot be caught under the Anglo-Saxon banner of 'public-private partnerships', because the different actors work together on a basis of trust and common interests rather than in strictly formalised partnerships. Marc Schuilenburg (2012) has proposed the term 'security assemblage' (after the philosopher Gilles Deleuze) to catch the empirical practice of community safety in the Netherlands. Schuilenburg outlines how, for example, the police collaborate with the tax administration and energy companies in the fight against large scale cannabis cultivation; with the transportation sector in the fight against human smuggling or the illegal dumping of waste; with shop owners and local authorities with respect to shop prohibitions; and with a range of officials (such as social security agencies, housing corporations, child care, energy companies, debt control agencies and social workers) in so-called intervention teams that pay unannounced home visits to families labelled as 'problematic'.

Initially, most community safety plans were embedded in a politics of social welfare and inclusion, but the dominant trend from the mid-1990s on clearly echoes a mere *exclusive* discourse (van Swaaningen 2002). The buzz of 'broken windows' and 'zero-tolerance policing' have reshaped the notion of social crime prevention in a repressive direction (Koemans 2011). The widening of the scope to so-called 'pre-crime' – problematic behaviour that is not yet punishable as such, but which, according to life-course criminological risk assessments will eventually lead to crime – and to feelings of insecurity is yet another major policy change with respect to preventative programmes. The above-mentioned multi-disciplinary intervention teams are installed to offer 'help' in latently criminogenic situations. Reassurance policing is the clearest response to an anxious citizenry, to show that 'something' is being done about their fears and complaints. With the populist political adagio that 'the citizen is always right', feelings of insecurity have actually become a more important incentive for penal intervention than crime as such.

Next to these political changes, the shift in crime prevention politics can also be explained by the fact that evaluation studies designed in the 'what works' framework offer less support for the effectiveness of social crime prevention than for situational prevention or interventions based on life-course criminological risk assessments (van Noije and Wittebrood 2008). This does not mean that social crime prevention actually *is* less effective; it is, because the effects are more indirect, just more difficult to measure.

Nonetheless, social crime prevention is still taking place. Social renewal is still taking place under the banner of crime prevention – albeit increasingly as a means to gentrify deprived areas. Some good old initiatives with restorative aims, such as Neighbourhood Justice (*Justitie in de Buurt*), that had by 2000 gradually crumbled, because the different collaborating parties (Prosecution Service, Victim Support Schemes, Child Protection, Probation and such) were more occupied with their own institutional targets than with the communal goal of crime prevention and restorative justice, have in 2004 been re-established as 'Safety Houses' (*Veiligheidshuizen*). Because such 'communal' goals are also subscribed to in crime prevention politics, Hans Boutellier (2004) is more positive about the current 'safety utopia' than most Dutch criminologists. According to Boutellier, the care for a reasonable measure of security is a matter of civilisation.

Ten years ago, we were more positive about crime prevention (van Swaaningen 2002), but now that 'inclusive' measures have become extremely intrusive and the 'exclusive' policy-line has become more dominant we have become more sceptical. The inclusive policy-line generally aims to 'persuade' 'outsiders' (e.g. drug addicts, prostitutes, homeless, anti-social families) to adopt a 'decent' lifestyle. Sociologists Godfried Engbersen et al. (2005) have coined this deployment of welfare provisions in the fight against nuisance and insecurity as 'social recapture' (*sociale herovering*). If such a social recapture fails, a sheer exclusive trajectory comes to the surface, in which people are actually 'banished' from certain areas – to lend the term Katherine Beckett and Steve Herbert (2010) have introduced to characterise the complex of off-limit orders, anti-loitering ordinances, park exclusion orders, civil gang injunctions and such in the USA. In the Dutch case, Henk van de Bunt and René van Swaaningen (2012) have used this concept to catch the complex of measures to ban beggars from city centres, 'hooligans' from football stadiums and festivals, nasty boys from swimming pools, shoplifters from shops and paedophiles from playgrounds.

It is probably mainly a matter of appreciation, but according to us, the development of crime prevention in the Netherlands predominantly reaffirms the Foucauldian story of a 'penal-welfare complex' in which welfare provisions serve to discipline the population. It is reminiscent of

Stanley Cohen's (1979) notion of the 'punitive city'. Maybe the Dutch prison population has merely decreased because we have creatively transformed policing and community safety politics into the main strategies of crime control. The merger of prevention and repression Willem Schinkel (2011) identified in Dutch local safety politics, strongly oriented at so-called 'pre-crimes' of the 'underclasses' (immigrants, homeless, drug addicts, prostitutes) makes the thesis of an urban revanchism that got hold of penal politics quite plausible (van Swaaningen 2008).

Collateral sentencing

Another measure to prevent ex-offenders from committing further crime is to hold them from occupying certain jobs and positions. In the Netherlands, employers rarely have direct access to criminal records. They do, however, have the possibility, and sometimes the legal duty, to require a 'certificate of conduct' before they employ somebody. Since 2004, the policy of submitting a certificate of conduct has become much stricter, whilst at the same time the categories of jobs for which such a certificate is needed has increased impressively. At present, conduct certificates are required for all jobs in the educational, child care and nursery sector, but also in branches where ex-convicts traditionally could easily find a job, as for example the security or the transportation sector. In case you would want to start your own enterprise or if you want to do business with the national or local government, you often need a conduct certificate as well. Moreover, there are no legal obstacles to require a conduct certificate for employers. In a society in which avoiding risk becomes very dominant, it is predictable that this lack of prescriptions only leads to an increase of the number of jobs a conduct certificate is needed for. Since 2004, the number of applications for a conduct certificate more than doubled to over half a million applications a year and this increase is far from coming to an end. (Boone 2011).

Conclusions

The recent decrease of the Dutch prison population immediately catches the eye when studying recent developments concerning punishment in the Netherlands. This is, indeed, a very interesting phenomenon, in particular after a steady increase of the prison population for thirty years and because, until now, no similar trend can be observed in surrounding countries. The direct causes for this downfall cannot, however, be interpreted as a sign of a renewed tolerant penal climate. On the contrary, the decrease can be partly attributed to factors that are the consequence of the same policy causing the growth of the prison population in first instance.

Therefore we do not hesitate to characterise Dutch society as less tolerant than it was in 1995, the year the first edition of *Western European Penal Systems* was published. In 1995, we still had a rather stable political situation. Since 2002, we have had five elections in which two different extreme Rightwing parties participated. They both managed to win the votes of more than 20 per cent of the population. Their opinions and vocabulary concerning crime and offenders have become common amongst *all* other political parties. Moreover, many developments in penal policy clearly show a more punitive attitude towards deviant behaviour. The process of defining crime up, for example, has resulted in a range of new activities, that were previously judged as rather innocent, being brought under the realm of criminal law. Not the intrinsic 'evil-ness' of the behaviour seems to be guiding for the process of criminalisa-tion, but the degree to which the group amongst whom that behaviour is the most common is an irritant to the law-abiding citizen: that is youngsters, Muslims, irregular migrants and possible terrorists. Other examples of recently introduced punitive measures are the increase of the maximum duration of the temporary prison sentence, the abolition of the policy to evaluate life sentences after a certain number of years, the categorical exclusion of violent and sexual offences from community service orders, the introduction of a 'long stay department' for mentally ill offenders who stay in penal-psychiatric TBS-clinics and the establish-ment of many special regimes for offenders who are not considered to be eligible for rehabilitation. Also in a preventative context many measures are introduced that aim to diminish crime and nuisance. Most typical for the last decade is that the emphasis has shifted from social welfare and inclusive measures to measures that exclude and incapacitate – like for example 'banning orders' or measures that restrict the access to the labour market for ex-offenders.

Despite all this, the rehabilitative orientation that has been character-istic of the Dutch sentencing approach has not been totally lost. After the introduction of the community service orders in the 1970s, many other measures followed that primarily have a rehabilitative aim, such as penitentiary programmes that can be applied in the last phase of a detention, the conditional release system and the introduction of an extensive after care programme in prison. These still aim at smoothly returning prisoners to society, whilst recent efforts to replace short prison sentences with suspended conditional sentences definitely try to keep offenders out of prison. A characteristic of all these measures, however, is that they are applied to an already relatively successful, harmless group of white offenders and that those categories of offenders who would probably profit most are not qualified for them and, worse still, are transferred to the farthest corners of the penitentiary system where a rehabilitative approach totally lacks. The Dutch attitude that David Downes once interpreted as tolerance has turned into indifference towards those people who do not belong to 'us'.

Note

1. We will leave out the whole field of juvenile criminal justice, for it is completely different. For juvenile delinquents, for example, some five times as many non-custodial sanctions (23,583) are meted out as prison sentences.

References

Beckett, Katherine and Steve Herbert (2010) *Banished: The New Social Control in Urban America* (New York: Oxford University Press).

Beijerse, Jolande uit and René van Swaaningen (2007) 'Non-Custodial Sanctions', in Miranda Boone and Martin Moerings (eds), *Dutch Prisons* (The Hague: BoomJu) 77–98.

Boone, Miranda (2012) *Our Own Rascals First!: Inclusion and Exclusion in the Use of Penal Sanctions* (inaugural lecture RUG) (The Hague : Eleven International Publishers).

Boone, Miranda (2011) 'Judicial Rehabilitation in the Netherlands: Balancing between Safety and Privacy', *European Journal of Probation*, 2: 63–77.

Boone, Miranda (2010) 'Only for Minor Offences: Community Service in the Netherlands', *European Journal of Probation*, 2: 22–40.

Boone, Miranda and Mieke Kox (2012) 'What Works for Irregular Migrants in the Netherlands', *European Journal on Probation*, 3: 54–68.

Boone, Miranda and Martin Moerings (2008) 'Detentiecapaciteit en detentieomstandigheden in Nederland', *Fatik*, 120: 5–10.

Boone, Miranda and Martin Moerings (2007) 'Growing Prison Rates', in Miranda Boone and Martin Moerings (eds), *Dutch Prisons* (The Hague: BoomJu) 51–76.

Bovenkerk, Frank (2009) *Etniciteit, Criminaliteit en Het Strafrecht.* (Den Haag: Boom Juridische Uitgevers).

Boutellier, Hans (2004) *The Safety Utopia: Contemporary Discontent and Desire as to Crime and Punishment* (Dordrecht: Kluwer).

Bunt, Henk van de and René van Swaaningen (2012) 'Van Criminaliteitsbestrijding Naar Angstmanagement En Van Preventie Naar Verbanning', in Erwin Muller (ed.), *Veiligheid: Studies Over Inhoud, Organisatie En Maatregelen* (Deventer: Kluwer) 663–76.

Bunt, Henk van de and René van Swaaningen (2005) 'Privatisering Van de Veiligheidszorg', in Laurens W. Winkel, Jacques Jacques M. Jansen, Heiko O.

Kerkmeester, Ruud J.P. Kottenhagen and Vincent Mul (eds), *Privatisering Van Veiligheid* (The Hague: BoomJu) 5–19.

Buruma, Ybo (2004) 'Onoprechte Handhaving', in Bas van Stokkom and Lodewijk Gunther Moor (eds), *Onoprechte Handhaving? Prestatiecontracten, Beleidsvrijheid En Politie-Ethiek* (Dordrecht: Stichting Maatschappij, Veiligheid en Politie) 19–33.

Cavadino, Michael and James Dignan (2006) *Penal Systems: A Comparative Approach* (London: Sage).

Cohen, Stanley (1979) 'The Punitive City: Notes on the Dispersal of Social Control', *Contemporary Crises* 3 (4): 339–63.

Dienst Justitiële Inrichtingen (2012) *Gevangeniswezen in Getal 2007–2011* (The Hague: Dienst Justitiële Inrichtingen).

Downes, David (1988) *Contrasts in Tolerance: Post-War Policy in the Netherlands and England & Wales* (Oxford: Clarendon Press).

Downes, David and René van Swaaningen (2007) 'The Road to Dystopia? Changes in the Penal Climate of the Netherlands', in Michael Tonry and Catrien Bijleveld (eds), *Crime and Justice in the Netherlands* (Chicago: The University of Chicago Press) 31–72.

Engbersen, Godfried, Erik Snel and Afke Weltevrede (2005) *Sociale Herovering in Amsterdam en Rotterdam: Één Verhaal Over Twee Wijken* (Amsterdam: Amsterdam University Press/WRR).

Feeley, Malcolm M . and Jonathan Simon (1992) 'The New Penology', *Criminology*, 30 (4): 452–74.

Fischer, Tamar, Miriam Captein and Barbara Zwirs (2012) *Gedragsinterventies voor volwassen justitiabelen. Stand van zaken en mogelijkheden voor innovatie* (The Hague: BoomJu) WODC Research and Policy series no (302).

Flight, Sander, Oberon Nauta and Jolien Terpstra (2011) *Voorwaardelijk Vrij. Evaluatie van de Wet Voorwaardelijke Invrijheidstelling* (The Hague: WODC).

Garland, David (2001) *The Culture of Control: Crime and Social Order in Contemporary Society* (Oxford: Oxford University Press).

Heide, Wibren van der, Frank van Tulder and Cas Wiebrens (2007) 'Strafrechter en strafketen: de gang van zaken 1995–2006', *Rechtstreeks* 2007, nr. 3.

Kalidien, Sandra and Nynke de Heer-de Lange (eds) (2011) *Criminaliteit en Rechtshandhaving 2010: Ontwikkelingen en Samenhange* (The Hague: BoomJu).

Keijzers, Arjan P.H . (2005) *Nederland: Vrij Veilig. De Opkomst Van Het Thema Veiligheid in de Nederlandse Samenleving* (Unpublished master thesis in Sociology, Erasmus University Rotterdam).

Klijn, Albert, Frank van Tulder, Ralph Beaujean, Toon van der Heijden and Gerdien Rodenburg (2008) *Moord, Doodslag, Taakstraf?: Een Zembla-Uitzending Nader Bekeken*, Raad voor de Rechtspraak, Research Memoranda, 4 (1).

Koemans, Monique (2011) *The War on Antisocial Behaviour: Rationales Underlying Antisocial Behaviour Policies. Comparing British and Dutch Discourse Analyses* (Leiden: Meijers Research Institute and Graduate School of the Leiden Law School).

Kruttschnitt, Candace and Anja Dirkzwager (2011) 'Are there Still Contrasts in Tolerance? Imprisonment in the Netherlands and England 20 Years Later', *Punishment & Society*, 13: 283–306.

Laan, Peter H. van der (1993) 'Het Publiek En de Taakstraf, Een Maatschappelijk Draagvlak Voor de Taakstraf', *Justitiële Verkenningen*, 19 (9): 89–110.

Leun, Joanne van der and Maartje van der Woude (2012) 'A Reflection on Crimmigration in the Netherlands', in Maria João Guia, Maartje van der Woude and Joanne van der Leun (eds), *Social Control and Justice: Crimmigration in the Age of Fear* (The Hague: Eleven International Publishers).

Nelen, Hans (2008) *Evidence Maze: Het Doolhof Van Het Evaluatieonderzoek* (Maastricht: Maastricht University).

Noije, Lonneke van and Karin Wittebrood (2008) *Sociale Veiligheid Ontsleuteld: Veronderstelde en Werkelijke Effecten Van Veiligheidsbeleid* (The Hague: Sociaal en Cultureel Planbureau).

Raad voor Strafrechtstoepassing en Jeugdbescherming (2008a) *Advies: Gedetineerden met een verstandelijke beperking* (The Hague: Raad voor Strafrechtstoepassing en Jeugdbescherming).

Raad voor Strafrechtstoepassing en Jeugdbescherming (2007) *Advies: De zorg aan gedetineerden met een ernstige psychische stoornis of verslaving* (The Hague: Raad voor Strafrechtstoepassing en Jeugdbescherming).

Rovers, Ben (2008) 'Ze Deugen Nergens Voor: Het Belief-Effect in Justitiële Jeugdinterventies', in Hans Moors and Ben Rovers, *Geloven in Veiligheid: Tegendraadse Perspectieven* (Den Haag: Boom Juridische Uitgevers).

Ruiter, Stijn, Jochem Tolsma, Marloes de Hoon, Henk Elffers and Peter van der Laan (2011) *De Burger Als Rechter. Een Onderzoek Naar Geprefereerde Sancties Voor Misdrijven in Nederland* (The Hague: Boom Lemma).

Ruggiero Vincenzo, Mick Ryan and Joe Sim (eds) (1995) *Western European Penal Systems A Critical Anatomy* (London: Sage).

Sackers, Henny J. B. (2011) 'De afschaffing van de Terroristenafdeling', *Sancties*, 6: 333–7.

Schinkel, Willem (2011) 'Prepression: The Actuarial Archive and New Technologies of Security', *Theoretical Criminology*, 15: 365–80.

Schuilenburg, Marc (2012) *Orde in Veiligheid: Een Dynamisch Perspectief* (The Hague: Boom/Lemma).

Sonnenschein, Anne, Susan van den Braak, Debora Moolenaar and Paul Smit (2011) *Trendwatch: Introductie En Eerste Resultaten Van Een Instrument Ter Verbetering Van Justitiële Capaciteitsramingen* (The Hague: WODC).

Spaans, Eric C . (1995) *Werken of Zitten: De Toepassing Van Werkstraffen En Korte Vrijheidsstraffen in 1992* (Arnhem: Gouda Quint).

Swaaningen, René van (2013) 'Reversing the Punitive Turn', in Tom Daems, Sonja Snacken and Dirk Van Zyl Smit (eds), *European Penology?* (Oxford: Hart), 329–50.

Swaaningen, René van (2008) 'Sweeping the Street: Civil Society and Community Safety in Rotterdam', in Joanna Shapland (ed.), *Justice, Community and Civil Society: A Contested Terrain across Europe* (Cullompton: Willan) 87–106.

Swaaningen, René van (2005) 'Public Safety and the Management of Fear', *Theoretical Criminology*, 9 (3): 289–305.

Swaaningen, René van (2002) 'Towards a Replacement Discourse on Community Safety: Lessons from the Netherlands', in Gordon Hughes, Eugene McLaughlin and John Muncie (eds), *Crime Prevention and Community Safety: New Directions* (London: Sage) 260–78.

Swaaningen, René van (2000) 'Back to the Iron Cage: The Example of the Dutch Probation Service', in Penny Green and Andrew Rutherford (eds), *Criminal Policy in Transition* (Oxford: Hart) 91–108.

Swaaningen, René van and Jolande uit Beijerse (2013) 'Bars in Your Head. Electronic Monitoring in the Netherlands', in Mike Nellis, Kristel Beyens and Dan Kaminski (eds), *Electronically Monitored Punishment: International and Critical Perspectives* (London: Routledge) 172–90.

Swaaningen, René van and Gerard de Jonge (1995) 'The Dutch Prison System and Penal Policy in the 1990s: From Humanitarian Paternalism to Penal Business Management', in Ruggiero Vincenzo, Mick Ryan and Joe Sim (eds), *Western European Penal Systems: A Critical Anatomy* (London: Sage) 24–45.

Tonry, Michael (2001) 'Why are U.S. Incarceration Rates so High?', in Michael Tonry (ed.), *Penal Reform in Overcrowded Times* (Oxford: Oxford University Press) 52–64.

Van Zyl Smit, Dirk and Frieder Dünkel (eds) (1991) *Imprisonment Today and Tomorrow: International Perspectives on Prisoner's Rights and Prison Conditions* (Deventer: Kluwer Law International).

Veldhuis, Tinka M. et al. (2010) *Terroristen in Detentie. Evaluatie van de Terroristenafdeling* (University of Groningen: Department of Behavioural and Social Sciences).

Verhagen, Jos (2011) *Gedetineerden ontmaskerd. Hoe in Nederland over gedetineerden wordt gedacht en hoe het werkelijk 'zit'* (Veenhuizen: Nationaal Gevangenismuseum).

Wilms, Peter, Rafiq Friperson and Jamie Weda (2011) *Literatuuronderzoek Privatisering Gevangeniswezen* (The Hague: WODC).

3
Punishment in Sweden: A Changing Penal Landscape

Hanns von Hofer and Henrik Tham

Imprisonment trends: an overview

Europe has abolished the death penalty. Imprisonment has thereby become the most severe available sanction. The level of, and trends in, imprisonment are also often used as a simple way of describing penal control, although it should be noted that fines have always been the dominant penal sanction in Sweden.

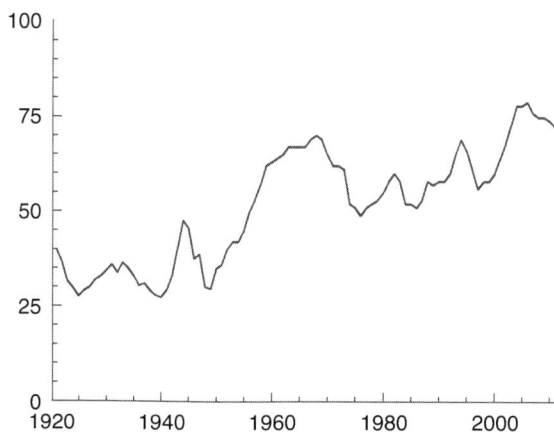

Figure 3.1 Number of prisoners, including remand prisoners, per 100,000 population, 1921–2011. Stock data

Source: Official Swedish Criminal Justice Statistics, compiled by the authors.

Along with the other Scandinavian countries, Sweden is counted among those with the lowest number of prisoners in the world (ICPS 2012). However, as in most other European countries, imprisonment has been on the rise. Figure 3.1 shows the numbers of prisoners and remand prisoners in Sweden over the course of almost a century, 1921–2011. The number of prisoners rose sharply after the Second World War, which was then followed by a marked decrease during the first part of the 1970s. Since that time, however, the trend has been towards an increase. This increase was particularly marked during the first years of the new millennium.

Table 3.1 shows, in turn, that the recent increase in inmate numbers is for the most part associated with drug offences, violence and sexual crimes. Both the numbers sentenced to a prison term and the length of prison sentences have increased. Further, the actual time served in prison has also increased as a result of the abolition in 1999 of the final remnants of the system of release on parole once half the sentence had been served. Inmates can today be released on parole only once they have served two-thirds of their sentence.

To understand the dominance of drug, violent and sexual offences among Swedish prisoners, some further description is required of the policy trends regarding the use of imprisonment for these types of crime.

Table 3.1   Number of prison inmates in Sweden, 1 October 1997, 2004 and 2011 respectively, by offence type. Stock data. Remand prisoners excluded

	1997	**2004**	**2011**
Drug offences (incl. smuggling)	932	1 630	1 637
Violent offences (incl. robbery)	1 255	2 009	1 877
Sexual offences	196	311	425
Other offences	1 683	1 772	1 435
All offences	4 066	5 722	5 374

Note: The figure for 1997 represents the lowest number of inmates in the period 1995–2011. The maximum was reached in 2004 with a total of 5,722 inmates.
Source: Official Swedish Prison Statistics, compiled by the authors.

The impact of sentencing policies on drug, violent and sexual offences

As in other countries, Swedish drug policy has exerted a powerful influence over the development of the entire crime policy field (Träskman 1995, 2004). In contrast to Sweden's traditionally *restrictive* alcohol policy, Swedish drug policy is based on a repressive *total prohibition* model. All non-medical use and handling of drugs is now criminalised. Almost 40,000 compulsory drug tests are administered each year in order to detect drug consumption. In practice, drugs policy has become one of the most powerful driving forces underlying the introduction of increasingly repressive crime policy measures. This trend can be seen in the work of both police and prosecutors (Kassman 1998) and in the praxis of the courts, which is characterised – by Scandinavian standards – by unusually long custodial sentences in drugs cases (Träskman 2004). The changes have also affected the prisons themselves. The establishment of drug-free prisons has become an explicit political objective (Krantz and Hagman 2004), in relation to which there is an acceptance of increasingly stringent security measures (Tham 2003).

Figure 3.2 shows the trend in years of imprisonment meted out by courts of first instance in drug cases – a measure that combines the number of prison sentences and their length.

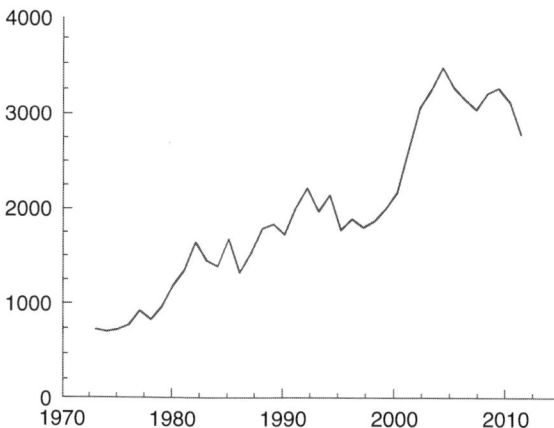

Figure 3.2 Sum of years meted out by the courts of first instance in drug cases, 1973–2011

Source: Official Swedish Criminal Justice Statistics, compiled by the authors.

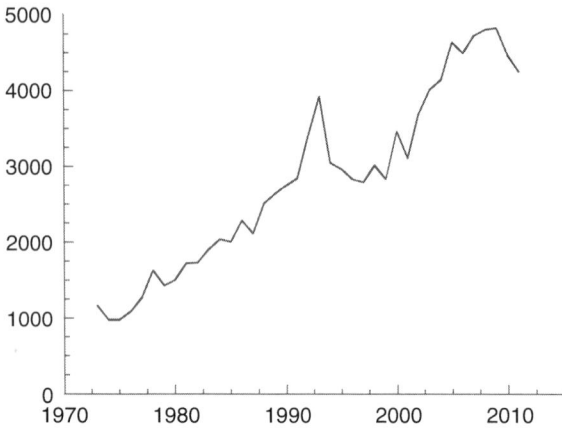

Figure 3.3   Aggregate number of years of imprisonment meted out by courts of first instance in cases involving violence and sex crimes, 1973–2011

Source: Official Swedish Criminal Justice Statistics, compiled by the authors.

The vast majority of both politicians and the public view the idea that there has been an increase in the level of violent crime as an indisputable fact, even though there is no systematic criminological evidence to support this view. The majority of indicators, with the exception of the crime statistics collected by the police and sentencing statistics, indicate rather stable levels of violence.[1] At the same time, the fact that people's perceptions as to what should be defined as violence, and strategies to control violence, have changed, may now be regarded as well-established (von Hofer 2004). In turn, these factors lead to a greater number of both convictions and prison sentences. The rise in imprisonment for crimes of violence is particularly marked by an increase in the length of prison sentences. Figure 3.3 shows the trend in the aggregate number of years of imprisonment meted out by the courts for crimes of violence, including robbery and sexual crimes.

Lifers

Similar shifts may be found in relation to the use of life imprisonment for murder. Despite the fact that murder and manslaughter rates have decreased somewhat since the 1980s, the number of inmates in Swedish prisons sentenced to life imprisonment has increased sharply. In 1983, there were 15 such inmates in Sweden, whereas this number had increased to 159 in 2012 – a tenfold increase, for which there are two explanations. On the one hand, the courts now more often sentence offenders to a prison term instead of sentencing them to secure forensic psychiatric care.[2] On the other hand, the Ministry of Justice, which until recently was responsible for granting pardons and reprieves, has shifted its praxis since the beginning of the 1990s. During the 1980s, the average length of time actually served in prison in connection with a life sentence was approximately eight years. This average has since risen to approximately seventeen years.[3]

Alternatives to custody and the use of imprisonment

A correct description of the trend in the use of imprisonment should also consider various alternatives to prison that involve some deprivation of liberty. If, for example, there had been a shift in sentencing practice in favour of secure psychiatric care or different forms of youth custody, an exclusive focus on prisons would underestimate the use of custodial sanctions. If a shift had occurred in the opposite direction, of course, the resulting increase in prison numbers would constitute a corresponding overestimate.

The question of which sanctions should be regarded as alternatives to a custodial sentence that contain an element of deprivation of liberty is not entirely straightforward. Home detention under electronic monitoring, for example, is in pure legal terms a custodial sentence that is served in the home. Contract treatment usually involves treatment for alcohol or drug abusers, in connection with which part of the sanction is implemented at a non-secure treatment facility. Community service involves a deprivation of liberty in that it involves compulsory labour (albeit with the consent of the convicted individual) even though such sentences are usually served in the form of work at a voluntary organisation.

Comparisons over time are also difficult. Some alternatives to imprisonment have recently been introduced, others have disappeared. Given these reservations, it is nonetheless possible to conclude from official statistics and other sources[4] that Figure 3.1 at least does not overestimate the increase in the use of imprisonment. The increase since the beginning of the 1980s is real, i.e. it is not due to a shift to prison from other forms of sanction involving a deprivation of liberty.

The impact of treatment programmes and parole

There are presently 52 correctional institutions in Sweden. Her prisons remain small, usually with less than 100 inmates. The largest prison – Kumla – has 330 places. Single cells of six square metres are the rule. Open prisons, where security is minimal, account for about a quarter of all prison places. Closed institutions have a high degree of security to prevent inmates from escaping; some of them are held in special high-security units. Inmates are placed in accordance with risk assessments. There is no overcrowding and the staff/inmate relationship is – as in other Scandinavian countries – high. Prisoners are obliged to work. Work can be substituted by studies and treatment.

The most common treatment programmes are the 12-step programme for alcohol and drug abuse, in accordance with the AA-model and other models, programmes to increase the inmates' motivation to desist from crime, and special programmes for convicted sex offenders. In 2011, a total of 4,728 participants in programmes of between 6 and 360 hours in length were completed in prisons (L. Krantz, personal communication, 12 April 2012). The programmes have been chosen on the basis of certain criteria relating to their evidence base. Evaluations have found that cognitive skills and programmes based on the therapeutic communities' model have produced a certain level of positive effects (BRÅ 2002, 2008). These positive programme effects do not, however, appear to be sufficiently large to have produced any positive effect on aggregate levels of recidivism within society at large. The cumulative recidivism frequencies presented in official statistics are characterised by a substantial degree of stability over time.

There are no private sector prisons in Sweden. However, care measures outside prison are often provided by private individuals, associations or foundations. These measures may involve therapy, foster care or institutional substance-abuse treatment.

Following a parole release after two-thirds of the prison sentence has been served, former inmates are subject to a probationary period of at least one year. This usually means that the former inmates are given a probationary supervisor, with half of released inmates being assigned lay-supervisors (BRÅ 2012a: 17). The first part of the post-release period may involve being subject to home detention curfew. Treatment programmes are also conducted within the probation system. The programmes themselves are largely the same as those provided within the prison system. In 2010 a total of 3,686 participants in such treatment programmes were followed to completion within the probation system (L. Krantz, personal communication, 12 April 2012). An evaluation has shown positive effects on recidivism for a project involving a collaboration between the Prison and Probation Service, the Public Employment Service and municipal authorities, which is based on work-focused rehabilitation and job coaching (Nyström et al. 2002). Aggregate recidivism rates for those awarded probationary sanctions have also been very stable over time, however.

The inmates

Women constitute just less than six per cent of Swedish prison inmates. This proportion has remained stable for the past ten years. Following the expansion of illicit drug use in Sweden in the 1960s, however, the proportion of female prison inmates doubled. All other things being equal, women face a lower risk of being sentenced to prison compared with men (von Hofer and Bogestam 2012). There are five prisons for women with altogether 305 beds; about two-thirds are for medium risk prisoners and one-third ("open prisons") for low-risk prisoners. There is no high-security prison for women. As regards recidivism, the differences are small between women and men released from prison. Recent official statistics show that imprisonment for both women and men is followed by higher rates of recidivism, compared with non-custodial sanctions, even if age, prior criminal record and type of crime are held constant (BRÅ 2012b).

Foreign citizens comprise 28 percent of prison inmates. This proportion has remained fairly stable over the past decade and is a clear over-representation. A study from the 1990s found that foreign citizens were three times more likely to be prison inmates than Swedish citizens, based on the size of the two groups in the Swedish population as a whole. The level of over-representation in the prison population was largely similar for the naturalised immigrant population, whereas it was only 1.5 times for second-generation immigrants (Nilsson 2002: 71; Kardell 2011).

The proportion of high status persons sentenced to imprisonment is low. The calls from some leftists in the 1970s to use prisons for the powerful members of society have not borne any fruit. There has, however, been an increase in the level of ambition focused on curbing tax offences and other economic crimes. The Swedish Economic Crime Authority was established in 1998, and has some 400 employees. The Swedish Tax Authority has also established a number of independent tax crime units. Around 100 persons per year are sentenced to imprisonment for tax crimes; the figure has not changed over the course of recent decades. It is not clear, however, that these sentences are primarily focused on high status or powerful individuals. A 2003 analysis of economic crime in Sweden concluded that the most typical crime investigated by the authorities involved accounting offences in connection with the bankruptcy of small and vulnerable businesses (Korsell 2003). Insider offences may constitute an example of more serious economic crime. Even though there has been an increase in the number of sentences for this type of crime, no more than 17 individuals were sentenced for insider offences in 2010, and none of these were given a prison term.

An interview study into the social and economic backgrounds of prison inmates was conducted in 1997. It was possible to compare the findings with a representative sample of the population at large, with data from this group also being collected in the form of face-to-face interviews. Table 3.2 presents a number of the findings, and shows very clearly the level of disadvantage found among the inmates. When problems relating to different aspects of the study participants' social and economic backgrounds were viewed together, it was also found that the situation of female prison inmates is considerably worse than that of their male counterparts. The incidence of incomplete education is striking. Unemployment[5] is almost three times as common among prison inmates. The incidence is quite marked, not only for mental but also for bodily illnesses. And so on for other areas of life.

Table 3.2   Social and economic backgrounds of prisoners and general population, 1997

	Prison inmates (%)	General population (%)
Incomplete education	15	0.3
Unemployed	62	22
Homeless	15	0
Difficulties coping with everyday expenses	42	21
Severe difficulties due to chronic illness	37	11
Mental health problems	49	8
Did not grow up with both parents	56	16

Note: The general population has been made comparable with the prison inmates by controlling for the different distributions according to age and sex.
Source: Nilsson (2002: chapters 5 and 6).

There are a number of comparisons that can also be made with the situation of earlier groups of prison inmates. By comparison with data from 1969, the proportion of prison inmates who were in employment prior to their prison admission has declined. The proportion with substance-abuse problems has increased, and drugs have replaced alcohol. Overall, then, the group of prison inmates has become more disadvantaged over time (Nilsson 2002: 168).

The 1970's: critics of imprisonment turn the tide

While our evidence demonstrates that there has been more than a doubling in the level of imprisonment in Sweden since 1945, and that in important respects some inmates are now even worse off when compared with the wider community than they once were, these developments have not been without their critics. For example, the sustained rise in the use of imprisonment in the 25-year period after the Second World War, the result of sharp increases in theft, met harsh criticism (see below) and the early 1970s saw a marked reduction in the use of imprisonment. One of the present authors then made a prognosis that imprisonment would eventually more or less disappear – as did the Minister of Justice of the time (Geijer 1974). It was not only the decline in the number of prisoners that justified such a prognosis at that time, there were also a number of other circumstances that made the prognosis appear reasonable.

First, the late 1960s and the 1970s were characterised by a clear tendency towards de-criminalisation and de-penalisation (see below). Some of these changes in penal and prison administrative law directly influenced the number of prisoners. They also promised to undermine the prisons from within, via the introduction of more liberal laws regulating furloughs and prison visits and also work and treatment outside the prison.

Second, crime policy became a public issue in Scandinavia for the first time during the 1960s and 1970s, with the emergence of the prisoners' movement and other clientele organisations (Mathiesen 1974; Adamson et al. 2004). At the same time, the media was showing a growing interest in social and crime policy issues and also backed-up the demands for decarceration. The success of the prisoners' movement must be understood against the general, prevailing political critique of society at the time, but it undoubtedly also had an effect of its own.

Third, prior to the late 1960s, crime policy had not been viewed as a political issue and the political parties did not have specific crime policy programmes. The critique of imprisonment influenced the established political parties. They all came to agree that imprisonment was harmful and that it was important to find alternatives. This was the general position in spite of the increase witnessed at the time in the number of serious crimes being committed.

Fourth, in addition to these more immediate circumstances, there were also underlying trends which contributed to a belief that the prison population would decline. Prisons had for a long time been dominated by individuals sentenced for theft offences. The sharp rise in theft crime following the Second World War had by this time started showing clear signs of decline in relative terms (von Hofer and Tham 1989). In spite of the media and political rhetoric, youth crime had started to decline (Estrada 1999). Over time, this also produced an effect on levels of adult crime, as fewer individuals initiated criminal careers. This was shown by analyses of cohort statistics in the early 1980s (von Hofer et al. 1983).

Finally, in an even longer perspective, the civilisation process (Elias 1980) might lead us to expect a decrease in the use of force and incarceration as a means of correcting behaviour. A good example of this in Sweden is that the legal basis for the corporal punishment of wives, servants, children, pupils etc. gradually disappeared after the mid-nineteenth century (von Hofer 2011: 49). In 1979 the explicit prohibition of the corporal punishment of children was written into the Children and Parents' Code.

More punitive times

However, contrary to these developments and the prognosis that the prison population would decrease, there has instead been an increase. A number of conditions that promote imprisonment have gained the upper hand since the late 1970s. Thus the earlier trend towards de-criminalisation and de-penalisation came to a halt, and was replaced by an expansion of the use of penal law. In the process of politisation, an increasing number of interest groups and changing cultural values have come to influence crime policy in a more punitive direction. Further, the conditions for politics in general changed in a manner that led to an increase in the use of a more repressive crime policy. These new conditions will be illustrated briefly by reference to the influence of the media, the crime victim, the drug issue, and the issue of immigrants.

The media

The media played an important role in the process that led to the reorientation of crime policy. This was the period during which parts of the radio and television services became privatised in Sweden. To an increasing extent, the media came to manifest an interest of its own in crime policy issues (Pollack 2003; Heber 2007; Demker et al. 2008), and it did so in a way that was characterised by a clear bias towards punishment and retribution. This also manifested itself in a growing criticism by the media of the allegedly too-lenient judgments and sentences passed by courts at all levels of the justice system, including the Supreme Court.[6] According to the latest European Survey of Crime and Safety, the Swedish public is increasingly more in favour of imprisonment than is the case in the EU on average (van Dijk et al. 2007:149). Nonetheless, in-depth Scandinavian, including Swedish, comparative research on attitudes towards punishment clearly shows that an informed public is hesitant about imprisonment (Balvig et al. 2010).

The crime victim

Recent decades have witnessed the emergence of the crime victim as a public issue in the majority of Western countries. This is also the case in Sweden where the focus on this issue may be even stronger than it is in comparable countries. The crime victim issue has manifested itself in the emergence of numerous voluntary organisations, in legislation, and in the establishment of a new and powerful government agency, The Crime Victim Compensation and Support Authority. The central focus of the crime victim issue is directed at the victims of violence, particularly at women as the victims of men's violence. Analyses of penal legislation and imprisonment for crimes of violence show this issue to have had a substantial effect on the number of prisoners (Table 3.3 below and Figure 3.3 above) (Tham, in collaboration with Rönneling and Rytterbro 2011).

There are a number of factors that can serve to explain the crime victim's rise to prominence. General explanations that have been proposed include, the process of civilisation and a decline in the level of tolerance for violence (Elias 1980), a view that the crime victim serves as a symbolic means of re-establishing a lost consensus in modern and secularised society (Boutellier 1989), the rise to prominence of human rights (Doak 2008) and a general tendency towards defining-up deviance and intensifying reactions to rule-breaking (Young 2007; Tonry 2010). These explanations appear to be valid for Sweden, and their effects may have been further intensified by Sweden's interventionist welfare state tradition, which focuses on doing good and helping the suffering, her pronounced policy of promoting gender equality and, in particular, the Swedish movement to combat men's violence against women (Tham, in collaboration with Rönneling and Rytterbro 2011).

The drug issue

This has been the dominant theme in Swedish criminal policy since the 1960s, in terms of both the discourse and distribution of criminal justice resources. Its impact on imprisonment has been shown above.

From around 1980 the slogan "Sweden – a drug free society" became the guideline for Swedish drug policy. The policy is thus in contrast with the, relatively speaking, more liberal policies of other European countries. Claims of success of Swedish governments[7] are not supported by indicators of harmful drug use, including drug-related deaths (Tham 1998b; EMCDDA 2011: 88; Olsson 2011).

The development from the 1980s of this increasingly interventionist and repressive drug policy coincided with growing criticisms of the welfare state. The concept of the "Swedish model", which had originally referred to active labour market policies and a generous social insurance system, was given a new meaning. It instead came to be used to refer to the allegedly successful drug policy that Sweden now was going to export to the rest of the world. One interpretation of this development is that the policy became a means for reinforcing a threatened national identity that could no longer be constructed around the welfare state project. The drug discourse increasingly became formulated in terms of traditional moral values, the people, mobilisation, and Sweden vs. abroad. A total consensus was created around the Swedish drug policy (Tham 1995a).

Immigrants

"The immigrant criminal" deserves to be regarded as a theme in its own right. Successive Swedish Governments and the political parties have generally taken a clear stance against racist and xenophobic tendencies. However, in 1991 a new party, New Democracy, entered the Parliament on an anti-immigration platform. Another of the party's focal issues was crime and the two questions were usually linked together. The New Democracy party almost dissolved during the three-year period in which it was represented in parliament and actually disappeared shortly afterwards. In 2010 a new anti-immigration party, the Sweden Democrats, won a number of seats in Parliament. Like their forerunners, crime is one of the party's most high-profile issues, and this is clearly linked to immigrants and particularly to Muslims.

The issue of the immigrant criminal also taps into other discourses. One is the gender question. Rapes committed by immigrant men are viewed as an expression of a foreign culture and of a lack of equality between the sexes. The theme of "honour killings" clearly depicts certain immigrant groups as being responsible for crimes that particularly provoke public outrage. These types of crimes are seen as part of the more general issue of men's violence against women – an issue that has special prominence in a country with perhaps the strongest policy of gender equality in the world (Borchorst et al. 1999).

The other discourse is that of "them" and "us". The immigrants are clearly overrepresented among the unemployed, which contributes further to their relative poverty. Earlier, this might not have contributed to a tendency towards polarisation. Solidarity was a central value for the Social Democrats and Social Democratic Prime Ministers stressed the importance of getting everyone aboard the train towards the good society. In today's politics this is less self-evident. Income inequality has risen since around 1980 and has become increasingly notable in the size of the differential between the top and bottom deciles. Since the early 1990s, unemployment has multiplied and residential segregation has become more marked. These economic and material trends are linked to a new discourse focused on the 'deserving' and the 'undeserving' and on individualisation and responsibilisation.

The Politicians

Ultimately, however, national politicians are the sources of crime policy. Above, public issues and special interests have been suggested as the driving forces behind crime policy. These processes should not, though, be regarded as something to which politicians only respond. Politicians actively exploit and influence issues that are put forward. Policies relating to the three central types of crime that influence the size of the prison population, drugs, violence and sex, have very clearly been politically driven. The rise in prisons is not an unavoidable development in relation to which politicians have been forced in certain directions. The prison populations and crime policy in general are clear political constructs (von Hofer 2003). The question is, however, why politicians increasingly formulated crime policy in an expansionist and punitive direction. One possible explanation might be formulated in terms of state legitimacy.

The nation-state is under threat. For countries like Sweden, decisions that were previously taken by politicians in parliament have now been moved to the European Union and the global market. National politicians still want to make political decisions, and particularly so in Sweden with her strong tradition of an interventionist welfare state. Moral issues, including law-and-order, become tempting as a means of demonstrating concern and action (Tham 1995b, 2001; see also Chapter 4 by Emma Bell in this volume).

Geographical borders and national identities have become increasingly diffuse as a result of migration and EU decisions. Tough measures against illegal immigrants and foreign criminals can also be perceived as a means of strengthening national sovereignty (Barker 2012: 118). The threat from abroad is clearly demonstrated in the rise to prominence of "serious international organized crime" as a political and public issue. This notoriously diffuse and illusive phenomenon constitutes a perfect motivation for expanding penal and procedural law and the powers of the police. In the process of bifurcation in criminal policy (Garland 2001) serious crimes, and particularly serious *organised* crimes, are those that remain the preserve of the state once everyday crimes have been assigned to the guardianship of the local community and responsible citizens (Andersson 2010). When welfare state ambitions crumble the state will try to (re-) establish its legitimacy through law-and-order.

Consequences

Against the background of the changes described above, it is perhaps understandable that punishment has once again become fashionable. The old liberal idea that punishment and penal law should be viewed as a last resort (*ultima ratio*), once other measures have been exhausted without producing an effect (Träskman 2009), is increasingly losing its political value. The punitive approach is – at least ideologically – acquiring the status of a *prima ratio*, since the use of the criminal law is the ultimate expression of individualisation and responsibilisation.

This trend may[8] have been – unintentionally – facilitated by the reforms in Sweden that were implemented in 1989 under the label "straffvärdesreform" ("penal value reform") through their renewed emphasis on retribution in the guise of "just deserts".

Between 1965 and 1988 the courts were obliged, with an eye to general prevention (deterrence), to give special consideration to rehabilitation in relation to sentencing. In 1989 this was replaced with the principle of just deserts. According to the *travaux préparatoires*, the new regulations were not intended either to increase or diminish the use of imprisonment. Instead, the basic aim was to increase the predictability and uniformity of penal decision-making (Lundqvist 1990:103).[9]

Irrespective of the intentions of the reform, the reform made it *de facto* much more difficult to criticise the use of specific sanctions on the basis of empirical arguments as to their effectiveness or otherwise, since the idea of just deserts is a purely *legal* doctrine. It requires that offences be followed by proportional and equivalent punishments and – for reasons of justice – it also requires that as many offences as possible are punished. Furthermore, the *rhetoric* of the reform itself conveyed no strong arguments to counter the demands for more and harsher punishments that were subsequently raised in the less liberal times of the 1990s and 2000s. The good intentions of the reform[10] have been hijacked by a different sort of political reality, as is illustrated in Table 3.3.

Table 3.3 provides an overview of central penal legislation in Sweden since the late 1960s. It is based on government bills presented to the Swedish Parliament. The bills are broadly classified according to whether they imply an expansion or a contraction of penal legislation. The table refers both to criminalisation/decriminalisation and penalisation/de-penalisation. The legislation is also classified according to the political complexion of the government of the time: social democratic or centre-right.[11]

Table 3.3 Expansion and contraction of penal law 1968–2011 and type of government

Government	Expansion of penal law	Contraction of penal law
1968–1976 Social democratic	1968:7 Drugs 1971:10 Tax fraud 1971:99 Aircraft hijacking 1972:67 Drugs 1972:96 Gambling 1973:37 Terrorism 1973:115 Temporary arrest 1975/76:82 Debtor crimes	1970:125 Pornography 1972:138 Military arrest 1972:138 Death penalty in war 1974:20 Prison regime 1974:70 Abortion 1975/76:42 Recidivism 1975/76:42 Theft and robbery 1975/76:113 Drunkenness
1976–1982 Centre-right	1978/79:62 Prison regime 1980/81:46 Drugs 1980/81:108 Environmental crime 1981/82:43 Battery of women 1981/82:85 Economic crime 1981/82:187 Pornography	1976/77:104 Conversion of fines 1978/79:212 Youth prison abolished 1980/81:1 Prison regime 1980/81:44 Prison two weeks 1981/82:153 Parole 1980/81:46 Internment abolished

Continued

Table 3.3   Continued

Government	Expansion of penal law	Contraction of penal law
1982–1991 Social democratic	1982/83:141 Drugs 1983/84:135 Prison regime 1983/84:105 Sex crimes 1984/85:116 Pornography 1987/88:71 Consumption of drugs 1987/88:120 Recidivism 1987/88:137 Battery of women	1982/83:85 Half time parole 1982/83:90 Conversion of fines 1986/87:106 Contract treatment 1986/87:112 Pre-trial detention 1989/90:2 Drink-driving
1991–1994 Centre-right	1991/92:35 Sex with children 1992/93:4 Parole 1992/93:141 Assault, threats etc. 1992/93:142 Consumption of drugs 1993/94:44 Drink-driving 1993/94:101 Hate crimes	1991/92:109 Community service 1993/94:184 Electronic supervision
1994–2006 Social democratic	1996:97:135 Witness threats etc. 1997/98:55 Abuse of women 1997/98:55 Buying sex 1997/98:96 Parole 1997/98:97 Criminal records etc. 1998/99:43 Drugs while driving 1999/00:109 Insider trading 1999/00:124 Smuggling 2001/02:124 Trafficking, sex. 2002/03:138 Graffiti 2004/05:45 Rape 2005/06:177 Special powers	2001/02:126 Restorative justice 2004/05:34 Electronic supervision
2006–2012 Centre-right	2007/08:97 Drink-driving 2007/08:163 Special powers 2008/09:118 Murder 2008/09:141 Grooming 2009/10:50 Statue of limitation 2009/10:70 Child pornography 2009/10:105 Drug testing children 2009/10:147 Serious violent crimes 2009/10:152 Trafficking 2010/11:45 Stalking 2010/11:77 Buying sex	2009/10:191 Criminal records

As is quite clear from the table, there is a marked decrease in legislation involving a contraction of penal measures. Since the beginning of the 1990s there have only been a few such examples. With the exception of the first social democratic period, it is also clear that the contractions relate to penalties and not behaviours or acts. It is always politically tempting to expand the penal law but doing so will be economically costly in terms of increased levels of imprisonment. The economic effects of political action in the form of criminalisations and penalisations can be reduced by introducing alternatives to imprisonment. Finally, at this general level, the analysis does not reveal any clear differences between social democratic and centre-right governments in terms of the expansion or restriction of the use of penal legislation. However, taking the length of government periods into consideration the centre-right governments seem to be more active in the expansion of penal law. The present Government has also explicitly stated its intention to consider the needs for further sharpening of punishments as a means of fighting crime (Proposition 2011/2012: 1, 19).

Today, all political parties – of both the right and the left – are agreed that police, prosecutors, courts and also prisons must be given more resources. Between 2000 and 2011 annual expenditures increased from 125 to 207 million EUR (+66 per cent) for the police, and from 39 to 75 million EUR (+92 per cent) for the prison and probation service. These increases lie far above the general trend for the total State budget (+15 per cent) (ESV 2012: table 11).

Conclusion

It can perhaps be argued that the "punitive turn" in terms of the development of imprisonment is not all that sharp after all (cf. Pratt 2008a, 2008b; Uglevik and Dullum 2012). Taking population growth into account, the increase since the mid-1960s is not particularly large. The increase in Sweden relative to other European and Anglo-American countries is fairly limited, and Sweden still has one of the smallest prison populations in the world.

However, what has clearly changed is the discourse on crime and punishment and the way in which public policy in this field is formulated. The welfare state model still occupies a strong position but it is now being challenged by politicians, the media, the legal discourse, and by various interest groups. What all this means for practical crime policy is the following.

As in other countries (Haggerty 2004; Ryan 2005; Loader 2006) until the mid-1960s the conduct of crime policy at the political level essentially took place at the Ministry of Justice in consultation with various experts. Crime policy did not constitute part of day-to-day politics nor was it an issue of party political disagreement (Lexbro 2000: 48). However, from the 1980s onward, the Swedish parties of the centre-right also placed the theme of crime and punishment on their political agendas (Estrada 2004). The most marked law-and-order election took place in 1991. The Social Democrats were criticised by the opposition as being soft on crime. This theme, together with the main issue – the attack on the welfare state model – was quite similar to the British election of 1979 (Tham 1998a). In both countries the neoliberals and conservatives came to power and the question of punishment was placed on the political agenda.

With the new principle for sanctioning in place, the question became how to decide what constitutes just deserts or a just punishment. This was answered by reference to the public. Increasingly, the government justifies criminal policy by reference to the general sense of justice (Andersson 2002), and this strengthens the role of the politicians.[12] In a parliamentary democracy, the elected representatives of the people, and in particular the Prime Minister and the Minister of Justice, must almost by definition reflect the general sense of justice (Andersson 2002; Tham 2011).

These tendencies are further intensified by the popular conception that the perpetrator violates the victim's *human rights* in committing the offence, and that the victim receives redress through the punishment of the perpetrator (i.e. her/his being sent to prison). These ideas were introduced at the governmental level in a document produced in 1993 by the conservative Minister of Justice, but they have since become common currency. For example, the proposal to abolish the statute of limitations in relation to murder and manslaughter offences was welcomed by the then chairperson of the Justice Committee (a member of the liberal *Folkpartiet*) with the following justification:

> I think it is very important [and the proposal should also include other serious violent offences and in particular serious sexual offences; *added by the authors*] as a means of being able to provide redress to crime victims and their families in a completely different way … and I think that the legitimate interests of the perpetrator are very, very little and that therefore, nobody should be able to evade punishment simply because time has passed.[13]

In a 2006 parliamentary debate, even the Social Democratic Minister of Justice expressed a positive view on the punitive use of criminal sanctions, in a way that would have been quite unthinkable a couple of decades earlier:

> Then it's the case that we want to violate the integrity of people who commit serious crimes. It's not just about us wanting to use wires and phone-taps against them; we want people who commit serious crimes to be locked away for many, many years. That, if anything, has to be seen as a violation of integrity.14

The new developments are well illustrated by a government bill from 2010, which widened the punishment scale for serious crimes of violence. It has been calculated that it will have the effect of increasing the prison population by 400, which represents an increase of seven per cent. The bill was motivated exclusively by reference to public demands for stiffer penalties – for which there was no empirical evidence – and with no reference being made to expected effects on crime (SOU 2008: 85; Proposition 2009/2010: 147). In 2012, the National Council for Crime Prevention was instructed by the Ministry of Justice to evaluate the new law (Justitiedepartementet 2012). Again, the purpose was not to evaluate whether the increase in sentencing severity has resulted in a decrease in violent crimes but rather to ensure that the courts are in fact meting out more punishment.

In summary, while the Ministry of Justice formerly had the task of finding a balance between the relatively diffuse interests of the criminal justice authorities and more general interests (which included those of victims, offenders and the public at large), this process has become much more complicated. A "two-party" relationship has been replaced by a "multi-party" one, in which widely differing interests must be balanced: those of public authorities, political parties, interest groups, the media and what is deemed to be public opinion. At the same time, an increasing number of crime policy questions are being dealt with in the full glare of the public gaze, which promotes solutions that serve *many* different interests and in which the traditional restrictive legal principles of the *Rechtsstaat*[15] no longer constitute the self-evident frame of reference for the competing parties. The influence of traditional legal thinking and of legal experts is diminishing, and the real losers in this new game are the lawbreakers.

The prison sanction is in practice focused on "truly poor" citizens. It is not uncommon for them not even to be citizens at all, but rather mere foreigners. We have long known that it is the truly poor that are sent to prison (Snare 1992; Nilsson, R. 2003), and evidence in support of this knowledge is produced time and again in systematic level-of-living surveys (above, Table 3.2; Nilsson, A. 2003). Poverty is associated with, amongst other things, political powerlessness (Vogel et al. 1988), which in the case of foreigners is also regulated in law: foreign citizens lack the right to vote or to stand in parliamentary elections. Previously, there were interest groups and political parties that were still prepared, at least in part, to safeguard the interests of even these powerless groups.

Today the situation is quite different. When it comes to drug addicts, drug dealers, robbers, murderers, rapists, paedophiles, pimps, Russian *mafiosi*, people traffickers and other thugs, villains and riff-raff, who would want to restrict penal law to being used only as a last resort? These often impoverished people have nothing of value to offer in this trade: neither in the form of economic or social capital, nor even in the sense of any meaningful form of electoral support. Thus, the criminal of today's Sweden has become a true "public enemy".[16]

Notes

1. Alternative data series are based on self-report studies, victim surveys, hospital admissions, and cause of death statistics. For a recent analysis, see Estrada (2006) which by all accounts invalidates studies that are entirely based on criminal justice data (e.g. Thome 2007; Thome and Birkel 2007).
2. The question of how this change is to be explained (as the result of changes in practice, legislation and/or actual circumstances) has yet to be investigated. The fact that a shift was taking place became clear as early as the end of the 1980s (Belfrage 1995: 51).
3. In 2010 the sentence for murder was changed from 10 years or life imprisonment to 10–18 years or life imprisonment. This has led to a reduction in the number of life sentences.
4. Various publications of official statistics, information from Government authorities, and von Hofer and Tham (1988).
5. An inmate's unemployment refers to the situation before entering prison.
6. This has led to recent attempts from the judiciary – together with prosecutors and barristers – to counteract this criticism by means of a more explicit media strategy (Engelbrektson 2006).
7. Swedish National Institute for Public Health (1998); Junior Minister of Social Affairs Maria Larsson (28 October 2010. Retrieved from http://www.tv4play.se/nyheter_och_debatt/nyhetsmorgon?title=debatt_om_narkotika&videoid=1105593).
8. For a contrasting view see for example von Hirsch (1994).
9. Others (e.g. Jareborg 1995: 119) believe that the reform has helped to (marginally) counter-balance the increased use of incarceration and that there has been a considerable 'hidden' redistribution of sanctions.

10. Cf. von Hirsch (1994: 476): '[P]roportionate sentences do not have to be severe ones; indeed, a policy of proportionality can (and should) be implemented with significantly *reduced* sanction levels'.
11. The number of bills is larger than shown in the table. In order to present a simplified rundown, some bills that have been judged as less important have been left out. Legislation resulting from directives from the European Union has been excluded.
12. General prevention (deterrence) and rehabilitation were relative sanctions in that they are seen as means of reducing crime. This gave experts such as the criminologist a role in criminal policy in order to test the effects of sanctions. On the other hand, just deserts is an absolute principle where the expert has no special authority and cannot contribute. In this context, the politicians are able to, so to speak, get rid of the expert (Andersson 2002; Balvig et al. 2010).
13. Interview with Johan Persson, Sveriges Radio, Dagens eko 16:45, 4 January 2006. [Authors' transcription and translation.]
14. Parliamentary debate 31 May 2006. Retrieved from http://www.riksdagen.se/sv/Dokument-Lagar/Kammaren/Protokoll/Riksdagens-protokoll-2005061_GT09132/. [Authors' translation; emphasis added.]
15. The basic idea of the *Rechtsstaat* is to safeguard the individual (including the lawbreaker) against encroachments of the State.
16. On the distinction between 'friend and foe', see for example Schmitt (1927); Jakobs (1985, 2004).

References

Adamson, M., Grip, L., Modig, C., and Nestius, H. (eds) (2004) *När botten stack upp. Om de utslagnas kamp för frihet och människovärde* (Hedemora: Gidlunds).
Andersson, R. (2002) *Kriminalpolitikens väsen*. Avhandlingsserie nr 10. Kriminologiska institutionen (Stockholm: Stockholms universitet).
Andersson, R. (2010) 'Tryggare kan ingen vara – en svensk kriminalpolitik för 2010-talet?', in T. Hjort, P. Lalander, and R. Nilsson (eds), *Den ifrågasatte medborgaren – om utsatta gruppers förhållande till välfärdssystemen* (Växjö: Linnéuniversitetet) 139–63.
Balvig, F., Gunnlaugsson, H., Jerre, K., Olaussen, L.P., and Tham, H. (2010) 'Den nordiske retsbevidsthedsundersøgelse', *Nordisk Tidsskrift for Kriminalvidenskab*, 97 (3): 232–50.
Barker, V. (2012) 'Global Mobility and the Penal Order: Criminalizing Migration. A View from Europe', *Sociology Compass*, 6 (2): 113–21.
Belfrage, H. (1995) *Brottsligheten, psykiatrin och samhället. Introduktion till den medicinska kriminologin* (Stockholm: Liber utbildning/Wiksell medicin).
Borchorst, A., Christiensen, A.-D., and Raum, N. (1999) 'Ligestilede demokratier? Opsamling og perspektivisering', in C. Bergqvist, A. Borchorst, A.-D. Christiensen, N. Raum, V. Ramstedt-Silén, and A. Styrkársdóttir (eds), *Likestilte demokratier? Kjönn og politikk i Norden* (Oslo: Universitetsforlaget) 253–65.
Boutellier, H. (1989) *Crime and Morality: The Significance of Criminal Justice in the Post-Modern Culture* (London: Kluwer Academic).

BRÅ. (2002) *Att lära ut ett nytt sätt att tänka. Utvärdering av Cognitive Skills-programmet i kriminalvården 1995–2000* (Stockholm: Brottsförebyggande rådet).

BRÅ. (2008) *Behandling av narkotikamissbrukare i fängelse* (Stockholm: Brottsförebyggande Rådet).

BRÅ. (2012a) *Lekmannaövervakare inom frivården* (Stockholm: Brottsförebyggande rådet).

BRÅ. (2012b) *Återfall i brott. Slutgiltig statistik för 2003–2005. Sveriges officiella statistik* (Stockholm: Brottsförebyggande rådet). Retrieved from http://www.bra.se/download/18.1ff479c3135e8540b29800013250/Sammanfattning_aterfall_slutl_2003–2005.pdf.

Demker, M., Towns, A., Duus-Otterström, G., and Sebring, J. (2008) 'Fear and Punishment in Sweden', *Punishment & Society*, 10 (3): 319–32.

van Dijk, J., van Kesteren, J., and Smit, P. (2007) *Criminal Victimisation in International Perspective. Key findings from the 2004–2005 ICVS and EU ICS* (The Hague: Boom Juridische uitgevers).

Doak, J. (2008) *Victims' Rights, Human Rights and Criminal Justice: Reconceiving the Role of Third Parties* (Portland, OH: Hart).

Elias, N. (1980) *Über den Prozeß der Zivilisation* (Frankfurt a.M.: Suhrkamp).

EMCDDA. (2011) *Annual Report on the State of the Drugs Problem in Europe.* European Monitoring Centre for Drugs and Drug Addiction (Luxembourg: Publication Office of the European Union). Retrieved from http://www.emcdda.europa.eu/attachements.cfm/att_143743_EN_EMCDDA_AR2011_EN.pdf.

Engelbrektson, L. (2006) 'Han vill att domarna ska höras', *Apropå*, (1): 30.

Estrada, F. (1999) 'Juvenile Crime Trends in Post-War Europe', *European Journal on Criminal Policy and Research*, 7 (1): 23–42.

Estrada, F. (2004) 'The Transformation of the Politics of Crime in High Crime Societies', *European Journal of Criminology*, 1 (4): 419–43.

Estrada, F. (2006) 'Trends in Violence in Scandinavia According to Different Indicators. An Exemplification of the Value of Swedish Hospital Data', *British Journal of Criminology*, 46 (3): 486–504.

ESV. (2012) *Tidsserier, statens budget m.m. 2011* (Stockholm: Ekonomistyrningsverket). Retrieved from http://www.esv.se/PageFiles/6085/rapport-slutgiltig-2012–06–11–2.pdf.

Garland, D. (2001) *The Culture of Control: Crime and Social Order in Contemporary Society* (Oxford: Oxford University Press).

Geijer, L. (1974) *Anförande vid svenska och finska socialtjänstemannaförbundens studiedagar* (Unpublished manuscript dated 5 August 1974.)

Haggerty, K.D. (2004) 'Displaced Expertise: Three Constraints on the Policy-Relevance of Criminological Thought', *Theoretical Criminology*, 8 (2): 211–31.

Heber, A. (2007) *Var rädd om dig! Rädsla för brott enligt forskning, intervjupersoner och dagspress.* Avhandlingsserie nr 23. Kriminologiska institutionen (Stockholm: Stockholms universitet).

von Hirsch, A. (1994) 'The logic of prison growth', *The Modern Law Review*, 57: 476–82.

von Hofer, H. (2003) 'Prison Populations as Political Constructs: The Case of Finland, Holland and Sweden', *Journal of Scandinavian Studies in Criminology and Crime Prevention*, 4 (1): 21–8.

von Hofer, H. (2004) 'Gewaltsensibilität, Gewaltschutzbewegung und Kriminalstatistik', in G. Hanak, and A. Pilgram (eds), *Phänomen Strafanzeige.*

Punishment in Sweden 55

Jahrbuch für Rechts- und Kriminalsoziologie '03 (Baden-Baden: Nomos Verlag) 7–29.
von Hofer, H. (2011) *Brott och straff i Sverige. Historisk kriminalstatistik 1750–2010. Diagram, tabeller och kommentarer* (4th ed.). Kriminologiska institutionen (Stockholm: Stockholms universitet).
von Hofer, H. and Bogestam, N. (2012) 'Påföljdsutvecklingen 1975–2011', in J. Hagstedt (ed.), *Brottsutvecklingen i Sverige 2008– 2011* (Stockholm: Brottsförebyggande rådet) 302–29.
von Hofer, H. and Tham, H. (1988) 'Brottslighet och kontroll', in U. Himmelstrand and G. Svensson (eds), *Sverige – vardag och struktur. Sociologer beskriver det svenska samhället* (Stockholm: Norstedts) 555–81.
von Hofer, H. and Tham, H. (1989) 'General Deterrence in a Longitudinal Perspective. A Swedish Case: Theft, 1841–1985', *European Sociological Review*, 5 (1): 25–45.
von Hofer, H., Lenke, L., and Thorsson, U. (1983) 'Criminality Among 13 Swedish Birth Cohorts', *British Journal of Criminology*, 23 (3): 263–69.
ICPS. (2012) *World Prison Brief.* International Centre for Prison Studies. Retrieved from http://www.prisonstudies.org/info/worldbrief/wpb_stats.php.
Jakobs, G. (1985) 'Kriminalisierung im Vorfeld einer Rechtsgutsverletzung', *Zeitschrift für die gesamte Strafrechtswissenschaft*, 97: 751–85.
Jakobs, G. (2004) 'Bürgerstrafecht und Feindstrafrecht', *hrr-strafrecht.de*, (3): 88–95. Retrieved from http://www.hrr-strafrecht.de/hrr/archiv/04–03/index.php3?seite=6.
Jareborg, N. (1995) 'The Swedish Sentencing Reform', in C.M.V. Clarkson and R. Morgan (eds), *The Politics of Sentencing Reform* (Oxford: Oxford University Press) 95–124.
Justitiedepartementet. (2012) *Utvärdering av 2010 års straffmätningsreform*, Ju2012/860/KRIM. Retrieved from http://www.regeringen.se/download/1fed10c9.pdf?major=1&minor=185470&cn=attachmentPublDuplicator_0_attachment.
Kardell, J. (2011) *Utländsk bakgrund och registrerad kriminalitet – överrepresentationen i den svenska kriminalstatistiken.* Kriminologiska institutionen (Stockholm: Stockholms universitet).
Kassman, A. (1998) *Polisen och narkotikaproblemet. Från nationella aktioner mot narkotikaprofitörer till lokala insatser för att störa missbruket.* Acta Universitatis Stockholmensis. Stockholm Studies in Sociology. N.S. 6 (Stockholm: Stockholms universitet).
Korsell, L.E. (2003) *Bokföringsbrott – en studie i selektion.* Avhandlingsserie nr 13. Kriminologiska institutionen (Stockholm: Stockholms universitet).
Krantz, L. and Hagman, K. (2004) *Kriminalvårdens redovisning om drogsituationen 2003* (Norrköping: Kriminalvården).
Lexbro, L (2000) 'Konflikt eller konsensus? Kriminalpolitiken och riksdagen 1946–1965', *Nordisk Tidsskrift for Kriminalvidenskab*, 87 (1): 48–58.
Loader, I. (2006) 'Fall of the "Platonic Guardians". Liberalism, criminology and political responses to crime in England and Wales', *British Journal of Criminology*, 46 (4): 561–86.
Lundqvist, A. (1990) 'Some Recent Developments in Swedish Criminal Policy', in N. Bishop (ed.), *Scandinavian Criminal Policy & Criminology* (Stockholm: Scandinavian Research Council for Criminology) 100–11.

Mathiesen, T. (1974) 'The Politics of Abolition. Essays in Political Action Theory', *Scandinavian Studies in Criminology*, 4 (Oslo: Universitetsforlaget).

Nilsson, A. (2002) *Fånge i marginalen. Uppväxtvillkor, levnadsförhållanden och återfall i brott bland fångar.* Avhandlingsserie nr 8. Kriminologiska institutionen (Stockholm: Stockholms universitet).

Nilsson, A. (2003) 'Living Conditions, Social Exclusion and Recidivism Among Prison Inmates', *Journal of Scandinavian Studies in Criminology and Crime Prevention*, 4 (1): 57–83.

Nilsson, R. (2003) 'The Swedish Prison System in Historical Perspective: A Story of Successful Failure?', *Journal of Scandinavian Studies in Criminology and Crime Prevention*, 4 (1): 1–20.

Nyström, S., Jess, K., and Soydan, H. (2002) *Med arbete som insats. Klienteffekter och samhällsekonomisk lönsamhet i socialt arbete* (Stockholm: Socialstyrelsen).

Olsson, B. (ed.) (2011) *Narkotika. Om problem och politik* (Stockholm. Norstedts Juridik).

Pollack, E. (2003) 'Juvenile Crime and the Swedish Media in an Historical Perspective. A Series of Contextualised, Cross-Sectional Studies of the Years 1955, 1975 and 1995', *Stockholm Media Studies*, 1: 184–202.

Pratt, J. (2008a) 'Scandinavian Exceptionalism in an Era of Penal Excess: Part I: The Nature and Roots of Scandinavian Exceptionalism', *British Journal of Criminology*, 48 (2): 119–37.

Pratt, J. (2008b) 'Scandinavian Exceptionalism in an Era of Penal Excess: Part II: Does Scandinavian Exceptionalism Have a Future?', *British Journal of Criminology*, 48 (3): 275–92.

Proposition (2009/2010: 147) *Skärpta straff för allvarliga våldsbrott m.m.* Retrieved from http://data.riksdagen.se/fil/C7C05A9B-794F-424D-84E4-BB9BB7CB464B.

Proposition (2011/2012: 1) *Utgiftsområdet 4. Rättsväsendet.* Retrieved from http://data.riksdagen.se/fil/C551E0E8–877E-49D8–996E-B325F21BAB4C.

Ryan, M. (2005) 'Engaging with Punitive Attitudes towards Crime and Punishment. Some Strategic Lessons from England and Wales', in J. Pratt, D. Brown, M. Brown, S. Hallsworth, and W. Morrison (eds), *The New Punitiveness. Trends, Theories, Perspectives* (Cullompton: Willan Publishing) 139–49.

Schmitt, C. (1927) 'Der Begriff des Politischen', *Archiv für Sozialwissenschaften und Sozialpolitik*, 58 (1): 1–33.

Snare, A. (1992) *Work, War, Prison and Welfare. Control of the Laboring Poor in Sweden.* (Copenhagen: Københavns universitet).

SOU. (2008) *Straff i proportion till brottets allvar. Slutbetänkande av Straffnivåutredningen.* Statens offentliga utredningar 2008 nr 85 (Stockholm: Fritzes).

Swedish National Institute for Public Health. (1998) *A Preventive Strategy. Swedish Drug Policy in the 1990s* (Stockholm: Regeringskansliet).

Tham, H. (1995a) 'Drug Control as a National Project: The Case of Sweden', *The Journal of Drug Issues*, 25 (1): 113–28.

Tham, H. (1995b) 'From Treatment to Just Deserts in a Changing Welfare State', in A. Snare (ed.), Beware of Punishment. *Scandinavian Studies in Criminology*, 14: 89–122.

Tham, H. (1998a) 'Crime and the Welfare State. The Case of the United Kingdom and Sweden', in V. Ruggiero, N. South, and I. Taylor (eds), *The New European Criminology. Crime and Social Order in Europe* (London: Routledge) 368–94.

Tham H. (1998b) 'Swedish Drug Policy: A Successful Model?' *European Journal on Criminal Policy and Research*, 3: 395–414.

Tham, H. (2001) 'Law and order as a leftist project? The case of Sweden', *Punishment & Society*, 3(3): 409–26.

Tham, H. (2003) 'Kriminalvårdslagens utveckling i Sverige', in K. Andenæs and K. Papendorf (eds), *Fortsatt uferdig* (Oslo: Unipax) 200–10.

Tham, H. (2011) 'Nej, svensken vill inte ha strängare straff', *Tvärsnitt*, (3–4): 12–6.

Tham, H. (in collaboration with A. Rönneling and L.-L. Rytterbro) (2011) 'The emergence of the crime victim: Sweden in a Scandinavian context', in M. Tonry and T. Lappi-Seppälä (eds), Crime and Justice in Scandinavia. *Crime and Justice,* 40 (Chicago, IL and London: The University of Chicago Press) 555–611.

Thome, H. (2007) 'Explaining the Long-Term Trend in Violent Crime: A Heuristic Scheme and Some Methodological Considerations', *International Journal of Conflict and Violence*, 1 (2): 185–202.

Thome, H. and Birkel, C. (2007) *Sozialer Wandel und Gewaltkriminalität. Deutschland, England und Schweden im Vergleich, 1950 bis 2000. Analysen zu gesellschaftlicher Integration und Desintegration* (Wiesbaden: VS Verlag für Sozialwissenschaften/ GWV Fachverlage GmbH).

Tonry, M. (2010) 'The Costly Consequences of Populist Posturing and Rhetorics: ASBOs, Victims, "Rebalancing", and Diminution of Support for Civil Liberties', *Punishment & Society*, 12 (4): 387–413.

Träskman, P.O. (1995) 'The Dragon's Egg – Drugs-Related Crime Control', in A. Snare (ed.), Beware of Punishment. *Scandinavian Studies in Criminology*, 14 (Oslo: Pax) 147–72.

Träskman, P.O. (2004) 'Drug Control and Drug Offences in the Nordic Countries: A Criminal Political Failure Too Often Interpreted as a Success', *Journal of Scandinavian Studies in Criminology and Crime Prevention*, 5 (2): 236–56.

Träskman, P.O. (2009) 'Purchase of a Sexual Service – a Lawful Private Delight or an Offence? A Study of Criminal Legislation in the Nordic Countries', *Scandinavian Studies in Law 54*, 289–303.

Uglevik, T. and Dullum, J. (eds) (2012) *Penal Exceptionalism? Nordic Prison Policy and Practice* (London and New York: Routledge).

Vogel, J., Andersson, L.-G., Davidsson, U., and Häll, L. (1988) *Inequality in Sweden. Trends and Current Situation. Living Conditions 1975–1985* (Stockholm: Statistics Sweden).

Young, J. (2007) *The Vertigo of Late Modernity* (Los Angeles: Sage).

4
Punishment as Politics: The Penal System in England and Wales

Emma Bell

Introduction

In the 1995 edited collection, *Western European Penal Systems*, Mick Ryan and Joe Sim concluded their chapter on the penal system in England and Wales by observing that 'the future looks bleak in England and Wales' (Ruggiero et al. 1995: 124). Without wishing to sound overly pessimistic, it would seem that their prediction was prescient. Indeed, many of the trends identified by Ryan and Sim in 1995 have deepened and a number of penal innovations have reinforced what they described as the 'disciplinary drive' (ibid.: 119). Most obviously, the prison population has continued to increase at an alarming rate, going far beyond the increases predicted in 1995. It now stands at record levels at over 87,000 prisoners (ICPS 2012). These figures omit the two to three thousand foreign nationals detained at any one time in 'immigration removal centres' or 'short term housing facilities' in England and Wales (Silverman and Hajela 2012), bringing the total incarcerated population closer to 90,000.

Despite the development of human rights legislation and ongoing criticism from European institutions (see, for example, CTP 2008), conditions in English prisons in the main continue to be 'overcrowded, unhygienic and brutalizing' (Ryan and Sim 1995: 110), ensuring that offenders go to prison *for* punishment not simply *as* punishment. Furthermore, the social composition of those detained has changed little, penal establishments generally being reserved for the poorest and most economically and socially marginalised members of society. Ethnic minorities also continue to be disproportionately represented in prison. Outside prison too, Muslims have become a new 'suspect community' (Pantazis and Pemberton 2009), bearing the brunt of new anti-terrorist legislation, which has been extended even further than when it was first designed to neutralise the risks posed by Irish terrorism in the 1970s. In addition, the trend toward managerialism has intensified since 1995, encouraged by the reorganisation of the Prison and Probation Services into a new National Offender Management Service.

Yet, there are some novelties. Whilst Ryan and Sim noted that prosecution and imprisonment for the minor offences of the poor, such as vagrancy and begging, had already increased significantly by the early 1990s (Ryan and Sim 1995: 107), it was only in 1998 – with the passing of the *Crime and Disorder Act* under a New Labour government – that new hybrid penalties were created, specifically to target such nuisance offences and any other behaviour that could be construed as 'anti-social'. New civil penalties – such as the now infamous Anti-Social Behaviour Order (ASBO) – were put in place, backed up by the threat of imprisonment, thus extending the reach of the criminal law even further than before. Such penalties, justified by a misinterpretation of left realism (Lea and Young 1993), have often been presented as a way of improving the lives of the poor. Yet, in practice, they have often entailed their increased surveillance and coercive attempts have been made to force them to change their behaviour.

Penal and social interventions have become increasingly blurred, particularly under the New Labour government, as social problems, such as educational failure and family breakdown, have come to be associated with delinquency. Many social interventions, intended to remedy these problems, are often underpinned by the threat of coercion, creating a contemporary 'welfare sanction' (Garland 1985). Such interventions reflect the continued obsession with responsibilising offenders and the poor in general, whilst the wealthy and powerful continue to escape responsibility, most flagrantly in the wake of the latest financial crisis.

In 1995, Ryan and Sim noted, following researchers such as Fitzgerald and Sim (1982), that the English penal system was still 'in crisis' (Ryan and Sim 1995: 93). It can certainly be said that this is still the case today, with the prisons full to bursting and the population set to rise still further. Prisons are experiencing a severe crisis of legitimacy. The government is faced with the dilemma of how to ensure that the public is convinced that 'justice is done' whilst preventing massive spending increases on the penal system during a deep recession. As we shall see, the private sector is being heralded as the magic solution to this specific conundrum. Meanwhile, the prison itself is being lambasted by the public and the tabloid press for being an ineffective remedy for crime. It also continues to face severe criticism from human rights organisations and from penal reform groups. Other penal interventions, such as those designed to tackle anti-social behaviour, have been ridiculed and lampooned for their ineffectiveness. Yet, despite an apparent change of rhetoric following the appointment of a new Minister for Justice (Kenneth Clarke) after the 2010 elections, the penal system of England and Wales seems to be set on the same fatalistic collision course as it was in 1995. This chapter will seek to analyse the key trends identified above before seeking to determine what are the key pressures driving penal policy toward a never-ending state of crisis.

The expansionist prison system

With the exception of the period 1910–1940, when it more than halved, the prison population of England and Wales has been on a constant upward trajectory throughout the past 100 years and more – never more so than since the early 1990s, when it began to rise exponentially, reaching a record high of 88,179 prisoners in December 2011 (Berman 2012). The population shot up by over 58 per cent between 1995 and 2012.[1] The projected increase of over 5,000 prisoners between 1995 and 2001[2] was surpassed by almost 10,000 prisoners – an increase of over 15,000 prisoners in the space of just six years (ICPS 2012). See Figure 4.1. It is expected that the prison population will continue to rise and could reach as many as 94,800 people by 2017 (Ministry of Justice 2011a).

The rate of imprisonment currently stands at 155 people per 100,000 of the total population, placing England and Wales very high up the

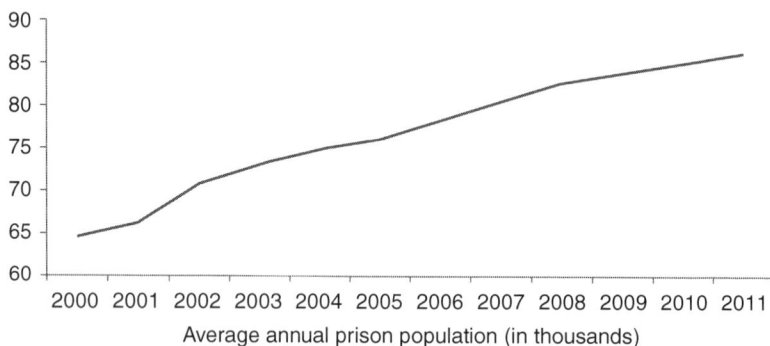

Figure 4.1   Average annual prison population
Source: Chart compiled from statistics provided by Berman 2012.

scale compared to other European countries – just below Scotland and Hungary but far above Western European countries such as France (151/100,000), Iceland (47/100,000) and even Northern Ireland (99/100,000) (ICPS 2012). In terms of total population, England and Wales are placed at number four in the imprisonment league tables, just below Russia, the Ukraine and Turkey (ICPS 2012).

Of course, only a small number of offenders are sentenced to imprisonment, but overall the custody rate has increased over the past two decades, from 4.1 per cent in 1989 (Ministry of Justice 2010a: 30) to 7.9 per cent at the time of writing in 2012 (Ministry of Justice 2012: 8). These increases are particularly notable for serious offenders, especially those convicted of violent and sexual offences (Ministry of Justice 2010a: 30). Simultaneously, the use of community sentences has increased by a massive 83 per cent (Ministry of Justice 2010a: 31), suggesting that these non-custodial sentences have failed to act as alternatives to custody. On the contrary, it is shown below that they have actually contributed to an increase in the prison population. Whilst the fine remains by far the most common disposal handed down by the courts (Ministry of Justice 2012: 53), imposed on over 65 per cent of all convicted offenders (Ministry of Justice 2012 10), its use has decreased by 20 per cent since 1989 (Ministry of Justice 2010a: 31). This would suggest a preference for increasingly demanding penalties which are often backed up by the threat of imprisonment (see Figure 4.2).

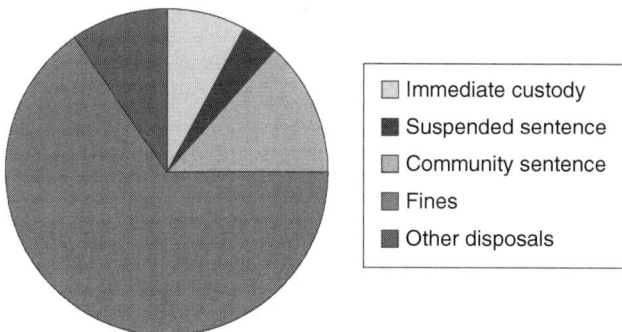

Figure 4.2   Sentences handed down by all Criminal Courts in England and Wales in 2011 (%)

Source: Chart compiled from Ministry of Justice statistics (see Ministry of Justice 2012: 9.)

The direct causes of prison expansion

There is a number of factors which would appear to have directly fuelled the increase in the prison population, not least the increase in the custody rate over the past couple of decades. Firstly, prison sentences have lengthened considerably: the average custodial sentence length handed down by the courts was 13.7 months in 2009, compared to 11.5 months in 1999 (Ministry of Justice 2010a: 32). This trend has in part been encouraged by the increasing use of indeterminate sentencing, notably via the creation of Indeterminate Sentences for Public Protection (IPPs) by the *Criminal Justice Act 2003*. Prisoners sentenced to IPPs must serve a minimum period of time in custody (stipulated by the sentencing judge) and thereafter may only be released at the discretion of the Parole Board. Between 2005 and 2011, just 320 IPP prisoners were released (PRT 2011: 21). As of 31 December 2011 there were 6,162 offenders in prison serving an IPP sentence (Hansard 2012a).

The *Legal Aid, Sentencing and Punishment of Offenders Act* which received Royal Assent on 1 May 2012 has effectively abolished IPPs, although it is not retroactive and therefore leaves thousands of IPP prisoners behind bars. Furthermore, the same Act reintroduces the so-called 'two-strikes' mandatory life sentence for those aged over 18, who are convicted for a second time of certain scheduled offences (laid out in the *Criminal Justice Act 2003*) which are deemed serious enough to justify a sentence of ten years or more.[3] In addition, new mandatory minimum sentences have been created for those who threaten others with a knife in public (six months for adults and 4 months for 16 and 17-year-olds). This confirms a trend toward mandatory minimum sentencing begun under the New Labour government in 1997. Previously, there had only been one mandatory minimum sentence in England and Wales: the life sentence for murder, created after the definitive abolition of the death penalty in 1965.

These trends have greatly eroded the principle of proportionality in the criminal justice system which has guided criminal procedure (in theory, at least) since the Enlightenment. Increasingly, offenders are finding themselves facing longer jail terms, not just for the offence they committed but also for breach of the conditions of an order imposed for relatively minor offences which were not initially deemed worthy of imprisonment (see below). Disproportionate sentencing was particularly notable in the wake of the English riots of summer 2011. For example, those who were convicted of theft found themselves facing prison terms of 7.1 months whilst the average sentence length for the same offence is 2.4 months (Ministry of Justice 2011b).

Another driver of an increased prison population has been the limitation of parole. The system of parole has undergone many changes over the past hundred years. Prior to the 1990s, most prisoners were eligible to apply for release after having served one third of their sentence. In the 1990s, a series of reforms led to the limitation of parole (Bell 2011). Today, prisoners still benefit from early release on parole (more commonly known today as release on licence), but usually only after having served half of their sentence. In addition, they can expect to be placed under surveillance until the entirety of their sentence has expired (previously, surveillance ended after an offender had reached the two thirds point of their sentence). The Ministry of Justice specifically cited the large numbers of offenders recalled to custody for failure to comply with their conditions of release on licence as one of the main drivers of the increase in the prison population (Ministry of Justice 2009: 3).

It is not just breach of licence which has led to increasing numbers of people finding themselves behind bars, but also breach of non-custodial penalties. The number of people imprisoned for breach of a non-custodial penalty increased by 470 per cent between 1995 and 2009 (Ministry of Justice 2009: 7). These non-custodial penalties include the Single Community Order, the Suspended Sentence Order (also introduced by the 2003 Act) and civil penalties such as the Anti-Social Behaviour Order (ASBO – created by the *Crime and Disorder Act 1998*). The conditions of these various orders may be extremely onerous, ranging from requirements to attend treatment programmes for drug and alcohol abuse, to carry out unpaid work in the community and/or to be subject to curfews and electronic surveillance. The *Legal Aid, Sentencing and Punishment of Offenders Act* sought to toughen up these sentences, notably by extending the maximum curfew period from six to twelve months.

With regard to ASBOs, there is no limit to the conditions which may be imposed on a person subject to such a measure, these not being defined by law. Any conditions may be imposed which are thought to prevent the offender from engaging in behaviour considered 'to be likely to cause harassment, alarm or distress to one or more persons not of the same household as himself'. These may entail exclusion from a certain area, for example. Anyone who fails to respect the conditions of their ASBO may be subject to anywhere up to five years' imprisonment. Whilst imprisonment for breach of ASBOs has not been a principal driver of the prison population, it is certainly a small factor: in 2010, 52.5 per cent of all those who breached their ASBO received a custodial sentence, whilst only 1.9 per cent were discharged (Home Office 2010).[4]

Despite an express desire on the part of the Justice Minister to see a reduction in the prison population (*The Guardian* 2010), it would seem that there is unlikely to be a significant departure from the trends which have helped to fuel it over the past couple of decades. Any small measures to reduce it, such as lowering the remand population[5] by enabling defendants who have 'no real prospect' of receiving a custodial sentence to be released on bail – are likely to be cancelled out by severe sentencing and the continued creation of ever-more new imprisonable offences. The New Labour government had already created a record number of new offences, some of which have directly contributed to an increase in the prison population (Ministry of Justice 2009: 11). The concept of criminal behaviour was broadened by the creation of new inchoate offences, such as that of assisting or encouraging another person to commit a criminal offence, regardless of whether or not there is a direct causal link between the two acts or whether the other person actually goes on to offend (*Serious Crime Act 2007*). The anti-terrorism legislation also criminalises not just those responsible for acts of terrorism but also those who may be considered to be inciting such acts (*Terrorism Act 2006*). The current government has also created new imprisonable offences, for example, converting the civil offence of squatting into a criminal one. The coalition's lack of interest in reducing the prison population was made clear by its decision to drop the initial proposal made by the Justice Minister to grant sentence discounts of 50 per cent to defendants who make early guilty pleas.

Austere regimes?

For those who do find themselves behind bars, the conditions of detention remain poor. Prisoners are, in theory, protected from 'cruel, inhuman or degrading treatment or punishment' under the *European Convention on Human Rights* and the *Human Rights Act 1998*. Prison authorities are obliged to take reasonable measures to ensure that the basic physical needs of prisoners are cared for, to provide adequate healthcare facilities, to ensure the physical safety of prisoners and to prevent detainees from taking their own lives in custody. In the UK today, prisoners tend to receive adequate nourishment, even though the food served does not always meet government standards (House of Commons 2006a). All prisons are also obliged to provide medical care to their inmates. Yet, despite some improvements, the Prisons Inspectorate has raised concerns about the standard of healthcare, which is often considered to be inadequate, especially with regard to treatment for drug users and those suffering from mental health problems (HM Inspectorate of Prisons 2011: 42–3). Prison authorities sometimes fail in their task of ensuring the physical safety of their inmates. It is estimated that there were over 1,700 deaths in prison in England and Wales in the years 1997–2007, 900 of which were self-inflicted (INQUEST 2012; Scott 2008: 117–9).

A situation contributing to deaths in custody, as well as an overall degradation of prison conditions, is that of overcrowding. In April 2012, 85 prisons in England and Wales (representing 62% of the total) were considered to be overcrowded (Berman 2012: 11). In June 2007, it was estimated that overcrowding causes two suicides a week in penal establishments in England and Wales (*The Guardian* 2007). The serious consequences of forced cell-sharing were revealed in 2000 with the brutal murder of Zahid Mubarek – a young Asian offender detained at Feltham prison – who was beaten to death by his violent and racist cell-mate. The official inquest into his death highlighted the problem of overcrowding, which made the circulation of information regarding individual offenders rather difficult (House of Commons 2006b.: 438).

Finally, prisoners who do not conform to the prison rules may still find themselves subject to particularly brutal punishment. Recently, the Prisons Inspectorate raised concerns about the operation of an unofficial punishment wing at HMP Liverpool in which a number of vulnerable prisoners, including those at risk of suicide, had been placed in solitary confinement for long periods of time (HM Inspectorate of Prisons 2012). All this would suggest that the 'pains of imprisonment' continue to be severe. Even if some physical conditions have improved, the practical and psychological effects of prison remain similar to those which Fitzgerald and Sim indentified in 1982 (Fitzgerald and Sim 1982: 149). It would seem that, 'for prisoners, the institution continue[s] to be an alien place of often-bearable pain and desperate tension' (Sim 2009: 110). This is particularly the case for certain groups of people, notably minority ethnic groups, who tend to be more vulnerable than others.

Who is targeted by the 'disciplinary drive'?

In 1995, Ryan and Sim noted, 'those who are punished overwhelmingly come from the economically and politically marginalized and the racially disadvantaged' (1995: 105). Again, little would seem to have changed in this respect.

Black, Asian and minority ethnic groups

In terms of race, ethnic minorities continue to be disproportionately represented in prison. In 2010, almost 26 per cent of all prisoners were from Black, Asian and Minority Ethnic (BME) groups (Ministry of Justice 2011c: 66), whereas it is estimated that 'not White-British' people represent just 16.7 per cent of the total population in England and Wales (Office for National Statistics 2011: 4). Black people represent the largest minority ethnic group in prison – 14.5 per cent in 2009 (Ministry of Justice 2011c: 70) – compared to under three per cent of the total population (Office for National Statistics 2011: 6). The number of foreign prisoners is also significant in English and Welsh prisons. In the early/mid 1990s foreign prisoners accounted for eight per cent of the total prison population, increasing to approximately 14 per cent by June 2006 (Berman 2012: 8). Since then, the proportion of foreign nationals in prisons has fallen slightly and was 13 per cent in March 2012 (ibid.). Sixty-two per cent of these prisoners are from a minority ethnic group (ibid.).

It is not just that minority ethnic groups are disproportionately represented in prison but they are also subject to longer sentences. Whilst the average custodial sentence length stands at 14.9 months for White offenders, it increases to 19.9 months for Asian offenders and 20.8 months for Black offenders (Ministry of Justice 2011c: 52). These groups are also likely to be subject to racism whilst in detention: a 2010 study of racist incidents in prison found that over one third of those interviewed said that racist incidents occur daily or often (PRT 2010a).

BME groups are also more likely to be targeted by a range of other penal measures. Indeed, some measures have been specifically designed to target foreign nationals, many of whom are likely to belong to a BME group. For example, the *Anti-Terrorism Crime and Security Act 2001* allowed foreign nationals to be detained indefinitely in prison, until the House of Lords ruled the practice unlawful. Subsequently, the *Prevention of Terrorism Act 2005* introduced Control Orders, which may require those subject to them to be placed under house arrest for an indefinite period of time. These were replaced in 2011 by Terrorism Prevention and Investigation Measures, but the new measure differs little from the previous orders. Whilst those placed under such an order will be subject to less restrictive conditions and the order is generally limited to a maximum of two years, terrorist suspects will still not be permitted to hear the evidence against them, and any breach of the order may result in imprisonment of up to five years.

Immigrants

The number of people detained under the immigration laws has also increased significantly: as of 31 March 2012, there were 3,034 people detained in custody, the highest number since records began in 2001 (Home Office 2012b).[6] This represents an increase of 14 per cent on the previous year (ibid.). Previously, there was a considerable number of children also held in immigration detention. Although child detention under immigration law has not been ended completely – as pledged by the coalition government (HM Government 2010: 21) – the number of children detained has declined considerably: as of 31 March 2012, there was just one child detained awaiting deportation (Home Office 2012b). Nonetheless, the number of children entering detention has actually been increasing since early 2011 (ibid.).

Children and young people

In general, there are significant numbers of children and young people in the criminal justice system – those aged under 18 account for 21 per cent of first-time entrants to the prison system (Youth Justice Board/ Ministry of Justice 2012: 47). Although the numbers of children in custody[7] have fallen considerably – since reaching a peak of 2,807 in 2002–2003, in 2010–2011 there were still 2,040 children under the age of 18 held in the youth secure estate, in secure children's homes, secure training centres and young offender institutions (Youth Justice Board/ Ministry of Justice 2012: 29). In addition, there are very high numbers of young people aged between 18 and 21 held in custody – 7,816 as of the end of March 2012 (Ministry of Justice 2012b). The number of children in custody is significantly higher than in 1995 when the number of 15 to 17-year-olds in prison stood at less than 988 (Home Office 2006: 116). The proportion of children in prison is also higher than in many other European countries: the number of children under 18 incarcerated represents 1.6 per cent of the total prison population in England and Wales,[8] compared to 0.7 per cent in Italy or zero per cent in Spain (ICPS 2012). Also, the age of criminal responsibility – ten – is lower than the average age of 14 or 15 elsewhere in Europe, attracting the criticism of the European Commissioner for Human Rights (Council of Europe 2012). The latter has also criticised the high numbers of children and young people who continue to be remanded in custody, accounting for 26 per cent of the total custodial population (Youth Justice Board/ Ministry of Justice 2012: 26). It is, however, possible that new limitations on the use of remand introduced by the *Legal Aid, Sentencing and*

Punishment of Offenders Act 2012 (see above) will encourage a reduction in the juvenile remand population.

Yet, this same Act brings in other changes to the sentencing of young offenders which could potentially cause the youth custodial population to increase again. Firstly, the new mandatory minimum sentence for those who threaten others with a knife in public will also apply to 16 and 17-year-olds. Secondly, young people sentenced to a Detention and Training Order[9] will be subject to penalty for breach even *after* the order has finished its term. Finally, penalties for breach of Youth Rehabilitation Orders[10] are to be made more stringent: the maximum fine which can be imposed has been increased to £2,500 (from £250 for offenders under 14 and £1,000 for all other offenders) and curfews may now be imposed for 16 hours per day for a maximum of 12 months (previously 12 hours per day for six months). This would suggest that the process of 'dejuvenilisation' (Pitts 2001: 48) of the youth justice system – whereby the latter comes to resemble more closely the adult justice system in its harshness – may be set to continue.

Indeed, the drive to clamp down on 'anti-social' behaviour, which disproportionately targets young people, shows no signs of abating. In all likelihood, the new Crime Prevention Injunctions (see above) will have an impact on young people to the same extent as ASBOs – perhaps even more so, given the fact that they will be easier to obtain. Between 2000 and 2010, there were 7,785 ASBOs issued to young people, 68 per cent of which were breached (Youth Justice Board/Ministry of Justice 2012: 13). Of these, 25 per cent resulted in a custodial sentence.

Women

Another significant characteristic of the prison population in England and Wales, as in other countries, is that it is predominantly made up of men, women only representing 4.8 per cent of the total prison population (Youth Justice Board/Ministry of Justice 2012: 5). This figure has been falling every year since reaching a high of 6.1 per cent in 2002 (ibid.). Whilst this number is low compared to the number of women in the general population, it is significantly higher than its low of 2.5 per cent in the late 1960s, or even its 1992 rate of 3.4 per cent (Home Office 2003). This does not reflect increased offending rates on the part of women, but rather increasing sentencing severity (Home Office 2004: 3). In some ways, women are treated more harshly than men by the criminal justice system. For example, in 2009, more first-time female offenders than first-time male offenders were sentenced to custody for indictable offences – 16 per cent and 9 per cent respectively (Ministry of

Justice 2010b: 42) – yet, overall, they tend to serve shorter community and custodial sentences than men (ibid.: 45). There are higher proportions of men than women sentenced to custody for theft and drugs offences (ibid.: 50–3). This perhaps reflects the fact that more female crimes than male are financially motivated – 28 per cent and 20 per cent respectively (Cabinet Office 2009: 15) – and that women are more likely to be affected by serious drugs misuse problems (27% of female prisoners compared to 20% of male prisoners – ibid.: 11). Indeed, women who find themselves in custody are particularly vulnerable, often suffering from a complex set of problems, such as victimisation and abuse, financial problems, mental health disorders, substance abuse problems, high rates of unemployment coupled with low skills (ibid.: 10–5).

Gay, lesbian, bisexual and transgender people

There are no official statistics available on the number of lesbian, gay, bisexual and transgender (LGBT) people currently held in prisons in England and Wales but it is estimated that they represent approximately 5,000 people (*The Independent* 2011). The way in which LGBT people interact with the criminal justice system remains under-researched, most research focusing on the prosecution of crimes against them – notably hate crime – rather than on how they may be treated as defendants or prisoners. In prison, they tend to be particularly vulnerable to victimisation (ibid.). Yet, these problems are often ignored by prison staff. Whilst prison authorities are obliged to make an effort to tackle discrimination with relation to gender, race, religion, disability and sexual orientation – in compliance with equality legislation – those responsible seem ignorant of issues relating to the latter: a report by the Inspectorate of Prisons, noted, 'Even diversity managers frequently shrugged their shoulders [when asked about diversity policies with regard to sexuality] and said or implied that issues of gay identity were 'too difficult' (HM Inspectorate of Prisons 2011: 33). Only a few prisons had sought to tackle homophobia (ibid.: 39). Outside prison, LGBT people generally expect to be discriminated against by the police and by the judiciary, regardless of whether they are suspected of a crime or merely reporting one (Hunt and Dick 2008).

Marshalling the disadvantaged

Overall, prisoners tend to suffer disproportionately from a host of different problems: family breakdown (7% of male sentenced prisoners and 50% of female sentenced prisoners had run away from home as a child, whilst more than 25% of prisoners had been taken into care as a child); educational failure (50% of male prisoners and 33% of female prisoners had been excluded from school whilst the same proportion of male prisoners and 70% of female prisoners have no formal quali-fications); unemployment (66% of all prisoners were unemployed in the month immediately preceding their incarceration); homelessness (approximately one third of all prisoners were living in temporary accommodation or sleeping rough immediately before their imprison-ment); mental health problems (approximately 70% of all prisoners suffer from two or more mental disorders) (Berman 2012: 16). Young people are particularly vulnerable: those who end up in custody 'experi-ence multiple layers of different types of complex disadvantage ... both in terms of home and family and in terms of psycho-social and educa-tional problems' (PRT 2010a).

These complex problems are often regarded as being the principal causes of crime. For Prime Minister David Cameron, they are also regarded as the key indicators of a 'broken society'. In his own words, 'The broken society is not one thing alone. It is not just the crime. It is a whole stew of violence, anti-social behaviour, debt, addiction, family breakdown, educational failure, poverty and despair' (Cameron 2010). These interconnected problems are to be addressed, not by tackling their structural causes, but instead by measures which seek to reinforce individual responsibility. So, for example, following the English riots of summer 2011, Cameron announced that interventions to reinforce parental responsibility would be strengthened, extending the family intervention programmes initially introduced under New Labour. These projects focus on 'anti-social families' – bringing together a range of serv-ices to tackle problems of poor parenting, truanting and addiction, for example. Whilst participation in these projects is voluntary, 'problem' families who refuse to co-operate may face eviction, have their children taken into care or find themselves subject to anti-social behaviour orders. So, social interventions can rapidly transpose into penal interventions.

In many cases, social and penal sanctions are actually combined into one penalty. For example, the Detention and Training Order aimed at young recidivists (see above) and a range of community sanctions seek to address the causes of offending behaviour, as well as punishing by making attendance at drug and alcohol addiction programmes, for example, conditions of formal sanctions. Yet, as suggested above, such penalties tend to encourage an escalation of the penal sanction rather than effectively tackling offenders' problems. The emphasis on indi-vidual responsibility renders these welfare initiatives extremely coercive. It is in this way that the 'welfare sanction' that Garland originally wrote of – with reference to the beginning of the twentieth century (Garland 1985) – has truly come of age at the beginning of the twenty-first century (Bell 2011).

Perhaps this is the most significant penal novelty since Ryan and Sim wrote their overview of the English penal system in 1995. Yet, the fact that penal sanctions, notably imprisonment, tend to disproportionately target the poor is certainly not new. The difference is that the police arsenal against the poor has been greatly extended, with extraordinarily flexible measures such as ASBOs being used principally to punish the behaviour of the poor – notably begging and prostitution.[11] The whole penal apparatus in the UK may thus be regarded as being about 'punishing the poor', to borrow the words of Loïc Wacquant (2009).

It is perhaps more interesting to look not at who *is* targeted by the penal system but rather at who *is not*. Indeed, one historical continuity is that the middle-class and the wealthy tend to escape the penal net, despite the fact that the crimes they are most likely to be involved in, such as fraud, tend to cost much more to society than street crime (Tombs 2002: 18–20). Some of the most harmful activities – in terms of the social, economic and physical harm they may cause – are excluded from the formal definition of criminality. For example, numerous 'safety crimes', such as those perpetrated in the workplace, are not regarded as health and safety offences (Hillyard and Tombs 2008: 9). Rather than finding themselves targeted by the penal system, the privileged classes tend to be protected by it and, increasingly, are coming to profit from it.

The influence of the private sector on prisons in the UK

Delivering punishment to some of the UK's more difficult and vulnerable offenders is no longer the state's sole prerogative. Since the first privately-run prison in Britain, *HMP The Wolds*, opened its doors in 1992, the running of 13 more prisons and young offender institutions has been contracted out to the private sector in England and Wales (out of a total of 136 penal institutions as of June 2012). Nine prisons were put out to tender in 2011 – such as HMP Birmingham, which has become the first existing public sector prison to be handed over to a private company. In addition, seven of the ten immigration removal centres in England and Wales are run by the private sector. Although the majority of the prison estate continues to be managed by Her Majesty's Prison Service,[12] England and Wales now has 'the most privatised prison system in Europe', with 13.1 per cent of the prisoner population being held in privately-run institutions (PRT 2011: 71).

Privatisation, and the pressures of financial imperatives, have significant consequences for prison regimes. Problems of overcrowding, for example, are more likely to emerge where private companies seek to accommodate the maximum number of prisoners possible in a single prison. Indeed, the Prison Reform Trust's analysis of the latest prison performance statistics (Ministry of Justice 2012c) shows that private prisons have consistently held a higher percentage of their prisoners in overcrowded accommodation than the public sector (PRT 2011: 71). In addition, private prisons tend to perform five times less well than public prisons in terms of safety (defined as where 'prisoners, even the most vulnerable, are held safely'), largely on account of the large size of some private prisons (HM Inspectorate of Prisons 2009: 14). Safety may also be affected by low staff-to-prisoner ratios, compared to public sector prisons (3.03:1 compared to 3.78:1 respectively – PRT 2011: 72). This may be one factor contributing to the high rate of self-inflicted deaths in private prisons. There have been 75 such deaths in private prisons since 1992 (Hansard 2012b). This represents over five per cent of all such deaths in the prison estate in England and Wales since 1992 (INQUEST 2012), a very high figure, given that the last prison to be included in these statistics only opened in 2005. Furthermore, the use of unlawful restraint techniques for children detained at secure training centres, run by the private sector, was severely criticised by the High Court in January 2012 (*The Guardian* 2012).

In terms of regime, both public and private penal institutions have become increasingly permeated by 'managerialist' values, which tend to measure success against 'objective' management targets such as Key Performance Indicators (KPIs). Furthermore, the UK's coalition government has introduced the principle that those delivering these services will only be paid according to their ability to meet these narrow targets – 'payment by results' (PBR). In the case of the first private prison to pilot this PBR scheme, HMP Doncaster, 'results' are defined as 'running a safe, decent and secure prison and [reducing] the reoffending of their offenders on release' (Ministry of Justice 2011d: 7). Note that rehabilitation here is narrowly defined in terms of reducing offending, an ideal far removed from that of the 1895 Gladstone Report: that the prison authorities should aim to 'maintain, stimulate or awaken the higher susceptibilities of prisoners'. Prisoner management would appear to be much more important than rehabilitation, despite the current rhetoric about the need to institute a 'rehabilitation revolution'. This aim of managing offenders more effectively was made clear by the merging of the Probation and Prison Services into the executive agency[13] – tellingly known as the National Offender Management Service (NOMS) in 2004. It is alleged that the merging of the two services undermined the social work function of the Probation Service as its role became subsumed under the punishment function of the Prison Service.

Rehabilitation in prison is narrowly defined by engagement in work, even if efforts continue to be made to tackle drug abuse and other behavioural problems which may affect offenders. For the current Justice Secretary, prisons are to be transformed 'from places of idleness, into places of hard work and reform' (Clarke 2011). Consequently, he is seeking to develop a Working Prisons Programme, in collaboration with the private sector, to ensure that prisoners are working 40-hour weeks. The rehabilitative value of such work is questionable, given that the work provided is likely to be unskilled and not necessarily appropriately tailored to a particular offender's needs. In addition, given the high unemployment rates in the UK and the discrimination faced by ex-offenders, it is doubtful how far this working experience will serve offenders when it comes to obtaining employment on their release from prison (JRF 2001). Victim satisfaction appears to be at least as important as offender rehabilitation here: much of the money that prisoners will earn whilst in prison is to be used to compensate victims.

As under New Labour governments, a kind of neo-rehabilitative ideal – to borrow Rod Morgan's term (Morgan 1994) – seems to predominate, whereby emphasis is placed on the sole responsibility of the offender for his or her own rehabilitation. It is hard to see how the whole idea of 'payment by results' will succeed in reversing the trend toward seeing offenders as risks to be managed, rather than as people suffering from a host of social, financial or psychological problems that need attention. Given that success of rehabilitation programmes is to be measured solely in terms of their ability to prevent reoffending, they will emphasise the control and surveillance of the offender and the management of risk to the detriment of welfare and reintegration. It might be that private companies responsible for providing rehabilitative services in prisons simply cherry-pick the best candidates, deliberately excluding those who suffer from severe disadvantages and who will consequently be most difficult to 'rehabilitate'. On account of the fact that prisoner release is often determined by an offender's perceived ability to reintegrate into mainstream society (as is the case with Indeterminate Sentences for Public Protection – see above), the neo-rehabilitative penal system may turn out to be even more repressive than its predecessor, ensuring that offenders spend very long periods of time behind bars. The increasing involvement of the private sector, motivated solely by financial constraints, can only exacerbate this risk.

The wider pressures toward a disciplinary drive

It might be thought that high crime rates in England and Wales have elicited a punitive response from the British state, yet both police and self-report statistics show that crime has been falling since 1995 (Walker et al. 2009: 2–3). The most recent survey of 2011 statistics shows no significant statistical change from the previous year (Chaplin et al. 2011). Meanwhile, penal policy has become more severe, suggesting that there is no direct causal link between the phenomena (Bell 2011). It would seem that 'crime does not cause punishment' (Tonry 2004: 14).

It might also be thought that culture plays a role in influencing politicians to adopt punitive penal policies. Tonry has written, 'I believe a deeper strain of moralistic self-righteousness and punitiveness towards deviance and deviants characterizes British and American culture [...] than is the case in other countries' (2004: 64). In order to prove his affirmation, he cites the International Crime Victimisation Survey (ICVS) from 2000, which shows that 51 per cent of English people – compared to between 12 and 16 per cent of people questioned in other European countries – would impose a prison sentence for a recidivist burglar. The European Crime Survey from 2005 seems to confirm these results (Kühnrich and Kania 2007: 15), as do many British surveys on social attitudes (Hough and Roberts 2003; IPSOS/MORI 2005). Furthermore, if the tabloid press is taken as being representative of public opinion, English people would certainly appear to be highly punitive, constantly demanding tougher sentencing. Yet, even if this is the case, it has to be asked what has changed to make politicians respond to what they perceive to be popular opinion. In the past, when a more deferential political culture prevailed, those in power were able to implement policies which ran against the grain of public opinion (Ryan 2003: 27), the most striking example being the abolition of the death penalty in 1965 despite the fact that it was estimated that 76 per cent of British people remained in favour of it (Davies 1975: 41). Today, politicians are certainly much more responsive to the 'rise of the public voice' (Ryan 2004).

Yet, it would be wrong to think that government is directly responding to public demand. Rather than engaging in meaningful dialogue with the public about the best ways to tackle crime, governments are not above tapping into and encouraging public fears, whipping them up and using them to justify the adoption of ever-tougher penal policies.

Whilst not wishing to underplay the harm that crime can cause, it needs to be recognised that some crimes, namely those of the powerless, are as much about moral panic (Cohen 2002) as social reality. If government were serious about tackling the *harm* caused to the public, it would not just focus on street crime but instead make a more concerted effort to tackle white collar crime. Despite Prime Minister Cameron's recognition that 'the restoration of responsibility has to cut right across our society', highlighting the 'greed, irresponsibility and entitlement' of those involved in the banking crisis, in the MPs' expenses scandal and in the phone hacking scandal (Cameron 2012), the focus of the coalition government, like that of New Labour before it, has been on tackling the crimes of the poor, who belong to the 'broken society'.

This clampdown on the poor and disadvantaged needs to be understood as an attempt by the British governing elites to handle a crisis of state legitimacy prompted by neoliberalism. The legitimacy to govern has been undermined by the move from democracy, which sought primarily to provide economic and social security to the masses, to a plutocracy that primarily serves the interests of the economic elites by facilitating the forces of marketisation and commodification (Leys 2003; Harvey 2007; Reiner 2012; Bell 2011). Far from promoting democratic participation, as partisans of neoliberalism claim to do (invoking the language of public choice, for example), they have instead helped to 'de-democratise the state': government policies have increasingly come to serve the interests of capital rather than those of ordinary people (Leys 2003: 71–3). For example, the main beneficiaries of the introduction of market principles into public services, such as health, have not been the public they are meant to serve but rather the private investors and shareholders who seek to profit from such policies. All governments, but particularly those on the Left, consequently find themselves without a message, desperately searching for a platform from which they can appeal to the masses.

Crime is one of those issues which crosses class lines, affecting the population as a whole, but particularly the poor.[14] Tackling crime – and the social problems which are identified as the causes of crime – is an excellent way for British governments to be seen to be tackling a principal cause of insecurity whilst simultaneously attempting to repair some of the social effects of Thatcherite neoliberal policy. This was particularly important for New Labour which sought to represent a break from the selfish individualism of the Thatcher years whilst also dispelling its prior (unmerited) reputation for being 'soft on crime'. New Labour's hybrid social/penal interventions (such as the Family Intervention Programmes mentioned above) were an excellent way to be seen to be tackling both social and crime problems without addressing the potential structural causes of these same problems (such as the massive social inequalities exacerbated by neoliberalism).

Cameron's Conservatives have matched their 'security fightback' with a 'social fightback', aiming to give the party a more progressive image, just as New Labour sought to combine a tough and tender approach by promising to be 'tough on crime, tough on the causes of crime'. Yet, underlying both crime and social policy has been an attempt to reinforce personal responsibility at all costs, whilst absolving the state of responsibility for the disastrous social consequences of neoliberalism. Being tough on crime, of course, enables the neoliberal state to be seen to be doing something to provide physical security to the masses, at a time when it is no longer capable of providing them with economic and social security (Garland 2001). Yet, the British government also needs to show its desire to tackle social problems in order to mark itself out from its predecessors, namely the 'uncaring' Thatcher administrations. It is in this sense that penal policy must be understood as politics: it is an attempt to ensure that state legitimacy is not undermined by the economic problems and social dislocations engendered by neoliberalism by combining both social and penal interventions and fine-tuning the 'welfare sanction' (see above). In this way, penal policy is not regarded as brute authoritarianism but rather as a legitimate and effective attempt to tackle interconnected social and crime problems.

The crime question enables states to overcome the following conundrum. Whilst economic power has gone global, political power 'remains overwhelmingly tied to the level of the nation state' (Crouch 2011: 173). In other words, citizens still look to their national governments to protect them from the ravages of the global marketplace. Yet, at the same time as neoliberal globalisation heightens citizens' fears and insecurities (Beck 1992; Giddens 1998; Garland 2001; Young 2007), governments become even less powerful to protect the masses from these threats. Indeed, in a globalised economy, those governments are now relatively powerless. Even if they sought to change policy in such a way that their citizens would be better protected against the global marketplace, they would be constrained by 'disciplinary neoliberalism' (Gamble 2009: 87) in the form of international political and economic organisations, such as the IMF, which arguably now have more influence over policy-making than the citizens of nation states. Crouch explains just how such a situation might make governments more likely to turn to crime policy as a means of securing legitimacy: 'From here it is an easy slip to the defence of the public realm becoming the defence of a particular national population against foreigners, especially immigrants and ethnic minorities' and, one might add, against those White-British citizens who fail to conform to dominant norms and value systems. Whilst immigration policy becomes a new way of protecting the nation from the 'enemy without', crime policy becomes a good way of protecting it from the 'enemy within'. Thus, the incarceration of immigrants and poor English people can be seen as part and parcel of the same strategy – to secure state legitimacy in the face of political crisis. The 'undeserving' poor are stigmatised as criminal, diverting attention from the crimes of the economic elites, whilst the 'deserving poor' and the middle classes become willing participants in the fight against crime, the government tapping into their fears and insecurities for their own political ends. So, as Wacquant suggests, neoliberal penal policy is as much about governance as it is about punishment (2009). Yet, harsh penal policies are not so much about effectively governing the poor, as Wacquant suggests, but more about securing political legitimacy amongst the masses, thus more effectively governing the population as a whole. The welfare sanction may be an ineffective means of controlling the 'undeserving poor' (who continue to reject dominant value systems) but it is a very effective way of enabling government to be seen to be doing something – not just about crime but about social problems, allowing it to appeal to electors across the class divide.

Yet, the penal system is itself in a state of crisis, thought to be costly and ineffective. One way of making it appear to be more effective is by convincing the public that the idea of 'working prisons' will make them more effective reformative institutions and, together with tougher community sentences, a means of curbing recidivism and effectively protecting the public. The idea of working prisons of course chimes nicely with neoliberal rhetoric, which highlights the importance of work as a means of participating fully in the market society.

A way of tackling the massive costs of imprisonment is of course to contract punishment out to the private sector – and even to voluntary organisations – in line with the rhetoric of the 'big society', whereby communities should take over traditionally public functions. In reality, it is likely that the third sector will play a very small role in punishment delivery, largely on account of the fact that it cannot hope to muster the same level of finance and influence as the private sector. Where it does play a role, for example, as part of a privately-led consortium bid, as was the case with the 2008 Serco bid to run Belmarsh West and Maghull prisons, it has found itself aping the private sector, 'subject[ing]

[its] practices and outlook to the zeitgeist of change through "professionalization" and adaptation to the enterprise culture' (Corcoran 2011: 45). Consequently, voluntary institutions are unlikely to fundamentally change the way in which the penal system functions. It would appear that the government's chief motivation for involving the third sector has been to appear to be transferring power from the state to the 'big society' and 'to portray the privatisation of prisons as a potentially progressive initiative' (Moore and Scott 2012: 43). In reality, though, it is only government and the private sector that is profiting from the policy (in both pecuniary and political terms).

The privatisation drive overall and the discourse of the 'big society' may, therefore, be regarded as an attempt to legitimise the neoliberal shrinking of the public sector and as a (short-term) means of satisfying immediate financial concerns in times of recession (Ryan 2011). It should, however, also be seen as a way of satisfying the economic elites – enabling them to gain massive profits from the delivery of punishment whilst diverting the public gaze from the significant harms that they themselves inflict upon society.

Conclusions

The context of neoliberalism is of vital importance in explaining punitive trends in recent years, not just in the British context but also in a global one. Indeed, most Western nations are now, to a greater or lesser extent, subject to the forces of neoliberalism, causing severe crises of legitimacy for all governments, whether they are from the left or the right of the political spectrum, particularly given the current financial crisis. This would help to explain why punitive trends have been particularly widespread in recent years, with even the most liberal of penal regimes, such as the Netherlands and Scandinavia, experiencing a punitive turn (Van Swaaningen 2005; Tham 2001). These trends may appear to be responding to public demands but, in reality, are more about legitimising a particular ideological project and thus satisfying the interests of both political leaders and the economic elites.

This is not, however, to minimise national differences. Penal systems across the western world, or even within Europe, are far from uniform. Hence, it is essential to recognise that neoliberalism operates in different ways in different places, with practice often diverging from theory (Brenner and Theodore 2002). Penal policies, too, are determined by local judicial and institutional cultures (Lacey 2008). Even within the UK, there are significant divergences in the way that penal policies function.

Northern Ireland, for example, has a considerably lower rate of imprisonment than England and Wales (99/100,000: ICPS 2012), although it has been rising considerably since a low in 2001. Meanwhile, the Welsh Assembly has sought to diverge from its English neighbour in the field of youth justice, adopting a more welfarist, 'children first' approach to youth offending (Drakeford 2010).

Yet, despite these small differences, it seems irrefutable that, in England and Wales at least, if not the UK as a whole, the 'disciplinary drive' (Ryan and Sim 1995) has intensified over the past two decades. Furthermore, the recent crisis of neoliberalism has not heralded its demise (Crouch 2011), leaving very little room for manoeuvre within the disciplinary straight jacket. Given the current financial crisis, the legitimacy of the state is likely to be further called into question as it withdraws even further from its role as provider of public services and economic and social security. It is likely that both the Conservatives and Liberal Democrats in Britain will continue to use crime and immigration to ensure their political legitimacy in the face of serious social and economic insecurities.

Notes

1. This calculation is based on a prison population of 51,047 in 1995 and 87,028 at the time of writing in June 2012 (see ICPS 2012).
2. It was estimated in 1994 that the prison population would rise to 56,600 people by 2001 (Ryan and Sim 1995: 118).
3. The IPP was originally introduced to replace a similar mandatory minimum life sentence created under the Crime [Sentences] Act 1997 for those convicted for their second violent or sexual offence.
4. The Conservative-Liberal Democrat coalition government has proposed to replace the ASBO with a Crime Prevention Injunction which will actually be much easier to obtain since only the civil standard of proof will be necessary to trigger such a penalty (Home Office 2012a; Ireland 2011). Custody will remain an option for breach.
5. Prisoners awaiting trial currently account for 14 per cent of the prison population of England and Wales (Berman 2012: 3), compared to 22 per cent in 1992 (Ryan and Sim 1995: 100).
6. This compares to 920 people detained under the immigration laws in 1994, a number which had already increased three-fold since the previous year (Ryan and Sim 1995: 108).
7. 'Children' refers to young people under the age of 18. In 2010/2011, 95 per cent of children held in custody were aged between 15 and 17.
8. This figure is probably slightly higher since it does not include those held in secure training centres and in secure children's homes.
9. The Detention and Training Order (DTO) was created by the *Crime and Disorder Act 1998*. It is aimed at young people aged between 12 and 17 years

old who are considered by the court to be recidivists and dangerous. Half of the sentence must be served in prison and half in custody. In 2010/2011, 55 per cent of children aged under 18 who were held in custody were serving DTOs: see Youth Justice Board/Ministry of Justice (2012: 30).

10. The Youth Rehabilitation Order was introduced in November 2009 following the *Criminal Justice and Immigration Act 2008*. It is a community sentence which obliges young people subjected to it to accept any number of 18 different conditions, many of which may involve participation in programmes which seek to address problems such as drug and alcohol abuse. Breach may lead to a custodial sentence.

11. There are no official statistics available concerning the types of behaviour for which ASBOs have been issued but the evidence suggests that they have been disproportionately used to target the poor and vulnerable. See http://www.statewatch.org/asbo/ASBOwatch.html for a list of case-studies and the official Home Office typology which lists the kinds of behaviour which may be considered as being 'anti-social' (House of Commons 2007: 9).

12. All prisons, whether they are publicly or privately managed, are directly answerable to HM Prison Service within the Ministry of Justice. The Secretary of State for Justice remains responsible before Parliament for the running of all prisons in England and Wales. All detention facilities in England and Wales are subject to independent inspection by HM Inspectorate of Prisons.

13. An 'executive agency' is a public institution which carries out services for the UK government. It is still the Ministry of Justice which sets policy but NOMS looks after the day-to-day running of prison and probation services.

14. It was initially the Left Realists who put forward the theory that crime affects the poor more than other social classes (Lea and Young 1993). Consequently, they argued that it should be taken more seriously by left-wing parties who purport to represent the interests of the most disadvantaged members of society.

References

Beck, U. (1992) *Risk Society: Towards a New Modernity* (London and Thousand Oaks: Sage).

Bell, E. (2011) *Criminal Justice and Neoliberalism* (Basingstoke: Palgrave Macmillan).

Berman, G. (2012) *Prison Population Statistics*: http://www.parliament.uk/Templates/BriefingPapers/Pages/BPPdfDownload.aspx?bp-id=SN04334, accessed 6 June 2012.

Brenner, N. and Theodore, N . (2002) 'Cities and the Geographies of "Actually Existing Neoliberalism"', *Antipode* 34 (3): 349–79.

Cabinet Office (2009) *Short Study on Women Offenders*: http://webarchive.nationalarchives.gov.uk/+/http://www.cabinetoffice.gov.uk/media/209663/setf_shortstudy_womenoffenders.pdf, accessed 20 June 2012.

Cameron, D. (2012) 'PM's Speech on the Fightback after the Riots', 15 August 2011.

Cameron (2010) 'Let's Mend Our Broken Society', speech delivered Tuesday, 27 April 2010.

Chaplin, R., Flatley, J . and Smith, K . (2011) *Crime in England and Wales 2010/11: Findings from the British Crime Survey and Police Recorded Crime,* 2nd edn: http://www.homeoffice.gov.uk/publications/science-research-statistics/research-statistics/crime-research/hosb1011/hosb1011?view=Binary, accessed 20 June 2012.

Clarke, K. (2011) 'Speech Delivered to the Conservative Party Conference', 4 October 2011.

Cohen, S. (2002) *Folk Devils and Moral Panics,* 3rd edn (London: Routledge).

Corcoran, M . (2011) 'Dilemmas of Institutionalization in the Penal Voluntary Sector', *Critical Social Policy,* 31 (1): 30–52.

Council of Europe (2012) *Letter from the Commissioner of Human Rights to The Rt Hon Kenneth Clarke:* https://wcd.coe.int/com.instranet. InstraServlet?command=com.instranet.CmdBlobGet&InstranetImage=2048839&SecMode=1&DocId=1868640&Usage=2, accessed 20 June 2012.

Crouch, C. (2011) *The Strange Non-Death of Neoliberalism* (Cambridge: Policy Press).

CTP (2008) *Report to the Government of the United Kingdom on the visit to the United Kingdom carried out by the European Committee for the Prevention of Torture and Inhuman or Degrading Treatment or Punishment (CPT) from 18 November to 1 December 2008:* http://www.cpt.coe.int/documents/gbr/2009–30-inf-eng. htm#_Toc226775019, accessed 5 June 2012.

Davies, C. (1975) *Permissive Britain: Social Change in the Sixties and Seventies* (London: Pitman).

Drakeford, M. (2010) 'Devolution and Youth Justice in Wales', *Criminology and Criminal Justice,* 10: 137–54.

Fitzgerald, M . and Sim, J . (1982) *British Prisons,* 2nd edn (Oxford: Blackwell).

Garland, D. (2001) *The Culture of Control* (Oxford: Oxford University Press).

Garland, D. (1985) *Punishment and Welfare* (Aldershot: Gower).

Gamble, A. (2009) *The Spectre at the Feast: Capitalist Crisis and the Politics of Recession* (Basingstoke and New York: Palgrave Macmillan).

Giddens, A. (1998) 'Risk Society: The Context of British Politics', in Franklin, J. (ed.), *The Politics of Risk Society* (Cambridge and Malden: Polity Press/IPPR).

Hansard (2012a) 'Written Answers', 28 February 2012: Column 182W.

Hansard (2012b) 'Written Answers', 27 March 2012: Column 1077W.

Harvey, D. (2007) *A Brief History of Neoliberalism,* 2nd edn (Oxford and New York: Oxford University Press).

Hillyard, P. and Tombs, S . (2008) 'Beyond Criminology' in Dorling, D., Gordon, D., Hillyard, P., Pantazis, C., Pemberton, S. and Tombs, S. (eds), *Criminal Obsessions: Why Harm Matters More Than Crime,* 2nd edn (London: Centre for Crime and Justice Studies).

HM Government (2010) *The Coalition: Our Programme for Government:* http://webarchive.nationalarchives.gov.uk/20100919110641/http://programmeforgovernment.hmg.gov.uk, accessed 20 June 2012.

HM Inspectorate of Prisons (2012) *Report on an Unannounced Full Follow-Up Inspection of HMP Liverpool 8–16 December 2011:* Http://www.justice.gov.uk/ downloads/publications/hmipris/prison-and-yoi-inspections/liverpool/liverpool-2011.pdf, accessed 20 June 2012.

HM Inspectorate of Prisons (2011) *Annual Report 2010–11:* http://www.justice. gov.uk/downloads/publications/corporate-reports/hmi-prisons/hmip-annual-report-2010–11.pdf, accessed 20 June 2012.

HM Inspectorate of Prisons (2009) *The Prison Characteristics That Predict Prisons Being Assessed as Performing 'Well': A Thematic Review*: Http://www.justice.gov.uk/downloads/publications/hmipris/thematic-reports-and-research-publications/prison_performance_thematic-rps.pdf, accessed 20 June 2012.

Home Office (2012a) *Putting Victims First: More Effective Responses to Anti-Social Behaviour*: Http://www.official-documents.gov.uk/document/cm83/8367/8367.pdf, accessed 20 June 2012.

Home Office (2012b) *Immigration Detention Statistics January-March 2012*: http://www.homeoffice.gov.uk/publications/science-research-statistics/research-statistics/immigration-asylum-research/immigration-q1–2012/detention-q1–2012, accessed 20 June 2012.

Home Office (2010) *Anti-social Behaviour Order Statistics England and Wales 2010*: http://www.homeoffice.gov.uk/publications/science-research-statistics/research-statistics/crime-research/asbo-stats-england-wales-2010/, accessed 20 June 2012.

Home Office (2006) *Offender Management Caseload Statistics 2005*: http://webarchive.nationalarchives.gov.uk/20110220105210/rds.homeoffice.gov.uk/rds/pdfs06/hosb1806.pdf, accessed 20 June 2012.

Home Office (2004) *Women's Offending Reduction Programme: Action Plan*: http://webarchive.nationalarchives.gov.uk/+/http://www.homeoffice.gov.uk/documents/WORP-action-plan?view=Binary, accessed 20 June 2012.

Home Office (2003) *Statistics on Women and the Criminal Justice System*: http://www.homeoffice.gov.uk/rds/pdfs2/s95women03.pdf, accessed 6 June 2012.

Hough, M . and Roberts, J. V . (2003) *Youth Crime and Youth Justice: Public Opinion in England and Wales* (London: Institute for Criminal Policy Research/The Nuffield Foundation).

House of Commons (2007) *Tackling Anti-Social Behaviour*: http://www.publications.parliament.uk/pa/cm200607/cmselect/cmpubacc/246/246.pdf, accessed 20 June 2012.

House of Commons (2006a) *Serving Time: Prisoner Diet and Exercise*: Http://www.publications.parliament.uk/pa/cm200506/cmselect/cmpubacc/1063/1063.pdf, accessed 20 June 2012.

House of Commons (2006b) *Report of the Zahid Mubarek Inquiry*: http://www.official-documents.gov.uk/document/hc0506/hc10/1082/1082_ii.pdf, accessed 20 June 2012.

Hunt, R . and Dick, S . (2008) *Serves You Right: Lesbian and Gay People's Expectations of Discrimination*, Stonewall: http://www.stonewall.org.uk/documents/servesyouright.pdf, accessed 20 June 2012.

ICPS (2012) International Centre for Prison Studies, *Prison Brief*: http://www.prisonstudies.org/info/worldbrief/, accessed 20 June 2012.

INQUEST (2012) *Deaths in Prison 2001–11*: http://inquest.gn.apc.org/website/statistics/deaths-in-prison, accessed 20 June 2012.

IPSOS/MORI (2005) *Public Concern about ASB and Support for ASBOs*: http://www.ipsos-mori.com/researchpublications/researcharchive/poll.aspx?oItemId=412, accessed 20 June 2012.

Ireland, S . (2011) 'ASBOs are Dead, Long Live ASBOs', *Criminal Justice Matters*, 86: 26–7.

JRF (2001) Joseph Rowntree Foundation, *Recruiting and Employing Offenders :The Impact of the Police Act* (London: JRF).

Kühnrich, B. and Kania, H . (2007) *Attitudes Towards Punishment in the European Union: Results from the 2005 European Crime Survey*: http://www.europeansafety-observatory.eu/, accessed 20 June 2012.

Lacey, N. (2008) *The Prisoners' Dilemma: Political Economy and Punishment in Contemporary Democracies* (Cambridge and New York: Cambridge University Press).

Lea, J. and Young, J . (1993) *What Is to Be Done about Law and Order?*, 2nd edn (London: Pluto Press).

Leys, C. (2003) *Market-Driven Politics: Neoliberal Democracy and the Public Interest*, 2nd edn (London and New York: Verso).

Ministry of Justice (2012) *Criminal Justice Statistics Quarterly Update to December 2011*: http://www.justice.gov.uk/downloads/statistics/criminal-justice-stats/criminal-justice-stats-dec-2011.pdf, accessed 20 June 2012.

Ministry of Justice (2011a) *Prison Population Projections 2011–2017: England and Wales*: http://www.justice.gov.uk/downloads/statistics/mojstats/prison-pop-projections-2011-17.pdf, accessed 20 June 2012.

Ministry of Justice (2011b) *Statistical Bulletin on the Public Disorder of 6th-9th August 2011*, http://www.justice.gov.uk/downloads/statistics/criminal-justice-stats/august-public-disorder-stats-bulletin-230212.pdf, accessed 20 June 2012.

Ministry of Justice (2011c) *Statistics on Race and the Criminal Justice System 2010*: http://www.justice.gov.uk/downloads/statistics/mojstats/stats-race-cjs-2010.pdf, accessed 20 June 2012.

Ministry of Justice (2011d) *Breaking the Cycle: Government Response*: http://open.justice.gov.uk/breaking-the-cycle-response.pdf, accessed 20 June 2012.

Ministry of Justice (2010a) *Green Paper Evidence Report on Breaking the Cycle: Effective Punishment, Rehabilitation and Sentencing of Offenders*: http://www.justice.gov.uk/downloads/consultations/green-paper-evidence-a.pdf, accessed 20 June 2012.

Ministry of Justice (2010b) *Statistics on Women and the Criminal Justice System*: http://www.justice.gov.uk/downloads/statistics/mojstats/statistics-women-cjs-2010.pdf, accessed 20 June 2012.

Ministry of Justice (2009) *Story of the Prison Population 1995–2009 England and Wales*: Http://www.justice.gov.uk/downloads/statistics/mojstats/story-prison-population.pdf, accessed 20 June 2012.

Moore, J. and Scott, D . (2012) 'It's Not Just about the Profits: Privatisation, Social Enterprise and the "John Lewis" Prison', *Criminal Justice Matters*, 87 (1): 40–41.

Morgan, R. (1994) 'Just Prisons and Responsible Prisoners', in Duff, A., Marshall, S., Emerson Dobash, R. and Dobash, R., *Penal Theory and Practice: Tradition and Innovation in Criminal Justice* (Manchester: Manchester University Press).

Office for National Statistics (2011) *Population Estimates by Ethnic Group 2002–2009*: http://www.ons.gov.uk/ons/rel/peeg/population-estimates-by-ethnic-group – experimental-/current-estimates/population-density – change-and-concentration-in-great-britain.pdf, accessed 20 June 2012.

Pantazis, C. and Pemberton, S . (2009) 'From the "Old" to the "New" Suspect Community: Examining the Impacts of Recent UK Counter-Terrorist Legislation', *British Journal of Criminology*, 49: 646–66.

Pitts, J. (2001) *The New Politics of Youth Crime: Discipline or Solidarity?* (Basingstoke and New York: Palgrave Macmillan).

PRT (2011) Prison Reform Trust, *Bromley Briefings Prison Factfile: December 2011*: http://www.prisonreformtrust.org.uk/Portals/0/Documents/Bromley%20Briefing%20December%202011.pdf, accessed 20 June 2012.

PRT (2010a) Prison Reform Trust, *A Fair Response: Developing Responses to Racist Incidents That Earn the Confidence of Black and Minority Ethnic Prisoners*: Http://www.prisonreformtrust.org.uk/Portals/0/Documents/fair_response%20developing%20responses%20to%20racist%20incidents%20.pdf, accessed 20 June 2012.

PRT (2010b) *Prison Reform Trust*: http://www.outoftrouble.org.uk/sites/default/files/Punishing_Disadvantage.pdf, accessed 20 June 2012.

Reiner, R. (2012) 'The Return of the Nasty Party' in Silvestri, A. (ed.), *Critical Reflections: Social and Criminal Justice in the First Year of Coalition Government* (London: CCJS) 28–30.

Ruggiero, V., Ryan, M . and Sim, J . (eds) (1995) *Western European Penal Systems: a Critical Anatomy* (London: Sage).

Ryan, M. (2011), 'Counterblast: Understanding Penal Change: Towards the Big Society?', *The Howard Journal of Criminal Justice*, 50: 516–52.

Ryan, M. (2004) 'Red Tops, Populists and the Irresistible Rise of the Public Voice(s)', *Journal for Crime, Conflict and the Media*, 1 (3): 1–14.

Ryan, M. (2003) *Penal Policy and Political Culture in England and Wales* (Winchester: Winchester Press).

Ryan, M. and Sim, J . (1995) 'The Penal System in England and Wales: Round up the Usual Suspect' in Ruggiero, V., Ryan, M. and Sim, J. (eds), *Western European Penal Systems: A critical anatomy* (London: Sage).

Scott, D. (2008) *Penology* (London and Thousand Oaks: Sage).

Silverman, S. and Hajela, R . (2011) *Briefing: Immigration Detention in the UK*, Oxford, Migration Observatory: http://migrobs.vm.bytemark.co.uk/sites/files/migobs/Immigration%20Detention%20Briefing%20v2_0.pdf, accessed 5 June 2012.

Sim, J. (2009) *Punishment and Prisons: Power and the Carceral State* (London and Thousand Oaks: Sage).

Tham, H. (2001) 'Law and Order as a Leftist Project?: The Case of Sweden', *Punishment and Society*, 3 (3): 409–26.

The Guardian (2012) 'Unlawful Restraint Widespread in Child Jails for a Decade, Says Judge', Travis, A., Thursday 12 January 2012.

The Guardian (2010) 'Kenneth Clarke Pledges to Cut Daily Prison Population', Travis, A. and Hirsch, A., Wednesday 20 October.

The Guardian (2007) 'Prison Suicides Up to Two a Week as Jail Numbers Soar', Travis, A. 13 June.

The Independent (2011) 'Homophobic Crime: Unspoken scourge within Britain's prisons', Lakhani, N., 28 November.

Tombs, S. (2002) 'Focus on Crimes of Affluence: Beyond the usual suspects – crime, criminology and the powerful', *Safer Society*, NACRO, 15: 18–20

Tonry, M. (2004) *Thinking about Crime: Sense and Sensibility in American Penal Culture* (Oxford and New York: Oxford University Press).

van Swaaningen, R . (2005) 'Public Safety and the Management of Fear', *Theoretical Criminology*, 9 (3): 289–305.

Wacquant, L. (2009) *Punishing the Poor: The Neoliberal Government of Social Insecurity* (Durham and London: Duke University Press).

Walker, A. Flatley, J., Kershaw, C. and Moon, D. (eds) (2009) *Crime in England and Wales 2008/09 Volume 1: Findings from the British Crime Survey and Police Recorded Crime* (London: Home Office).

Young, J. (2007) *The Vertigo of Late Modernity* (London: Sage).

Youth Justice Board/Ministry of Justice (2012) *Youth Justice Statistics 2010/2011: England and Wales*: http://www.justice.gov.uk/downloads/statistics/youth-justice/yjb-statistics-10–11.pdf, accessed 20 June 2012.

5
The Irish Penal System: Pragmatism, Neglect and the Effects of Austerity

Mary Rogan

Introduction

Ireland has historically been at the low end of the European 'league table' in terms of prison numbers. However, since the 1960s the country has seen an upwards trend in the number of people being sent to prison, with notable increases occurring in the 1980s and early 1990s, along with a sharp upturn in numbers in the more recent past. Prison numbers and prison space have become the predominant topic on political agendas regarding penal policy, with many other pressing issues – such as conditions, accountability structures, and the use of alternatives to custody – being sidelined.

This chapter begins with analysis of the current prison population and trends in sentencing as well as a description of the Irish penal estate. The chapter moves on to consider the wider historical and political forces that have helped to shape the direction of Irish penal policy. Though the terms 'Ireland' or 'Irish' are used throughout, this chapter refers to the prison system in the Republic of Ireland, or Southern Ireland.

Contemporary Irish penal policy

The most recent official figures indicate that the Irish prison population currently stands at 4,390 (Irish Prison I. P. Service 2012). This translates to about 96 prisoners per 100,000 population. The prison population has been increasing since the late 1960s, with significant rises in the numbers sent to prison over the last five to ten years in particular (see Figure 5.1 and Figure 5.2). 2011 saw an increase in the numbers of persons sent to prison of 1.4 per cent, representing a slowdown after

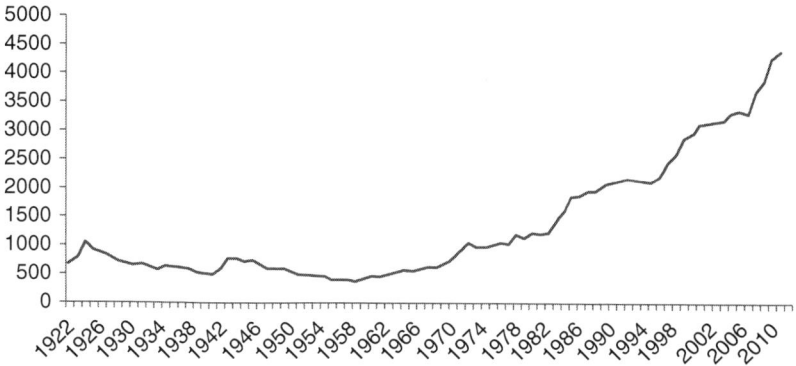

Figure 5.1   Average daily prison population, 1922–2012

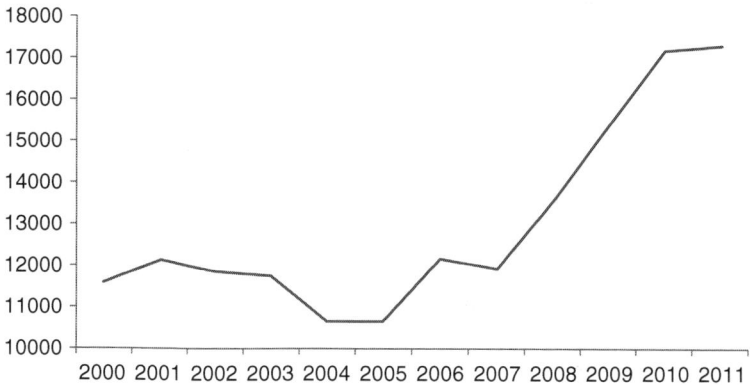

Figure 5.2   Committal rate, 2000–2011

a number of years in which the numbers incarcerated increased in the order of ten per cent each year.

The average cost per prisoner in 2011 was €65,359 – a figure which has been dropping because of the increasing number of prisoners and a reduction in expenditure.

The most recent figures (relating to 2011) also provide a snapshot of the nature of the Irish prison population: 86.4 per cent of those sent to prison in Ireland in 2011 were male and 13.6 per cent were female. Irish nationals represent 89.6 per cent of those in custody. Of all those sent to prison, 32.4 per cent were resident in Dublin – in and around Ireland's capital city – prior to incarceration. Other European Union nationals accounted for 12.5 per cent of the total numbers committed. What the official reports describe as 'African nationals' (with no further nuance, detail or breakdown provided) comprised 2.7 per cent of the total, with 'Asian nationals' representing 2.2 per cent, and 'Central/South American nationals' accounting for 0.6 percent. The deficiencies in official data recording should be obvious from the poor quality of data relating to country of origin and ethnicity. This problem is referred to in greater detail below.

In terms of the profile of those in Irish prisons, 7.9 per cent are serving life sentences, with 7.8 per cent serving sentences of ten years or more. The number of persons serving sentences of less than three months represents a small percentage of the average daily prison population, at around 1.2 per cent, but over 50 per cent of all those sent to prison by the courts.

The most commonly sentenced offence was those relating to road and traffic offences (27% or 3,495) of the total (see Figure 5.3). Public order and social code offences constituted the second most common category (13% or 1,745) with homicide offences accounting for 53 sentences (0.4%) and sexual offences at 0.94 per cent (122). Burglary and related offences represented 480 sentences (3.9%), with theft and related offences at 1410 (10.9%). Controlled drug offences amounted to 865 sentences (6.7%). Over 80% of those sent to prison are in for non-violent offences, which rises to over 90 per cent in the case of women.

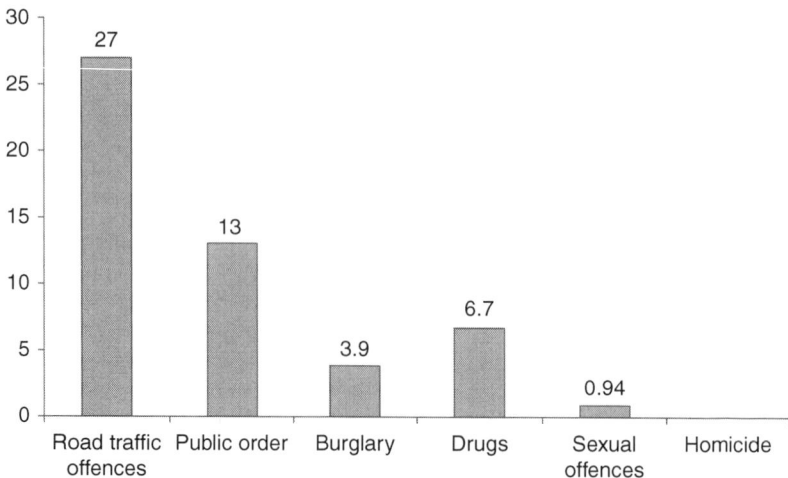

Figure 5.3   Types of crimes for which sentences were given in 2011(%)

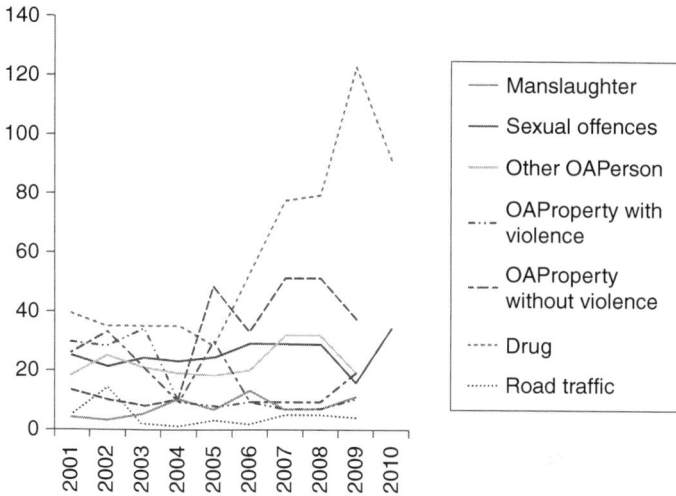

Figure 5.4 Offences with sentences in the five to ten-year range

Of the 17,318 committals to prison during 2011, 4,546 were on remand having been denied bail, comprising 26 per cent of all the committals for the year. There were 423 present under immigration laws. Current data sources do not permit the analysis of how many of those denied bail are eventually sentenced to prison, or for how long. The number of committals to prison as a result of failure to pay a court-ordered fine was, remarkably, 7,514, a figure which has been increasing since the beginning of Ireland's latest recession.

Most of those sent to prison are between the ages of 30 and 40 (27%) with 21.8 per cent of those committed to prison aged between 25 and 30 and 20.8 per cent between 21 and 25. Those over 50 years of age make up 5.9 per cent.

The rise in the Irish prison population – over the past decade in particular – has been driven by a rapidly increasing volume of short sentences and, most particularly, an increase in the number of longer sentences – particularly for drug offences. It appears that, at present, there is a levelling off of the numbers incarcerated for longer periods, but a continued increase in the use of imprisonment for less than three months. The number of sentences passed of three months or fewer has increased from around 2,000 in 2001 to just over 8,000 in 2011. The number of sentences of between five and ten years stood at around 150 in 2001, rising to over 250 in 2008, before dipping back again below the 250

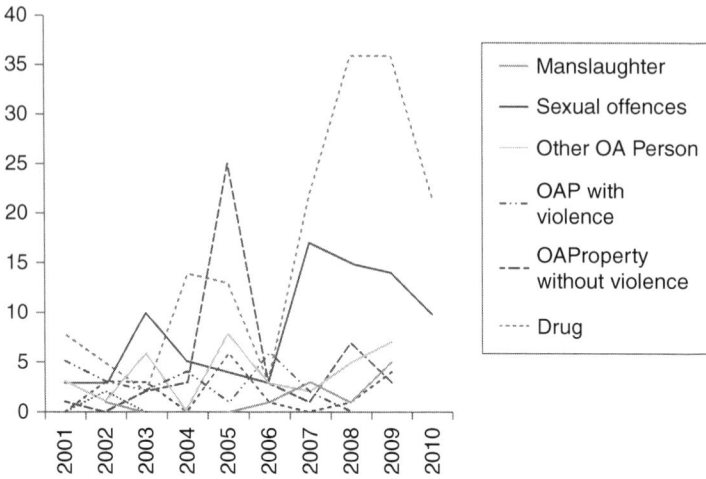

Figure 5.5   Offences with sentences in the ten years and more range

mark. Significant increases in the number of sentences of over ten years were registered in the years 2007–2010. Around 20–30 such sentences were given annually in the first part of the decade, but the numbers rose to over 60 by 2008. Life sentences, however, remained relatively stable at around 20 per year.

Recent changes to the manner in which data are presented in the official statistics make it impossible to compare the proportions of sentences handed down for particular offences since 2010. The available figures indicate, however, that longer sentences for drug offending have driven much of the increase in the numbers in Irish prisons.

The figures for the sentences in the five to ten year category are contained in Figure 5.4.

The relevant figures for the ten years or more sentences are contained in Figure 5.5. Again, the impact of sentencing for drug offences is evident.

The penal estate in Ireland

Ireland has 14 prisons. There is no official security categorisation though, in practice, there are two 'open' prisons, used mainly for those coming to the end of their sentences, and one 'semi-open' institution, called the 'Training Unit'. The uniform level of security in Irish prisons poses difficulties for those prisoners who do not require high levels of security, imposing unnecessary restrictions on such individuals.

There are two prisons for women in Ireland. One is situated in Limerick in an archaic building with poor conditions, including very little open space. The other was purpose-built in Dublin and opened in 1999, after decades of delay and official neglect of female prisoners. The Dóchas Centre, (Dóchas being the Irish word for 'hope') was designed around the principle of one person per cell in clusters of houses of varying levels of security, with communal dining and cooking facilities. The upsurge in the numbers of women sent to prison has led to the severe overcrowding of that prison, including the use of bunk-beds and the conversion of buildings to temporary accommodation.

Some prisons have become associated with particular categories of prisoner, with Arbour Hill in Dublin used mainly to detain prisoners serving long sentences, particularly for sexual offending. Cloverhill Prison was built to house the increased numbers of prisoners on remand, following the passing of a referendum in 1997 to change the Irish Constitution and allow for the denial of bail pending trial on the grounds that a person may commit a serious offence while on bail, in certain circumstances. Portlaoise Prison has a long association with those considered to be 'subversive' prisoners.

Until 2012 male children were sent to prison, usually to St. Patrick's Institution, an old building which is part of the Mountjoy complex; this practice was roundly condemned by the Council of Europe's Committee for the Prevention of Torture (CPT 2011), Ireland's Ombudsman for Children (OCO 2011), the United Nations' Commissioner for Human Rights – as well as various domestic human rights organisations. Female children have been dealt with outside the prison system for several years.

Alternatives to custody

For adults convicted of offences, the alternatives to a prison sentence are based on a variety of statute-based and informal mechanisms. There is little in the way of coherence to their implementation, or information on their use. Most have developed in an *ad hoc* manner. The data on the use of alternatives to custody, as is the case with sentencing generally (Hamilton 2005), is limited. The scheme of alternatives is underdeveloped (Seymour 2006), though there are indications that the use of community service orders has increased in the past year.

Probation orders were originally introduced in 1907 under legislation equivalent to that establishing their use in the United Kingdom. Community service was introduced in 1983. In 2011, its enabling legislation was amended to require judges to consider the imposition of a community service order whenever they are contemplating imposing a prison sentence of up to 12 months. Previously, a community service order could replace a sentence of up to six months only. In 2011, the Probation Service dealt with 14,845 persons convicted of a criminal offence, including 9,347 new referrals. Of the new referrals, 13.5 per cent were women. The number of community service orders imposed by the courts increased in 2011 (Probation P. Service 2012). While the increased use of this sanction is generally welcome, until the Irish prison population falls significantly there is the concern that the orders will be used to widen the net of the criminal justice system rather than truly act to divert convicted persons from custody.

Judges in the District Court, the lowest court in the Irish judicial hierarchy, which can impose a maximum sentence of 12 months for a single offence and up to 24 months in the case of multiple offences, may also use the 'Poor Box', an informal (and poorly regulated) system whereby a defendant can pay a sum of money to charity as part of their sentence. It can also be used when the Court does not record a conviction formally (Law Reform L. R. Commission 2005).

The fine is used by all courts, though is seen more frequently in the District and Circuit Courts. The number of people being committed to prison for non-payment of a fine has increased dramatically in recent years. Though few stay in prison for anything more than a few hours or days, the Department of Justice's own research details the negative effects of such committals on the lives of the individuals concerned (Redmond 2002) – as well as the prevalence of a lack of understanding about requirements to pay along with the simple inability to pay a fine.

Since 1993 judges may impose a compensation order in favour of the victim of a crime, either as an alternative to custody or in addition to it. Restorative justice is used as a response to offending but on a very small scale.

Electronic monitoring was introduced by the Criminal Justice Act 2006 as an alternative to a term of imprisonment for certain public order offences. It has yet to be used outside a pilot project, with the Department of Justice seemingly reluctant to pursue it as an option in sentencing.

A recent initiative was introduced in order to reduce the high levels of overcrowding in Irish prisons. Called 'Community Return' this scheme provides for early release for prisoners serving sentences of up to seven years to carry out community service under the supervision of probation staff (*Dáil Debates*, vol 764, 2 May 2012). It is a measure to reduce the prison population at the 'back end' – that is by releasing serving prisoners.

Under Article 13.6 of the Irish Constitution (Bunreacht na hÉireann), the President has a right of pardon, which can be delegated to the Executive. Under the Criminal Procedure Act 1993, a person may petition the minister for Justice for a pardon – but only in cases where a miscarriage of justice has occurred. Widespread use of pardons as a way of alleviating overcrowding is unknown in Irish penal practice. Remission is set in statute as one third of a sentence for 'good behaviour'. Temporary release is, however, regularly used to free up prison space (see further O'Malley 2010).

Post-custodial measures

Since 2001, Ireland has had a system of post-release measures to monitor those convicted of sexual offences after their release from prison. These requirements involve an obligation to inform the Gardaí (police) of the released person's address and changes of address.

Much more extensive requirements were introduced in 2006 and 2007. In 2006, a poorly debated law was enacted which enables judges at the time of sentence to impose a post-conviction order on a person (section 26 of the Criminal Justice Act 2006) in the case of certain serious offences. Such orders can be imposed for up to seven years. The types of orders which can be imposed are the 'monitoring order' and the 'protection of persons order'. These require a person to notify the Garda Síochána (police) of changes of address or to refrain from engaging in behaviour which would be threatening or harassing to a person named in the order. A breach of either order is a criminal offence, rendering a person liable to a fine and/ or a sentence of imprisonment of up to six months. Section 26A of the 2006 Act, inserted in 2007, introduced a single order which gives a great deal of flexibility to judges in fashioning a set of conditions or restrictions on activities or requirements to engage in certain behaviours.

It does not appear that Irish judges have taken up these orders with any great enthusiasm. Official data is not collected on their use, but experience indicates they are not well known in Irish legal circles. While this may be so, and represents an interesting example of how judges can mediate penal policy, the introduction of these orders is an important departure in Irish law. Such orders act as barriers to the integration of a person released from prison into the community and place Ireland, at least symbolically, amongst the countries where there is 'no such thing as an ex-offender' (Garland 2001: 142; on the Irish context see further Rogan 2011a).

Private sector and voluntary involvement

There are no privately run prisons in Ireland. A plan for a very large prison at Thornton Hall in north county Dublin, discussed further below, involved the building of the prison by a private consortium under a 'public private partnership', whereby the State would then lease the buildings from the private company over a long period. The collapse in the construction industry in Ireland meant that the consortium was not able to commence the project.

The Prisons Act 2007 allows for private companies to provide prisoner escort services. This has not been implemented to date. It would appear that the threat of privatisation was used at the time as a bargaining chip in an industrial relations dispute with prison officers in order to secure reforms in the area of overtime and sick leave.

Recently, the private security company 'G4S' acted as the sponsor for a conference on the criminal justice system in Ireland, which was addressed by the Minister for Justice, Director General of the Irish Prison Service and other high ranking public servants working in the criminal justice field.[1] G4S provided a presentation on its work around the world (http://www.eolasmagazine.ie/events/justice2012/programme.php).

There have been no official announcements of plans to privatise Irish prisons, or indeed whether privatisation is being examined as a viable option. It is clear, however, that the private security industry has turned its attentions to Ireland and is clearly seeking to gain the attention of the Government.

One of the features of Irish criminal justice has been the plethora of voluntary and community organisations involved in what can be described as the 'social care' aspects of dealing with those convicted of offences. Since the foundation of the State, the Irish government has relied heavily on charitable organisations – particularly those associated with religious organisations – to deliver core State services – including health and education (see generally Carey 2007; McCashin 2004). Many hospitals in Ireland are still run, at least nominally, by religious orders, as are very many schools. Within criminal justice, the forerunners of today's professionalised probation staff were often religiously motivated individuals taking those convicted of offences into their care. Probation officers – as they are known today – were very late to appear in Ireland, with the service developing only since the early 1970s in any mean-ingful way (Kilcommins 2004; Rogan 2011b). Religious organisations were also involved in the provision of assistance to those leaving prison. Since independence in 1922 Irish prisons have, however, always been run directly by the State. It is one of the puzzling features of Irish prison policy that the Catholic Church, so closely involved in the running of a vast network of institutions of confinement for children and unmarried mothers, did not become directly involved in the administration of the formal penal system. Irish prisons still all have chaplains, most, but not all, of whom are members of religious organisations. The chaplains have produced some of the most critical reports of the Irish prison system written by any organisation in the past decade (Chaplains 2011).

Today, charitable organisations such as the Society of St. Vincent de Paul and the Society of Friends continue to work within the prisons, assisting mainly in the area of prison visiting. Many voluntary organisations, most of which receive often highly uncertain state funding, work within communities, assisting with re-integration post-release or in crime prevention. The community sector's involvement is fragmented and highly localised.

Advocacy groups

Campaigning and advocacy organisations working on behalf of prisoners or for the reform of the penal system have been quite rare in Ireland and are historically associated with Ireland's troubled political history. The birth of the Irish state in 1922 was a difficult one, involving the outbreak of Civil War and a period of bitter division over a Treaty with Great Britain which, ultimately, gave independence to the 26 counties now forming the Republic of Ireland, but which also required an oath of allegiance to be taken by members of the Irish parliament to the British monarch (amongst a wealth of literature see Bew 2007; Ferriter 2004; Lee 1989).

The politically charged nature of the period played out within Irish prisons – and the debates about prisons and prison conditions during these years – were dominated by politically motivated groups linked to the broader debates about the future of Ireland and their stance on the Treaty with Great Britain. The advocacy and campaigning of these groups was focused on the treatment of those imprisoned for their actions in advancing these political goals, rather than being directed at penal reform more broadly.

Supporters of the prisoners who opposed the Treaty with Britain formed groups agitating for their release and improvements to the dire conditions in which they were being detained. Most of these organisations' aims were closely connected to the broader political objectives of the period. One of the most notable prisoners' support groups was the 'Women Prisoners' Defence League' – also known colloquially as 'the Mothers'. The group was established by Maud Gonne MacBride – a former prisoner herself, the subject of much poetry by W.B. Yeats and the mother of Seán MacBride, who went on to found Amnesty International and advocate penal reform also. The League was established and mainly worked in Dublin and engaged in protest and disruption through public demonstration and within the print media.

The League also featured high profile female Republican figures and the activities of the group revolved around protest and publicity. The League's members engaged in hunger strikes outside prisons; its leaders made public speeches – particularly around O'Connell Street and Cathal Brugha Street in Dublin. The League's members also engaged in prison visiting (Rogan 2011b).

Their impact on prison policy at the time was minimal and it appears they caused little but frustration and annoyance on the part of those in Government, with the gender of those involved clearly a factor. For example, Alec McCabe T.D. declared: 'why not let out these prisoners and put an end to the campaign of these wild women who spend their Sundays and the time they should spend in their homes, orating from the ruins in O'Connell Street?' (*Dáil Debates*, vol 7, col 1135, 21 May 1924).

While the impact of the organisation on the policy-making process was minimal, to analyse it solely from that point of view is misleading. The association of these groups with Republicans meant they were not 'acceptable' to policy-makers, to use Mick Ryan's term (Ryan 1978). The League was a protest movement aligned to a political agenda against a very particular backdrop in Irish political history.

In the 1970s, the Portlaoise Prisoners' Union was established by a group of serving prisoners. It later became the Prisoners' Union and produced a *Jail Journal*. The main focus of its actions was on the specific conditions in Portlaoise Prison, where many Republican prisoners were detained. Again, its impact on policy-makers was minimal, with the Government denying its existence. This is unsurprising, given that the Department of Justice during the Troubles was a highly insular and defensive place, fearful of threats from what it saw as subversive and deeply dangerous organisations.

Also in the 1970s the Prison Study Group was established. It comprised a number of law students, a solicitor, a priest and a psychologist. The group received a grant from the Department of Psychiatry at University College Dublin to carry out research on the Irish prison system. This group, despite its credentials as a non-political study group made up of professionals, found the Department of Justice unreceptive to its activity and most uncooperative with its efforts (Prison Study P. S. Group 1973). Efforts in the 1980s to engage in independent examination of the penal system were met with similar coldness (MacBride M. Commission, 1982).[2]

It was not, however, until 1994 that an organisation advocating reform of the penal system – with a more general and longer-term remit regarding prisoners' rights – was established. The Irish Penal Reform Trust (www.iprt.ie) is the country's leading non-governmental organisation, working for respect for the rights of all those in the penal system, for imprisonment to be a measure of last resort, and for penal policy to be based on a commitment to combating social injustice.[3] Like many NGOs in Ireland, its main source of funding is from the American philanthropic organisation 'Atlantic Philanthropies', with funding coming also from the UK's Joseph Rowntree Charitable Trust, and individual members and local grant-giving bodies. It receives no State funding.

Its impact on prison policy-making has yet to be formally measured, but in recent times many of the objectives on which it has campaigned have been adopted by Government – including the desire to reduce the prison population, to introduce in-cell sanitation into all prisons, and to develop an independent system for dealing with the complaints of prisoners; matters which are examined further below.

Those Ireland imprisons

The deficits in Irish criminal justice are perhaps most keenly felt in attempts to examine the nature of the Irish prison population. What we know about Irish prisoners is gleaned from a small number of important but one-off studies. The largest sample of prison records studied to date found that 52 per cent of the prison population had been unemployed prior to entering prison and 54 per cent had left school without completing any State examinations (O'Donnell et al. 2009). O'Donnell et al. also found that prisoners were 25 times more likely to live in a community categorised as 'seriously deprived' upon release than those who had not been in prison.

O'Mahony's study of prisoners in Dublin's main prison, Mountjoy – published in 1997 – found that 50 per cent of his research participants had a parent, sibling or child in prison, while 77 per cent had served a sentence in St. Patrick's Institution for men and male children between the ages of 16 and 21 (O'Mahony 1997).

Seymour and Costello have found that 33 per cent of women prisoners who participated in their study had been homeless immediately prior to their committal to prison, with the overall rate at 25 per cent. Of all prisoners, 54 per cent had at least one experience of homelessness in their lives. Other research has found that 24.4 per cent of male prisoners in their study had engaged in deliberate self harm, rising to 41.8 per cent in the case of women (Duffy et al. 2006).

It is clear that the Irish prison population is characterised by multiple forms of socio-economic disadvantage and that the most deprived communities in Ireland are bearing the greatest burden of imprisonment and release from imprisonment.

Recently, however, the Irish judiciary has signalled its intention to punish 'financial' crime more severely than had been the case heretofore. Though it is both too early to say – and difficult to examine in a scientific way, given the state of criminal justice data in Ireland – a number of judicial pronouncements have indicated that the Irish prison population may now include more first-time, older individuals, drawn from the more affluent parts of society. In the case of *DPP v. Murray* (2012 IEHC 60) – an appeal against the severity of a sentence on a person convicted of social welfare fraud – Finnegan J opined:

> How should a sentencing court treat offenders who have defrauded the public revenue by either engaging in unlawful tax evasion on the one hand or (as in this case) by making false social welfare claims on the other? Given the importance of such questions for the public wealth – not least at a time of financial emergency – it seems appropriate that this Court should now give some general guidance for future cases of this kind. (*DPP v. Murray* (2012 IEHC 60) at 1–2)

Finnegan J held further that, though financial crimes are not in the same category as those against the person, they are not victimless, 'quite the contrary: offences of this kind strike at the heart of the principles of equity, equality of treatment and social solidarity on which the entire edifice of the taxation and social security systems lean' (*DPP v. Murray* (2012 IEHC 60) at 7).

Overall, the Court of Criminal Appeal laid down some general principles to guide sentencing judges in future such cases. The court held:

> significant and systematic frauds directed upon the public revenue – whether illegal tax evasion on the one hand or social security fraud on the other – should generally meet with an immediate and appreciable custodial sentence, although naturally the sentence to be imposed in any given case must have appropriate regard to the individual circumstances of each accused. (*DPP v. Murray* (2012 IEHC 60) at 9)

While a single judicial pronouncement in the context of a social welfare fraud should not be used to draw too many conclusions, the attitude of the Court of Criminal Appeal in the *Murray* decision does, however, lay down a clear statement that sentencing courts should deal with financial crime in a more robust manner. It may be that, as Ireland sees more financial offences being prosecuted its prisons will be required to deal with first-time offenders at a more mature stage of life than is commonplace, and without the usual profile of prisoners within our penal system. However, the fact that these comments were made in the context of a case of social welfare fraud cannot be overlooked. Whether the same approach is in fact applied to those found guilty of financial crime, on a much larger scale within the corporate and banking environments, remains to be seen.

Moral panics and Irish penal policy

During the 1990s and early part of the 2000s, Ireland – historically a place blighted by *emigration* – witnessed levels of *immigration* which were utterly without precedent. While the number of people born outside Ireland has increased, there appears to be comparatively little in the way of sustained moral panic concerning crimes committed by those who have moved to Ireland. At the same time, it seems that the issue of ethnicity is somewhat invisible in Irish prison policy-making discourse. There is still no official strategy on diversity within prisons, though one is now promised. Researchers have also yet to turn their attentions to the experiences of those from outside Ireland incarcerated in its prisons. A great deal remains poorly understood and examined concerning the experiences of non-Irish nationals coming before the courts and entering the prison system.

Ireland's Traveller community –, a group with a shared history, culture and traditions including, historically, a nomadic way of life – face discrimination in everyday life and in their interactions with State institutions. Travellers were recognised as an ethnic group by legislation in 1997. Again, however, the number of Irish Travellers in prisons is not recorded separately and research on their experiences of prison is largely absent. A study conducted by the Irish Chaplaincy in Britain – of the experience of Irish Travellers in the British prison system – indicates that such prisoners come from backgrounds of serious socio-economic deprivation, and experience high levels of mental illness. Within prison, many reported instances of discrimination by other prisoners and staff (Irish Chaplaincy in Britain 2011). Irish Travellers make up 0.6 per cent of the British prison population. It is likely that the experiences of Travellers in Irish prisons is not far removed from that of those in the United Kingdom.

Though official statistics are deeply inadequate, it would appear that the Roma community in Ireland numbers around 3,000 (www.paveepoint.ie). Similarly, no studies of their experiences of Irish criminal justice exist.

While it cannot be said that long-lasting moral panics around immigration have been a discernable feature of Irish prison policy, moral panics have occurred, affecting the penal system – most notably during the 1990s, where a series of measures introduced at that time have had long-lasting results. In what O'Donnell and O'Sullivan describe as a 'textbook case' of moral panic (O'Donnell and O'Sullivan 2003), the summer of that year brought the killing of an investigative journalist who had written about crime in Ireland – particularly regarding what was seen as Ireland's growing organised or 'gangland' crime scene and the killing of a Detective Garda (police officer). These shocking incidents came at a time of concern about killings in rural areas, traditionally low in crime. While the events in the summer of 1996 – which led to a number of legislative responses which ultimately increased the numbers in prison – would, no doubt, have had an impact at any time on Irish politics and society, they occurred during a period which was particularly likely to lead to legislative change. The year 1996 was a politically charged one. The Government of the day was a coalition of three parties, one right of centre and two on the left. The main opposition party was Fianna Fáil – a party with a tradition of pragmatism and considered to be similar to Gaulism , and one enduring what was at that time an extremely rare period in opposition. Another opposition party was the Progressive Democrats, a right-of-centre party with a clear philosophy of laissez-faire economics. These two parties went on to win the 1997 General Election.

In the run-up to that election, political tempers were fraught and the issue of crime was an obvious line of attack in the circumstances. The Fianna Fáil opposition spokesperson on Justice, John O'Donoghue, regularly made searing and colourful criticism of the Government's approach to crime. For example, he described Ireland since 1994 (when Fianna Fáil had last been in power) as having been 'all but devastated by wave after wave of remorseless crime' (*Dáil Debates*, vol 452, col 653, 2 May 1995) and enduring a 'tide of criminal terror'. The Progressive Democrats sought to characterise the coalition Government as soft on crime, saying that such an approach was symptomatic of otherwise undesirable 'leftist' tendencies.

The combination of these attacks and the particular crimes in the summer of 1996 was to prompt the Government to rush through a legislative package, including a constitutional amendment to allow judges to deny bail more readily than had been the case. The Government in 1997 also announced plans to build an additional 840 prison spaces. Just three years earlier the then Government had said just 230–40 were required and advocated a cap on prison numbers. Once the Fianna Fáil–Progressive Democrat Government came to power, the number of spaces planned rose to 2,000. Prison building came to be seen as a sign of governmental strength, and with increased money available during the 'Celtic Tiger' years, could be carried out with relative ease.

The concern about gangland crime was most particularly felt in relation to drugs. In 1999 John O'Donoghue T.D. – now Minister for Justice – oversaw the enactment of new legislation which provided for a presumptive minimum penalty of ten years' imprisonment for those found guilty of possession of drugs with a value of €13,000 or more. Judges are required to impose the statutorily mandated ten year sentence unless exceptional and specific circumstances apply. In practice, it would seem that a guilty plea is considered to amount to such circumstances. However, the increase in the number of prisoners sentenced for five to ten years – and ten years or more for drugs offences – has had a marked effect on the prison population as a whole, providing further credence to the assertion that the mid- to late 1990s – the moral panics and political competition of the period – had long-lasting and negative impacts on the Irish penal system.

Contemporary Irish prison policy

Irish prison policy is undergoing something of a period of transition at present and its recent and ongoing experiences of fiscal austerity involving swingeing cuts to public services have been felt in prison policy also. The current Government – involving a coalition of the centre-right party Fine Gael and the centre-left party Labour – took power in 2011.

Ireland's economic crash has given rise to high levels of unemployment, crushing levels of public debt, cuts in public spending, and poor demand in the domestic economy (Honohan 2009). The almost bullish approach to prison policy of the 1990s and early 2000s has, in tandem, also given way to a much more muted and cautious tone. As well as this change in rhetoric, Ireland has seen a number of concrete policy changes indicating a desire to reduce the prison population. The first indication of this came in the Programme for Government, agreed on the formation of a coalition government. That document stated:

We are committed to a sentencing system that provides a safer society at a lower cost to the taxpayer. We will ensure that violent offenders and other serious offenders serve appropriate prison sentences while at the same time switching away from prison sentences and towards less costly non-custodial options for non-violent and less serious offenders. This will result in a reduction in the prison population and alleviate overcrowding. (Government of Ireland 2011)

Previous governments had also committed to the building of a prison which could hold up to 2,200 people at a site called Thornton Hall, in north county Dublin (Brangan 2009). The project was mired in controversy, not least due to its cost, but the plan for it was consistently held out, almost as a panacea, to the problems of overcrowding and poor conditions across the Irish penal estate. The new Government commissioned a review group to examine its continued feasibility and it also recommended an overall reduction in the size of the Irish prison population (Thornton Hall Review T. H. P. R. Group 2011).

Shortly after the establishment of the new Government, the Minister for Justice, Alan Shatter T.D., introduced the Criminal Justice (Community Service) (Amendment No. 2) Bill 2011, which aimed to increase the number of community service orders given by the Irish courts. The press release which accompanied the passing of the Bill into law gave prominence to the financial savings to be derived from the scheme (available at http://justice.ie/en/JELR/Pages/PR11000185).

In a startling move, The National Recovery Plan 2011–2014 – which contains the agreement between the Irish Government and the so-called 'troika', which is providing financial assistance to the Irish State – contains detailed commitments to reducing costs across the prison system. These include the diversion of those who default on fines from prison and the increased use of community service (Government of Ireland 2011: 70). Under the terms of the 'bailout' for the State, the cost of imprisonment also came in for scrutiny. That plan also envisages the reduction of staff in the Prison Service.

Other long overdue changes are also being made. Irish prison policy – long lamented for its lack of strategic objectives, and piecemeal and *ad hoc* approach to planning – has also seen the introduction of the first Strategic Plan for the Irish Prison Service, to cover the period 2012–2015. In April 2012 it was announced that the Inspector of Prisons would investigate the deaths of all those in the custody of the Irish Prison Service. Until now, the only independent investigation into a death took the form of an inquest. With no statutory basis for narrative verdicts and the limitations inherent in inquests, Ireland has arguably long been in breach of Article 2 of the European Convention on Human Rights.

In 2012 it was also announced that a new system of dealing with the complaints of prisoners would be put in place, involving, for the first time, independent examination of the most serious complaints.

While there are elements of the current picture of prison policy which signal a more reformist attitude on the part of the Government, there is much that remains outdated, regressive and in breach of human rights norms within the Irish penal system.

Overcrowding and poor conditions

Probably the most serious and pernicious issue facing the prison system concerns the levels of overcrowding and poor conditions in many of the State's prisons. The most recently available figures show that the bed capacity for the prison system as a whole, in 2011, was 4,486, while there were 4,390 prisoners on average. Bed capacity as officially defined hides, however, the reality in many prisons of doubling up or greater levels of multiple-occupancy. Overcrowding is particularly serious in some institutions – Cork prison has an official bed capacity of 272 while 295 prisoners were present in it, as an average measure, during 2011. Mountjoy male prison has a capacity of 602 (which fluctuates as the prison is renovated), but there were 616 prisoners there in 2011. The Inspector of Prisons has laid down a more realistic measure of what the bed capacity of each prison should be. This shows that individual prisons are far more overcrowded than the official statistics suggest. The Inspector, for example, considers the maximum capacity of Cork prison to be 194, meaning it is running at 152 per cent of its capacity, with higher figures reported at various times in the year (Inspector of Prisons 2010b).

Within Cork prison, only eight cells have in-cell sanitation. Mountjoy Prison has long been criticised for widespread slopping out. In 2010, of the 4,397 prisoners in custody across all Irish prisons, 1,003 people had to slop out and a further 1,866 had to use in-cell toilet facilities in the presence of others (*Dáil Debates*, vol 727, 27 January 2011). The Council of Europe's Committee for the Prevention of Torture has consistently criticised the Irish prison authorities on this front (CPT 2011), considering it to be inhuman and degrading treatment.

In another tardy move, the Irish government is engaged in the installation of in-cell sanitation into Mountjoy prison at present, and it is planned to replace Cork prison entirely with a prison of 150 capacity and a commitment to using community-based strategies to reduce the prison population.

Violence in Irish prisons is also a matter of serious concern. The Committee for the Prevention of Torture described stabbings and slashing occurring in Mountjoy on an almost daily basis. There is also a very high usage of 'protection' – up to a 23 hour lock up for prisoners about whom there are concerns regarding their safety.

Accountability deficits

Equally as concerning is the lack of adequate structures to ensure accountability for decisions taken and actions within Irish prisons. Decision-making – and guidelines thereon – are opaque, and prison circulars or instructions are not easily accessible publicly. There is no Ombudsman for Prisoners, or similar body, in Ireland who can receive complaints from prisoners and conduct investigations. The Inspector of Prisons is an independent body, visiting prisons on a regular basis and writing prison-specific and thematic reports. The Inspector cannot, however, receive complaints from prisoners directly. Visiting Committees are attached to each prison. These are groups of individuals whose role it is to visit prisons on a regular basis and hear complaints from prisoners, though they have no legal power whatever to resolve them.

Until very recently, children detained in St. Patrick's Institution were the only children excluded from the remit of the Ombudsman for Children in Ireland to hear complaints.

The Inspector of Prisons has expressed concern about the handling of complaints by prisoners internally – with inadequate recording of information, incomplete investigations and the lack of facility to assist prisoners in making complaints (Prisons 2010a). In its 2006 Report the Committee for the Prevention of Torture stated the view that many prisoners did not have confidence in the complaints system (Committee for the Prevention of Torture 2006).

In August 2012 the Irish Government announced the introduction of a new model of complaints, prompted by the criticisms of the Inspector of Prisons and organisations such as the Irish Penal Reform Trust. This model envisages independent investigators examining the most serious complaints such as those of excessive force by prison officers, racial discrimination, intimidation or threats, with a right to appeal to the Inspector of Prisons.

While improvements are in the offing, there remains a grave lack of transparency concerning how decisions are made within prisons – including around matters such as temporary release and in the decisions on early release. In Ireland, the Parole Board makes recommendations concerning the early release of prisoners who have served over seven years of their sentences. However, the final decision on release continues to rest with the Minister for Justice.

Data deficits

As is likely to have become clear from the above discussion, Ireland's data on its prisons and prisoners are seriously defective.

The Annual Reports of the Irish Prison Service and the publicly available data on our prison population is scant. We lack full information on sentence length and offence type, average sentence length, average amount of fines and other indicators. Full demographic information on who our prisoners are is not published. As has been described elsewhere (O'Donnell 2004; Rogan 2012), we are unable to link data across the criminal justice system.

The strengthening Irish criminological research community has the ability to turn its attentions more closely to the criminal justice and prison systems. However, as O'Donnell et al. correctly state, the hurdles to research 'make[s] it difficult to assemble and accumulate the basic knowledge about crime and justice issues that is required to put things into perspective for concerned citizens and to guide decisions by policy-makers' (O'Donnell et al. 2009: 124).

What drives penal policy in Ireland?

The Republic of Ireland has a population of around 4.2 million. Its voting system is that of proportional representation, which, since the 1970s in particular, has led to a succession of coalition governments. Historically, Irish politics has been dominated by Fianna Fáil, and party politics was borne largely out of parties' positions on the Treaty with the United Kingdom which gave rise to Irish independence, rather than along an ideological continuum reflecting the traditional tensions between capital and labour – as in most other western European countries. The Labour party has previously been very much the third party of the State. In the recent upheaval across Irish politics and society, the Irish left has grown with the rise of Sinn Féin, a Republican party, as a political force within the Republic and advocating more explicitly on social policy issues, as well as through the election of a number of left-wing independent and other members of parliament.

While Irish politics has something of a clearer ideological spectrum at present, this is very much a recent phenomenon. Ireland has proven difficult to compare to other countries across many indices. The peculiar nature of the Irish welfare state gives some indication of the ways of Irish politics. The welfare state in Ireland has been described as a 'mongrel', or a hybrid of various models (Carey 2007; McCashin 2004). Most welfarist initiatives have been prompted by the actions of individual reformist-minded and energetic politicians. The Irish welfare state itself did not take hold until at least the 1960s, with the State relying on the voluntary and charitable sectors for welfare provision. There has been a great deal of flexibility and fluidity in social and economic provision in Ireland, which is recognised as being distinctive or particularistic. The major parties have historically avoided ideological labels and there is a great deal of heterogeneity and fluidity within their support bases.

Irish politicians are also notably, perhaps exceptionally, close to their constituents and are well known for acting as brokers for gaining access to social benefits; this occurs across party lines. Ireland also has a great many politicians, at present 166 members of the lower house of parliament, the Dáil (O'Halpin 2010).

As is the case with many aspects of Irish economic and social life, it is difficult to state what precisely is the particular ideology – or political or penal philosophy – driving change within Irish prison policy. A confluence of factors must be examined: individual ministers and civil servants have enormous influence (Rogan 2010); the criminological research base has, until very recently, been extremely weak; prison policy is vulnerable to rapid change in the wake of high profile events of concern.

This fluid picture has meant, for example, that Ireland came to the penal-welfare movement – with its commitment to the rehabilitation of offenders, sometimes it must be said at the expense of attending to the needs of victims – very late and with less vigour or commitment than elsewhere. Ireland's penal-welfarist period commenced in the 1960s, driven largely by the efforts of an energetic and ambitious Minister for Justice. Such fluidity has also meant that Ireland was spared some of the excesses of the drive to austerity in prison conditions and mass incarceration witnessed in other countries; though, as the above makes clear, it did not escape entirely. O'Donnell has also provocatively argued that Ireland's lack of a criminological research base may have also acted as a form of insulation against penal excess. Moreover, Ireland does not have elected prosecutors or judges (O'Donnell 2011).

While the lack of ideology in Irish politics and prison policy may explain the start-stop nature of Irish penal planning, it certainly cannot be said that this has been benign. As Henderson has pointed out, pragmatic politics can act as a Trojan horse for regressive ends (Henderson 2012). The lack of ideological barriers allowed a minister in the 1960s to implement penal-welfarist policies, but the same lack enabled a minister in the 2000s to bring forward plans for a prison which would hold up to 2,200 people, at the time almost two thirds of the entire prison population. The drift which has been a feature of Irish prisons has allowed conditions to deteriorate unchecked and for clearly problematic policies – around mandatory sentencing for drug offences – to continue. The profile of the Irish prison population also indicates that incarceration cuts most deeply amongst communities already suffering marginalisation of multiple kinds. Irish prison policy-makers have, furthermore, shown themselves capable of decisive action against those seeking to overthrow the State.

Finally, no discussion of Irish prison policy can ignore the extraordinary and scandalous practices of confinement which took place for decades in Ireland – quite outside the formal, State-run penal system. Ireland had a vast network of institutions: for children deemed to be 'unruly' or whose welfare was at risk, for the detention of women who had children outside of marriage, and for the holding of people considered to be psychiatrically ill – whether by their family or others, sometimes on very dubious grounds. The precise legal basis for the detention of many of those held in these institutions is unclear, but around one per cent of the entire population of the state was held in some kind of institutional detention, with many experiencing neglect and abuse at the peak of its use (from around the 1920s until the 1950s). While this painful history is only now being explored in a meaningful way (for a seminal examination of the topic see O'Sullivan and O'Donnell 2012) it is clear that a deeply conservative society imposed a rigid view of what was 'acceptable' behaviour, particularly in the sexual domain – a view aimed at women through a series of institutions of confinement. Intertwined with views on morality, these institutions also upheld the often brutal system for the inheritance of land and of survival in Irish rural culture. A repressive ideology was clearly operative in such a system, and it will be some time yet before it is fully understood and assuaged within Irish society.

Conclusion: Irish prison policy in an age of austerity

The ebb and flow of Irish prison policy has entered another phase of development, prompted by its economic woes. Ireland's current period of austerity is having some interesting effects on Irish prison policy-makers. There is a clear appetite for a reduction in the prison population and the use of cheaper alternatives. Irish policy-makers are showing their pragmatic credentials once again. Cost cutting has been mandated across Irish public services – necessitated by the decision to provide gargantuan funding to Irish banks – and talk about prison building to show 'strength' on criminal justice matters is no longer an option.

It is perhaps in the area of sentencing that the greatest potential to change the nature of the Irish prison population is present. If, as they suggest, the Irish judiciary take a 'tough' approach to financial crime, the effect that will have on prison policy – in terms of conditions and the development of alternatives – will be both interesting and revealing of the Irish authorities' actual attitude to the questions: what prison is for?, and for whom should it be reserved?

Notes

1. The author spoke at this meeting on behalf of the Irish Penal Reform Trust, stating the Trust's opposition to the introduction of private prisons in Ireland.
2. Incidentally, the MacBride Commission comprised two individuals who went on to become Presidents of Ireland – Mary McAleese, who served from 1997–2012, and the current President of Ireland, Michael D. Higgins.
3. The author was the Chairperson of this organisation at the time of writing.

References

Bew, P. (2007) 'Ireland: The Politics of Enmity 1789–2006', *Oxford History of Modern Europe* (Oxford: Oxford University Press).

Brangan, L. (2009) 'Thornton Hall: A Policy Analysis – Uncaring or Unthinking?', in *Social Sciences* (Dublin: Dublin Institute of Technology).

Carey, S. (2007) *Social Security in Ireland, 1939–1952 : The Limits to Solidarity* (Dublin: Irish Academic Press).

Chaplains, I. P . (2011) *Annual Report* (Dublin: Irish Prison Chaplains).

Commission of Inquiry into the Penal System (2005) *Report on the Court Poor Box* (Dublin).

Commission, M. (1982) *Report on the Penal System* (Dublin: Profile Books).

CPT. (2011) *Report to the Irish Government on the Visit to Ireland Carried Out by the European Committee for the Prevention of Torture and Inhuman or Degrading Treatment or Punishment (CPT) from 25 January to 5 February 2010* (Strasbourg: Council of Europe).

Duffy, D., Linehan, S . and Kennedy, H . (2006) 'Psychiatric Morbidity in the Male Sentenced Irish Prisons Population', *Irish Journal of Psychological Medicine*, 23 (2): 54–62.

Ferriter, D. (2004) *The Transformation of Ireland: 1900–2000* (London: Profile Books).

Government of Ireland (2011) *National Recovery Plan 2011–2014* (Dublin: Government of Ireland).

Garland, D. (2001) *The Culture of Control : Crime and Social Order in Contemporary Society* (Oxford: Oxford University Press).

Group, P. S. (1973) *An Examination of the Irish Penal System* (Dublin: Department of Justice).

Group, T. H. P. R. (2011) *Report of the Thornton Hall Project Review Group* (Dublin: Department of Justice).

Hamilton, C. (2005) 'Sentencing in the District Court: Here Be Dragons', *Irish Criminal Law Journal*, 15 (3): 9–17.

Henderson, T.-N.Y. (2012) 'Review: Prison Policy in Ireland: Politics, Penal-Welfarism and Political Imprisonment', *Criminal Law and Criminal Justice Books* http://clcjbooks.rutgers.edu/books/prison_policy_in_ireland.html.

Honohan, P. (2009) 'Resolving Ireland's Banking Crisis', *Economic and Social Review*, 40 (2): 207–31.

Inspector of Prisons (2010a) *Guidance on Best Practice Relating to Prisoners Complaints and Prison Discipline* (Nenagh, County Tipperary: Inspector of Prisons).

Inspector of Prisons (2010b) *The Irish Prison Population – An Examination of Duties and Obligations Owed to Prisoners* (Nenagh, County Tipperary: Inspector of Prisons).

Irish Chaplaincy in Britain (2011) *Voices Unheard* (London: Law Reform Commission).

Irish Prison Service (2012) *Annual Report on Prisons* (Dublin: Irish Prison Service).

Kilcommins, S. (2004) *Crime, Punishment and the Search for Order in Ireland* (Dublin: Institute of Public Administration).

Lee, J. (1989) *Ireland, 1912–1985: Politics and Society* (Cambridge: Cambridge University Press).

McCashin, A. (2004) *Social security in Ireland* (Dublin: Gill and Macmillan).

O' Donnell, I. (2004) 'Imprisonment and Penal Policy in Ireland', *Howard Journal of Criminal Justice*, 43 (3): 253–66.

O' Donnell, I. (2011) 'Criminology, Bureaucracy and Unfinished Business', in M. Bosworth and C. Hoyle (eds), *What is Criminology?* (Oxford: Oxford University Press) 488–501.

O' Donnell, I., Hughes, N. and Baumer, E. P. (2009) 'Recidivism in the Republic of Ireland', *Criminology and Criminal Justice*, 8 (2): 123–46.

O' Donnell, I. and O' Sullivan, E. (2003) 'The Politics of Intolerance—Irish Style', *British Journal of Criminology*, 43 (1): 41–62, doi: 10.1093/bjc/43.1.41.

O' Halpin, E. (2010) 'Politics and the State 1922–1932', in J. R. Hill (ed.), *A New History of Ireland: VII, Ireland, 1921–1984* (Oxford: Oxford University Press) 86–126.

O' Mahony, P. (1997) *Mountjoy Prisoners : A Sociological and Criminological Profile* (Dublin: Stationery Office).

O' Malley, T. (2010) 'Early Release from Prison in Ireland', in D. van zyl Smit, N. Padfield and F. Dunkel (eds), *Release from Prison: European Policy and Practice* (Cullompton, Devon: Willan Publishing).

O' Sullivan, E. and O' Donnell, I . (2012) *Coercive Confinement in Ireland: Patients, Prisoners and Penitents* (Manchester: Manchester University Press).

OCO (2011) *Young People in St. Patrick's Institution* (Dublin: Ombudsman for Children Office).

Redmond, D. (2002) *Imprisonment for Fine Default and Civil Debt* (Dublin: Department of Justice).

Rogan, M. (2010) 'Yes or No Minister: The Importance of the Politician–Senior Civil Servant Dyad in Irish Prison Policy', *The Prison Journal*, 91: 32–56, doi: 10.1177/0032885510389560.

Rogan, M. (2011a) 'The Innocence Rights of Sentenced Offenders', *The Irish Journal of Legal Studies*, 2 (1): 55–66.

Rogan, M. (2011b) *Prison Policy in Ireland: Politics, Penal-Welfarism and Political Imprisonment* (London: Routledge).

Rogan, M. (2012) 'Improving Criminal Justice Data and Policy', *Economic and Social Review*, 43 (2): 303–23.

Ryan, M. (1978) *The Acceptable Pressure Group-Inequality in the Penal Lobby : A Case Study of the Howard League and RAP* (Farnborough: Saxon House).

Seymour, M. (2006) *Alternatives to Custody* (Dublin: Business in the Community and the Katharine Howard Foundation.).

6
The French Criminal Justice System[1]

Philippe Robert[2]

Understanding the characteristics of the French penal system entails looking at trends over time – in order to identify key changes – and making European comparisons to see what is specific to France.[3] We will adopt this method of analysis over the coming pages rather than undertaking a detailed elaboration of the penal system per se.

The stability of imprisonment, the decline in the use of the fine, the triumph of community sentencing?

The first key trend concerns the use of different kinds of sanctions (Table 6.1). Over the past 30 years and more, it is clear that their respective use has changed significantly, even if it is quite difficult to understand the reasons for these changes.

The relative use of imprisonment has remained quite stable over a 35-year period, representing approximately one fifth of all sentences. The distribution of sentences between various penalties has undergone serious change, mainly because of the transformation in the relative

Table 6.1 Sanctions (minor offences excluded), in %

sanctions	1975		2010	
	N	%	N	%
imprisonment	96,070	17.8	124,527	19.8
fine	303,569	56.2	224,224	35.7
community sentences	140,639	26.0	279,308	44.5
total	*540,278*	*100.0*	*628,059*	*100.0*

Source: Robert 2002; Justice, SDSE 2011: 18.

share of non-custodial sentences. Yet, the use of other kinds of sentences has changed significantly: the use of fines has strongly declined whilst recourse to community sentences has doubled. Contrary to what we may consider *prima facie*, this trend has been led by increased punitiveness: whilst more than half of offenders got away with a simple fine at the beginning of this period, only one-third can expect to do so today. This is confirmed when we examine the kinds of community sentences used. Indeed, more intrusive measures are being used – such as probation, community service and electronic monitoring. A comparison with France's main neighbours (Table 6.2) suggests that the apportionment of different sentences has national particularities. For France it is tempting to draw the simple conclusion that recent trends reveal stability in the use of imprisonment, a decline in the use of the fine and the triumph of community sentencing.

Yet, a closer analysis suggests that this conclusion needs to be qualified. Although recourse to imprisonment has hardly increased, relative to the use of other sanctions, it has increased significantly in terms of the absolute number of people imprisoned (Table 6.1). The growth in the detention rate that can be observed over the long term in France, as in neighbouring countries (Table 6.3), cannot only be explained by

Table 6.2   Distribution of different sanctions and measures according to country, in %

Countries	Admonition	Fines	Non-custodial sentence	Suspended sentence	Custodial sentence	Other measures
Germany	1.1	79.8		13.3	5.8	
England	6.6	71.5	9.8	2.5	6.8	2.8
France	1.0	37.9	11.1	30.8	19.3	

Source: European sourcebook 2010, tbl 3.2.3.1.

Table 6.3   Detention rate per 100,000 of the total population on 1 September

	1983	2010
England and Wales	87	154
Spain	37	165
Holland	28	71
France	70	104
Belgium	65	105

Source: 2010 council of Europe annual penal statistics space
1.The reunification of Germany renders comparison with this country impossible.

the increase in the number of entries. It is also in large part due to the increase in the length of sentences handed down. The passing of a new penal code in 1994 allowed a never-ending increase in the sentences that could be imposed.[4] This resulted in more punitive sentencing – especially as more recent laws have restricted judges' margin of discretion, notably by mandating minimum sentences for recidivists (Robert and Zauberman 2010). All in all, the French criminal justice system is characterised by chronic prison overcrowding.

Furthermore, the spectacular decline in the use of fines should not mask the fact that it is still the most commonly-used penalty for the mass of minor offences – notably road traffic offences,[5] the majority of which are never brought before a judge but are, instead, managed administratively by the police who, in these proceedings, enjoy the right – exorbitant in French law – to represent the public prosecutor.

Finally, the rise in the use of community sentences is misleading. Since the middle of the 1980s, prison overcrowding has led to prisons being given the lion's share of funding, particularly as the adoption of a semi-private model for the construction of new prisons turned out to be very costly for the public purse. Community sentences, on the other hand, have been underfunded, leading to a number of problems. Firstly, these sentences often cannot be enforced as soon as they become enforceable (an aspect of the legal system that is rarely studied). Secondly, the measure often lacks substance on account of the fact that an insufficient number of supervisory personnel are required to handle excessive caseloads (Chauvenet et al. 1999; Larminat 2012).

Yet, in order to fully understand the development of sanctions that are neither pecuniary nor custodial, it is necessary to also examine alternative measures, handed down by the public prosecutor as part of a policy of diversion from the courts. Table 6.4 shows that only one-sixth of cases dealt with by the public prosecutor end up before a judge.

Table 6.4   Classification of criminal cases by the public prosecutor, 2010

Offence not cleared up	2,617,860	58.1
No offence committed	481,831	10.7
Offence dismissed	163,039	03.6
Mediatory fine	72,785	01.6
Alternative measures	527,530	11.7
Prosecution	639,317	14.2
Total cases dealt with	4,502,364	100.0

Source: Justice, sdse 2011: 14.

Almost as many are dealt with using alternative penalties. The importance accorded to this institution – and the small role played by the
judge in these cases – is one particularity of the French penal system.[6]

Table 6.4 also reveals another significant characteristic in the French
system: three-fifths of cases handed over by the police to the public
prosecutor cannot be dealt with because the latter has not managed
to charge a suspect,[7] thus precluding all further legal action. Strangely,
this key fact has always been 'brushed under the carpet'. Politicians and
journalists constantly harangue the public prosecutor to find a criminal
response to all cases – whether by prosecuting the perpetrators or by
applying alternative measures – but no-one worries about the poor rate
of police success.

We will now turn to the nature of the cases dealt with by the French
criminal justice system, in order to understand this particularity in more
detail.

Public order and the safety of citizens

Over a 30-year period the use of imprisonment has changed greatly (see
Table 6.5): whilst in 1980 the typical inmate was likely to be a thief, in
2010 he or she is more likely to be a rapist, murderer or drug trafficker.

Table 6.5   Prisoners on 1 January, according to offence, 1980–2010

Type of crime prisoners were sentenced for (on 1 January)	1980		2010	
	N	%	N	%
Wilful offences against the person	4,639	22.0	15,984	31.5
Theft	10,090	50.0	9,034	17.8
Handling stolen goods, fraud, breach of trust	1,418	0.7	3,985	0.8
Drug and immigration offences	113	0.1	7,929	15.6
Other	3,936	19.5	5,860	11.5
Total	*20,196*	*100.0*	*36,330*	*100.0*

Source: Prisons administration service.

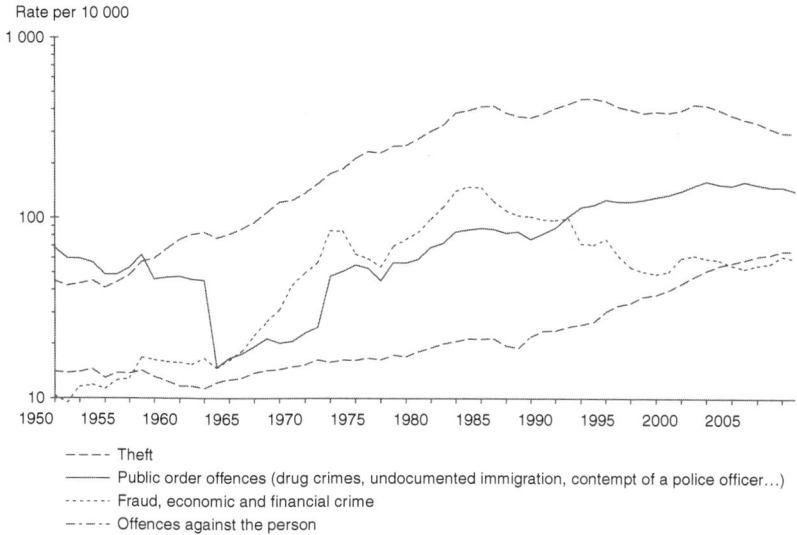

Figure 6.1 Police statistics of cases handed over to the public prosecutor, 1950–2009

Notes: Logarithmic scale, European France.

Source: Robert and Zauberman 2011: 26 based on data from the Ministry of the Interior.

The changes in the types of cases transmitted to the public prosecutor by the police[8] show that it is violent and public order offences (such as undocumented immigration or drug offences) which have increased most significantly over the past half-a-century (see Figure 6.1). This explains why offenders convicted for these offences represent an increasingly significant proportion of prisoners – particularly since this trend is accompanied by a 'stock effect': whilst thieves do not remain in prison for a long time, rapists, murderers and drug traffickers do, increasing their relative representation in the prison population.

Yet, this particular change in the nature of cases transmitted to the public prosecutor does not suffice to explain the change in the use of imprisonment. Firstly, the number of offences against the person in these statistics only started to rise significantly from the middle of the 1980s, and this rise often resulted from the proliferation of new laws which enlarged the scope of the offence of assault and battery to include minor violent incidents which would not previously have fallen within the legal definition (Robert and Zauberman 2011: 80–5). In fact, the murder rate has never been so low; as for cases of serious violence, their level has remained very low, if the legal definition is held constant through

Table 6.6   Recorded crime and people charged, European France, 2011

	% of all recorded crime	% of all people charged
Offences against the person	12.08	25.14
Property offences	65.53	29.35
Economic and financial crime	10.19	8.74
Public order offences: among which	14.20	36.77
Drug trafficking	0.17	0.99
Other drugs offences	5.19	15.19
Undocumented immigration	2.71	8.11
Contempt and assault against public authority holder	1.64	3.39
Other public order offences	4.48	9.09

Source: Based on data from the ministry of the interior.

time (Robert and Zauberman 2011: 76–8, 85). The rise in violence is in reality confined to relatively minor offences (less serious assault, threats, slander and racketeering) (Robert, Zauberman and Jouwahri 2013). As for theft and burglary, these offences seem to have soared between the 1960s and the 1980s: they remain the most common risk for the citizen (ibid.). Therefore, as already noted, changes in the types of offences recorded by the police do not suffice to explain the changes in the use of imprisonment.

Comparing two further kinds of police statistics may help to explain the changes in the use of imprisonment: recorded crime vs. suspected people (Table 6.6).

If property offences represent almost two-thirds of recorded crimes, they represent no more than one-third of all people charged: in five cases of theft or burglary out of six[9] the police do not succeed in identifying a suspect, with the result that the course of justice is immediately interrupted. This accounts in large part for the cases which the public prosecutor cannot follow up on, since no-one has been charged.

Crime is largely anonymous: neither the victim of theft nor the police can identify the thief. The problem is linked, in large part, to changes in social relations. In our society – where far-flung trips and communications are now easy – we often find ourselves face-to-face with strangers.

The thief and the burglar can now easily hide themselves under the veil of anonymity. To overcome this handicap, at least partially, the police ought to fulfil two conditions: have good relations and networks within the local community, place priority on this kind of offence. A centralised organisation, which manages recruitment and deployment at a national level, is unlikely to fulfil this first condition.[10] There are two national police forces in France, the *Police Nationale* (a civilian force) and the *Gendarmerie Nationale* (a military force). Despite its centralised organisational structure, the *gendarmerie* has nonetheless managed to implant itself within local communities, on account of the all-inclusive jurisdiction of the locally-based *brigades territoriales* and the integration of their members into local society. Although the *gendarmes* have retained their military status, since the end of the 1980s they have been subjected to less demanding on-call duties, which have negatively impacted on their relationship with the societies in which they operate. The *gendarmerie* has also moved away from its virtuous model of all-inclusive competence through increased recourse to specialised units. The renaissance of the municipal police could have been a chance to rebuild a local police service focused on public safety but, for the most part, local councils have been incapable of imposing professional guidelines which could prevent their officers from drifting towards the 'model' of the national police – of which they have become, as a matter of fact, plain auxiliaries. This is very comfortable for the national police, but ineffective with regard to public safety (Malochet 2011 a, b).

The second condition has no greater chance of being met. Repeating that *property crime is falling*, whilst overlooking that this is only a small decline after a significant rise, represents a euphemistic way of hiding the real message: that this kind of crime is insignificant. The professional is not particularly interested in these widespread, repetitive and hard-to-solve crimes: it is not by tackling burglaries that a police officer is likely to make a career as a 'great cop'. Since these crimes are unspectacular, it is also unlikely that the political-bureaucratic hierarchy will attach great importance to it – especially since it attracts little media attention. The trivialisation of this kind of *petty* crime contributes to the tendency to declare those crimes which the police do not want to deal with, or cannot deal with effectively, as negligible.[11] This trend is reinforced by focusing police performance indices on law enforcement and by disregarding the expectations of the public.

The reverse is true with regard to public order offences: they represent less than one-sixth of recorded crimes but over one-third of the people

Table 6.7 Sentenced prisoners (final sentence) on 1 September 2010 by main offence, in %

	Homicide	Assault	Rape	Robbery	Other thefts	Drug offences	Other offences
Belgium	(11.3)	(29.6)	(11.7)	(41.5)	(45.4)	(36.1)	(85.3)
France	6.7	25.6	14.8*	18.1		14.1	20.8
Germany	7.3	12.7	6.7	12.3	20.9	14.8	25.4
Italy	16.2	0.2	5.3	13.8	5.7	38.4	20.5
Netherlands	13.1	3.6	2.5*	14.2	12.1	17.3	37
Spain	5.2	5.3	4.1	30.3	3.7	28	23.4
England and Wales	10.1	18.4	6.4	12.4	15.1	15.6	21.9

For Belgium, the data is from 1 April and the total includes double counting.
* Including rapes and other sexual assaults.

Source: Council of Europe annual penal statistics space 1, 2010.

charged. Yet, these victimless crimes are only prosecuted if one or several suspects have first been identified.

To summarise briefly, the police pass the following cases onto the public prosecutor: (1) crimes with identifiable victims which are unlikely to be cleared up (2) victimless crimes which are almost always likely to be solved. The first type of crime concerns safety of the public, whilst the second concerns public order.

Offences against the person fall into a case somewhere in between safety and public order offences. They account for 12 per cent of recorded crimes and 25 per cent of charged persons. Just as with property crime, there is an identifiable victim but anonymity is less marked: the victim is more likely to know his or her assaulter than the victim of a theft. At the very least, he or she can more often provide some means of identifying the offender.[12] It should also be noted that the police are more motivated to look for the perpetrator of a murder than a theft, even if such violent crime only represents a very small part of all recorded crime. According to victimisation studies, violent crime mostly concerns minor assaults for which the propensity of victims to report is particularly low: reporting only occurs in the small minority of serious violent crimes (Robert and Zauberman 2011: 133). If violent crime nevertheless represents such a significant proportion of offences for which people are imprisoned, this is because serious violence is the largest part of reported violence and because legislation has considerably toughened up the penalties for these crimes.

A European comparison suggests that the apportionment of different offences in the sentencing statistics can vary significantly from one country to the next (Table 6.7): what we have argued with regard to the French system does not necessarily hold elsewhere. The following section will focus on the French case by taking a diachronic look at crime policy, from François Mitterrand through to M. Sarkozy.

Public Safety Policy – from François Mitterrand to M. Sarkozy

Since the 1960s, with the development of a mass consumer society, acquisitive crime (theft and burglary) has skyrocketed. Yet, this historical change did not become a significant cause for concern so long as the welfare state provided security and people believed that their lives – and especially their children's lives – could only improve. In the second half of the 1970s, however, feelings of insecurity emerged as the fracture of the labour market began to push more and more poorly-qualified people into chronic unemployment or job insecurity.

Following May 1968, those responsible for law and order were at first hypnotised by the fear of a spread of Maoist terrorism to France. When this did not materialise,[13] there was a renewed focus on ordinary crime in the 1970s. But theft and burglary were of little interest: the urgent need to restore order – following the aftermath of the colonial wars and May 1968 – had already turned attention away from them. It was Alain Peyrefitte who was to succeed in naming a new target: crimes of violence... first in 1977 as chair of a presidential commission on violence, crime and delinquency, and above all as Justice Minister, with the passing of the Act named *Sécurité et Libertés* in February 1981, the main purpose of which was to clamp down on violent offences. Regardless of the immediate political conjecture, this formed the basis of the Right's approach to law and order for the next 30 years.[14]

When the Left came to power in 1981, it had just been engaged in a political battle over the death penalty and the *Sécurité et Libertés* Act. It aimed to abolish both. However, urban riots in the deprived suburbs of Lyon erupted like a thunderbolt in the summer of that year. The riots showed that problems of security could not be resolved by the planned legislative measures alone. The government adopted an original approach and called on local representatives to reflect on the problem. This commission of mayors – known as Bonnemaison[15] – marked above all a return of local authorities into a field which had, since the Second World War, been the sole reserve of the state; helped, in certain cases, by a few associative sectors which enjoyed little autonomy. The Commission's report(Commission des maires 1982) sketched out an alternative law and order policy, which would link together crime prevention, law enforcement and social policy (solidarity). Yet, such an ambition went far beyond what certain branches of the central state were prepared to accept: they feared painful restructuring and unbearable loss of autonomy. There was, nonetheless, one part of the plan which could be implemented without offending these corporatist sensibilities – prevention. In practice, this entailed three significant ruptures from previous policy, with regard to: the type of crime prevention, its targets and the prevention schemes themselves.

Which type of crime prevention first? Since the 1960s, there had been a sort of national tradition whereby prevention was targeted at potential criminals; specialist crime prevention teams (*Clubs et équipes de prévention*) experienced their finest hours following the explosion of the youth subculture known as the *blousons noirs* (see Robert and Lascoumes 1974 Part II; Mohammed and Mucchielli 2007). But, with the later emergence of a host of young people excluded from the labour market, preventative measures were no longer deemed sufficient. The teams also suffered from the decentralisation of social policy, which deprived them of the active support of the central State's local agencies. The new preventative ideal no longer placed much importance on reforming the traditional method of crime prevention. Nor did it opt for situational crime prevention methods, which focused on helping potential victims of crime to improve self-protection against property crime and violence. Instead, it favoured a more general form of crime prevention – known as 'social crime prevention' – which entailed focusing on deprived areas in an attempt to improve conditions there and thus reduce crime. So, the target of crime prevention measures also changed – no longer did these measures focus on specific individuals or groups, such as youth gangs, but rather on specific urban and suburban areas. The schemes also changed. The base consisted of local mayors, who would be responsible for implementing policy by marshalling a partnership with the State's local agencies, municipal services and the voluntary sector in municipal crime prevention committees. At the summit of the system was a joint committee involving the mayors of the major cities and representatives from the ministries concerned.

There was much initial enthusiasm, which helped to protect the new system once the Right returned to power in 1986. Yet this enthusiasm masked two underlying problems. The social prevention model could not focus on precise targets and was only likely to have an impact in the long term. Yet, the social transformations which were taking place at that time – particularly the ever-increasing difficulty to gain access to a stable job – made it difficult to target specific populations. But disregarding targeted prevention also entailed abandoning programmes with possible short term impact. Furthermore, from the very beginning it was hard to reconcile these social prevention measures with tough law enforcement practices, as progress made in one area could cancel out success in another. There was no serious reflection concerning what priority was to be accorded to law enforcement. Nor was there any attempt to rein in the forces of law and order.

Yet, with the introduction of a new political configuration in 1988, an attempt was made to link prevention more closely to social policy, bringing them together under a single task force, the *Délégation inter-ministérielle à la Ville* (DIV, Interdepartmental Delegation for the City).[16] Prima facie, this reorganisation seemed logical to the extent that social prevention had been prioritised. Yet, in practice, rather than forging a genuine partnership the part of the task force dedicated to prevention was swallowed up. This situation was exacerbated when the highest State authorities panicked, following a new wave of riots in the deprived suburbs of Lyon and Paris in the early 1990s. They wavered between inter-ministerial cooperation and returning to the traditional ministerial organisation with the creation of a new Ministry for Urban Affairs, along with sub-prefects for urban affairs.

In such a context, it was impossible for the social prevention model to consolidate guidelines and procedures, despite having put in place a number of imaginative local programmes. Instead, it was situational crime prevention which became dominant. This development passed unnoticed, though, since it took place outside the public sector. The private security industry sought to enclose private spaces open to the public[17] in a 'security bubble' – using private security personnel and their equipment. It found it more difficult to control public transport. It was only later that the industry succeeded in convincing local authorities to contract security services out to private companies to which they had already handed over the management of a whole range of public serv-ices.[18] As for individuals, those who had the financial means were able to protect their homes to a certain extent from burglary; more intensive protection meant moving into a gated community, or at least to urban areas isolated from risk by high property prices.[19] As for public space – the street – it is amusing to note how easy it was to convince people that surveillance at a distance could compensate for the disappearance of the physical presence of the police.

Throughout the 1990s, urban policy became increasingly complex and multilayered, with mixed outcomes – as suggested by the surveys carried out by the *Institut national de la recherche statistique et des études économiques* (INSEE French National Institute of Statistics and Economic Studies) (Le Toqueux 2002–2003; Le Toqueux and Moreau 2002). Yet, the policy was up against growing problems – especially demographic changes in areas officially classified as underprivileged urban areas (*zones urbaines sensibles*[20]). The better-off were leaving, whilst ever-poorer people – especially new migrants – moved in. Furthermore, the 1990s were marked by numerous changes of government and associated successive policy initiatives – such as local security plans at the municipal and *department* level and local security contracts – which all aimed to establish some sort of coherence between crime prevention and law enforcement. For a while, towards the end of the 1990s, it was possible to believe that these two aims had been reconciled via three key measures:

- The adoption of a community policing model, more or less inspired directly by North American experience, with municipal police forces such as that of Chicago.
- The rapid spread of local social mediation workers (*agents locaux de médiation sociale*) backed up by a state policy of financing unskilled jobs for young unemployed people.[21]
- A policy of spreading the population more evenly across urban areas in order to halt the concentration of the poorest populations in the most deprived towns.

These measures were developed without following any clear methodology and without overall coordination at the highest level of the national government. They met with significant professional resistance and, in any case, failed to survive yet another political changeover in 2002.

Since then, urban policy has returned to its core function – namely, the renovation of public buildings and material – but, even with this limited function, it has been exposed to the divestiture of the state. In terms of crime prevention, there have been numerous local initiatives from local authorities and public services, in particular attempting to have diverse groups of people sharing a common space. For all that, official prevention policy increasingly limits itself to a defensive dimension, as is made clear in a law from 2007. Although it is officially aimed at prevention, this law contains only measures concerning surveillance and law enforcement. Indeed, in recent years local government has been under extraordinary pressure from the central government to adopt CCTV systems as the panacea of crime prevention.[22]

As a result, national security policies are reduced to law enforcement only (Roché 2012). Yet, the criminal justice machinery is poorly adapted to deal with minor offences. Its focus on victimless crime (drug crimes, undocumented immigration etc.) fails to hide its failure to provide public protection: robberies are just as unlikely to be cleared up as theft or burglary and minor incidences of expressive violence are rarely reported to the police.

This short-sighted policy – focusing only on law enforcement – can be understood as an electoral strategy: in the first round of the presidential elections of 2002, the right-wing candidate did not even gain 20 per cent of the vote and only managed to win the second round of the election because the extreme right gained more votes than the left-wing candidate, who was forced to withdraw after the first round. Since then, the Right has placed priority on regaining the votes the extreme right had confiscated from them since the municipal elections of 1983. In order to do so, it has played to xenophobic and punitive sentiments, enacting a veritable avalanche of new laws. In the presidential election of 2007 this strategy paid off: the Right succeeded in gaining votes from the extreme-right whilst the Left failed to control its most extreme elements. The same tactic was thus employed in the 2012 elections, but this time without success: the less the Right becomes distinguishable from the extreme right, the more likely it is that electors will swing between the two.

A system under threat: the uncertain future of the French criminal justice system

In practice, between 2002 and 2012 these politics resulted in an astonishing number of criminal laws. Every widely-reported crime provided the occasion for the President to make public declarations of sympathy to the victims, to criticise the judges for being too 'soft', and to pass new laws which toughened up penalties and limited the autonomy and the margin of appreciation of the magistrates.

The (often virulent[23]) criticism of judges served to mask the mixed results of this new tough crime policy. Yet, the judges did not oppose tougher sentencing (see Mouhanna 2012), as is evidenced by the trends in sentencing analysed above. Rather, disagreement emerged in specific cases where politicians attempted to prevent the judges from applying this harsh sentencing policy. Indeed, the aim was to prevent judges from assuming too much independence from politics, as they had begun to do in the 1990s with regard to criminal cases involving members of the political elite.

Certainly, judicial activism did not play any significant role in bringing these cases to light. Instead, they were often brought by victims who had not found any other political or administrative solution, by politicians seeking to settle a score, or else they resulted from unexpected detections in the course of routine investigations. Although a lot of cases were brought to court, very few ended up with a conviction, sentences tended to be moderate and, above all, were handed down very belatedly. Yet, these cases marked the beginning of a significant change in the French criminal justice system.

Whilst it is impossible here to trace the whole history of this development (see, for example, Bancaud and Robert 2001), it is necessary to at least underline the fact that in France the world of politics, high public office and the media treat the legal system as a simple administrative service under the control of the Executive. The cases of the 1990s challenged this position.

It was essentially via the abolition of the *juge d'instruction* (all cases such as these are examined by investigating judges) and by the decriminalisation of business law that containment of these political-financial scandals was attempted. Both failed. (The *juge d'instruction* is an independent examining magistrate that former President Sarkozy attempted to suppress but failed.)

Political control of the penal system is mainly exercised via the public prosecutor, whose legal status is rather peculiar: just like Germany, France is one of a minority (15) of European countries (European Commission for the Efficiency of Justice 2012) where the public prosecutor is under the control of the Ministry of Justice; furthermore – this time contrary to Germany – French public prosecutors belong to the same body of judges, a status that grants them quasi-jurisdictional powers beyond the initiation of criminal proceedings.[24] This ambiguity concerning the status of public prosecutors impacts upon the entire justice system. Resolving this ambiguity would entail suppressing either the hierarchical power of the Justice Minister (as in Italy), or separating prosecutors from the judicial corps (as in Germany). As the first solution would be unacceptable to politicians and the second to prosecutors, it is only envisaged that the powers of the High Judicial Council (*Conseil supérieur de la magistrature*) over their appointment be strengthened. Such a reform would have little impact if the composition of the Council, and the appointment procedure of its members, remained unchanged. Even if the Council was to be reformed, it is questionable whether reinforcing its control over the appointment of prosecutors would suffice to persuade the latter to change their usual relationship with the executive power. In any case, such a reform would not satisfy the European Court of Human Rights, which does not consider a prosecutor to be a magistrate.

Furthermore, despite their wide powers, there are very few public prosecutors in France compared to the European average (Table 6.8). Their dependency on the Executive aside, their limited numbers makes it impossible for them to control the police in any meaningful way. On the contrary, they can be easily manipulated.[25]

There are not just considerably fewer public prosecutors than the European average, but also, to a lesser extent, fewer judges (Table 6.8). To give some idea of their social status, the European Commission for the Efficiency of Justice (CEPEJ) used an indirect measure: a

Table 6.8 The French criminal justice system compared to that of the rest of Europe

	France	European average	European median
Proportion of public spending on criminal justice (%)	1.1	1.9	1.9
Number of professional judges per 100 000 inhabitants	10.7	21.3	18
Number of lay magistrates per 100 000 inhabitants	44.4	125.1	46.8
Gross starting salary for a judge compared to the national average salary	1.2	2.4	2.1
Gross starting salary for a Supreme Court judge compared to the national average salary	3.4	4.5	3.9
Number of public prosecutors per 100 000 inhabitants	3.0	11.1	9.8
Gross starting salary for a public prosecutor compared to the national average salary	1.2	1.9	1.8
Gross starting salary for a public prosecutor at the Supreme Court compared to the national average salary	3.4	3.6	3.6

Source: CEPEJ 2012: 26, 145, 153, 233, 262, 267.

comparison between judges' starting and finishing salaries and the national average. From this perspective, French judges appear to be less favourably remunerated than judges elsewhere in Europe. More generally, public spending on criminal justice is (considerably) lower than the European average. It is not therefore surprising if the legal system is very slow – it takes one year, on average, for minor or moderately serious offences to come to court, and three years for the most serious crimes (Justice 2012: 18). This is probably because the fast-tracking of some offences has slowed down the processing of the majority of crimes. Furthermore, the drive to make savings recently led to the redrawing of the boundaries of judicial districts; however, instead of reducing the high number of appellate courts, a decision was made to cut the number of lower courts – thus further complicating citizens' experience of the legal system.

Conclusion

All of these characteristics have undermined the French criminal justice system. In sum, these characteristics are as follows:

- A police service which is all the more powerful now that the two main bodies of which it is composed – the national police service and the *gendarmerie* – have recently been placed under the control of a single ministry.[26] It is a police service which is more concerned with upholding order than protecting citizens.
- A public prosecutor's office whose competence extends ever more beyond the sole initiation of criminal proceedings, towards functions which should be reserved to judges. The ambiguous status of public prosecutors is becoming less and less acceptable. Furthermore, they are not sufficiently numerous to prevent their tremendous powers from being manipulated by the police.
- Underfunded courts operated under an administrative model which is overly concerned with quantitative performance indicators focused on the number of cases to clear (see, for example, Ackermann and Bastard 1993; Deschamps and Mouhanna 2001).
- An intensified penal pressure, with overcrowded prisons and the increased use of community sentences.

Since 2002, the French criminal justice system (although it had tentatively begun to move away from its traditional role from the 1990s onwards) has been subjected to a number of attempts to forcibly push it back to its *status quo ante*. Which direction is it currently heading in?

It is too early to tell if the left-wing presidency and parliamentary majority which assumed power in 2012 will profoundly change the current state of the French criminal justice system.

It seems likely that this change of course will be slow, as new sentencing laws are required and as, with regard to the High Judicial Council and the office of the public prosecutor, the Constitution itself will have to be reformed.

With regard to the definition of public safety policy, the main difficulty resides in the failure to diagnose the nature of the crime problem (Robert et al. 2013): nowhere is it subjected to serious analysis. It is necessary to change policy but this can only be done based on serious evidence.

The French criminal justice system thus faces a particularly uncertain future. It is highly possible that it will change significantly in the coming years but it is too early to predict what form that change will take.

Notes

1. Thanks to Renée Zauberman, senior researcher at the CNRS (CESDIP), for her comments and suggestions on this chapter.
2. Emeritus Research Director at the CNRS/CESDIP (French National Centre for Scientific Research/ Centre for Sociological Research on Law and Criminal Justice Institutions).
3. Thanks to Annie Kensey, Head of the Planning and Research Bureau at the Prisons Administration Directorate and associate researcher at the CESDIP, for providing the data used to compile the tables used in this chapter. The analysis of these statistics is entirely my own.
4. Lascoumes (2009: 464) explains that it was at this price that the Senate accepted the bill.
5. Particularly with the proliferation of speed cameras.
6. European comparisons carried out by the European Commission for the Efficiency of Justice (CEPEJ 2012: 246) seem to indicate that the French criminal justice system leaves more room for alternative sanctions and measures to be handed down by the public prosecutor than the European average.
7. To which should be added 10 per cent of cases where the incident was not legally an offence or where the charges were insufficient to entail prosecution: overall, almost 70 per cent of the cases handed over by the police are not admissible in law.
8. These official statistics do not take into account traffic offences, neither homicides cases or physical harm caused through carelessness, 'contraventions' (a vast category of minor offences), nor proceedings in administrative law.

9. In 2010, the police and the *gendarmerie* succeeded in clearing up 13.7 per cent of all cases of recorded theft (13.5% in 2011), 14.1 per cent of robberies (13.8% in 2011) and 11.4 per cent of domestic burglaries (10.5% in 2011) (OND-RP 2012: 9, 16).

10. The violent rejection – as much by the police hierarchy as by professional organisations – of attempts (clumsily handled) to introduce 'community policing' in 2000 showed the strong resistance of the police organisation in the face of any locally-based policing model.

11. Garland 2001: *117*. Perhaps it is implicitly assumed that the possibility of relying on insurance policies to compensate for material loss makes up for the limited involvement of police forces in property crime. If national victimisation studies only provide piecemeal information about compensation (Névanen et al. 2010), the studies carried out in the *Île-de-France* region (Greater Paris) by the Institute for Urban Planning and Development (IAU-IdF) on the other hand show that even though three-quarters of all victims of car theft (theft of and from cars) are compensated, this is only the case for half of all victims of domestic burglary and one tenth of victims of assault or theft (Bon et al. 2011: 86, 110, 129, 172).

12. Many assaults are actually robberies which are generally anonymous but their clear-up rate is just as poor as that for other property crimes.

13. With the exception of the delayed episode of attacks carried out by the revolutionary group, *Action Directe*.

14. At the time, this focus on crimes of violence hardly seemed credible given that it seemed so obvious that property crime was the main problem. Yet, the Right and the Extreme-Right never wavered in their denunciation of violence. It was the only way of dramatising criminality in such a way as to make it an issue of national concern. In the end, all political parties – and most of the media – rallied around this questionable diagnosis.

15. The Commission took the name of its president who was also Member of Parliament and mayor of a deprived suburban town north of Paris.

16. Now known as the General Secretariat for Urban Affairs (*Secrétariat général à la Ville*).

17. Such as shopping centres and department stores.

18. Such as rubbish collection and water supply.

19. The fall in burglary from the middle of the 1980s onwards is often attributed to these situational crime prevention measures and spatial segregation. The decline in car theft began ten years later when an agreement signed on 10 February 1994 between insurance companies and automobile manufacturers brought a significant improvement to anti-theft security devices fitted to cars.

20. Since the 96_987 Act of 24 November 1996, 751 districts (34 of which are in the French overseas territories) have been categorised as '*zones urbaines sensibles*'.

21. See the analysis of the development of the security 'neo-proletariat' in Robert (1999: 252).

22. While deliberately avoiding any evaluative research living up to international standards: it might have exposed the weaknesses of this technology in terms of crime prevention (Le Goff and Heilman 2009).

23. For example, on one occasion the President described judges from the *Cour de Cassation* as 'green peas: all the same color, same size, same lack of flavour'.
24. Although this solution is regularly challenged by the ECHR which considers that the French public prosecutor's lack of independence means that they cannot be regarded as a judge, at least not in the sense intended by the ECHR (See Fifth Section *Medvedyev and others v. France*, 10 July 2008 and *Moulin v. France*, 23 November 2010, even if the ruling of the Grand Chamber *Medvedyev and others v. France*, 29 March 2010, did not directly examine this precise question). Thanks to René Lévy, research director at the CNRS, for drawing my attention to legal comment on these cases.
25. Take the recent example of the system for processing reported offences (the *système de traitement des infractions constatées* – STIC). When the French national commission for data protection (the *commission nationale de l'informatique et des libertés* (CNIL, 2009) published a critical report on this police database, it underlined the fact that it is placed under the control of the public prosecutor's office even though it is ill-equipped to exercise such control. Benoit Bastard and Christian Mouhanna (2007) note the perverse consequences of rapid ('real time') processing of cases on the relationship between the police and the Public prosecutor.
26. The Ministry of the Interior.

References

Ackermann W. and Bastard B. (1993) *Innovation et Géstion dans l'Institution Judiciaire* (Paris: LGDJ).

Aebi M., Aubusson de Cavarlay B., Barclay G., Gruszczynska B., Harrendorf S.. Heiskanen M.,, Hysi V., Jacquier V., Jehle G.M., Killias M., Shostko O., Smit P. and Borisbottir R. (2010) *European Sourcebook of Crime and Criminal Justice Statistics, Meppel,* (Boom: Juridische Uitgevers), www.wodc.nl/.

Bancaud A. and Robert Ph. (2001) 'La place de la Justice en France: un avenir incertain', in Robert Ph and Cottino A., (Dir.), *Les mutations de la Justice. Comparaisons Européennes* (Paris : L'Harmattan) 161–98.

Bastard, B. and Mouhanna, C . (2007) *Une Justice dans l'Urgence. Le Traitement en temps réel des Affaires Pénales* (Paris: PUF).

Bon D., Castelbajac M. de, Névanen S., Robert Ph. and Zauberman R.(2011) *Victimations et insécurité en Île-de-France, 2006–07_08, Analyse de la cinquième (2009) enquête de l'Institut d'aménagement et d'urbanisme d'Île-de-France* (Guyancourt: CESDIP) www.cesdip.fr/.

Chauvenet A., Gorgeon C., Mouhanna C. and Orlic F. (1999) *Contraintes et possibles: les pratiques d'exécution des mesures en milieu ouvert,* Centre de sociologie des organisations, Centre d'études des mouvements sociaux (Paris: Acadie).

Commission des maires sur la sécurité (1982) *Face À La Délinquance : Prévention, Répression, Solidarité* (Paris: La Documentation française).

Commission Nationale de l' Informatique et des Libertés (2009) (CNIL) *Conclusions du contrôle du Système de traitement des infractions constatées (STIC), Rapport remis au Premier ministre le 20 janvier 2009,* disponible sur le site internet: www.cnil.fr/.

Conseil de l'Europe (2010), *Statistique pénale annuelle, SPACE 1*, www.coe.int/prison.

Deschamps T. and Mouhanna C. (2001) *L'administration Française de la Justice* (Paris: Institut international d'administration publique).

European Commission for the Efficiency of Justice/ Commission Européenne pour l'efficacité de la Justice (2012) (ECEJ/CEPEJ) *European Judicial Systems/Systèmes Judiciaires Européens*, (Strasbourg: Council of Europe).

Garland D. (2001) *The Culture of Control: Crime and Social Order in Contemporary Society* (Oxford: Oxford University Press).

Justice (2011) *Sous-Direction de la Statistique et des Etudes, Les chiffres clés de la Justice* (Paris: Ministère de la Justice).

Larminat X. (2012) *La probation en quête d'approbation* (Guyancourt: Université de Versailles-Saint-Quentin (UVSQ), thèse de science politique.

Lascoumes P. (2009) 'Les compromis parlementaires, combinaisons de surpolitisation et de sous-politisation', *Revue Française de Science Politique*, 59 (3): 455–78.

Le Goff T. and Heilman E. (2009) *Vidéosurveillance : Un Rapport Qui Ne Prouve Rien*, www.laurent-mucchielli.org/.

Le Toqueux J.L. (2002–2003) *Le Chômage Dans Les Zones Urbaines Sensibles, Données Sociales* (Paris: INSEE) 539–44.

Le Toqueux J.-L. and Moreau J. (2002) 'Les zones urbaine sensibles', *INSEE Première*, mars, n° 835.

Malochet, V . (2011a) 'De la 'surveillance du bon ordre' au 'maintien de l'ordre'. L'action des polices municipales en question', *www.délinquance, justice et autres questions de société. fr/*, 8 Novembre 2010.

Malochet, V. (2011b) 'La socialisation professionnelle des policiers municipaux en France', *Déviance et Société*, 35 (3): 415–38.

Mohammed M. and Mucchielli L. (Dir.) (2007) *Les Bandes de Jeunes. Des Blousons Noirs À Nos Jours* (Paris: La Découverte).

Mouhanna C. (2012) 'Nicolas Sarkozy et la justice pénale. Les artifices d'une politique volontariste, in Maillard J. de and Surel Y. (eds), *Les Politiques Publiques Sous Sarkozy* (Paris: Presses de Sciences Po) 259–78.

Névanen S., Robert Ph. and Zauberman R. (2010) Cadre de vie et sécurité. Analyse des enquêtes pour 2005–2006 et 2006–2007 (Guyancourt: CESDIP), www.cesdip.fr/.

Observatoire National de La Délinquance Et des Réponses Pénales (OND-RP) (2012) *Les Tableaux de bord de l'OND-RP* (Paris: OND-RP).

Peyrefitte A. (1977) *Réponses à la Violence* (Paris: Presses Pocket).

Robert P. (2002) *L'insécurité en France* (Paris: La Découverte).

Robert P. (1999) *Le Citoyen, Le Crime Et l'Etat* (Genève-Paris: Droz).

Robert P. and Lascoumes P. (1974) *Les bandes d'adolescents. une théorie de la ségrégation* (Paris: Editions Ouvrières).

Robert P. and Zauberman R. (2010) 'Crise Sécuritaire Et Alarme À La Récidive : Entre Étude Savante Et Fébrilité Législative', in Allinne J.P. and Soula M., (eds) *Les Récidivistes. Représentations Et Traitements de La Récidive. XIXe–XXIe Siècle* (Rennes: Presses universitaires de Rennes) 211–26.

Robert P. and Zauberman R. (2011) *Mesurer La Délinquance* (Paris: Presses de Sciences Po).

Robert P., Zauberman R. and Jouwahri F. (2013) 'Délinquance Et Action Publique: Les Illusions D'un Diagnostic', *Politix,* 26 (1): 219–45.

Roché S. (2012) 'Les Politiques de Sécurité Intérieure. Une Approche Technicienne, Une Efficacité Douteuse', in Maillard J. de and Surel Y. (eds), *Les Politiques Publiques Sous Sarkozy* (Paris: Presses de Sciences Po) 237–58.

7

Contradictions in German Penal Practices: The Long Goodbye from the Rehabilitation Principle

Bernd Dollinger and Andrea Kretschmann

Introduction

Drawing on Esping-Andersen's work on different types of welfare regimes (1990), penal systems are often grouped in accordance to their defining characteristics. For example, regarding the treatment of juvenile delinquency Winterdyk (2002) identifies six groups or models: participatory, welfare, corporatism, modified justice, justice, and crime control. For him, Germany belongs to the 'justice' model whose defining features comprise adherence to the rule of law, the lawyer as a crucial actor, and the principle that punishment should also take into account educational aspects. The typology of Cavadino and Dignan (2006), on the other hand, distinguishes five models (welfare, justice, minimum intervention, restorative justice, and neo-correctionalist). Germany is seen as a case of 'archetypical corporatism' (ibid.: 101), due to the crucial role played by professionals and traditional institutions, the emphasis on social rights, as well as the integration of the individual into corporatist structures. Despite recent changes in a more punitive direction, the German system still seems to be characterised by a 'remarkably firm and stable attachment to a mildly welfarist approach' (ibid.: 260). Therefore, whereas Winterdyk focuses primarily on the country's adherence to the rule of law and the role of actors within the legal system, Cavadino and Dignan emphasise historically grown institutional structures and the importance of social policy objectives. There are good arguments in support of both approaches, although the philosophies underlying them differ considerably.

These two examples demonstrate that typologies of national penal systems are neither really 'right' nor 'wrong', the question is rather what variables they are based upon, how they are weighted and what purposes they set out to achieve. Moreover, we would contend that because such penal typologies often disregard internal contradictions and regional particularities, they rarely do justice to the multifaceted nature of national penal systems (Muncie 2009). The world is not 'flooded by sameness' (Sparks 2011: 94).

This is particularly relevant to Germany, where it can be argued that cultures of punishment are highly contradictory. Long-term developments have created structures that seek to balance diverging interests and penal philosophies. Only by placing these developments in their historical context can we hope to understand their importance (Savelsberg 1994, 2002). We begin by observing an example of this complex process in juvenile justice.

Contradictions and ambiguities: juvenile justice

The German penal code (*Strafgesetzbuch* or StGB), together with accessory criminal law (such as the narcotics law, *Betäubungsmittelgesetz* or BtMG), is the substantive criminal law that determines the specific legal consequences faced by persons who are found guilty of a crime. Procedural issues are regulated separately in the code of criminal procedure (*Strafprozessordnung* or StPO). The Juvenile Court Act (*Jugendgerichtsgesetz* or JGG), on the other hand, determines the treatment of young offenders, that is, of adolescents (who are between 14 to 17 years of age at the time of their offence) and young adults (between 18 to 20 years), though there are no statutory offenses in German criminal law that would apply to young offenders only. However, the legal consequences differ: for adolescents – and normally also for young adults – legal responses cover an intentionally broad range, with the objective (according to § 2 Para. 1 JGG) of preventing recidivism through educational means; whereas, for adults a 'therapeutic model' (P.A. Albrecht 2010b: 46) and the rehabilitation principle are of primary significance (§ 3 of the Treatment of Offenders Act – *Gesetz über den Vollzug der Freiheitsstrafe und der freiheitsentziehenden Maßregeln der Besserung und Sicherung* or StVollzG). For adults, the law also stresses that punishment should aim to 'protect the general public from further offences' (§ 2 StVollzG). The simultaneous emphasis on education on the one hand, and protection of society on the other aptly illustrates the ambiguities of German penal policy and criminal justice.

The way in which juvenile delinquency is dealt with is seen by German criminologists as having a pioneering role with regard to the institutional treatment of criminality in general. Penal reforms have often found their first expression in the treatment of juvenile delinquency to subsequently become role models for the treatment of adults (Ostendorf 2008: 243). Therefore, we will first discuss the basics of the treatment of juvenile delinquency so as to illustrate the above-mentioned ambiguities.

The year 1882 is important here because that is when the German Empire published its first-ever crime statistics (Roth 1991: 27–8). These statistics attracted particular attention because they showed an increase in the proportion of juvenile recidivists: 107.4 young persons with previous convictions (for every 100,000 young persons in the total population) were sentenced in 1890, whereas there were 138.7 of them in 1900 (Peukert 1986: 323). These numbers decreased in subsequent years, but it became clear nonetheless that the established ways of fighting crime were not just ineffective, but sometimes counterproductive (Liszt 1900/1969: 40). This perception led to the demand that the uniqueness of young offenders, who were seen as having limited criminal responsibility, should be taken into account. Through education, it was suggested, they should be rehabilitated and supported in their personal development. In accordance with these goals, the treatment of criminality in general was to be guided by instrumental rationality and targeted prevention. Punishment was to be proportional (as defined by the 'justice' model) and have a clearly defined goal – that is the 'education' of young offenders (as defined by the 'welfarist approach'). After the creation of the first juvenile court in 1908, and of the first prison for juvenile delinquents in 1912, the 1920s saw the creation of a legal double structure that exists to this day: the *Imperial Juvenile Court Act* (*Reichsjugendgerichtsgesetz*) was introduced in 1923 and the *Imperial Youth Welfare Act* (*Reichsjugendwohlfahrtsgesetz*) in 1922 and 1924 (Kreuzer 2008; Oberwittler 2000). Two things are especially noteworthy: the mingling of the objectives of support and punishment, and a typology of offenders that has systematic exclusionary effects.

First, education was introduced as a principle of criminal law (Roth 1991). The educational principle of juvenile criminal law was formulated in a way that 'retain[ed] punitive elements' (Kreuzer 2008: 124) while leaving only 'marginal' room for a strict welfare-orientation (H.-J. Albrecht 2004: 450). Education was implemented in the context of juvenile delinquency, but primarily with the aim of socially disciplining young people (Weyel 2008). In reality, the education practises in the juvenile penal system were hardly different from punitive measures.

There were far-reaching interventions into family life and forms of forced education in care institutions. Yet, there have been considerable amendments to this state of affairs, since the 1970s in particular: following reforms that were led by practitioners, the scope for diversion and alternative measures was expanded and incarceration was reduced (Heinz 2011). There is, at the moment, widespread agreement among experts that the educational principle can open up a space for treatment that is appropriate for the individual young person (Hassemer 2008: 157). Not all punishments available within the general criminal law are used against adolescents and young adults, which would suggest a certain degree of leniency towards them. Nonetheless, young offenders have sometimes received harsher sentences than adults – for example, when recidivists were involved, or in cases of violent offending (Heinz 2012: 549–51; Kemme and Stoll 2012).

Welfarist principles of punishment have been criticised for endangering the legal status of defendants and placing them at a disadvantage (e.g. Muncie 2009: 288–9). As we can see, such allegations are not unjustified with regard to the treatment of juvenile offenders in Germany.

Second, the discussion over crime statistics, since 1882, has focused on recidivists in particular. As mentioned above, they provided an important motivation for reform and for the (more programmatic than actual) introduction of welfare principles. There was, however, a crucial flipside: in spite of reform efforts, crime and social deviance among young people did not decrease – they increased instead. In the context of financial constraints, this made an obvious solution appear quite attractive: to address educational means and resources to those young people who seemed most receptive to them, while labelling others as 'incapable' or 'barely capable' of being educated (Peukert 1986). Peukert shows that this kind of offender typology was widely used in the 1920s and 1930s by professionals trying to deflect claims that their reforms were futile. By the late nineteenth century well-known reformers of criminal law, such as Franz von Liszt, had already used such labels. His demands were (1883/1968, 31–2): 1. Correction for those criminals who are capable and in need of it; 2: Deterrence for those criminals who do not require correction; 3. Keeping in check those criminals who are incapable of correction.' He saw no use in trying to rehabilitate offenders who were presumably incapable of correction and dismissed this as a waste of money (Liszt 1883/1968, 33). Such typologies of offender groups were taken up again later. Members of the underclass in particular were regarded as problem cases, making them a focus for criminal law and repressive corrective education (Baumann 2006).

Reformist tendencies have been influential since the 1970s – young offenders were supposed to receive help and support, but the enduring punishment of recidivists and members of marginalised groups continued unabated. As in other countries, high-profile individual cases served as 'proof' that 'tough measures' were necessary against groups of offenders that did not appear responsive to a helping hand. Marginal groups were, and continue to be, the target of moral panics. Since the Second World War, there has been – according to Cavadino and Dignan (2006: 259) – a continuing 'succession of moral panics over youth crime issues, culminating during the 1990s in concerns relating to violent and persistent juvenile offenders, young immigrant offenders, and chronic child offenders who appear to be beyond the control of conventional juvenile justice and welfare measures' (see also Cremer-Schäfer 2010: 195). The topic of the 'foreign repeat offender' has become particularly salient since the 1990s (H.-J. Albrecht 2004; Dollinger and Schmidt-Semisch 2010; Geißler 2008). Currently, dramatised mass-media portrayals of individual violent crimes create the impression that there is an increase in brutal acts of violence committed by adolescents and young adults. In particular, violent offences by male youths from Turkish or Arab migrant families are perceived as a problem. Together with sexual offenders, the perceived threat posed by violent youths from migrant families is seen as a crucial factor behind the tightening of punishment since the 1990s (Pfeiffer et al. 2005: 276).

Various commentators have recently claimed that, in a punitive-minded political environment, the educational principle in juvenile criminal law is increasingly being used as a gateway for repressive tendencies, because there is less hope for the rehabilitation of offenders and a stronger emphasis on the principle of protecting society (Boers and Schaerff 2008; Oelkers et al. 2008). Recent years have seen numerous legislative initiatives that aim at tougher treatment of offenders with a view to strengthening the protection of society. This has led to the claim that German penal policy is now more strongly determined by the intention of reinforcing internal security (Ostendorf 2010: 92; regarding individual laws and regulations see P.-A. Albrecht 2010a: 179–84).[1]

Institutional context and professional practice

The claim we have made so far – that penal policy in Germany has become increasingly repressive – primarily applies to the area of criminal law. This tendency has significantly influenced the institutional framework of the criminal justice system, as well as professional practices. German prosecutors and judges are usually life-long, unelected, civil servants, recruited in a highly academic and formalised fashion; they enjoy special privileges and can only be fired under certain narrowly defined conditions. This creates a strong professional identity that enables them to resist political reform projects if they happen to disagree with them. International studies have found that professional actors tend to use their discretion to resist unwanted reforms (Fielding 2011; Steiner et al. 2011), and this clearly applies to Germany. It has to be kept in mind that judicial independence is highly protected; public prosecutors enjoy considerable latitude but, unlike judges, they are answerable to their superiors (Albrecht 2010b: 204).

The German court system provides the structural foundation for the work of public prosecutors and judges. It comprises the *local courts*, the *district* (or *regional*) *courts* and the *higher regional courts*. In cases of serious crime, regional courts act as first instance tribunals, but they also function as second instance when the decisions of local courts are appealed. The higher regional courts, on the other hand, 'examine the legality and the appropriateness of the procedure adopted by the previous two courts' (Messner and Ruggiero 1995: 131). The *Federal Court of Justice* (*Bundesgerichtshof*) functions as court of the highest level, while the *Federal Constitutional Court* (*Bundesverfassungsgericht*) oversees compliance with the principles of the German constitution.

Nicola Lacey's theoretical work can be used to make sense of the remarkable stability of the German criminal justice system in the face of a more punitive environment. Drawing on comparative political economy, Lacey describes German society – and the institutions that are relevant in the context of criminal justice – as shaped by a strong corporatism. She contrasts the German *coordinated market economy* with the *liberal market economy* of which the US is the prime example. According to this view, German society typically places a high value on training for skilled workers and on safeguarding their interests through corporatist arrangements, granting them a higher degree of protection from purely market-oriented interests than would be the case in liberal production regimes. Coordinated market economies such as Germany rely on 'long-term relationships and stable structures of investment, not least in education and training oriented to company- or sector-specific skills', and incorporate 'a wide range of social groups and institutions into a highly co-ordinated governmental structure' (Lacey 2012: 11). Since the 1990s, a neoliberal flexibilisation of social security has occurred (Brütt 2011) that has also affected penal policy (Wichmann 2012). Nonetheless, social policies continue to be shaped to a much

higher degree than in liberal market economies by corporatist structures and by the goal of protecting people's social status. (The latter is
achieved in Germany through the crucial social policy tool of national
social insurance.) This makes it hard for outsiders to attain positions of
high social status in German society, because corporatist associations
manage recruitment processes in accordance with their own views and
interests and because inclusion in the system of social insurance requires
certain previous achievements (Lacey 2012: 22). Thus, the very same
mechanisms that grant considerable scope for professional latitude to
actors in the criminal justice system also raise the barrier stopping access
to outsiders.

According to Lacy, each production model is connected to certain
structural conditions, creating path-dependencies that also affect the
theories and practices of criminal justice and systematically impede
radical structural change. In the German case, those conditions comprise
the existence of a welfare state that is relatively strong in comparison to
liberal regimes, comparatively low levels of social inequality, a consen-
sus-oriented style of politics, and proportional representation. Moreover,
although mass-media portrayals of crime also tend towards the punitive
(Dollinger 2011; Reichert 2009) they do so less than in the UK or the US.
In opposition to theories that explain different punishment preferences
through cultural features (e.g. Green 2009), Lacey emphasises structural
conditions. In coordinated market economies these conditions suggest,
according to her, more integrative styles of politics and criminal policy.
This may explain why significant differences exist between coordinated
and liberal market economies, with the latter characterised by higher
incarceration rates (Lacey 2012: 12). Contrary to what one would expect
to see on the basis of Lacey's arguments concerning the exclusive nature
of Germany's coordinated market economy, however, the incarceration
rate in Germany for migrants and non-German nationals is not higher
than the rate observed in countries with different economic models
(Melossi 2011; see also below). In addition to that, there are considerable differences between the German states regarding the application of
criminal law (Heinz 2012). General structural features of German society
cannot account for these differences; neither do they explain why particular groups of people and particular crimes are treated more punitively
at certain times than others. An adequate understanding requires attention to the interdependence between historical developments, structural
features, contemporary discourses and professional practices. Discourses
and normative decisions determine the foundations and functional logic
of institutional and penal arrangements; their cultural and structural

implications have to be examined in order to evaluate penal policy and the criminal justice system in Germany in their full complexity.

Different risks of criminalisation: selectivities in the context of police investigations and criminal proceedings

To understand the punitive changes – as well as the continuities – it is necessary to look at the selection that occurs in the process of criminalisation. This process starts with the police arresting a suspect, continues with judicial prosecution, and ends with a decision regarding the defendant. Following the *ultima ratio* principle of German criminal law – according to which imprisonment must only be used as a last resort – criminalisation is portrayed as a funnel in which the number of admitted persons decreases continuously: 'Out of 100 suspects identified by police, 30 are on average sentenced, and three of those are detained' (Heinz 2012a: 50). Prosecutors and judges play an important role here: whereas German police are bound by the legality principle, that is the requirement that any reasonable suspicion must be investigated (§ 152 of the code of criminal procedure – *Strafprozessordnung* or StPO), prosecutors and courts may refrain from prosecution on the basis of the opportunity principle (P.-A. Albrecht 2010b). Informal settlement through diversion (frequently with conditions attached) is the most important decriminalising tool in the German criminal justice system. In the past 20 years, about 50 per cent of proceedings have been stopped (Dünkel and Morgenstern 2003: 24). However, the funnel does not treat everyone equally: processes of selection work to the disadvantage of marginalised groups, which is why Kerner (1976: 137) talks of 'differential decriminalisation'.

This is most easily observed when we turn to reported crime. Reports to police by the general public, or the police's own investigations, show above-average inclination to stigmatise marginalised groups (Baier et al. 2010: 41–3; Mansel and Albrecht 2003). Social and media discourses influence the population's readiness to report offences. Together with additional factors like the current trends in penal policy, legal guidelines and institutional capabilities (Dünkel and Snacken 2001; Lappi-Seppälä 2010), those discourses also influence the decision-making practices of police and the judiciary. Therefore, neither official crime figures, nor the number of people incarcerated accurately reflect the 'reality of crime' (Oberwittler 2012: 777), and their decrease or increase is rarely connected to changes in the occurrence of crime. The police's own crime statistics (*Polizeiliche Kriminalstatistik* or PKS) are traditionally biased with regard to class, gender, age and (presumed) ethnicity. This cannot be solely explained through specific crime rates among these groups (Sack 1972). The most important reason lies in 'realities of control that diverge systematically for different social groups' (Walter 2010: 44). Socio-economically disadvantaged groups of offenders are more strongly represented in police crime statistics, and women normally exhibit lower than average crimes rates due to certain structural factors – gender-specific socialisation, at times a more restricted freedom of movement, as well as the assumption that offenders are normally male (Althoff and Kappel 1995). Women are therefore less likely than men to be charged with an offence, although the number of female suspects (especially adolescents) has slowly risen in recent years (Köhler 2012: 18). Adolescents, on the other hand, exhibit consistently high crime rates, partially because the general population is strongly inclined to report offences committed by them (Mansel and Raithel 2003: 17).

Particular attention should be paid to non-German nationals because of their over-representation in the prison population. Studies show that, for many years now, they consistently exhibit a criminalisation rate that is up to three-and-a-half times higher than for Germans (e.g. Albrecht and Pfeiffer 1979; Mansel and Albrecht 2003: 697). Notwithstanding this fact, non-German nationals are a very heterogeneous group and, depending on their countries of origin, they differ considerably in the likeliness of being charged (Walter and Trautmann 2003: 67). Individuals with a Turkish or ex-Yugoslav background, for example, are particularly disadvantaged throughout the entire system of criminal prosecution (BMI and BMJ 2006: 426–7). The socio-economic and legal integration of non-German nationals is, on average, worse and does force some of them into illegal occupations. But their high crime rate is also explained by the fact that the majority of the population is strongly inclined to report non-German nationals to the police (Wilmers et al. 2002: 34–6; Mansel 2003: 274–6). Racial profiling and other discriminatory police practices (Schweer 2004: 15) further contribute to this. Moreover, the socio-economic condition of many non-German nationals tends to impede their mobility and force them to concentrate in certain areas, normally those more intensely policed (Walter 2010: 44). Finally, owing to Germany's repressive migration policy, the offence in many cases consists simply in the uncertainty of their status as migrants.

The selectivity inherent in the practices of prosecutors and judges in criminal proceedings only partly mirror those of police crime statistics. In this context one must distinguish preliminary investigations, interlocutory proceedings and the main trial. When facing a case, pros-ecutors first have to determine whether evidence is sufficiently strong for charges to be pressed (preliminary investigations). If, during inter-locutory proceedings, the judge deems a conviction more likely than acquittal he/she will decide whether to move on to the main trial (Messner and Ruggiero 1995: 130). During preliminary investigations, charges are less often brought against female than male suspects, and proceedings are stopped less frequently for young adults than they are for adults (Mansel and Albrecht 2003: 688). The higher crime rate among non-German nationals shown by police statistics is corrected downwards during criminal proceedings because initial suspicions are dropped more frequently for non-German than German nationals (Mansel and Albrecht 2003 690–1). Overall, however, non-Germans are prosecuted more than Germans, even though 'in the vast majority of cases this cannot be explained by features of either the offence or the offender' (Pfeiffer et al. 2004: 84; BMI and BMJ 2006: 426). Schüler-Springorum (1983: 536) has pointed out that linguistic difficulties in the court room encourage judges to choose detention rather than non-custodial measures, and Buckolt has found that German judges often display limited sensitivity when punishing non-German adolescents (2009: 266). In addition, non-German nationals are also often found to be poorly integrated into society, which forces the use of detention measures – especially pre-trial detention (BMI/BMJ 2006: 426–7; Pfeiffer et al. 2004: 77–9; Schott 2004: 391).[2] Regarding the age of defendants, it should be noted that diversion rates are usually higher for adoles-cents than adults and that rates of formal punishment are accordingly lower (Dünkel 2010: 569–70, 575). Practices of criminal prosecution also exhibit spatial selectivities across all social groups because different cultures of justice (Dünkel and Pruin 2012: 140) lead to regionally varied diversion rates, often in the form of a North-South divide Dünkel 2010: 559. Regional differences in reporting behaviours add to this (Baier et al. 2009: 42).

As a consequence of this criminalisation process, the average pris-oner in Germany is male and below 30 years of age (Statistisches Bundesamt, Federal Statistical Office of Germany, 2011). Only a small part of the prison population – about five per cent – is female (Köhler 2012). Since the mid-1990s, the share of migrants in that population is between two and two-and-a-half times as high as their share of the total population: at about 25 per cent (Dünkel 2005; Laubenthal 2010: 36; Statistisches Bundesamt 2011). They also serve comparatively longer prison sentences (Schott et al. 2004). However, not all convicted persons are actually imprisoned in Germany. Only 9.4 per cent of those who were found guilty in 2010 received a prison sentence (Heinz 2012a: 52). In accordance with the goal of decriminalisation most convicts receive punishment without detention, especially in the area of juvenile criminal law, where a wider range of non-custodial measures is available (Dünkel 2010: 580–5). Therefore, when one examines the presence of various social groups in the prison system, the discretion of judges and prosecutors choosing between forms of punishment must also be taken into account. For example: non-German nationals benefit a lot less than Germans from non-custodial forms of punishment (Müller-Dietz 1999 in Walter 2010: 41). In what follows, the system of criminal penalties is presented in more detail.

The system of criminal penalties: prison and alternative forms of punishment

In line with the general trend in Europe (Dünkel and Morgenstern 2003: 25), there is now a continuously widening range of alternative forms of punishment in Germany. The foundations of the current system of criminal penalties go back to the penal reform of 1969 (Meier 2009: 39) which included those alternatives as part of the criminal justice system.

For decades, the monetary fine has been the most widely used form of punishment (Dünkel and Morgenstern 2003: 24). It was created mainly with the intention of reducing short-term prison sentences – whose incidence had traditionally been high, but whose educational value was generally deemed low: nearly 32 per cent of all prison sentences in 2010 were shorter than six months (Heinz 2012a: 182). Fines usually replace prison sentences of up to three months (Messner and Ruggiero 1995: 132), and since the penal reform of 1969, about 80 per cent of all convictions each year result in fines (Heinz 2012a: 66). In the past 20 years, however, the deterioration of the social and economic situation of disadvantaged social groups has led to a renewed increase in imprisonment for failure to pay a fine (Wikitzki 2000: 448; Statistisches Bundesamt 2012). This is why community service is now a form of punishment frequently applied to the poor and, moreover, the most widely used form of punishment in juvenile criminal law (Kaiser and Schöch 2002: 133; Dünkel 2010: 576).

Probation is also available, as is the suspension of a sentence after two-thirds of the period has been served (one-third for juveniles). Probation constitutes about 70 per cent of all sentences (Kury et al. 2009: 74), while suspension of remainder time to be served is applied in about 60 per cent of the cases. (Dünkel and Pruin 2012: 140). When violent and sexual offenders are given the latter alternative measure they may be electronically monitored – a practice introduced in 2011 in accordance with § 162 of the German penal code (StGB) (Heinz 2012a: 23). Doubts have been raised about the educational or rehabilitational effectiveness of some of the newer alternatives to prison sentences (Streng 2000: 213–4) – such as community service or the ankle electronic device – on the grounds that the purposes of the punishments and proportionality are unclear. Community service, on the other hand, seems questionable because of its similarity to (unconstitutional) forced labour. In 2010, 575,068 convicts (81.6%) from a total of 704,802 received a fine; of the 129,717 (18.4%) prison sentences, more than two-thirds (71.0%) were suspended on probation (Heinz 2012a: 66).

There is a whole range of other – rarely used – forms of alternative penal measures, such as cautioning and remittance of sentence (Dünkel and Morgenstern 2003: 25). For instance, victim-offender mediation offers the possibility of conviction without punishment, or of sentence mitigation (Dünkel and Morgenstern 2003). This is the only tool that utilises the autonomy of the parties involved in the conflict, but is rarely used despite the growing emphasis on the victims of crime in recent years (H.-J. Albrecht 2010).

In brief, fines, probation and conditional sentences make up the bulk of penal measures while imprisonment, though remaining a crucial form of punishment, is decreasing (Heinz 2012a: 54; Kaiser and Schöch 2002). Therefore, the argument can be made that alternatives do not always replace prison sentences, but – inasmuch as they are imposed *in addition to* other measures – they indicate that state control is intensifying and becoming more refined (Heinz 2012: 560; Kemme and Stoll 2012). The highly invasive ankle electronic device is an example, as is the suspension of a sentence on probation which is ever more strongly complemented by a series of restrictions. Moreover, because few obstacles hamper their application, alternative measures are frequently deployed in cases where charges would otherwise have been dropped (Messner and Ruggiero 1995: 140).

Imprisonment: forms and figures

In Germany, there are custodial institutions for adult, juvenile, and adolescent offenders. Those awaiting trial can be remanded in custody if they are deemed likely to abscond or re-offend. This also applies to refugees awaiting possible deportation (pre-deportation detention).[3] Pre-trial and pre-deportation custody are not considered punishment, although they share significant aspects of imprisonment. Not all forms of detention require a (full) guilty verdict, as offenders who are partially guilty and regarded as dangerous incur *correction and prevention measures* as a form of 'protecting the public'. In accordance with §§ 63 and 64 of the German penal code (StGB), offenders with no (or diminished) responsibility are committed to one of a number of correctional institutions delivering prevention measures: psychiatric hospitals, detoxification clinics or preventive detention centres (cf. Section 2 above).

On 31 March 2012, 54,787 individuals were serving prison sentences in adult or juvenile institutions, 1,556 of which were in socio-therapeutic institutions. By contrast, 11,195 individuals were remanded in custody, marking a considerable decrease since the 1990s (see the data in Messner and Ruggiero 1995: 134–5). Another 1,689 individuals were the recipient of 'other detention measures', which include pre-deportation detention (Statistisches Bundesamt 2012a). Following the rehabilitation objective, open prison (day-release) has been the programmatic standard form of punishment in most German states for more than 30 years. In actual fact, however, non-open detention is still the standard treatment, with an ascendant trend in this respect (Puschke 2011: 21). On 31 March 2012, Germany had 171 closed institutions holding 60,362 prisoners, and only fifteen open prisons with 7,309 inmates (Statistisches Bundesamt 2012a: 5). There are, however, large regional differences between German states with respect to decisions between open or closed prison (Dünkel 2010a: 8). This demonstrates that different forms of punishment are chosen more on the basis of political criteria than the suitability of offenders (Puschke 2011: 21). Currently, restrictive policies in the juvenile prison system have caused overcrowding of closed institutions on the one hand, with spare capacity in open prisons on the other (Walkenhorst 2010: 23).

On 31 March 2012, a total of 67,617 individuals were imprisoned in Germany, which is less than 0.1 per cent of the total population. Compared with other European countries, Germany has, therefore, a relatively low incarceration rate (Dünkel 2010a; Heinz 2012a: 150), although this has not always been the case. The rate has decreased since 2005, but long-run trends do not appear to be consistent. The expansion of alternative forms of punishment in the 1980s (especially in juvenile criminal justice) had indeed led to a decrease, but this was reversed in the 1990s, partly as a result of external factors – such as German reunification and increased migration – and partly due to an increase in the number of convictions for violent and drug-related offences (Dünkel 2010a). The current decrease of the incarceration rate is primarily connected to a reduction in the number of people remanded in custody where occupancy rates have gone down by half since the mid-1990s (Dünkel 2010a; Puschke 2011: 18). The continuous decrease of occupancy rates in juvenile prisons is a contributing factor, as is the massive reduction of prisoner figures in pre-deportation detention (Dünkel and Morgenstern 2010: 98), which is itself caused by lower numbers of asylum-seekers in Germany (due to the 1993 tightening of asylum laws). Non-German nationals are considerably overrepresented in pre-trial custody. Therefore, the reduction in the asylum-seekers figure has had a strong impact on the reduction in the number of pre-trial detainees mentioned above (Dünkel 2010: 556; 2010a; Puschke 2011: 18).

If we take a closer look at different forms of punishment and classes of offence, the above-mentioned decriminalising tendency looks weaker. Occupancy rates in the correction and prevention sector have been on the rise almost continuously since the 1990s (Puschke 2011: 18–9), primarily in the areas of violent and sexual offences. In 2009, the number of individuals in preventive detention was above 500 for the first time (Statistisches Bundesamt 2012a: 47), while in Western Germany the threshold of 10,000 individuals committed to psychiatric hospitals or detoxification centres was crossed (Statistisches Bundesamt 2011a) – a twofold increase over the past ten years (Stolpmann 2010: 29). The relative figure may be small, but a clear tendency emerges nonetheless, which has been described in the literature as 'bifurcation' (Dünkel and Morgenstern 2010). Whereas certain classes of offences – especially the less serious property offences – have tended to become decriminalised since the 1990s due to the increasing use of alternative forms of punishment, such as diversion, there is more pressure on other offences – particularly those of a violent or sexual nature (Dünkel 2010b). There appears to be an increasing tendency to see detention for correction and prevention as an alternative to imprisonment: there are now more convicts with long-term sentences of more than five years in correction and prevention than there are in prison (Heinz 2012b: 69).

This development is the combined effect of a number of factors that come into play at more or less all the stages of the criminalisation process. For example, alarm towards certain violent crimes has considerably risen among the general public (Reuband 2004: 93), and there is (as discussed in Section 2) strong media attention on violent and sexual offences. Moreover, a series of amendments since 1998 has increased minimum penalties and raised the thresholds for the suspension of sentences and for conditional release – especially for sex offences, but also for grievous bodily harm (Streng 2000: 207). At the same time, conditions for preventive detention were loosened and the rather invasive punishment method of electronic monitoring of suspended sentences was introduced. Some of those amendments were directly motivated by spectacular media portrayals of a few extreme cases, especially of sexual violence against children (Kury et al. 2009: 75). Moreover, violent and sexual offenders are also more often sentenced to some form of detention and their terms are longer (Dünkel 2010b; Dünkel et al. 2008: 303). The tendency of penal policy seems to be that a certain group of offenders is not imprisoned anymore solely for the purpose of rehabilitation, but also to protect the public from crime. For preventative reasons, this can extend beyond the term of imprisonment. Back in 1999, legal developments already prompted H.-J. Albrecht (1999: 876) to observe a 'reordering of the balance between the security principle and civil rights [...] in which security is clearly dominant' (see also Streng 2000: 207). This analysis also applies to contemporary practices with regard to a particular group of recidivists who are deemed especially dangerous, and generally to the development of punishment – as we shall see below.

The prison system

In principle, all prisons in Germany are publicly run. The constitution only allows partial privatisation – for example, in the construction of new facilities or the provision of certain goods and services – though this is subject to the requirement of demonstrably better efficiency. Therefore, privatisation only plays a small role in German prisons. Some deportation centres are an exception because private companies are involved in guard duties alongside public servants (Lindenberg and Schmidt-Semisch 1995: 45–6; Rüppel 2010: 51). Following the reform of the German federal system in 2006, administrative authority over the prison system now lies with individual states. Prior to this reform, substantive criminal law, the law of criminal procedure and the law of prison administration were uniformly regulated at the federal level. The intention was to preserve the legally guaranteed equality of opportunities for all prisoners by making their conditions as similar as possible regardless of their place of domicile (Dünkel 2010a). The new regulation initiated a new direction in the prison policy that was inaugurated since the criminal law reform of 1969. Thanks to differences in policy, finance and staffing decisions, practices in the prison system had already varied between states prior to the reform. The amendment, however, has provided a more solid institutional foundation to such differences (Dünkel 2010a: 7).

There is now also modest diversification with regard to punishment purposes and notions about rehabilitation: in some states, for example, open prison was explicitly renounced as the programmatic standard form of imprisonment (Dünkel 2009), while security constitutes an equally relevant feature. Instead of preparing prisoners for a socially responsible life, in accordance with the rehabilitation principle, some states now see protection of the general public as equally important. Thus, the granting of privileges to prisoners depends, in theory, more strongly than before on 'vague security criteria' (Puschke 2011: 29), though it will have to be empirically tested how far this will have an impact in practice. Following the reform of the federal system, a reduction can be seen with regard to rehabilitation measures that prepare prisoners for release (open prison, privileges and prison leave; see Dünkel 2009: 29; Dünkel and Schüler-Springorum 2006; Dünkel 2010a: 13), especially in the case of violent and sex offences (Niemz 2011: 26). In connection with the differentiation of custodial penalties, we can also observe a departure from an educational role towards a conception of prison as a provider of 'opportunity structures', drawing on the offenders' ability to act in a self-responsible manner (*Chancenvollzug*). This opportunity-oriented model is only interested in supporting prisoners who are considered cooperative, while it offers nothing but detention to 'passive' prisoners. In some states, existing regulations no longer include the option of granting discretionary privileges to prisoners who are uncooperative (and therefore considered incapable of rehabilitation) (Dressel 2008: 131–3). This model systematically disadvantages prisoners who are not considered dangerous, but who are unable or unwilling to cooperate – or who require support in this respect.[4]

Officially, conditions in prison should be led by the goal of re-integration, and life in custody should approximate as closely as possible to life on the outside. Theoretically, it is for the authorities to counter any negative consequences of imprisonment. Moreover, custody is meant to enable individuals to live 'a socially responsible life free of crime in the future' (§ 2 Para. 1 Treatment of Offenders Act – StVollzG). However, the theory and practice of punishment often diverge. This is due, above all, to the ambivalence surrounding the goal of rehabilitation, on the one hand, and protection of society, on the other – as well as to the mixture of support and control delivered by the system. The possibilities of reviewing treatment under the law of prison administration still give scant legal protection to prisoners. Prisoners' representatives have very limited influence, external controls only play a marginal role (Koeppel 1999; Becker 2008: 84), and initiating legal proceedings is very unlikely to yield success (Laubenthal 2002: 50). Therefore, the task of checking whether prison conditions comply with the protection of human rights has so far been mainly undertaken by trans- or international institutions, such as the European Committee for the Prevention of Torture and Inhuman or Degrading Treatment or Punishment (CPT).

Locking-up for long hours and offering limited leisure facilities are still the rule in many prisons – especially in remand and pre-deportation centres (Dünkel 2010a), where prisoners, moreover, do not have the right to choose a doctor and doctor-patient confidentiality is revoked (Stolpmann 2010: 31). The 'protecting the public' principle, however, provides insufficient justification for the suspension of certain fundamental human and civil rights. Among these is the right to political participation, which is denied through the exclusion of prisoners from the electorate, but also to the lifting of the ban on forced labour (that is enshrined in the German Constitution) and the right to be treated fairly when working as an employee (this includes wages in accordance with agreements, and compensation for pension and long-term care insurance by the employer) (Hillebrand 2009: 49). With a €1.36 per hour wage (Laubenthal 2011: 259–60), prisoners are barely compensated for their work. Those who defend this state of affairs cite in their support the difficulties in finding appropriate companies willing to run production in prison. In 2009, inmates at work were between 20–46 per cent of the prison population, depending on the specific Federal state (Hillebrand 2009: 177–8).

Health conditions among the prison population continue to be a crucial issue: in comparative terms, inmates are disproportionately exposed to illnesses and diseases. The rate of HIV infections, for instance, is 20 times higher in prison than outside, for Hepatitis C it is 40 times higher, while the suicide rate is five times higher (Stöver 2010: 86). This is partly caused by, among other things, the impossibility of anonymously obtaining condoms and of 'safe drug use' (e.g. through provision of sterilised syringes). Due to public pressure – and in line with common understandings – prisons are considered to be drug-free spaces; available therapies (if any exist at all) are strongly focused on abstinence. Another possible cause is the fact that medical care in prison follows a 'traditional curative' (Stöver 2010a: 16) rather than preventative orientation. The number of prisoners with drug problems is rising continuously, and there are now more drug addicts locked up in German prisons than ever before (Stöver 2010: 22–4; cf. Schulte et al. 2009). However, there is also a growing tendency to transfer drug addicts to therapeutic institutions (Kury et al. 2009: 77).

Minorities are structurally disadvantaged in the prison system because existing facilities are focused more on the needs of the average inmate than on theirs – both in organisational and conceptual terms. The problems faced by the heterogeneous group of non-German nationals transcend those experienced by the indigenous prison population. The former do not enjoy the benefits of rehabilitation programmes (Walter 2010: 43) because their residential status is often uncertain or because, in many cases, a prison sentence is followed by deportation (Kleespies 2006: 170–2; Laubenthal 2010: 37). For those who are not deported, however, the risk of recidivism is as high as that for all other prisoners (of any nationality) who are not offered education and training opportunities (Jehle et al. 2003).

Turning to the female prison population, there are few separate women's prisons in Germany: which means, for example, that two-thirds of female prisoners are housed in separate sections of large men's prisons; female adolescents are put into facilities for adult female prisoners, disregarding the principle that they should be looked after separately (Zolondek 2005: 15; Walkenhorst 2010). This has some negative consequences: for instance, it is often impossible to put a woman in a facility close to her place of residence (Keppler 2010: 74). There is also a lack of specialised treatment, adequate opportunities for education and training as well as work opportunities that are 'specifically female'. It is only in recent years that attempts have been made to offer women similar work opportunities to those available to men (Boogaart et al. 2004: 183–5).

Conclusion

There is no empirical evidence of a general trend towards growing punitiveness in the German criminal justice system. The existence of a 'positive feedback loop between politics and journalism' that 'transforms crime into a comprehensive problem' (Obermöller and Gosch 1995: 54), and therefore directly affects incarceration rates cannot be demonstrated. Despite the clear punitive tendencies prevailing in the media and in the political sphere, it is more plausible to argue that the process of criminalisation and the criminal justice system in Germany are marked by the co-existence of older, as well as more recent, orientations. Punitive tendencies do exist, but they mostly affect social groups that are marginalised, as well as offenders who are particularly stigmatised. We have described the unequal treatment of marginalised social groups throughout the entire criminalisation process, as well as the growing attention paid to violent and sexual offences – in particular since the 1990s – which are accompanied by the prevalence of protection principles over rehabilitation. Today, the core target of the criminal justice apparatus is a small group of serious criminals who are seen as highly dangerous and at a high risk of recidivism; hence, tougher laws and longer sentences are aimed at excluding them from society for as long as possible. Signs of the growing emphasis on security can also be detected in how the general purposes of punishment are rewritten in some German states. However, for the majority of individuals who are processed through (parts of) the criminal justice system, relative primacy of decriminalising measures and punishments is retained or even reinforced, though there are also considerable regional divergences, as well as differential treatment on the basis of individual features and of membership of particular social groups.

If one were to describe or even conceptualise recent changes in German penal policy, one may well use the phrase 'targeted governance'. This encompasses, on the one hand, the punitive tendencies that affect certain stigmatised classes of offences and traditionally marginalised groups and, on the other hand, the selectivity that economising efforts has introduced into rehabilitation practices. It remains to be seen whether the prison-as-opportunity concept – which is steeped in the doctrine of neoliberalism – can catch on in the German Federation as a whole.

Notes

1. Take as example the expansion of preventive detention since the late 1990s, some elements of which were later annulled by the European Court of Human Rights (in 2009 and 2011) and Germany's Federal Constitutional Court (2011). Preventive detention aims to detain offenders beyond their prison term in accordance with how dangerous they are assumed to be. Its use was also allowed for young adults and, in 2008, for adolescents, subject to certain conditions. This amounts to a decisive 'break with the educational principle' (H.-J. Albrecht 2010: 53) because protecting society from criminal offences is the stated goal.
2. On top of that, the laws concerning legal aliens are an additional punishment insofar as imprisonment is followed by deportation or a downgrading of their residential status (Walter 2001: 255).
3. The practice of detention prior to deportation raises questions of legal policy because it is merely a means for the execution of an obligation to leave the country. Adolescents are at times detained here, too (Grimm 2007: 141).
4. Thus, a new form of detention practice is introduced that is very similar to the repressively activating social policies introduced in the 1990s and 2000s whose exclusionary effects on disadvantaged social groups have been amply described. In both cases, the individual is required to cooperate and

actively submit to the expectations of professionals while passive behaviour is 'punished' (Dollinger and Ziegler 2009).

References

H.-J. Albrecht (2010) 'Internationale Tendenzen in der Entwicklung des Jugendstrafrechts', in B. Dollinger and H. Schmidt-Semisch (eds), *Handbuch Jugendkriminalität* (Wiesbaden: VS) 43–59.

H.-J. Albrecht (2004) 'Youth Justice in Germany', in M. H. Tonry and A. N. Doob (eds), *Youth Crime and Youth Justice: Comparative and Cross-National Perspectives* (Chicago: University of Chicago Press) 443–93.

H.-J. Albrecht (1999) 'Die Determinanten Der Sexualstrafrechtsreform', *Zeitschrift Für Die Gesamte Strafrechtswissenschaft,* 111: 863–88.

P.-A. Albrecht (2010a) *Der Weg in die Sicherheitsgesellschaft* (Berlin: BVW).

P.-A. Albrecht (2010b) *Kriminologie,* 4th edn (München: CH Beck).

P.-A. Albrecht and C. Pfeiffer (1979) *Die Kriminalisierung Junger Ausländer: Befunde und Reaktionen Sozialer Kontrollinstanzen* (Weinheim: Juventa).

M. Althoff and S. Kappel (1995) *Geschlechterverhältnis und Kriminologie* (Weinheim: Juventa).

D. Baier, C. Pfeiffer, J. Simonson and S. Rabold (2009) 'Jugendliche in Deutschland als Opfer und Täter von Gewalt', *Forschungsbericht 107* (Hannover: KFN).

D. Baier, C. Pfeiffer, S. Rabold, J. Simonson and C. Kappes (2010) *Kinder und Jugendliche in Deutschland: Gewalterfahrungen, Integration, Medienkonsum,* http://www.kfn.de/versions/kfn/assets/fob109.pdf, date accessed 26 August 2012.

I. Baumann (2006) *Dem Verbrechen auf der Spur. Eine Geschichte der Kriminologie und Kriminalpolitik in Deutschland 1880 bis 1980* (Göttingen: Wallstein).

H. Becker (2008) *Ritual Knast. Die Niederlage des Gefängnisses* (Leipzig: Forum).

K. Boers and M. Schaerff (2008) 'Abschied vom Primat der Resozialisierung im Jugendstrafvollzug?', *Zeitschrift für Jugendkriminalrecht und Jugendhilfe,* 19: 316–24.

H.v.d. Boogaart, M. Kleber and R. Nanninga (2004) 'Arbeit und Qualifikation von Gefangenen in kleinen Vollzugseinheiten', in G. Rehn, R. Nanninga and A. Thiel (eds), *Freiheit und Unfreiheit. Arbeit mit Straftätern innerhalb und außerhalb des Justizvollzuges* (Herbolzheim: Centaurus) 183–99.

C. Brütt (2011) *Workfare als Mindestsicherung. Von der Sozialhilfe zu Hartz IV, deutsche Sozialpolitik 1962 bis 2005* (Bielefeld: transcript).

O. Buckolt (2009) *Die Zumessung der Jugendstrafe* (Baden-Baden: Nomos).

Bundesministerium des Inneren und Bundesministerium der Justiz (BMI and BMJ) (2006) *Zweiter Periodischer Sicherheitsbericht* (Berlin).

M. Cavadino and J. Dignan (2006) *Penal systems* (London: Sage).

H. Cremer-Schäfer (2010) 'Die Jugendkriminalitätswelle und andere Kriminalisierungsereignisse', in B. Dollinger and H. Schmidt-Semisch (eds), *Handbuch Jugendkriminalität* (Wiesbaden: VS) 187–201.

B. Dollinger (2011) '"Punitivität" in der Diskussion. Konzeptionelle, Theoretische und Empirische Referenzen', in B. Dollinger and H. Schmidt-Semisch (eds), *Gerechte Ausgrenzung? Wohlfahrtsproduktion und die neue Lust am Strafen* (Wiesbaden: VS) 25–73.

B. Dollinger and H. Schmidt-Semisch (2010) 'Den Ausländischen Intensivtäter an der Wurzel Packen? Eine Kollektivsymbolanalytische Analyse Populistischer

Tendenzen bei der Thematisierung Von Jugendkriminalität', *kulturRevolution*, 29: 71–6.

B. Dollinger and H. Ziegler (2009) 'Investive Kriminalpolitik und die Rückkehr der Défense Sociale', *Sozial Extra*, 28: 42–6.

B. Dressel (2008) *Das Hamburger Strafvollzugsgesetz* (Berlin: LIT).

F. Dünkel (2009) 'Vollzugslockerungen und offener Vollzug – die Bedeutung entlassungsvorbereitender Maßnahmen für die Wiedereingliederung', *Forum Strafvollzug*, 58 (4): 192–6.

F. Dünkel (2010) 'Germany', in F. Dünkel, J. Grzywa, P. Horsfield and I. Pruin (eds), *Juvenile Justice Systems in Europe* (Mönchengladbach: Forum) 547–621.

F. Dünkel (2010a) 'Strafvollzug in Deutschland – Rechtstatsächliche Befunde', *Aus Politik und Zeitgeschichte*, 7: 7–14.

F. Dünkel (2010b) Gefangenenraten im Internationalen und Nationalen Vergleich, http://www.neue-kriminalpolitik.nomos.de/?id=1462 (home page), date accessed 26 August 2012.

F. Dünkel (2005) 'Migration and Ethnic Minorities: Impacts on the Phenomenon of Youth Crime', in N. Queloz, F. Bütikofer Repond, D. Pittet, R. Brossard and B. Meyer-Bisch (eds), *Youth Crime and Juvenile Justice* (Bern: Staempfli) 45–71.

F. Dünkel, D. Gebauer and B. Geng (2008) *Jugendgewalt und Möglichkeiten der Prävention* (Mönchengladbach: Forum).

F. Dünkel and C. Morgenstern (2010) 'Deutschland', in F. Dünkel, T. Lappi-Seppälä, C. Morgenstern and D. van Zyl Smit (eds), *Kriminalität, Kriminalpolitik, strafrechtliche Sanktionspraxis und Gefangenenraten im europäischen Vergleich* (Mönchengladbach: Forum) 97–204.

F. Dünkel and C. Morgenstern (2003) 'Aktuelle Probleme und Reformfragen des Sanktionen- rechts in Deutschland', *Juridica International*, 8: 35–24.

F. Dünkel and I. Pruin (2012) 'Die bedingte/vorzeitige Entlassung aus dem Strafvollzug im Europäischen Vergleich', in E. Matt (ed.), *Bedingte Entlassung, Übergangsmanagement und die Wiedereingliederung von Ex-Strafgefangenen* (Münster: LIT) 125–46.

F. Dünkel and H. Schüler-Springorum (2006) 'Strafvollzug als Ländersache? Der „Wettbewerb der Schäbigkeit" ist schon im Gange!', *Zeitschrift für Strafvollzug und Straffälligenhilfe*, 5: 145–9.

F. Dünkel and S. Snacken (2001) 'Strafvollzug im europäischen Vergleich: Probleme, Praxis und Perspektiven ' , Zeitschrift für Strafvollzug und Straffälligenhilfe 50, 195–212.

G. Esping-Andersen (1990) *The Three Worlds of Welfare Capitalism* (Princeton: Princeton University Press).

N. G. Fielding (2011) 'Judges and Their Work', *Social & Legal Studies*, 20: 97–115.

R. Geißler (2008) ' „Ausländerkriminalität"? Realitäten und Vorurteile', *IDA-NRW*, 14: 3–9.

D. A. Green (2009) 'Feeding Wolves: Punitiveness and Culture', *European Journal of Criminology*, 6: 517–36.

S. Grimm (2007) *Die Rückführung von Flüchtlingen in Deutschland* (Berlin: BWV).

W. Hassemer (2008) *Strafrecht* (Berlin: BWV).

W. Heinz (2012) 'Aktuelle Entwicklungen in der Sanktionierungspraxis der Jugendkriminalrechtspflege', in DVJJ (ed.), *Achtung (für) Jugend! Praxis und Perspektiven des Jugendkriminalrechts* (Mönchengladbach : Forum) 513–62.

W. Heinz (2012a) *Das strafrechtliche Sanktionensystem und die Sanktionierungspraxis in Deutschland*, http://www.ki.uni-konstanz.de/kis/ (home page) date accessed 26 August 2012.

W. Heinz (1/2012b) *Freiheitsentziehende Maßregeln – Struktur und Entwicklung der Sanktionierungspraxis*, http://www.ki.uni-konstanz.de/kis/ (home page) date accessed 26 August 2012.

W. Heinz (2011) 'Neue Straflust der Strafjustiz – Realität oder Mythos?', *Neue Kriminalpolitik*, 23: 14–27.

J. Hillebrand (2009) *Organisation und Ausgestaltung der Gefangenenarbeit in Deutschland*, 2nd edn (Mönchengladbach: Forum).

J.-H. Jehle, W. Heinz and P. Sutterer (2003) *Legalbewährung nach strafrechtlichen Sanktionen – Eine Kommentierte Rückfallstatistik*, edited by Bundesministerium der Justiz (Mönchengladbach: Forum Verlag Goedesberg).

G. Kaiser and H. Schöch (2002) *Strafvollzug*, 5th edn (Heidelberg: Müller).

S. Kemme and K. Stoll (2012) 'Bestehende Benachteiligungen junger Straftäter im Lichte der Forderungen nach Verschärfungen im Jugendstrafrecht', *Monatsschrift für Kriminologie und Strafrechtsreform*, 95: 32–51.

L. Keppler (2010) 'Von der Gesundheitsfürsorge zur Gesundheitsförderung im Gefängnis. Hat sich die Gefängnismedizin gewandelt?', in H. Bögemann, K. Keppler and H. Stöver (eds), *Gesundheit im Gefängnis: Ansätze und Erfahrungen mit Gesundheitsförderung in Totalen Institutionen* (Weinheim: Juventa) 49–58.

H.-J. Kerner (1976) 'Normbruch und Auslese der Bestraften – Ansätze zu einem Modell der differentiellen Entkriminalisierung', in H.-E. Göppinger and G. Kaiser (eds), *Kriminologie und Strafverfahren* (Stuttgart: Enke) 137–55.

S. Kleespies (2006) *Kriminalität von Spätaussiedlern: Erscheinungsformen, Ursachen, Prävention*, (Frankfurt a.M.: Peter Lang).

T. Koeppel (1999): *Kontrolle des Strafvollzugs – Individueller Rechtsschutz und generelle Aufsicht: Ein Rechtsvergleich* (Mönchengladbach: Forum).

T. Köhler (2012) *Straffällige Frauen* (Göttingen: Universitätsverlag Göttingen).

A. Kreuzer (2008) 'Ursprünge, Gegenwart und Entwicklungen des deutschen Jugendstrafrechts', *Zeitschrift für Jugendkriminalrecht und Jugendhilfe*, 19: 122–34.

H. Kury, M. Brandenstein and J. Obergfell-Fuchs (2009) 'Dimensions of Punitiveness in Germany', *European Journal on Criminal Policy and Research*, 15: 63–81.

N. Lacey (2012) 'Punishment in the Perspective of Comparative Political Economy', *Kriminologisches Journal*, 44: 9–31.

T. Lappi-Seppälä (2010) 'Vertrauen, Wohlfahrt und politikwissenschaftliche Aspekte – International vergleichende Perspektiven zur Punitivität', in F. Dünkel, T. Lappi-Seppälä, C. Morgenstern and D.v. Zyl Smit (eds), *Kriminalität, Kriminalpolitik, strafrechtliche Sanktionspraxis und Gefangenenraten im europäischen Vergleich* (Mönchengladbach: Forum) 937–96.

K. Laubenthal (2002) 'Rechtsschutz im Strafvollzug – Reform aus Sicht von Wissenschaft und', in Praxis R. Herrfahrdt (ed.), *Sicherheit und Behandlung – Strafvollzug im Wandel* (Schriftenreihe der Bundesvereinigung der Anstaltsleiter im Strafvollzug 5) (Hannover: Eigenverlag der Bundesvereinigung der Anstaltsleiter im Strafvollzug) 43–61.

K. Laubenthal (2011) *Strafvollzug*, 6th edn (Würzburg: Springer).

K. Laubenthal (2010) 'Gefangenensubkulturen', *Aus Politik und Zeitgeschichte*, 7: 34.

Lindenberg and Schmidt-Semisch (1995) '"Über alles andere kann man reden"'. Privatisierung des Strafvollzugs und das Staatliche Gewaltmonopol', *Neue Kriminalpolitik*, 7 (2): 45–7.

F. Liszt (1900/1969) ' Die Kriminalität der Jugendlichen' , in: B. Simonsohn (ed), Jugendkriminalität, Strafjustiz und Sozialpädagogik (Frankfurt a.M.: Surhkamp) 40 – 2.

F. Liszt (1883/1968) *Der Zweckgedanke im Strafrecht*, 3rd edn (Frankfurt a.M.: Klostermann).

J. Mansel (2003) 'Konfliktregulierung bei Straftaten', in A. Groenemeyer and J. Mansel (eds), *Die Ethnisierung von Alltagskonflikten* (Opladen: Leske+Budrich) 261–84.

J. Mansel and G. Albrecht (2003) 'Migration und das kriminalpolitische Handeln staatlicher Strafverfolgungsorgane. Ausländer als polizeilich Tatverdächtige und gerichtlich Abgeurteilte', *Kölner Zeitschrift für Soziologie und Sozialpsychologie*, 55 (4): 679–715.

J. Mansel and J. Raithel (2003) 'Verzerrungsfaktoren im Hell- und Dunkelfeld und die Gewaltentwicklung', in J. Mansel and J. Raithel (eds), *Kriminalität und Gewalt im Jugendalter* (Weinheim: Juventa) 7–24.

B.-D. Meier (2009) *Strafrechtliche Sanktionen* (Heidelberg: Springer).

D. Melossi (2011) *The Processes of Criminalization of Migrants and the Borders of 'Fortress Europe'* (Unpublished Manuscript).

C. Messner and V. Ruggiero (1995) 'Germany: The Penal System between Past and Future', in V. Ruggiero, M. Ryan and J. Sim (eds), *Western European Penal Systems* (London: Sage) 128–48.

J. Muncie (2009) *Youth and Crime*, 3rd edn (London: Sage).

S. Niemz (2011) *Sozialtherapie im Strafvollzug 2011: Ergebnisübersicht zur Stichtagserhebung zum 31.03.2011* (Wiesbaden: KrimZ), website http://www. krimz.de/texte.html date accessed 26 August 2012.

B. Obermöller and M. Gosch (1995) 'Kriminalitätsberichterstattung als Kriminologisches Problem', *Kritische Justiz*, 28: 45–59.

D. Oberwittler (2000) *Von der Strafe zur Erziehung? Jugendkriminalpolitik in England und Deutschland (1850–1920)* (Frankfurt a.M.: Campus).

D. Oberwittler (2012): 'Delinquenz und Kriminalität als soziales Problem', in G. Albrecht and A. Groenemeyer (eds), *Handbuch Soziale Probleme*, Vol 2, 2nd edn (Wiesbaden: VS) 772–860.

N. Oelkers, H.-U. Otto, M. Schrödter and H. Ziegler (2008) '„Unerziehbarkeit" – Zur Aktualität einer Aussonderungskategorie', in M. Brumlik and S.K. Amos (eds), *Ab nach Sibirien? Wie gefährlich ist unsere Jugend?* (Weinheim: Beltz) 184–216.

H. Ostendorf (2008) *Jugendstrafrecht – Reform statt Abkehr*, http://www.strafverteidi-gervereinigungen.de/Material/Jugendstrafrecht/Ostendorf_ReformstattAbkehr. pdf date accessed 26 August 2012.

H. Ostendorf (2010) ' Strafverschärfungen im Umgang mit Jugendkriminalität', in B. Dollinger and H. Schmidt-Semisch (eds), Handbuch Jugendkriminalität (Wiesbaden: VS) 91 – 104.

D. J. K Peukert (1986) *Grenzen der Sozialdisziplinierung. Aufstieg und Krise der deut-schen Jugendfürsorge 1878 bis 1932* (Köln: Bund).

C. Pfeiffer, M. Kleimann, S. Petersen and T. Schott (2004) *Probleme der Kriminalität bei Immigranten und Politische Konsequenzen. Expertise für den Sachverständigenrat für Zuwanderung und Integration (Zuwanderungsrat) der Bundesregierung* (Hannover: KFN).

C. Pfeiffer, M. Windzio and M. Kleimann (2005) 'Media Use and its Impacts on Crime Perception, Sentencing Attitudes and Crime Policy', *European Journal of Criminology*, 2: 259–85.

J. Puschke (2011) 'Strafvollzug in Deutschland – eine Bestandsaufnahme' in J. Puschke (ed.), *Strafvollzug in Deutschland. Strukturelle Defizite, Reformbedarf und Alternativen* (Berlin: Berliner Wissenschaftsverlag) 15–36.

F. Reichert (2009) 'Straflust in Zeitungsmedien: Gibt es in der Presse eine „Punitivität im weiteren Sinn"? ', *Kriminologisches Journal*, 41: 100–14.

K.-H. Reuband (2004) 'Konstanz und Wandel im Strafbedürfnis der Bundesbürger – 1970 bis 2003', in R. Lautmann, D. Klimke and F. Sack (eds), *Punitivität* (Weinheim: Juventa) 89–103.

A. Roth (1991) 'Die Entstehung eines Jugendstrafrechts', *Zeitschrift für Neuere Rechtsgeschichte*, 13: 17–40.

S. Rüppel (2010) *Privatisierung des Strafvollzugs. Rechtliche und praktische Problemstellungen als Chance zur normativen Entkriminalisierung* (Frankfurt a.M.: Peter Lang).

F. Sack (1972) 'Definition von Kriminalität als politisches Handeln. Der labeling approach', *Kriminologisches Journal*, 4: 1–31.

J. J. Savelsberg (1994) 'Knowledge, Domination, and Criminal Punishment', *American Journal of Sociology*, 9: 911–43.

J. J. Savelsberg (2002) 'Cultures of Control in Contemporary Societies', *Law & Social Inquiry*, 27: 685–710.

T. Schott (2004) 'Ausländer vor Gericht', *Zeitschrift für Jugendkriminalrecht und Jugendhilfe*, 15: 385–95.

T. Schott, S. Suhling, T. Görgen, R. Löbmann and C. Pfeiffer (2004) *Der Anstieg der Belegung im Justizvollzug Niedersachsens und Schleswig-Holsteins* (Hannover: KFN).

H. Schüler-Springorum (1983) 'Ausländerkriminalität', *Neue Zeitschrift für Strafrecht*, 3: 529–36.

B. Schulte, H. Stoever, K. Thane, C. Schreiter, D. Gansefort and J. Reimer (2009) 'Substitution Treatment and HCV / HIV Infection in German Prisons', *International Journal of Prisoner Health*, 5: 39–44.

T. Schweer (2004) *Polizisten im Konflikt mit ethnischen Minderheiten und sozialen Randgruppen in Interkulturelle Kompetenz in der Polizeiausbildung*, http://www.amnesty-polizei.de/d/wp-content/uploads/interkulturelle_kompetenz_polizei.pdf date accessed 26. August 2012.

R. Sparks (2011) 'Preface: Review Symposium on Nicola Lacey, The Prisoners' Dilemma: Political Economy and Punishment in Contemporary Democracies' *Punishment & Society*, 13: 93–5.

Statistisches Bundesamt (2012) Bestand der Gefangenen und Verwahrten in den deutschen Justizvollzugsanstalten nach ihrer Unterbringung auf Haftplätzen des geschlossenen und offenen Vollzugs jeweils zu den Stichtagen 31. März, 31. August und 30 November eines Jahres, Stand 03/2012, www.destatis.de, (home page), date accessed 26 August 2012.

Statistisches Bundesamt (2012a) Strafvollzug: Demographische und Kriminologische Merkmale der Strafgefangenen zum Stichtag 31.3.2011 www.destatis.de, (home page), date accessed 26 August 2012.

Statistisches Bundesamt (2011) Fachserie 10, Reihe 4.1, Demographische und kriminologische Merkmale der Strafgefangenen zum Stichtag 31.3.2011, www. destatis.de, (home page), date accessed 26 August 2012.

Statistisches Bundesamt (2011a) Strafvollzugsstatistik. Im psychiatrischen Krankenhaus und in der Entziehungsanstalt aufgrund strafrichterlicher Anordnung Untergebrachte (Maßregelvollzug), 2010/2011 (Stand: 31.10.2011), www.destatis.de, (home page), date accessed 26 August 2012.

B. Steiner, L. F. Travis and M. B. Makarios (2011) 'Understanding Parole Officers Responses to Sanctioning Reform', *Crime & Delinquency*, 57: 222–46.

G. Stolpmann (2010) 'Psychiatrische Maßregelbehandlungin', *Aus Politik und Zeitgeschichte*, 7: 28–33.

H. Stöver (2010) 'Drogenkonsum und Infektionskrankheuten: Grundsätzliche Herausforderungen für Gesundheit in Gefängnissen', in H Bögemann, K Keppler and H. Stöver (eds), *Gesundheit im Gefängnis: Ansätze und Erfahrungen mit Gesundheitsförderung in totalen Institutionen* (Weinheim: Juventa) 85–102.

H. Stöver (2010a) 'Gesundheitsversorgung und Gesundheitsförderung im Gefängnis', in H *Bögemann, K. Keppler* and H. Stöver (eds), *Gesundheit im Gefängnis: Ansätze und Erfahrungen mit Gesundheitsförderung in totalen Institutionen* (Weinheim: Juventa) 11–32.

F. Streng (2000) 'Entwicklung neuer Sanktionsformen in Deutschland', in J.-M. Jehle (ed.), *Täterbehandlung und neue Sanktionsformen* (Mönchengladbach: Forum) 207–34.

P. Walkenhorst (2010) 'Jugendstrafvollzug', *Aus Politik und Zeitgeschichte*, 7: 22–8.

J. Walter (2010) 'Minoritäten im Strafvollzug', *Aus Politik und Zeitgeschichte*, 7: 40–6.

M. Walter (2001) *Jugendkriminalität*, 2nd edn (Stuttgart: Boorberg).

M. Walter and S. Trautmann (2003) 'Kriminalität Junger Migranten – Strafrecht und Gesellschaftlichen (Des-)Integration', in J. Mansel and J. Raithel (eds), *Dies Kriminalität und Gewalt im Jugendalter* (Weinheim: Juventa) 64–86.

F. H. Weyel (2008) 'Geschichte und Wandel des Erziehungsgedankens', *Zeitschrift für Jugendkriminalrecht und Jugendhilfe*, 19: 132–36.

C. Wichmann (2012): 'Sozial- und Kriminalpolitik und die Praxis der Freien Straffälligenhilfe', *Kriminologisches Journal*, 44: 49–64.

N. Wilmers, D. Enzmann, D. Schaefer, K. Herbers, W. Greve and P. Wetzels (2002) *Jugendliche in Deutschland zur Jahrtausendwende: Gefährlich Oder Gefährdet?* (Baden-Baden: Nomos).

J. A. Winterdyk (2002) 'Introduction', in J. A. Winterdyk (ed.), *Juvenile Justice Systems. International Perspectives*, 2nd edn (Toronto: Canadian Scholar's Press) XI–XL.

P. Wikitzki (2000) 'Neue Kriminalpolitische Akzente in Deutschland', in J.-M. Jehle (ed.), *Täterbehandlung und neue Sanktionsformen* (Mönchengladbach: Forum) 447–54.

J. Zolondek (2005) *Rechtliche Rahmenbedingungen des Frauenstrafvollzugs in Europa Internationale Studie zum Frauenstrafvollzug Bestandsaufnahme, Bedarfsanalyse und „best practice"* (Reader of Greifswald University) 12–18.

8
The Russian Penal System

Laura Piacentini

Introduction

In 2012, criminal justice, sentencing, political governance, activism, punk music and free speech all met and meshed to create a veritable avalanche of debate and discord about Russia's political culture and its criminal justice system. Events since March 2012 have dominated world headlines on an unprecedented scale, not seen since the collapse of the Soviet Union in 1991. The sentencing of three young women, two of them mothers, from the Russian feminist punk collective Pussy Riot to two years imprisonment each for hooliganism by a Moscow court on 17 August 2012 attracted, and continues to attract, considerable political, public and international criticism. Angry at what Pussy Riot perceive as government policies that discriminate against women and the increasing restrictions over free speech and a free press in Russia under the recently re-elected President Vladimir Putin, the Pussy Riot collective held the kinds of unsanctioned concerts and spontaneous protests that are more familiar to Western 'Riot Grrrl'[1] bands. The detention of the female performance artists has raised numerous questions about Russia's direction of political travel, with some commentators mocking Putin, in cartoons and in discourse in an often critical and outraged global media, as the chief architect of a return to Russia's past. What happens to 'women like them' has been the subject of much internal debate, with commentators calling for them to receive 'a good slap'. Inside Russia the discourse tends to train attention not on judicial overreach – or on Pussy Riot's claims to be the New Soviet Dissidents – but on the acceptable limits of badly behaved women. Media images of Putin supporters and anti-Pussy Riot campaigners pitching up at court, show Russia in a slightly ugly light – a place where church and state are not odd bedfellows but together in their universal, hysterical indigna-tion at abnormal deviancy 'against all things innately Russian'. Yet, in the West the response is markedly different.

As gender equality and the rights of ethnic minorities and gays remain marginalised, the appeal of Pussy Riot is hugely seductive in the West. They have, in a sense, become pop-stars whose incarceration leaves many in the West dumbfounded at the trajectory Russian political culture has taken. Has Russia now swung fully to the right – or to the extreme Soviet left? Whatever the direction, the view from the West is not shared inside Russia, where it is felt that young women in Russia have become *too* westernised – an irony if it is considered that Russia is a country where 'Westernisation' has produced a dangerous and corrupt Oligarch culture, with close connections to the political leadership. However, it is the unfolding internal debate about womanhood, western influences, crime and incarceration in a post-Soviet Russia, which is now as close as it has ever been to 'The West', that is fascinating. The notion of general deterrence in punishment was taken to the extreme during Soviet Russia and this case – if we can draw anything meaningfully criminological from it – reveals to us exactly how far down that path of penal, criminal justice and political reform Russia has travelled – or not as this case seems to suggest. How do they fit together: the jailed artists and the unmovable, orthodox president? What is the temperature of political reform (away from the corridors of power in Europe), and what next for the judicial fairness, rule of law and due process that Russia fought so hard to activate in the early 1990s?

Over the last 15 years, Russia has experienced legislative and penal reform, and a genuine political and social commitment to 'ending the Gulag'. Yet, opportunities for modernisation and a conceptual and mean-ingful re-mapping of penal ideology have come to very little, due largely to the often-reported swing toward more centralised political govern-ance under the newly-reappointed President Vladimir Putin (McAuley and Macdonald 2007). We see this with the various Directors of the Prison Service who were leading penal reform debates, only to find their time in office coming to a speedy end – sometimes too speedily for us to fully comprehend the reasons. For it has to be said that Russia's prison system is not a 'European penal system' in any conventional sense of the term. Where commonalties do exist, they are found in the universal legal commitments that tie Russia to a European project of human rights (Van Zyl Smit 2006). Further areas of commonality between the Russian jurisdiction and her European neighbours can be found in the rapid rise in heavier sentences over the last 15 years and, much more importantly, in the extension of prison as a measure of incapacitation for resolving the crippling welfare system (Pallot and Piacentini 2012).

The penal system in Russia is like none other in the entire world. Human rights disasters in prisons have scarred the Russian people and the country. In its sheer scale, its geographical shape, its landscape domination, brutalising history and the culture of punishment and politics that came together to create what can only be described as a vast penal turbine, it is unique. This uniqueness has led only a few scholars, including myself, to enter its uncharted waters – its heart of darkness, to reach its peripheral locations in an effort to expand criminological and sociological knowledge about how Russia has come to terms with its penal archipelago past, and expand its range of alternatives to Soviet penal philosophy, which 'officially' ended in 1991.

In this chapter, I map out some of the key trends in imprisonment in Russia since 1991 and I highlight how the penal system (including staff, prisoners and also modes of punishment) has changed – or otherwise, in light of the Europeanisation project that marked the 1990s and early noughties (see Piacentini 2004). I make the point that it is Russia's penal history, and arising from that, its penal geography, that marks it out from other penal systems. It was only in 2010 that the last piece of the 'Gulag jigsaw' was dismantled from the post-Soviet penal ideological monolith. It must be noted from the outset that gaining reliable and valid data on prisoners and prison operations in Russia is fraught with difficulties, as the country often does not report to World Prison Population lists, and human rights monitors often report a failure by justice officials to respond to their visits.[2] The picture of the penal system provided in this chapter, therefore, insofar as it is possible, will use the best data that is obtainable.

Key penal reform 'occasions'

On 14 October, 2010, a *concept paper* called 'The Concept Document' became a government decree in Russia (decree no. 1772-r, "On a Concept for the Development of the Criminal Correctional System of the Russian Federation to 2010"). In it some of the most thorough and far-reaching reforms of the correctional penal system were outlined: a cessation of the correctional labour colony structure, a modelling of prisons on a graded scale from maximum to minimum security prisons and, importantly, cellular confinement – not unlike the style and type found in many Western and North-European prisons. (Though it must be added that cellular confinement is reserved for very serious offenders, with less serious offenders continuing to be held in the large dormitory detachment blocks.) The reforms also included maximum use of surveillance technology, the introduction of probation across the country, an expansion of the range of non-custodial sentences, and greater emphasis on rehabilitation of offenders in the community. We have been here before – reforms in developing a probation service, re-integration projects, educational work, and alternatives to incarceration have been on the penal reform agenda for over 20 years (King and Piacentini 2005).

However, the latest round of reform planning is distinctive in one core area – it deals with Russia's painful penal past. Russia's Justice Minister, Alexander Konovalov, stated publicly on Norwegian television that it was time for Russia to get rid of Gulag sensibilities and the Stalinist heritage that marks the country's contemporary penal estate (see *Dagsnytt* [Daily News], 29 January, 2010; *http://www.nrk.no/nett-tv/indeks/199403/) (*Pallot and Piacentini 2012). The Minister is here referring to the combat and criminal gangs who are trying to control other sub-criminal groups – such as the 'thieves in law' (the *vory)* – and who have thrived since the Gulag era. The gangs, as the concept paper notes, thrive because of the conditions of communalism encouraged by the cramped penal architecture that favours not individualism but collectivism in the penal colonies – as a result, many prison officers, the paper reports, are overworked and experience regular violent attacks (page 5). The entire structure of the penal system, therefore, must be changed (page 6). Thus, the reforms were to include, for the first time, a geographical re-structuring of prison facilities in order to 'optimize the distribution of places of incarceration over the country' (Kontseptsiya 2009: 8). I will touch on Russia's distinctive penal geography further on in the chapter, but firstly I would like to go back to 1991 and outline some of the key penal reform moments, or 'occasions' as I have referred to them elsewhere due to their highly fluid, contingent and fleeting nature (Piacentini 2004, 2008). It is my intention here to provide readers with a visual picture, of what Russian prisons look like, as well as a narrative account of how the Russian penal enigma came out of the cold and engaged with Western penal sensibilities.

When the Soviet Union collapsed in 1991, human rights campaigners, former dissidents, political reformers and academics working on criminal justice began to ask searching questions on exactly how the collapse of the USSR would affect the penal system. Its population, in 1991, was sitting at over one million prisoners – held in all places of confinement, including remand prisons – or around 750 prisoners per 100,000 of the population, (Bowring 1997, 2009; Piacentini 2004; King and Piacentini 2005; Van Syl Smit 2006; Piacentini 2008; Pallot and Piacentini 2012).

A heavily militarised penal culture, widespread and common abuse of prisoners and an absence of both the rule of law and 'natural justice' were just some of many alarming hallmarks of Russia's penal system (Piacentini 2004). Violence, illness, internal rioting, and arbitrary treatment by guards were all the more inevitable, due to a legal system that lacked procedural or judicial fairness, a police and prison service that routinely abused detainees and prisoners and a political culture that ruled with an iron fist, dispensing penal punishment as a default response to the socio-economic crisis (Piacentini 2005; Applebaum 2003).

Massive overcrowding in the Sizo remand prisons produced some of the most enduring images of Russian penal reform. Prison cells in Butyrka prison in Moscow designed for 20 were holding 60 plus prisoners. Staff rarely entered these squalid rooms, and with less than one square metre of space for each prisoner, weaker (physically and mentally) prisoners became vulnerable to the internal orders of cell bosses (*blatniye)* and the *thieves in law* culture (*vory-v-zakone*). Cells that in England and Wales would be intended for 3, held 13 prisoners. By the mid-1990's, conditions in penal colonies were marginally better but dilapidated fencing, subsidence of internal walls, peeling paint with rusting wire and steel panels, guard dogs and unmanned wooden watch towers featured everywhere. And HIV, AIDS, and TB had now joined the penal system (King and Piacentini 2005).

The process of reform to address these problems began in the 1990s and has continued ever since. Among the 32 significant landmarks was the transfer to the prison system of a justice framework, in 1998, to reflect European penal and legal norms and practice (Pallot and Piacentini 2012). Russia's accession into the Council of Europe in 1996 brought in its train 2,000 legislative amendments and acts, including laws on the Status of Judges, the agencies of the Judicial Community, State Forensic Activity, the Work of Defence Lawyers and the Bar, Freedom of Conscience and Religious Association, and proportionate sentencing. More spaces were provided in remand prisons to accompany the new criminal procedure code of 2002, and federal funding increased alongside considerable efforts to combat the problems of disease, squalor, and human rights abuses. Meanwhile, prison officer salaries were doubled in the early 2000s, and housing and a network of health and holiday spas were provided for staff. There was a concerted attempt to get a 'new message' across to penal staff and to Russian society: that in this widely scattered prison system, major investment in changing penal sensibilities would follow changes to infrastructure (ibid.). But, despite all the changes described above, powerful interests and institutional inertia continued to maintain Soviet models of penal management and norms in Russia. It used to be said of the Soviet Union that the clearest evidence that reform efforts were being frustrated was the frequency with which successive rounds of reform were announced. The past 20 years have witnessed a profusion of new regulations, laws, and 'concepts'. The latest is the one that was mentioned earlier in the chapter, which is 'finally' going to eliminate the vestiges of the gulag – it is claimed.[3]

Types of regime and imprisonment rates

On the eve of the collapse of the USSR, there were between 1.3 and 1.6 million prisoners in various penal institutions, the majority in the Russian Republic. An immediate task associated with the creation of 15 independent states was the repatriation of prisoners to their relevant sovereign states, a process which took place during the early 1990s. The prison population in the newly created Russian Federation hovered around 750,000 in the early 1990s, with an incarceration rate (number of prisoners per 100,000 population) of under 500; but thereafter the numbers began to rise, exceeding 1,000,000 in 1996 to 1997, when, albeit for a brief period, Russia became the country with the highest rate of imprisonment in the world. Numbers fluctuated thereafter, but the overall trend has been downwards – to 568 per 100,000 in 2008–2011. Currently the Russian Federation stands third in the world in terms of its incarceration rate, behind the USA and Rwanda.

The structure of the penal system descends directly from the Gulag system, but with modification in key areas – namely, the dropping of the 'labour colony' from the title of each colony, which came into force in 1993. Table 8.1 outlines the penal institutions in which these prisoners are held. They are administered by FSIN and its territorial branches – or UFSINs (*upravleniia federal'noi sluzhbi ispolneniia nakazanii*), one for each subject (*oblast* or republic) of the Federation (see Pallot and Piacentini 2012). Alongside the network, clusters of regimes belonging to UFSIN are the local, smaller jails managed by the Ministry of Internal Affairs (MVD) and administered by local militia (Russian police); people can be held here before they are transferred to the FSIN system. Under new proposals and, specifically, the concept paper, these institutions will be given enhanced roles to detain persons who receive short sentences, which is an interesting development as it will lead to more persons being held in their place of domicile. This could affect women and juvenile offenders quite significantly who, because of Russia's exceptional penal geography, are sent to disproportionally further regions to serve sentences.

Table 8.1   Types of penal facilities in Russia

Abbreviation	Full name	Number in April 2009
Sizo	*Sledstvennii Izoliator* Investigative isolator for people awaiting trial	225
VK	*Vospitatel'nie Kolonii* Educational colonies for juvenile offenders (now being re-named 'educational centres' vospitatel'nie tsentri)	62 (of which 3 for girls)
IK758	*Ispravitel'nie Kolonii* (Correctional colonies for adult offenders) comprising: *Obshchii rezhim* (Standard regime) Minimum security colony for adult men and women *Strogii rezhim* (Strict regime) Medium to maximum security colony for men, including first-time offenders convicted of particularly grave crimes, and repeat offenders who have previously served prison sentences. *Osobii rezhim* (Special regime) Maximum security colony for male offenders convicted of particularly dangerous repeat crimes, or who have been sentenced to life KP	758
KP	*Kolonii-Poseleniia* 'Colony-settlements', for male and female offenders given custodial sentences for minor offences, and other offenders nearing the end of their sentence	138
Tiur'ma	*Tiur'ma* Prison: a maximum security facility for men with cellular or galleried accommodation	7
LIU	*Lechebnie Ispravitel'nie Uchrezhdeniia* 'Medical isolation colony' for male prisoners with tuberculosis and other infectious diseases or requiring treatment for drug addiction	68

Source: See Pallot and Piacentini (2012).

According to a basic classification, there are remand prisons (pre-trial facilities) and correctional facilities for convicted prisoners. These latter are divided according to the severity of regime and there are, in addition, specialist facilities for prisoners suffering from TB and other infectious diseases, foreigners from 'far abroad' (that is, not including people from the former Soviet republics), juveniles, and former members of the security services. The official classification of penal institutions, in fact, masks a much 'messier' picture in which different categories of offender are held together in the same facility.

In men's correctional colonies there can also be a variety of prisoners of different categories – as is the case in all women's colonies, in which prisoners are not differentiated (Pallot and Piacentini 2012). Each of the different types of penal facility described in the table has its own geography. Typically, pre-trial facilities are located in the metropolitan centres, and are found in every *oblast* and republic. Most regions also have at least one standard regime colony for men, although this does not imply that there is sufficient capacity to accommodate local 'demand'. The distribution of facilities catering for juveniles, TB or AIDS sufferers, and other specialist categories is less even between Russia's regions. When these specialist facilities are taken together with the more ubiquitous standard regime colonies, the pattern of geographical distribution that emerges can be described as one of 'dispersed concentration', with particular places in the peripheries accommodating clusters of facilities.

Russia's prison population since 1991 is shown in Table 8.2. Of note is the fact that, in the immediate aftermath of the collapse of the USSR, the Russian prison population was not as high as some commentators had expected (Piacentini 2004; King and Piacentini 2005) – sitting at around 500 per 100,000. However, numbers did rise to the million mark in 1996–1997, when Russia had the highest prison population in the world, with 730 prisoners per 100,000 (Moran et al.. 2011). Russia, China and the USA now dominate world prison population figures with a collective total prison population of eight million (Walmsley 2009).

Of key note is the significant reduction of juvenile offenders sentenced to a period of confinement, which has nearly halved between 2005 and 2009. The sentencing of women to a period of custody has increased by over 20,000.

Table 8.2 Russia's prison population 1993–2009

Year	Total prison population	Of which are women	Of which are juveniles
01.04.09	889, 948	69,200	7,700
01.11.08	891, 700	68,200	8,800
01.12.07	888,200	64,100	10,700
01.03.07	883,500	61,500	12,500
01.12.06	874,200	59,800	13,100
01.04.06	847,000	55,400	14,600
01.02.06	828,900	52,900	14,700
01.12.05	819,100	51,600	14,700
01.07.05	797,400	48,600	14,500
01.01.04[4]	763,115	–	–
01.10.03	820,000	–	–
01.07.03	866,600	39,600	14,000
01.01.03	877,000	50,000	–
2003[5]	847,000	39,500	16,500
2002	877,393	40,800	11,000
2001	980,151	47,700	18,700
2000	925,072	39,700	17,200
1995	1,017,900	32,400	20,800
1993	772,000	–	–

Source: Data gathered from a variety of sources and websites of the Russian Penal Service (www.fsin.ru) and the Moscow Centre for Prison Reform (MCPR: www.prison.org). See King and Piacentini (2005) and Moran et al. (2011).

Alternatives to custody and post-custodial measures

There is a paucity of research into non-custodial punishments in the Russian Federation, most probably because the use of alternatives is, at best, patchy and remains very much a commitment on paper. The latest 'concept paper' provides the most detailed discussion of alternatives to date. These alternatives include greater use of open prisons, day release, half-way houses, and the formation of prison work brigades for community projects. Many of these changes are predicated on the participation of local communities in overcoming fellow citizens' offending behaviours. But present arrangements of penal zones hidden away in rural Russia are not well-suited to these proposals (Pallot and Piacentini 2012), and with the Russian Orthodox Church increasing and intensifying its penal reach inside the system, prisoners engagement with civil society groups is limited to religious groups.

Russia operates a continental law system, has a Criminal Code and a Code of Criminal Procedure. Despite several redrafts over the 1990s (King and Piacentini 2005), the Codes today still classify many minor actions (such as theft) as 'serious' or 'very serious' offences, although it must be added that the new 'concept paper' seeks to reform the classification of crimes and sentencing. Increasingly it is the case that repeat offences or group offences carry heavy penalties. This is largely due to the practice of sentencing all offenders as adults, which therefore means that children are hit the hardest because the codes are designed with adults in mind (McAuley and Macdonald 2007). Secondly, compulsory detention is often the only choice – there is no probation service in Russia and no national embedded criminal justice social work system that seeks to divert offenders away from imprisonment. As a result, judges – despite showing responsiveness toward educational measures – are inclined toward policing and prosecutorial practices (Pallot and Piacentini 2012). More concerning is that the Russian police, unlike their European counterparts, have no powers to monitor offenders in the community because electronic tagging, fines and community service are issued by judges, still, in a hesitant and arbitrary way. Juvenile courts are starting to appear here and there in Russia but, to quote McAuley (2009, the future looks bleak:

> The introduction of juvenile courts has headed the agenda for the past ten years, and a draft even passed a first reading in the Duma in 2002. Yet the federal authorities, the Supreme Court, and the Prosecutor General's Office have dragged their feet, and now the Orthodox Church is arguing that juvenile justice is an alien concept, promoted by foreign money, aimed at undermining Russian morality, the Russian family, and Russian society. Duma politicians seem poorly informed, and unenthusiastic. Medvedev could move the agenda forward, but is it worth his while to take on the conservative and entrenched justice ministries and legal establishment? McAuley (2010)

Spotlight on women prisoners

Pallot, Piacentini and Moran conducted the first major, multi-disciplinary project into women prisoners in Russia funded by the UK's Economic and Social Research Council. Their findings, published in Pallot and Piacentini (2012), are startling for showing the extremities that operate in Russia's penal service. On the one hand, the Gulag 'metaphor' exists still as a concept (nostalgia in peripheral regions for Soviet practices) and as a practice (banishment and exile) to create a unique carceral geography. On the other hand, there continues to be openness to 'Western' penal thinking and policy. In the project just mentioned the research team, time and again, came across prison officials, prison colony governors and senior staff allied to the professions of social work and psychology who endorsed alternatives to custody and post-custodial measures that reduced re-offending and returned prisoners to their families and communities. It is also true to say that Russian prisoners *are* prepared for release. In many respects, preparation for release is similar in Russian colonies to what happens in most jurisdictions, where a balance is sought between creating employment opportunities and personal development, and contact with families is taken as an essential part of rehabilitation toward home. However, many prisoners, women in particular, are denied – through distance – regular contact with relatives and friends on the outside. Many women's colonies, and some colonies for men, have what can be loosely called 'Schools of Freedom', which are attached to the colonies but operate as half-way houses. Here, prisoners learn domestic skills such as cooking and 'looking after the home', which they add to other work-related skills wherever it is possible to acquire these. But, again, the picture is very patchy – there is no national standard or directive providing for these in every institution. It is, indeed, often the case that donor money from NGO civil society partnerships is used to build and maintain these centres.

In Russian women's prisons, where we have the most conclusive and in-depth data, behavioural change is, indeed, a goal – but it is secondary to targeting a woman's emotions and her psychological attitudes about being a woman, a mother, and a wife. In various ways, therapy and basic psychological analysis, coupled with semi-compulsory cultural interventions, such as pageants and amateur dramatic shows, occupy the centre ground of re-socialisation doctrine and are the focus of women offenders' rehabilitation.

Any discussion of alternatives to custody in Russia cannot be divorced from understanding the importance of how a woman or a juvenile responds to the unique penal geography of the country. The majority of the respondents presented in Pallot and Piacentini (2012) were intending to return to their original place of domicile and, the researchers found, had intended to find a job or enrol to study, live a 'normal life' free of crime, and devote themselves to the triad of home, family, children (*dom, sem'ia, rebenek*). However, upon re-entry they are vulnerable to becoming stuck in a perpetual liminal state because the quality of their life, at the final stage of re-integration, is stamped by the formative experience of incarceration. This is especially the case for those women who remain in the areas where the prisons are located and who do not make it back to their former place of domicile, through either desire, or absence of documentation, or lack of somewhere to go. Such women become frozen in a perpetual state of geographical inertia and pain, because punishment has disconnected them from their previous self, family, and kin. Todd Clear's (2009) observation, made in relation to the American penal system, is particularly apposite for Russia: that incarceration punches deep holes in women's networks. This is the case, too, for some male offenders who have committed more serious crimes and who are sentenced to penal colonies in peripheral locations.

The most recent research conducted into Russian imprisonment reveals poor relationships between prisoners and staff, serious deficiencies in medical care, ineffective social work due to small numbers of relevantly trained personnel in badly overcrowded colonies, a 'rehabilitation' effort that is confined to a few lectures, and narrowly focused skills training, which, in the case of women, focus on psychological 'emotion therapy' and cultural activities. These are delivered in a way that reinforce traditional gender stereotypes and create an image for post-prison life of motherhood, home, and wifely rule at odds with what awaits prisoners when they are released (Pallot and Piacentini 2012). On the contrary, a pessimistic view of Russian imprisonment is a well-founded view (see Bowring 2009).

Recent attempts at introducing non-custodial measures

In 2007 a team of UK-based probation scholars and academics conducted an evaluation – funded by a European Aid grant – into establishing, and embedding, a genuinely meaningful and culturally-specific alternative to Russia's imprisonment regime.[6] There have been no studies conducted since that date into alternatives, but if this study is considered alongside the prison research conducted by Pallot, Piacentini and Moran (2006–2010) some interesting observations and findings emerge on Russian criminal justice in the second decade of the new millennium.

The evaluation into alternatives is particularly interesting because it aimed at determining the effectiveness and viability of electronic monitoring and supervision orders for offenders in the community. The Minister for Justice himself, judges, prosecutors, representatives from law-related groups, NGOs and the prison service's (FSIN) senior administrative and managerial staff were targeted to assess the extent to which a culture-shift could take place in terms of delivering non-custodial sentences. The researchers were able to launch a meaningful societal debate about the potential for penal change, making new penal choices and establishing better support frameworks for alternatives across the country, and – because NGOs and other civil society groups were a core element of the evaluation – the debates, particularly on the harmful effects of imprisonment, were able to reach many sections of the Russian media.

There were specific operational challenges to overcome, including: changes in the leadership at the top of FSIN at the time when the project began and significant, 'embarrassing' internal delays in getting electronic monitoring pilots up and running, identifying key Russian experts in the field, and populating a steering group with a diverse range of partners from both inside Russia and the EC Delegation. However, a more significant challenge was finding some convergence with European-style probation services at a time when diplomatic relations between Russia and the West had deteriorated (King and Piacentini 2005; Pallot and Piacentini 2012). The Director of the Russian prison service, General Reimar, stated on record, and publicly, that the leadership of FSIN must work to sustain new policy directions toward using imprisonment less and alternatives to imprisonment more. This led to the implementation of a Department of Alternative Sanctions in FSIN; it has already made some significant progress in training up staff to deliver European-style offender rehabilitation services, rather than 'passive offender monitoring'. With new ways of thinking about punishment and rehabilitation, coupled with new legislation passed in 2009, the policy debates are leading to some positive changes and achievements in practice.

Further post-custodial measures – including anger-management programmes – rolled out across all prisons and were implemented through NGO groups. Offender behaviour programmes and workshops aimed at Cognitive Behavioural Therapy are completely new for Russian criminal justice practitioners, who are seeking to comprehend how they have embraced the notion that prison 'corrects', 'treats' and 'cures'. Post-custodial policies provide services for prisoners with drug problems, employment programmes and training workshops, which run alongside motivational workshops. There have been numerous events aimed at bringing together senior Russian figures in the criminal justice system with European counterparts to build a momentum toward European convergence (Piacentini 2004; King and Piacentini 2005). Progress has been slow, and whilst great interest was shown in the 1990s and early noughties toward European principles and practices, the shift toward a more authoritarian orthodoxy – under the outgoing President Medvedev and the recently re-elected Putin – should give scholars and specialists in the region some cause for concern. Nevertheless, the current Director of the Prison Service has made consistent and un-contested (internally at least) statements in support of a European-style probation service, and with a number of regional capitals implementing the new directives under the Department for Alternative Sanctions the hoped-for 'end to the Gulag' might just be happening, albeit slowly.

Turning our attention toward the implementation of alternatives, the most recent 2007 evaluation – outlined above – explains how delays of nearly two years, which had a negative effect on getting programmes off the ground, may also have damaged the momentum to deliver a more European-style probation service.[7] The evaluation cites difficulty in accounting for delays and premature announcements of success happening at the same time. The Russian Parliament did, in 2009, pass legislation to authorise electronic monitoring of offenders, but only one modest experiment was conducted – in Voronezh. Unfortunately, this was curtailed by the severe limitations to what can be achieved imposed by Russia's outdated – and very outmoded – criminal justice infrastructure. It must also be noted that 'big brother' technologies, both inside and outside jails, are thin on the ground, with the Russian penal practice of Soviet-style watch towers and guards very much the modus operandi of surveillance and security, inside and immediately beyond the perimeter fences.[8]

The socio-economic context of crime and punishment in Russia

In the immediate post-Soviet years, the economic situation in Russia declined sharply, with a total collapse of the Russian economy in 1998. Crime became, and continues to be, a significant problem with racially motivated violence increasing alongside theft,[9] vandalism, robbery, physical and sexual assault, and murder. Although Russia is a multi-ethnic society, according to the 2002 census, 79.8 per cent of the Russian population describe themselves as Ethnic Russians (UNHCR 2009). Human rights organisations, media sources and the United Nations Committee for the Elimination of Racial Discrimination (UNCERD) report increased racial discrimination, xenophobia, and racially motivated violence against ethnic minorities. According to the Moscow-based NGO, SOVA, 'anyone with non-Slavic features may be assaulted by racists in Russia' (SOVA, quoted in the UNHCR 2009).[10] According to the Moscow Bureau of Human Rights, which monitors hate crimes, racist violence and racist murders increased significantly between 2004 and 2008, with 113 deaths and 334 injuries resulting from hate crime reported over just nine months (between January and October 2008) (UNHCR 2009).

Racist violence, discrimination, social and economic marginalisation of women and children have all increased exponentially in Russia since the collapse of the USSR. As mentioned earlier, in the early post-Soviet years, the country was in the grip of chaos, political uncertainty, exposés of corruption at the highest levels of office and a complete absence of the rule of law. Procedural fairness and judicial rights for offenders, and all those detained in the criminal justice system, were routinely violated. As the new Russia was signing up – with rapacious speed – to commitments toward penal and judicial reform, it was simultaneously engaging in a firestorm of aggressive military action that created a military quagmire among its satellites in Eurasia and to the East. Like two tectonic plates angrily rubbing against each other, the invasions of the Caucasus were pursued with a hyper-nationalist political discourse, vengefully and aggressively – alongside the implantation of progressive, articulate reformers in the corridors of power in the European Union. The veritable tsunami that one would expect to happen following the dismantling of the Soviet criminal justice and legal infra-structure proceeded instead as a form of political and cultural turbulence that was slower and more piecemeal. This was, after all, Russia, an enigmatic nation well used to terror, autocrats, and fluctuating nationalist tendencies from the extreme to the benign. Russia's unique geographical positioning straddling Europe and Asia, but in a unique blend of its own, was played out in the penal sphere in an almost perfect storm.

Since the first invasion of Chechnya, under Yel'tsin in 1994, the deteriorating security and fragile political settlements in the North Caucasus have led to acute identity loss and, at best, a weak process of assimilation of smaller minorities into the Russian North, Siberia, the Far East and the North Caucasus. The United Nations Development Programme's Russia Representative said in 2009 'unresolved issues, including migratory imbalance, cultural and social integration and cohesion, competition at labour markets and labour outflows' (Vyshnevsky and Bobylev 2008),[11] have created acute imbalances in the cultural, social and economic sphere, heightening marginalisation, poverty and unemployment. Migration is increasingly politicised, with Russia looking increasingly a deeply divided society. With government attempts to downgrade administrative entitlements for some of the smaller ethnic minority groups – thus creating a cultural vacuum and a resurgence of Soviet-style nationalism – under the current re-elected President, Vladimir Putin (see UNHCR 2009), we are seeing signs of a police state, with daily harassment of minorities, disproportionate identity checks, unlawful detention and physical abuse (see UNHCR 2009). There are four to nine million migrant workers in Russia and over 80 per cent come from the former USSR (UNHCR 2009). Just under half of all migrants work in construction, and human rights organisations have catalogued detailed cases of daily abuse, denial of contracts, confiscation of passports and unsafe working conditions. Legislation has been passed to improve the working rights of migrants in Russia but there is much room for improvement.

The post-Soviet Russian government has had a very patchy track record in implementing both safeguards and opportunities that target women's needs – their professional lives, their home lives and their cultural status. Officially, Russia remains committed to expanding opportunities for women in the social and economic spheres and in the labour market. In a UN concept paper, *National Human Development Report Russian Federation 2008 Russia Facing Demographic Challenges*,[12] the demographic challenges facing the Russian Federation are explicitly stated as three-fold: dealing with declining birth rates, poverty and ageing. According to the report:

> Regrettably, life expectancy indicators pull down Russian HDI [Human Development Index]. Russia has been grappling for some time with demographic developments, which must be qualified as a crisis. Short life expectancy is the main feature of this crisis, though by no means its only feature. The birth rate is too low, the population is shrinking and ageing, and Russia is on the threshold of rapid loss of able-bodied population, which will be accompanied by a growing demographic burden per able-bodied individual.[13]

Among the basic goals of this report is the future development of a system of providing benefits in connection with childbirth and childrearing and also creating mechanisms of supplementary support for families of various kinds – single-parent, multi-child, families providing education for children who have been left without a guardian, and those having disabled children. Among the other goals: creating conditions for improving access to housing, developing mortgage credits, assisting in providing employment, creating favourable conditions for carrying out family and professional responsibilities, the creation of a system of advanced training and retraining for new professions for women who are returning from maternity leave, and expanding flexible patterns of employment (UNHCR 2009).[14] As is the case in most countries, women and children feature significantly in official data on poverty. In Russia, there is a high level of poverty among citizens of working age and this can be explained essentially by the low level of pay in various areas and the multi-month delays in paying out state pensions that marked the entire 1990s period. According to the most recent figures, around 30 per cent of poor people are made up of families where all working-age persons have regularly worked in agriculture, trade, and the financial sector. Women with children are more often faced with the problem of poverty than women without children (UNHCR 2009). In Russia, among women aged 31–54, 21 per cent are from an underprivileged population, while for men aged 31–59, it is 18.9 per cent. A special risk group is made up of young families, since the birth of a child significantly lowers their standard of living.

The effect of these social and economic issues on crime and punishment in Russia has not been well documented (Piacentini 2004) as there is an acute paucity of research in the area. However, key points of note are that the prison system has been creaking under the immense weight of the penal past and because of acute shortfalls in funding and reform. For over 20 years, Russia has re-structured its judicial system to ensure defendants' rights are safe-guarded, human rights law is followed and good governance trickled down from the legislation through to sentencing practices. But the penal system itself has remained virtually unchanged, particularly its architecture and the cultural characteristics of staff. The picture we have of crime and punishment in Russia is fragmented and often contradictory, with official crime statistics subject to varied interpretation and gaps in data gathering.

Focusing attention on youth justice and criminalisation, as McAuley (2009: 43) notes:

Russia looked different [to other European countries] in the early 1990s (when it experienced a rapid increase in offending behaviour (both crimes and administrative offences) by children under the age of 18; by 1997 the figures were stabilizing but the financial crisis of 1998/9 brought another upsurge; since 2000 the figures have flattened out again to bring Russia in line with other countries.

McAuley adds:

In Russia the number of violent crimes has risen significantly since 1997 and continues to rise, although at a slower rate. The homicide figures are high (higher than in Europe, if not in the USA). In this respect, and not only in this, Russian youth seems to be behaving as its counterparts in many other countries....As a percentage of all convictions violent crimes remain very small. The percentage increases over the period – from 6 to 12 per cent – but this should be seen in context: the total number of criminal convictions is less than it was in the mid-1990s. Theft, everywhere the key to youth crime, has fallen sharply and, very recently, hooliganism has been reclassified in such a way as to take many activities out of the criminal code. Hence the percentage of violent crime will surely rise, regardless of actual numbers. (ibid.: 53)

McAuley's findings are drawn from government statistics and, as the author has also noted, should therefore be treated with some caution.[15] It is also worth noting that, in what has been described as 'the lost generation', Russia has now been ranked by the World Health Organisation as having the highest youth crime rate in the world. Stabbings account for almost half of the homicides carried out by youngsters in the European and Central Asian region. The WHO puts Russia top of the table, with the highest rate of violence among the surveyed age group of ten to 29-year-olds. Children and young people, it is argued in a United Nations Children's Fund Report, are at unprecedented risk of abuse, poverty, alcohol- and drug-related violence in the home.

The economic backdrop to the extraordinary shifts in crime in Russia is marked by the crisis of the rouble – throughout the 1990s and early noughties – that led to significant and rapid increases in poverty and homelessness. The consequences included family breakdown, rises in alcoholism (and other poverty related illnesses), the hardening of organised crime – and *mafiya*-related activity that permeated into mainstream politics, and ineffectiveness and corruption within the police, brought about by the chaos of perestroika and the transition from communism. Despite the acute economic and social upheaval (brought on by chaotic labour markets) experienced by Russians during the years immediately following the collapse of the USSR, the trends on *who* commits the majority of offences show remarkable similarities with Western Europe. The majority of crimes committed by young people in Russia are thefts (McAuley 2009). Yet Russian legislators have been slow to respond to the needs of young people and have employed adult, adversarial punishments on the young offending population. Young offenders – particularly female offenders – are, therefore, acutely more marginalised than adults (Piacentini et al. 2010).

Punishment in Russia: contrasting philosophies or synergised beliefs?

Since the collapse of the Soviet Union in 2001, human rights in imprisonment have been at the forefront of all judicial and penal reform processes in Russia – and remain so today. The 'long and complex relationship' (Bowring 2009: 259) between human rights and penal and legal reform can be explained, in part, by the complexity of the Russian Federation.

> The subjects [of the Russian Federation] are as follows. First, and most significant from the point of view of human rights, Russia has 21 ethnic republics, the successors of the "autonomous republics" of the USSR, named after their "titular" people, with their own presidents, constitutions, and, in many cases, constitutional courts. There has been no reduction in the number of ethnic republics, not least because of the potential strength of their resistance. Next, there are 9 enormous krais, a word often translated as "region", with their own appointed governors. In 2000 there were 6, with elected governors. The most numerous subjects of the Federation are the 46 oblasts, territorial formations inhabited primarily by ethnic Russians, also with governors. There were 49 oblasts in 2000. The 4 "autonomous okrugs" are also ethnic formations, and reflect a relative concentration of the indigenous peoples which give them their name. There were 10 of these in 2000, and the six which have disappeared have been "united" with larger neighbours, often in very controversial circumstances. For all their formal constitutional equality under the 1993 Constitution, they were for the most part located within other formations (krais and oblasts), with consequences which will be explored later in this chapter. There is a Jewish autonomous oblast, located in the Russian Far East. Finally, two "cities of federal significance", Moscow and St Petersburg, are also subjects of the federation. It is important to remember that of at least 150 nationalities in the Russian Federation, only 32 had their own territorial units 7 including the Chechens. This number has now shrunk. (Bowring 2009: 260)

To answer questions, therefore, about penal reform is to take a historical perspective on Russia's traditions, roots and multi-cultures. Human rights are not anathema to Russia's giant territories – despite Russia being a law-governed state and the extreme, grotesque and murderous violations of rights and of people that took place during the Stalin era. Indeed a culture did permeate, throughout the twentieth century, that human rights should be universal – just not necessarily an internal matter that might interfere with internal governance (see Bowring 2009). In Russia the complete legal overhaul that took place over the early post-Soviet years was, crucially, shaped by *European* norms, with the European Prison Rules (1987, 2006) framing intellectual debates between senior justice figures and the international law communities of Europe. Russia could no longer avoid submitting herself to international scrutiny and processes that sought to, amongst other things, abolish the death penalty (there was a moratorium in 1997).

Prisoners' rights in Russia have long been campaigned for and did not just surface as a serious international humanitarian matter once the USSR had collapsed (Al'pern 2004). What mattered in 1991 was that Russia – with breath-taking speed – engaged in a penal reform process that was unprecedented. Russia's commitment could be evidenced in its active encouragement to change conditions, standards and laws for the betterment of all those who fall under the care and custody of law and criminal justice. Observers, monitors and Rapporteurs were invited – welcomed even. Russia's penal codes discussed 'European standards' and human rights for the very first-time. The First Chechen War was in full swing in 1996, yet Russia accepted intervention, external legal rules, compulsory judgments and large payments of compensation. The celebrated doctrines of human rights from outside – from the West and from Europe – became enshrined in legal parables. Officials accepted wider briefs for inspections and welcomed international lawyers to feed into the process of reform and provide new knowledge that would make real legislative impact.

The one group that was missing, however, from the lines of engagement with the West were the academics – while journalists, meanwhile, were venturing forth into the vast penal territories to conduct meaningful and reliable academic-related work. Searching questions were put to all those involved in imprisonment, such as 'What does it mean to be a prisoner today in post-Soviet Russia?' and What does a prison officer do now that s/he is no longer engaged in a process of 'Soviet political correction'? There were many other questions about how penal change is experienced by people receiving prison sentences and those administering it. Whilst the corridors of power in Europe were saturated with experts on penal reform, in Russia's giant penal territories themselves – as late as 2003, some 12 years after the collapse of the USSR – prison officers were making far from benign statements about how European 'colonisation' was ruling and ruining the penal system (see Piacentini

2008). Although much of the Europeanisation of Russian penality is not legally binding law, its application and incorporation did bring the project – to concretise Russia's 'penal unity' with Europe – all the more closer.

This was, without question, a political process of penal reform that sought to improve the operation of the penal system, but which also sought to drag Russia into the twenty-first century geo-political European space. And it did happen with, as mentioned earlier, Russia entering the Council of Europe in 1996, and prisoners taking cases to internal appeals courts and the European Court of Human Rights (ECHR). For the first-time ever in Russia, prisoners were entitled to meet with their lawyers! The accused in every part of Russia now has the right to a trial by jury. The point to emphasise here is that the EU has actively sought to contribute to the prison debate in Russia and to develop and maintain a penal system based on the rule of law and respect for the fundamental rights of prisoners. This is further evidenced in countries in transition – such as Georgia, where the EU has engaged a permanent representative tasked with overseeing penal reform.

Conclusion

The Russian penal system is not like any in Europe, yet Europe lies as its direct neighbour and direct partner in cultural, political and economic matters. There are several problems with synergising Russian prisons with European values, and these emanate from two key developments: how Russia has positioned herself politically within, and beyond, Russia under Putin; and secondly, how Russia has responded to case law challenges post-2000, which is the year that marks the end of the legal and penal reform process that began in 1991 (see Bowring 2009). The enactment of new procedural codes came to an end in 2003, simultaneously with the arrest Mikhael Khodorkovsky and the dismantling of YUKOS.

The first difficulty with the Europeanisation of penal punishment in Russia is not only how the practice of human rights is delivered on the ground, but also, how it is *understood* on the ground. Research has documented that there is a fragmentary and problematic policy transfer process across Russia with many in the prison officer field feeling isolated, over-scrutinised and surveilled to ensure that boxes are ticked and bureaucratic external priorities are met (see Piacentini 2004,2008; Bowring 2009). When everyday lives and professional activities are thrown into chaos following radical political 'change', identities of old times can appear ever-alluring, with the need for a leader's voice absorbed into the collective chorus (McEvoy 2001; Smith 2009). Prison officers and prisoners are a case in point. Their lives are often caught betwixt and between vast political changes that can affect them both fleetingly and deeply, particularly as the officers are charged with the professional role of guarding those society deems deviants. The defensive position of many in Russia today suggests a feeling of outrage – not at conditions, but at posturing from outside. Russian prisons could, therefore, be described as locked into a state of reactive and defensive penal politics.

Secondly, penality – as an apparatus of social control, and as a process where social and philosophical responses to punishment meet politics and the economy – has a fraught and tainted history in Russia. Throughout the Soviet period, penal law blew crime up to grotesque and infinite proportions in order to meet the wholly ambitious – and indeed unachievable – economic plans of the Communist regime (Applebaum 2003; Piacentini 2004). In contemporary Russia, interesting and complex contradictions exist in the penal realm. Punishment is pursued ruthlessly, yet the jurisprudence of the ECHR is still applied. Generally recognised penal principles from Europe, and norms organised around human rights, have a problematic reception in many jurisdictions, yet in Russia – where penality was manufactured for economic purposes, and where conventional notions of criminality were supplanted, establishing an internal, from below, perspective on what punishment 'means' – there continue to be a huge problem for a culture embracing Soviet nostalgia (see Pallot and Piacentini 2012).

Third, if 'Europeanness' is promoted mainly through law, there is another dilemma, which is related to the previous point, about which mode of penality is being followed? That which flows through *from below* – via policy transfer and international research – or that which is demanded of Russia *from above*, through legal obligations? With prison populations increasing, concerns over freedom of speech, and a crackdown on civil society groups attracting relentless worldwide media, the fragile balance between integrating the jurisprudence of the ECHR (which is a positive sign and *is* happening) and the loosening up of Russia's ideological ties – with its brutal penal legacy, might tip toward ideological retrenchment. We do not yet know the implications of this for the penal system in Russia as a whole, but clues about the direction of Russia's next stage can be found in the most recent research on its carceral geography – a continuation of penal banishment and exile that appears to have not undergone any major reform (Pallot and Piacentini 2012).

Russia does recognise the general principle of international penal law (see Van Zyl Smit 2006; Pallot and Piacentini 2012). However, as is often the case with histories of punishment, the mobilisation of ideas and legal commitments have not dimmed Russian culture's grip on mass incarceration. As mentioned in the brief opening outline of the Pussy Riot trial, there are many more citizens, social groups, political organisations and governments who are asking the same question: where does Russia go now in its commitment to human rights and penal and judicial reform? The hurdles Russia must overcome in the coming years are not only confined to the diversification of its economy, the safeguarding of a free press and the building of an independent judiciary. On the other hand, the *penal imagination* confronting Russia this decade and the next will not, perhaps, be of the kind led by NGOs, policy makers and academics in European jurisdictions, where debates centre on rehabilitation, recidivism, policy transfer or 'governmentality' (see Garland 2002 for comparisons to the USA). Russia has not become awakened to the important philosophical question – Why punish? Instead, Russia will continue to face urgent questions on how prisons have yet again become tangled in a complex and authoritarian political web.

Notes

1. The term Riot Grrrl refers to all women punk music that came out of Washington D.C. and the North West of the USA in the 1990s. Known as the third wave of feminism, Riot Grrrl music addressed issues of rape, domestic violence, and patriarchy.
2. The World Prison Brief, published through the International Centre for Prison Studies at King's College London, has from time to time, not reported prison figures for Russia due to delays and difficulties in obtaining figures.
3. Although it must be added that Phase 1 of implementation of the concept paper was due to take place over the period 2009–2012, with the several key tasks to be completed: the re-structuring of the penal estate into two types of prison and three types of penal colony and the establishment of children's centres. The main change from the present was to have much smaller cells for eight people. At the time of writing, there is no information available with regard to whether these changes have taken place. Further on in the chapter I outline a programme of evaluation research conducted in the 2009 period, which set out a programme to establish a meaningful and viable criminal justice probation service.
4. The – note denotes that no data are available for women and juveniles for this year.
5. The figures for the years 2003, 2002, 2001, 2000, 1995 exclude women in investigative isolation facilities awaiting trial.

6. The document, Russia Alternatives to Imprisonment Completion Report Summary the report of the *Research Evaluation, Alternatives to Custody in the Russian Federation (2007–2009)* and was passed to the author by Martin Seddon, who led the project. The document has not been published. The project number is: EuropeAid/123578/C/SER/RU

7. Whilst this is not stated as fact in the evaluation report, it is difficult to see how the near on two years delay to developing alternatives had anything but a negative effect on developing a change culture especially when it is considered that at this time relations between Russia and the west, especially the United Kingdom, were very poor indeed (see Pallot and Piacentini, 2012 for a detailed account of conducting academic research in the period between 2006–2009 in Russia).

8. The evaluation report outlined above, that the European Commission Delegation donated electronic equipment to the value of 500,000 euros. The money was used to test out surveillance technologies in a settlement colony in the event of legislative delay. It is also worth noting that there are currently no private sector companies involved in Russian criminal justice EM provision or any other criminal justice services in the country.

9. Most of the violence is targeted at ethnic and inter-ethnic groups from the Caucasus and Central Asia but African students studying in the big cities are reporting increases in racial violence (see 'Where is the Justice, Human Rights Watch, 2010 at http://www.hrw.org/sites/default/files/reports/kyrgyzstan0810webwcover_1.pdf, accessed June 2012).

10. SOVA, quoted in the UNHCR 2009) Russia: Situation and treatment of visible ethnic minorities; availability of state protection, 2009: 1).

11. Cited in http://www.undp.ru/documents/NHDR_2008_Eng.pdf

12. http://www.undp.ru/documents/NHDR_2008_Eng.pdf (accessed June 2012)

13. http://www.undp.ru/documents/NHDR_2008_Eng.pdf (accessed June 2012: 7).

14. Full title: Consideration of reports submitted by States parties under article 18 of the Convention on the Elimination of All Forms of Discrimination against Women: 6th and 7th periodic reports of States parties: Russian Federation

15. In conversation, 2010.

References

Al'pern, L. (2004) *Son I Yav' Zhenskoi Tyurmy [Dreams and Reality in Women's Prisons]* (Aletiya: St Petersburg).

Applebaum, A. (2003) *GULAG: A History* (DoubleDay: Random House).

Bowring, B. (ed.) (1997) *Prisons Law and Human Rights* (Moscow: Erebus Publishers).

Bowring, B., Levina, M . (eds) (2000) *Sotsilanoye Zakonodatelstvo Rossii i Velikobritanii* (Social Legislation in Russia and Great Britain) (Moscow: Russian European Trust).

Bowring, B. (2009) 'Russia and Human Rights: Incompatible Opposites?', *Göttingen Journal*, 1 (2).

Clear, T. (2009) *Imprisoning Communities: How Mass Incarceration Makes Disadvantaged Neighborhoods Worse* (New York: Oxford University Press).

'Concept Document' *Kontseptsiya*, The Decree no. 1772-r, "On a Concept for the Development of the Criminal Correctional System of the Russian Federation to 2010".

Dagsnytt [Daily News], 29 January, 2010, http://www.nrk.no/nett-tv/indeks/199403/.

European Prison Rules, The (1987), The Council of Europe.

European Prison Rules, The (2006), The Council of Europe.

Garland, D. (2002) *The Culture of Control: Crime and Social Order in Contemporary Society* (Oxford: Oxford University Press).

Human Rights Watch (2010) *Human Rights Watch World Report*, http://www.hrw.org/world-report-2010.

Kontseptsiia razvitiia ugolov'no-ispolnitel'noi sistemy Rossiskoi Federatsii do 2020, utverzhdena rasporiazheniem Pravitel'stva Rossiskoi Federatsii Ot 14oko oktabria 2010 g. No. 1772-R (The conception of the development of the Russian correctional system to 2020. Validated by the Russian government 14 October 2010); accessible at http://www.president-soviet-ru/structure/group_10/materials/concept_of_reform/index.php [accessed August 2012]

King, R.D. and Piacentini, L. (2005) 'The Correctional System during Transition', in W.A. Pridemore (ed.), *Ruling Russia: Law, Crime and Justice in a Changing Society* (New York: Rowman and Littlefield Pub, Inc).

McAuley, M. (2009) *Children in Custody: Anglo Russian Perspectives* (London: Bloomsbury).

McAuley, M. (2010) *Children in Prisons,* at http://www.opendemocracy.net/od-russia/mary-mcauley/children-in-prison, 28 May 2010, accessed May 2011.

McAuley, M. and Macdonald, M. (2007) 'Russia and Youth Crime: A Comparative Study of Attitudes and their Implications', *British Journal of Criminology*, 47 (1): 2–22.

McEvoy, K. (2001) 'Paramilitary Imprisonment in Northern Ireland: Resistance, Management, and Release', *Clarendon Studies in Criminology* (Oxford: Oxford University Press).

Moran, D., Piacentini, L . and Pallot, J . (2011) 'Disciplined Mobility and Carceral Geography: Prisoner Transport in Russia', *Transactions of The Institute of British Geographers*, 37 (3): 446–60.

Pallot, J. (2007) 'Gde Muzh, Tam Zhena' (Where the Husband Is, So Is the Wife): Space and Gender in Post-Soviet Patterns of Penality', *Environment and Planning*, 39 (3): 570–89.

Pallot, J. and Piacentini, L . (2012) *Gender, Geography and Punishment: The Experience of Women in Carceral Russia* (Oxford: Oxford University Press).

Piacentini, L. (2004) *Surviving Russian Prisons: Punishment, Economy and Politics in Transition* (Devon: Willan Publishing).

Piacentini, L. (2005) 'Cultural Talk and Other Intimate Acquaintances with Russian Prisons', *Crime Media Culture*, 1: 189–208.

Piacentini, L. (2008) 'Burden or Benefit: Paradoxes of Penal Transition in Russia', in McEvoy, K. and L. McGregor (eds), *Transitional Justice from Below: Grassroots Activism and the Struggle for Change* (Oxford: Hart Publishing).

Piacentini, L. Pallot, J . And Moran. D. (2010) 'Welcome to Malaya Rodina: Gender and Penal Order in a Russian Prisons', *Social and Legal Studies,* 18 (4): 523–42.

Pratt J, (2011) 'Penal Excess and Penal Exceptionalism: Welfare and Imprisonment in Scandinavian and Anglophone Societies', in A. Crawford (ed.), *International*

Governance and Comparative Criminal Justice and Urban Governance (Cambridge: Cambridge University Press) 251–75.

Robertson, A. (2012) 'The Role of the Police in Building Justice in Russia: Problems and Prospects', in M. Malloch and B. Munro, *Building Justice in Post-Transition Europe? Processes of Criminalisation within Central and Eastern European Societies* (London: Routledge).

UNHCR (2009) Russia: Situation and Treatment of Visible Ethnic Minorities; Availability of State Protection.

UNHCR (2009) Russia: Situation and Treatment of Visible Ethnic Minorities; Availability of State Protection.

Smith, C. (2009) *The Prison in the American Imagination* (USA: Yale University Press).

Van Zyl Smit, D. (2006) 'Humanising imprisonment: a European project?', *European Journal of Criminal Policy Research*, 12: 107–20.

Vyshnevsky, A. G. And Bobylev, S. N. (2008) National Human Development Report of the Russian Federation: Rusisa Facing Demographic Challenges (Moscow: United Nations).

Walmsley, R. (2009) *World Prison Population List*, 8th edn, http://www.prisonstudies.org/info/downloads/wppl-8th_41.pdf.

9
Poland: The Political Legacy and Penal Practice

Monika Płatek[1]

Introduction

In addition to describing the judicial and political contexts in which Poland's penal system operates, this paper also raises a central question that is directly opposite to the one that usually surfaces in this context. Instead of simply asking how far the political situation in Poland has shaped the criminal justice system, it also asks how much, in their turn, criminal justice routines, penal traditions, habits and practices, have infused Poland's politics and squeezed out more rational and supportive actions in response to crime.

Poland is the ninth largest country in area in Europe. It has a population of over 38 million, which makes it the sixth most populous country in the European Union (EU) and the most populous of the old Soviet Union's satellite states in Eastern Europe. In the form of Solidarity, Poland was in the vanguard of the struggle to end the Soviet domination of Eastern Europe.

Embracing democracy

A totalitarian society might have some trouble distinguishing where prison ends, for no matter where you are, in or out, you still feel like you are behind bars. However, the period 1980–1982 was the era of *Solidarity*. There had been periods of protest against autocratic regimes before, but *Solidarity* gave a specific feel to the protests: it created a unique feeling of unity that gave rise to work for, and a push towards, the reform of prisons. The meaning of terms such as 'community' – as well as 'local community' – were hard to grasp for a Pole. But, during 'solidarity' they did have meaning. It was genuinely a time, when the average citizen was aware that prisons should be more just, and should be reformed because prisoners are part of society – not just outcasts. Later, with the backlash against *Solidarity* and, in particular, with the Martial Law of 1982 these warm feelings of unity and solidarity evaporated – but work on evaluating how to reform the prison system continued. It brought with it what is today the essence of the European Prison Rules of 11 January 2006 [EPR-2006]. When quoting these basic rules, one may associate them with the standards campaigned for in Poland at the dawn of 1982. The campaign was built around the idea that Prison conditions that infringe prisoners' human rights are not justified by lack of resources [rule 4 of EPR-2006], and life in prison shall resemble as closely as possible the positive aspects of life in the community [rule 5 of EPR-2006]. This plan of action – written in 1980 – was in place in 1989 when wider, major political changes started with the collapse of the old Soviet Union.

Institutional reform was rapid. In June 1989 Poland elected its first democratic Parliament, and the new Constitution was implemented in 1997. It declared the country a democracy based on the rule of law. The institution of the Polish Ombudsman had already been introduced in 1987 and The Constitutional Tribunal, theoretically initiated in 1982, began working in 1986. The elementary tools for executing the law – and for controlling those in power, had therefore been in place by the late 1980s, and had begun to operate.

In Poland, taking the law seriously is a fairly new phenomenon. Prior to 1918 Poland was divided between Russia, Prussia and Austria for more than 100 years. Polish people survived often thanks to being disobedient towards the rules. The short period between the two World Wars – when Poland regained its national sovereignty – was too short a time for its citizens to internalise a respect for the law. The period of the Second World War and the years until 1989 were marked by dependence, first on Nazi Germany and then on Soviet Russia. Contravening, violating and defying the law was, therefore, often perceived as brave and patriotic. In addition, the law has been mostly declarative and difficult to exercise through the usual legal channels. The harm of prison demonstrates itself through learned helplessness and a learned sense of entitlement acquired by inmates. The period 1944–1989 very much strengthened this feeling among the non-imprisoned population. It was thought that, while the Constitution should continue to exist, it did not necessarily need to be applied. The so called 'lex-telex', was produced not by the Parliament but by the boss and apart from the actual letter of law. The order from someone high in the power structure was worth more than the letter of the law. Not what you know but whom you know was what counted – or, at least, that was the working assumption. The sense of hopelessness was mollified by pointing at those behind the bars as being responsible for all the misery around. Many were content, not to say eager, to embrace such a perspective. This is why demands for wide-ranging reforms during the 'Solidarity' era were so exceptional. With the collapse of the old Soviet Union in 1989 Poland hoped, for a second time, to say farewell to the totalitarian order.

It 1997 a major reform of the criminal justice system brought a new criminal code and a new criminal executive code. According to the new rules imprisonment is meant to be the last resort – punishment at the 'deep end' though, interestingly, prison sentences/regimes are no longer considered to be tough enough. In Poland, there is a saying that a year of imprisonment is a joke – not a punishment: two years is what you would give to your brother to treat him leniently, and three years is just short enough to stroll down the prison corridors. It seems that we never get enough. Accustomed to harsh, long punishments we have trouble changing our perspective. It is not only the length of imprisonment, it is also the deep conviction that with no imprisonment there is no real punishment at all. Punishment and imprisonment can be seen as synonyms. It was Montesquieu who warned those in power not to abuse the harshness of the penalty, for people would get used to it. We did. What was supposed to be severe becomes – after a while – average. By continuing the Soviet practice of being generous with its use of long-term imprisonment, Poland well illustrates this point.

Despite legislators' efforts to put an emphasis on fines and probation, imprisonment prevails. It is often imposed in the form of a suspended sentence. In this way, judges hope to reconcile common sense and the will of vocal hard-line members of the public. It makes judges feel alright about themselves, but it does not make sense as far as criminal justice is concerned. Judges pay little attention to the numbers of revoked suspensions. This is significant. It results in a vicious circle. According to public opinion, a suspended sentence is no sentence at all, and is not justice. This opinion is not unreasonable, because a suspended sentence is rarely coupled with any sensible obligation – other than to remain sober. True, this in itself is not that easy in a country where most people believe that any alcoholic drink is very good. The data on revocation of suspension proves that it is not so much a newly committed crime, but rather the consumption of alcohol that puts people behind bars. Such cases are very frequent and they contribute to the problem of the constant over-crowding of Polish prisons.

The changes in the new criminal code of 1997 were aimed at cutting down the severity of punishment and changing the penal priorities. Instead of the previous emphasis on the priority of imprisonment, it gave precedence to fines and the limitation of liberty (art. 32 of the Polish Criminal code [further: k.k.]). The last amnesty, in 1989 – a direct result of the fundamental changes that had taken place in Poland's political system – let many inmates out of prison. In addition to amnesty law, the broad use of conditional release brought a phenomenal decrease in the prison population. With more than 100,000 inmates at the beginning of 1989 the number dropped to less than 45,000 by the end of the year. The success of prison depopulation was spectacular – and spectacularly short. With no criminal and social policy accompanying the release from prison, those released were soon back behind bars.

The prison estate

Poland has 80 prisons and 75 temporary detention centres. The system detained over 140,000 people in the 1970s. This number dropped to 40,000 in the 1990s. It is now over 84,000 and over 200 per 100 000 citizens. Sentenced inmates account for, on average, three in four inmates. The highest proportion of those remanded in custody was in 1990 (32%) (Siemaszko 2000). Despite the decrease, temporary detention is a problem. It is used too often, for too long, often mixed-up with punishment, and is too often used routinely and on the edge of legality. People are kept in detention as meat or cabbage is kept in a barrel – to make them softer. The European Court for Human Rights [ECHR] announced – in the case Kauczor v. Poland – that Poland has a structural problem with the over-use of pre-trial detention measures [Kauczor v. Poland 45219/06].

The system planned for no more than 45–55,000 inmates (assuming 4m² per person) now houses over 80,000 inmates. The Polish Constitutional Court in unity with the ECHR stresses that inhuman conditions dominate Polish prisons (see Orchowski v. Poland 17885/04, Służewiec v. Poland 17599/05 – judgment in both cases – October 2009). The Polish Constitutional Court reiterated the ECHR's position. However, it held that the text of the law provided the limit, but also gave permission to breach it. The court stressed that the provision lacked clarity and precision – which allowed for a very broad interpretation (Orchowski v. Poland 17885/04).

The Constitutional Court found that, in effect, the provision in question allowed for an indefinite and arbitrary placement of detainees in cells below the statutory size of three m² per person, thus causing chronic overcrowding in Polish prisons and exposing detainees to the risk of inhuman treatment (Pawłowska 2007). ECHR, in several cases evaluated in recent years, has clearly stated that overcrowded prison conditions actually do constitute inhuman treatment of prisoners. ECHR observed that each time a cell provides less than four m² per person it is perceived as a breach of article 3 of the European Convention on Human Rights (3 ECHR) is on the prohibition of torture, degrading or/and inhuman punishment or treatment]. In the view of the Constitutional Court and ECHR, the overcrowding itself could qualify as inhuman and degrading treatment. And if combined with additional aggravating circumstances, it might even be considered to be torture. The court also noted that already the minimum statutory standard of three m² per person was one of the lowest in Europe:

The postulate of humane treatment entails also the requirement of assuring for the detainees educational activities, which [would] prepare them for life after their release from prison and prevent them from relapsing into crime, and thus allowing for the achievement of the aims of a punishment (Orchowski v. Poland 17885/04). The courts question the possibility of prisoners' rehabilitation in such conditions. However, treating prisoners in this way is a regular practice in the contemporary Polish prison system.

The three musicians: prison conditions

At dusk on last New Year's eve three men got together in the shabby back room of the old café near Służewiec prison in Warsaw to play once more the music they used to play. They sat, smiled at each other, talked a little and played the music from the time they were inseparable. Things had happened. It happened that for years they had shared their life behind bars. Sometimes they had shared a cell but, like all prisoners, they had been shunted – rather like the package holiday tourists who flocked to Poland after 1989 – from one location to another. This was (and is) sometimes done to cope with overcrowding, sometimes to cope with specific needs or requirements, most often to semi-punish and/or get rid of annoying inmates. Penitentiary tourism is both costly and very characteristic of the Polish prison system.

The three musicians shared the awful smell of the place, the food that could be better, and the narrow space of the cell where all of them had been placed. A cell planned for a single inmate, but with the three of them living in it, was overcrowded. As we have already touched on, overcrowding is characteristic of the Polish prison business. Under communist rule prisoners were allowed eleven cubic metres per person. This was the WHO minimum of air to prevent a person from suffocation. In 1980 – with the rise of 'Solidarity' – sound arguments for prison reform addressed the issue of quarantined space per prisoner. The new criminal executive code of 1997 introduced, already under the democratic regime, a minimum of three m² per prisoner. Yet it also introduced an exception that allowed, in extraordinary cases, a limit of 2.5 m². Soon this exception became the norm and overcrowding grew.

The musicians remembered this unique time. In 1989 the initial numbers of inmates dropped from almost 100,000 to 40,000, then rose to 62,000 in 1994, dropping to 61,000 in 1995, 55,000 in 1996, then back up to over 84,000 in 2012. The prison population thus used to be for some time about half of what it was before 1989. The average time served had not changed significantly, although it dropped to 18 months from 27 months. With over 200 per 100,000 of the population in its prisons, the country has, by European standards, a high imprisonment rate. It is lower than during the previous regime, when it reached over 340 per 100,000, but much higher than it has been (160 per 100,000) prior to 2000.

The musicians observed that conditions in prison under the new regime changed significantly for an average inmate. It did not become significantly better, but was much more humane and safe – even the sanitary system was a bit better. It was said that the reform was done. From an inmate's perspective it meant actual changes in attitudes and communication between staff and inmates – not perfect, but almost civilised. The orders and shouting stopped, replaced by conversation and firm but polite communication. It was almost as though they were treated like average citizens should be treated while outside the institution. The language of everyday communication between staff and inmates became more refined and one could feel that both sides tried to minimise conflicts and help each other. Those three playing together are the best evidence that it is possible to build positive relations behind the bars. It is also possible to reach for freedom and become free while in prison. You simply have to take responsibility for yourself. They did. The system however did not manage to uphold the positive stream. It turned towards overcrowding, and like a water flow destroyed a lot with that wave.

It is hard to believe how easily one can spoil work prepared by many and for so long. When in prison, the three musicians shared their dreams. Dreams are so easily dreamt in a place like that. Prison is like an enchanted castle, full of yearning for an escape from the reality of incarceration. They did notice that fleeing to freedom in their dreams, decorated with picture-perfect visions, bound them to the prison more securely than bars. Freedom is always pretty while in prison and rarely bearable outside it. Before 2000 they could limit dreaming as the real windows were opened. It was possible because prisons before 2000 were filled with a variety of programmes, education paths and work opportunities – not well paid, but at least available. Alcoholics anonymous and special units for drug addicts were put in place and functioned well. But work? school? education? It is hard to get these opportunities. During the years of 2009–2011 the number of school participants fell in 2009 there were 1,172 courses with 13,755 participants, in 2010 – 1,177 courses with 13,291 participants, and in 2011 – 1,104 courses with 12,808 participants.[2] Then, in 2000 a new Minister of Justice arrived. He came only for a year, but it was sufficient to ruin a lot. The Minister of Justice was at the same time the Prosecutor General and his idea of a solution to corruption was that all suspects should remain in detention. Soon prisons had to give way to detention centres. Preliminary arrest was back to stay, this time for good. The use of preliminary detention turned into overuse of it. European Court of Human Rights in the case Kauczor v. Poland (Case Nr 45219/06) decided that Poland has structural problem with abusing preliminary detention. It is used far too often and far for too long. We know about it, yet this practice of overusing it, continues. The minister that has started that process of using arrest as tool to make people provide any evidence the prosecutor needs, was soon gone [and later became the President], but the practice he had started remained in place. So, while Poland repeatedly lost cases at the ECHR due to unreasonable periods of detention, the practice of keeping people behind bars remains in place.

The three musicians thought they were lucky. They were given a real chance. During the years of 2005–2007 the EU project called Equal: 'Back to Future Freedom' ['Powrót do wolności'] was operating in the Mazowsze region of Poland in more than ten prisons, including the Służewiec one. The project offered diverse activities to prisoners, prison staff and inmates' families. It was aimed at introducing routines and practices that would build paths out of prison and prepare prisoners for release and remaining in open society.

Służewiec is quite an ordinary prison. It was converted from a barracks built on the then outskirts of Warsaw, shortly after the Second World War, to accommodate German prisoners of war. It was meant to be temporary. It is still in use today and hosts Polish prisoners. Prisoners are the ones who renovated the old wings and constructed new ones – extra security wings. The new modern wings are meant for extremely dangerous inmates. Yet, since overcrowding is a systemic problem, some not so dangerous prisoners are labelled as such to help with the proper accommodation of inmates.

Two of the three inmates had a long prison history. They remembered a time – before 1989 – when work had been used as an excuse for re-socialisation. They worked in prison factories and the production was part of the state budget. The money they were paid for the work was meagre, but enough to buy cigarettes and tea in the prison canteen. At the dawn of the new era, the prison relaxed discipline a little, but jobs disappeared. The previous system lost ground; the new one was not yet stable. It was making humane promises but missing humane practice. At the same time, one can hardly find another place with so many programmes oriented at helping inmates to do useful things and work for the future. Each year, there are more than 200 different programmes, some very spectacular – as, for example, inmates working in hospices, in houses for the elderly or institutions for children with special needs. There are fantastic initiatives of inmates working in agriculture – they do everything from growing flowers to breeding animals. There are programmes for alcoholics, for drug addicts, for sexual offenders, for those with artistic minds who love to write, paint, write poetry, print and publish. There are over 20,000 staff and more than a quarter of them with university education in preparation for this kind of work. There are real enthusiasts among them and they manage to get space to do the work that suits inmates and gives true meaning to their actions. There are actually plenty of diverse, different programmes. One can hardly find a country in Europe with more. At the same time, so very few are able to profit from that rich offer. It is more often that one fights for years before getting access to a school. It is easier with sport, but still no more that 20 per cent participate in any such activities. The long list of activities looks short when numbers of participants are taken into consideration.

It has to be firmly stated – once there is serious overcrowding, rehabilitation is very difficult, if not impossible. A prison switches from working with inmates to supervising them. Priorities change. Orientation towards a future outside of prison turns into security here and now. The Polish prison system had a short period of time, after 1989, for exercising orientation toward inmates' future, and stable routines. Usually, due to the structural problem with overcrowding, became security obsessed.

The prison experience has an impact on practices in civil society. There are different forms of controlling people in the name of safety. The changes in criminal law are almost constant. There are over 100 amendments to the criminal code of 1997; most introducing more severe measures and criminalising new conducts. Many are introduced with vague language and loose concepts.

The changes in the criminal code aimed at increasing penal sanctions brought further scarcity of work in prison. Idleness and smelly melancholy sneaked in through the prison corridors. The prison that used to be open to visitors did not welcome them any more – for security reasons. Instead, more space was given to arguing for repression as a just goal of imprisonment. Therefore, the EU so called Equal Project 'Back to Freedom' was a chance worth taking.

The three musicians took part in the integration process. They often travelled from prison to prison, from villages to small towns all over Poland with a folklore dance group of men and women also brought together by the very same EU Project. 'Back to Freedom' initiated many activities oriented at mutual integration of the outside world with the inside of prison. Art and music was often the toll for crossing the border of 'otherness'. The musicians performed together with a female dancing group. They recall the feeling of equality with the audience: a rare feeling, absent while in prison. The big words 'freedom', 'integration', 'responsibility' translated themselves into everyday contacts where they shared handshakes, washing duties, taking care of themselves and others in the group, and conversations where barriers between 'them' as prisoners and 'others' – both staff and outsiders – were gone. They had names and talents, and were doing their work. Some had a great sense of humour, others were good in settling conflicts – one, to his own dismay, turned out to be a great cook. All of them were well aware that without this project this would not have happened. All of them were concerned about making sure that the process continues after the EU umbrella is taken away. The new routine – adjustment to prisoners' activities, inclusion practices – that's what they wanted to keep. The three musicians actually paid with the money they earned the damages and fines they owed because of the offences they committed. And yes, for the first time in their prison history they felt that their life had changed. They experienced the time before and after the big change, getting away from the system called 'socialist' or 'communist', and transformation towards what is called 'democracy', 'capitalism', or a 'neoliberal system'. Hardly anyone asked them what it means to be in prison under each of those umbrellas? This seems wrong. That is why this paper includes inmates' experiences.

Polish criminal justice: the reality

In July 2011 a family judge in the regional court in Bilgoraj – using the Juvenile Justice Act (Dz.Uof 2010 No. 33, item.178) – started an investigation to determine whether the circumstances of the case before him proved the involvement of four accused minors, and whether the measures provided by the Act (including the deprivation of liberty) need be applied. The four boys were accused of acting together and in conspiracy to the detriment of W. R. by stealing potatoes worth 1 zł 50 gr (0.30 euro) from his field. If this was in England some centuries ago perhaps even the death penalty – or transportation to Australia – could have been considered. But in modern Poland, in order to claim the act criminal it is not enough to have someone's behaviour fit into the specific situation described by the criminal code. A prohibited act, whose social consequences are insignificant, does not constitute an offence. No one suggests ignoring examples of potentially improper behaviour – they should be noted and corrected. The very same law, however, stresses the need to use other means than courts, especially criminal court procedures, when the case concerns a child.

A year later, while 'the potato case' was still pending, a prosecutor in Warsaw charged a popular pop singer with possession of three grams of marihuana, and the court decided to apply psychiatric tests in order to verify the singer's ability to stand trial. There are several thousands of mostly young people deprived of their liberty for possession of small amounts of drugs. It is mostly marihuana. The young people keep on going to prison despite the changes in the law allowing the police and the prosecutor to withdraw charges in cases of possession of a trivial amount of drugs.

The same over-reaction applies to the over 2,000 people imprisoned for drunken driving while riding a bicycle – on country roads after having consumed a beer or two. Sometimes they have not even been riding the bicycle – just pushing it. They are nevertheless punished for potential use of wheeled transportation while under the influence of alcohol.

The case of the man who allegedly stole electricity worth 70 groszy (20 cents) and which cost the Polish tax payer 7000 zł (1600 euro) closes this short list of examples. The above cases – even if they seem unlikely, not to say absurd – accurately illustrate Poland's direction of travel.

'The potato' case demonstrates how criminal measures are being used as a heavy-handed tool of social control. Other mechanisms of support – the educational sector, for example – are all squeezed out and marginalised to give more space for criminal justice responses. What would be – some time ago – a case for the school director, today becomes a case for a policeman and a judge. This is not the consequence of ambitious criminal justice professionals, but rather the result of a misconceived plan for school reform. The plan to harmonise the educational system simply brought distress. Fifteen years after the last reform we are now admitting that closing small schools and gathering masses of children in unfriendly, anonymous institutions does not benefit children or secure their safety. It is similar to the atomisation phenomenon described by Nils Christie (2004). Needless to say, the savings on the education budget arising from this policy have been paralleled by an increase in funds for criminal justice.

'The bicycle' case illustrates the perversion within the criminal justice system. Drunken driving is a severe problem in a country with one million alcoholics and four million daily abusing alcohol. There are less than 900 homicides per year in Poland. But the number of those killed in car accidents exceeds 5,000. Over 70,000 are injured in car accidents. It is far too often because of drunken driving. It was therefore sensible to amend the law [amendment from 4 April 2000] and change drunken driving from a misdemeanour (from five up to 30 days of imprisonment) to an offence (punished by fine, probation or imprisonment from one month up to one year). There are about 140,000 people sentenced per year for drunken driving with some 5,000 being imprisoned. The cyclists make up about 2,000 of these.[3] They usually go to prison for six months and spend it in idleness. School, therapy, and any consciousness raising sessions, none of these things are made available.

These offenders often end up in prison as a result of reversing a suspended imprisonment. But why are they stopped in the first place? It is an offence to drive a vehicle while under the influence of alcohol; the bicycle is a vehicle and the competence of the police and prosecutors is evaluated based on statistics – the more sentences, the better. Cyclists are easy to prove guilty. One does not need to catch them on the road. It is enough to place a police car near a country pub. It is easier, safer and nicer to catch countryside cyclists than to look for drunken drivers on the roads. It does not serve the purpose of law, it is genuinely opposite to the *ratio legis* of the amendment, but it serves the police well.

The situation is very similar with regards to punishing for the possession of small amounts of drugs. You can be imprisoned for up to two years for being caught with a joint. The amendment of 2000 was supposed to help fight drug addiction. It did not. It helped police, prosecutors and judges instead. The 5,000–7,000 sentenced to imprisonment for having a joint of marihuana allow the authorities to claim that they are effective.

The expense of going to trial over such petty offences exposes the superficial character of what effective justice means.

It is evident that, although we are a democratic society, we face the type of criminal justice problems that characterised the communist era. We also keep the same category of people in prisons that used to be imprisoned during the communist era.

They are young, badly educated and without sound prospects for their future. They were free manpower under communism; they are the unwanted labour surplus in today's market economy. The structure of convictions is as it was before. Taking into considerations just the most common offences – most inmates serve the term for crimes against property (over 43%). There are those who are convicted for crime against life and health (10%) and against safety, including wheeled – car and bicycle traffic (8%).There are very few convicted for domestic violence and sexual crime. Rape is prosecuted only at the victim's request. With the tendency to blame the victim very few victims are brave enough to demand justice. The same is the case with domestic violence. It is officially, but unwillingly, prosecuted. Perceived as a private matter, it rarely reaches the court. The Ministry of Justice – together with Catholic Church representatives – are officially against signing and ratifying the Council of Europe's Convention on preventing and combating violence against women and domestic violence. Therefore, when it comes to breaking the law a family prison hosts mostly those who do not pay their alimony. There are more than 30,000 sentenced for not paying alimony, over 2,500 of them in prison.

There are foreigners and minority groups among the inmates, but they currently constitute less than two per cent of the prison population. This is not because of Polish tolerance, it is rather because there are not many foreigners in Poland. Polish Roma are very few in number, when compared with the numbers in Hungary or Slovakia. Other minority groups – Chechen, Vietnamese or Ukrainian – are poorly integrated and deal with problems they face within their own community. It does not mean there is no crime there – we simply have very little knowledge of it.

It is interesting to see who is in prison but it is equally interesting to see who is not there. There are over 80,000 inmates behind bars. At the same time there are over 30,000 of those sentenced to imprisonment who are not in prison. Some of them got permission from the court to wait in a queue in order to prevent further overcrowding. Most, however, simply did not appear at the prison gate. Some of these convicts have been sentenced for ten years or more.

Crime statistics are not rising – just the opposite, they are falling. It is because we, as a society, are getting older. The lousy conditions for women (a strict abortion law, unfairly low wages, and for many, the meagre chance of a good career) and not much better conditions for men are probably partially the cause of a low birth rate. It is also partly because of one of the lowest levels, in Europe, of trust in the police and the criminal justice system. But even taking all that into consideration one can ask is it really necessary to send so many for so long to prison? The society that is so eager for democracy keeps, when it comes to criminal justice, its totalitarian roots. What are the possible reasons for this?

Being part of Eastern and Central Europe

While mere numbers do not reflect the processes behind them, Eastern and Central European countries are easily distinguished by much higher imprisonment rates than West European Countries (excluding the USA), and much lower numbers of crimes per 100,000 people than in most Western countries (Walmsley 2010). But this pattern is not set in stone. For example, Finland, which once had comparable rates of imprisonment to Poland under the communist-socialist regime, has put a brake on prison expansion and is arguably out-performing its Scandinavian neighbours. Finland accomplished what Poland had an ambition to do. Finland had a genuine will to become a more Scandinavian country instead of a Soviet one. Poland, with its negative sentiments towards the 'Soviet system', overlooked the similarities shared with that very system. The importance of the prison system is one of them. While criminal justice writings and ideas in Poland were mostly copied from western literature after the Second World War, practice followed the Soviet example. This mixture complicated the discourse on criminal justice in Poland. Similar contradictions were apparent elsewhere in the region.

As the result of expected difference between criminal policy of East and Western European countries there were few endeavors to study the common grounds and the existing difference.[4] These remain mostly invisible, unnoticed, and highly introspective. Expelled from consideration by the mainstream, texts dealing with criminal justice in Eastern countries are limited to analysing local or regional issues.[5] They look for similarities to the West rather than studying the 'Eastern' particularity and its causes (Filar and Frankowski 1982).

'West', in Eastern Europe, is associated with freedom, democracy, respect for liberty and economic wealth. 'East' appears to represent striving towards betterment, but bearing the weight of past negligence of human rights and the experience of totalitarian and authoritarian systems. 'West' is associated with progress and reform in the name of reverence for each individual's quality of life. 'East' – and to some extent 'Central' – continues to carry the burden of a place where ideology shattered entire communities and caused the erasure of the significance of an individual life. It results in the present overcrowding and heavy reliance on criminal law as major tools of social control. The so-called socialist countries followed the Soviet Union pattern, and therefore shared similarities in the law and in the criminal justice practices. This is partly correct. The data indicating similarities in the prison population and severe punishment are, however, not sufficient for drawing far-reaching conclusions, even when similarities prevail.[6] One should rather admit that we tend to know very little about each other, and frankly – for a long time – the mutual interest was a rather modest one. Lack of academic contact, lack of a common language add to the phenomenon of one side striving towards the other's standards and the other largely ignoring it.[7]

This approach was, to some extent, mutual and shared also by western experts. The predominance of the English language adds to that phenomenon. The Iron Curtain cut a large portion of Europe out of sight of western sociologists, lawyers, and criminologists. The Russian language never became the *lingua franca* of Eastern Europe and Russia. Soviet criminal justice was thought of as being so overwhelmed with ideology that it ceased to serve as a vibrant source for intellectual discourse. And even interesting developments actually present in the region were mostly neglected.[8] They were treated as intellectually tedious and dreary by both Eastern, as well as Western, experts. (Płatek, 2004)[9]

In accordance with the Soviet one-track ideology, until the end of the Stalinist era, criminology was banned in Eastern and Central countries, and criminal justice was saturated with demagogical slogans. The Soviet residual theory proclaimed the end of crime in the new communist society. It only needed, as was believed, the time necessary to get rid of all those affected by bourgeois vices, and lacking the new approach to society. Soviet propaganda put a ban on criminology and excluded criminal justice policies assuming that eradicating crime is just a question of time. Despite the ban on criminology and research, Poland observed interesting developments in criminology and criminal justice work and ideas.[10]

The Soviet Union criminal justice system popped up from time to time in the criminal justice literature as an exotic subject, and stayed on the margin of criminal justice analysis in Western literature. Eastern and Central European countries looked towards the West for inspiration and were eager to identify problems described by Western experts as similar to the ones observed in their countries. The West exuded intellectual freedom and attraction (Pratt et al. 2005; Hudson 2003; Garland 2001). Yet, when criminal justice and Europe is mentioned, it is in fact the conglomerate of the British and the American – or more broadly the Commonwealth perspective on what is specific for these two places – rather than broad inclusion of the diverse practices from different European countries.[11] What is specific to the USA and/or England and Wales sociology, law and/or criminology is, in fact, treated as general and representative of all of Europe.

The gulag factory devoured millions, and as the number of those killed grew, so too did the number of crimes. Almost anything could be an offence, for the definitions were blurred, imprecise and politically tainted. It is not that they are not politically tainted elsewhere, including in the West. People in Eastern and Central Europe tend to believe that political over-use and abuse of the penal system is not present in Western European democracies. It might be a bit naïve[12] but probably the scale on which the state justified killing, torture, inhuman and degrading treatment in the East and Central parts of Europe was not comparable with experiences faced by Western European countries. Spain had a destructive time under the Franco regime yet this was mitigated by an active opposition and the presence of a strong civil society. The Soviet repression commenced by Lenin and Stalin and continued through the twentieth century was developed as part of a heritage of the Russian Empire. No civil practice of balance of power was really practised. Empire is possibly quite an artificial concept, but the terror of the penal system was real (Hobsbawn 2008).

I cannot responsibly evaluate the level of intellectual freedom between 1956–1989 in Central and European countries other than Poland. Poland, however, seems to be specific because of the level of actual intellectual freedom experienced under the communist regime. It is believed to have been broader than in other countries. There might be several reasons for this: membership of the communist party helped in one's career but was not obligatory, Polish farmers owned their land and only some of it was unified in the state agriculture units, the church played a role of mitigating power, and probably the nobility tradition of being free and independent influenced the social atmosphere. Consequently, academia was thought to be irrelevant politically – until the protests of 1968. The scarcity of research and funds delegated to academia and science did not narrow the intellectual ideas developed within the criminal justice field. Academic work did not influence practice much but developed a criminal justice reform strategy, ready to be put in place when the political change of 1989 happened.

Concentration on the negative effect of communism took slavery away from both the conscious and unconscious sphere. The heritage of slavery is almost unnoticed. And yet slavery is part of the tradition of most of the Central and Eastern European countries. The history of political dependence is blamed for repressive aspects of the Polish penal system. Only in the year 1861 were Polish peasants freed, with the decree proclaimed by the Russian Tsar who, rightly, hoped thus to discourage them from joining the Polish nobility in the fight against the Tsar. The phenomenon of slavery and its historical impact on the contemporary penal system seems to be vital and yet overlooked (Domańska 2008a; 2008b).

Lack of independence cannot be the single most important issue when the distinctive characteristic of a penal system is discussed. It has been also part of the history of several Western European countries – including Finland, Norway and Belgium. The same, however, is not true with regards to slavery. Slavery, known also as feudal serfdom and equal in practice to enslavement, referred to a large population of those who lived and worked in villages. Memories of enslavement are not easily identified as a source of contemporary penal developments, but it is worth considering this when the critical anatomy of the penal system is at stake. Is it enough to have the burden of a Soviet type of administration or are the roots of criminal law embedded in and attributed to the slavery system? Is it, just, as Zygmunt Bauman stresses, the effect of neoliberal globalisation, a consequence of joining the common policy of European Union, or the cultural adjustment to exclude and divide people rather than practise solidarity? Those issues might have some common ground with other Eastern and Central European countries, but might also be very specific for Poland. My argument here is that it is difficult to explain the propensity for using imprisonment as a tool of social control without noticing the legacy of the system prone to cherish exclusion. It is only when our long tradition of exclusion, to the extent of perceiving others as unwanted strangers, is considered that we can, in my opinion, explain the failure of efforts to bring inmates into the mainstream.

Fitting in?

In a series of interesting texts on comparative criminal law and penal policy Michael Cavadino and James Dignan demonstrated that countries that operate broadly similar political and economic systems are inclined to operate broadly similar, though not identical (Cavadino and Dignan 2006a; 2007), social and penal programmes. (The authors were looking to synthesise aspects of the Marxist, Durkheimian and Weberian traditions to overcome the shortcomings of the 'singular' theories of Michel Foucault and Emile Durkheim.)

The authors carried out studies of penal systems in 12 contemporary capitalist countries (The USA, England and Wales, Australia, New Zealand, South Africa, Germany, The Netherlands, France, Italy, Sweden, Finland and Japan). The political economies of those countries were then categorised as being neoliberal (USA, England and Wales, Australia, New Zealand, South Africa), conservative corporatist (Germany, France, Italy, The Netherlands), social democratic (Sweden, Finland) and oriental corporatists (Japan). Cavadino and Dignan then argued that each of these categories could be linked to levels of punitiveness using rates of imprisonment as an index. On this restricted measure, neoliberal countries turned out to be the most punitive, social democratic societies much less so, and so on. Commenting on the results of their research both authors indicated the relationship between political economies and their penal tendencies was both highly complex and individual, depending on: economic and social policy organisation, income differentials and status differentials, citizen-state relations, level of social inclusivity/exclusivity, political orientation, and dominant penal ideology. Those values have an immense impact on: the mode of punishment, imprisonment rate and receptiveness to prison privatisation (Cavadino and Dignan 2006). The authors point out the degree to which societies with different types of political economy are inclusive or exclusive as a key factor with regards to the treatment of those perceived as deviant (Cavadino and Dignan 2006a).

The proposed categorisation seems to be both interesting and plausible. Criminal justice and criminal policy is like a human personality; you cannot explain it with a single gene. Yet Poland, an example of an Eastern and Central European country, does not fit in to any of the proposed categories. It should be closer, because of its origins, to social democracy, but it is not. Social democracy was advocated before 1989 but actually hardly practised. Neoliberalism is the classification that would nowadays, after 1989, be more appropriately applied. Poland can be characterised as a country with a residual welfare state; a country with a declared free market but without the culture required for its implementation. Because of the constant changes within the law and the unstable regulation, it misses out on business stability. It has pronounced – and to some extent extreme – income differences. Unemployment: rising, decreasing, and then rising again is a new phenomenon and not fully covered in the work of Cavadino and Dignan.

Unemployment was concealed in the previous system. Then just everyone could find a job, was paid the meagre salary, but had a sense of stability and safety. But this was arguably overprized – with no political freedom, no freedom of expression and no economic freedom. The change of the political system in 1989 brought unexpected developments for many. The changes initiated by the *Solidarity* movement in 1980 were meant to bring better quality of life for masses of workers, farmers in the state agriculture enterprises and for older citizens tired of the communist regime. 'Freedom' was not supposed to be just another word for 'nothing left to lose', yet, somehow, this indeed has happened. What was previously 'modest life conditions' after 1989 turned into social exclusion. The economic and material exclusion of individuals who are denied access to paid, full-time employment goes together with isolation from relationships provoked by social and special segregation. Education, taken for granted to be free and available for all and at all levels, became costly and hierarchical. And although more people are studying now than before, the gap between those who can afford education and those deprived of it, is growing. There is no immediate correlation between the number of academies and the number of prisons. There is no absolute truth in what Victor Hugo said – by opening libraries you start shutting down prisons – but the *Solidarity* promise was to reform prisons and open the chance for education. There were 310 universities in 2000 and this number increased to 467 in 2010 with 1.5 million students in 2000 to over two million in 2010 (Rocznik Statystyczny (2011). Therefore, from seven per cent of the population with a university degree before 1989, this percentage increased to 17.5.[13] At the end of the communist regime Poland had over 130,000 prisoners, and the average penalty lasted 27 months. A year later there were no more than 40,000 in prison with a sharp cut in the term of average imprisonment. Twenty years later we have doubled the prison population to over 80,000.[14]

The *Solidarity* movement created a vision of an all-inclusive society when people demanded not only political and economic freedom but also clearly articulated the need for criminal justice reform and a step back from the punitive tendency and traditions. It seems however, that tradition is stronger than the movement. Those who started it all became the most defeated and disappointed. The slogans of inclusion and unity were replaced by concern about the situation of one's bank account. Freedom – mistaken by many for material consumption, credit bank politics mistaken for care, and church strivings to gain material and political hegemony mistaken for consideration – raised political and social divisions. Poland has one of the highest long-term unemployment rates in the age group 15–64 in Europe (Levay 2007). The statistics were mitigated once Poland entered the EU. The almost allegorical 'Polish plumber' and 'polish nurse' improved the statistics by leaving the country, but did not affect the employment developments within the country.

It is often stressed that countries with a well-established democracy have better instruments to repress the tendency of increasing the role of the penal system as a main tool of social control. I would, however, argue that states with well-developed penal systems, serving as a major tool of penal control, have less incentive to strengthen democratic instruments. It is Zygmunt Baumann's argument that globalisation is responsible for steadily increasing the role of the penal system as a device of public control. But, in the case of Poland the increase of the penal system's role is not self-evident, for the country had become used to such a form of governance previously. It is also hard to call it a transition period. It rather that we are regressing while a transition presupposes forward movement. Poland is, therefore, a mixture between neoliberalism and conservative corporatism.

New developments

One of the three musicians had spent some time in a Swedish prison. He thought the conditions good, but could not bear the level of personal control exercised there. He also had the chance to experience electronic monitoring in both countries and saw no difference. Electronic monitoring was introduced into Poland several years ago as an adjunct to imprisonment and there are plans to extend its role in the wider sentencing process. It is evaluated as a positive experiment worth becoming a common practice.[15]

The second musician agreed to mediation with the victim. Mediation, used in the Polish criminal system for adults since 1997, is slowly gaining support. It is not fixed within the executive law, but is allowed in practice.

The three musicians, while playing, felt quite moved. As strange as it sounds they shared the feeling that when they were involved while in prison in the EU project called Equal they had the time of their lives. Prison is a lousy, slow place where time hangs like a smelly sock. Yet a place so apathetic and indolent while frozen still and idle, was full of actual purpose when they were allowed to do things that seemed right and meaningful. When they played, when the group started performing, time got on a speedy horse. The three years went like a day. And what a day it was! People were around, and among them women! Women – those from outside and inside – all of them watching them playing and asking for more.

The first musician was back in prison. The second had been out for a year already. With no chance of finding legal employment, he was working illegally. The third coped well. He had a job, but missed his family. He had come just for one night from England. He was in prison for killing his mother-in-law. He got released conditionally, but the family had already broken up. His wife took the two children and did not even want to talk to him. Caarmen danced in the female group created in prison for women. She got released a year before him, and left for Germany. She also had a good life there. Oh, well – maybe not so good. She found employment as a sexworker, and could imagine a better job, but not a better paid one. You earn less when you are a woman, and it is hard to earn anything when you have been to prison. It is equally hard for men and women, especially in Poland.

They got together to play with this one who was about to go back to prison next day. Friendship is not common even outside prison and, therefore, even more valued when it is found on the inside.

Prison resembles a toxic relationship; it destroys you while turning you into an addict. It makes promises and it breaks them. It cheats, tears away your dignity. It takes the potential of a Persian carpet's fine ornaments and turns it into a worn rag. It is like that everywhere, no matter the country, but in some countries it is worn thin more than in others. Things are relative. Bearable prison conditions in one country could be perceived as unbearable in another. In Poland, constantly struggling with problems, permanently dealing with overcrowding and new prison reforms – none of which are really effective – the carpet requires a lot of sewing and mending to fix the rag it has become. However, it seems that simple but important changes in attitude and practice, which would allow prisoners to simply feel dignified, are the first and most important steps to take.

Notes

1. I would like to thank Maria Pawłowska and Natalia Pawłowska for their comments and immense help during my work on this text.

2. All the statistics concerning prisons for the years 2009–2011 come from Prison statistical information: Informacja Statystyczna o ewidencji spraw i orzecznictwie w sądach powszechnych oraz o więziennictwie. Cz. VII Więziennictwo 2011, MinisterstwoSprawiedliwości Warszawa 2012

3. Police statistics and Ministry of Justice statistics for 2001: http://statystyka. policja.pl/portal/st/1104/63464/Prowadzenie_pojazdu_w_stanie_nietrzez-woscI_lub_pod_wplywem_srodka_odurzajacego_a.html [15/11/2012].

4. I am aware that thie is a general comment, and one can find data and even articles referring to Central and Easter part of Europe, but this is a more common now, from the down of XXI century, see for example: vanZylSmit and Dunkel (2001).

5. And when describing and comparing the region it is usually not analytical but limited to descriptive presentation of specific countries. See: Lelental and Wierzbicki (1975).

6. See for example developments described by Helena Valkova which are very common also for Poland; Valkova (2007).

7. This way built up tradition, had nothing to do with mischievous ignorance. The omission however was present. We did not share the specific criminal justice developments in our countries. We did not reckon them valid. We were much more concentrated on structural vices understanding that even interesting programmes and institutions have no chance to become the mainstream and influence the existing criminal policy. We also did not cherish the achievements we had. Anything that had western label meant to be better, of better quality, more interesting and more wanted. At the same time it was obvious it is out of reach. Why it was obvious? "West" as the Polish Constitution was supposed to be, but not to be reached.

8. See: for example Criminology: Yesterday, Today, Tomorrow – works of the so-called St Petersburg Criminology Club including Saint Petersburg University of Interior Ministry of Russia but also Russian State Pedagogical University of Herzen, Krgyz-Russian Slavonic University and Indiana University of Pennsylvania; or "Nevolja" [Slavery] Russian critical, very interesting, high quality journal on criminal policy and penitentiary practice.

9. I write about it in depth in M. Płatek Penal Practice and Social Theory in Poland Before and after 1989……op.cit.

10. It is enough just to mention the work concentrated on traditional criminology continued, for example, by the pupil of great criminal law lawyer Wacław Makowski, Stanisław Batawia and his school, or the interesting and innovative ideas of Adam Podgórecki with regards to sociology of law. Podgórecki ideas were derived from Leon Petrażycki, who was one of the world pioneers of legal sociology criminal justice philosophy. Podgórecki developed his social theory in opposition to the Marxist theory of law and the state. He stressed the importance of empirical comparative material guided by theoretical hypothesis.The good example of the process one can observe in original work of Leszek Lernell, an interesting Polish criminologist who at the time responsible for discontinuing criminology in academia later not only developed original theory of crime but eagerly propagated the ideas developed in criminal justice, criminology and penology in Western world; see: Batawia (1931); Ostrichańska (1982); Batawia (1965); Fajst (2006); Podgórecki (1991); Milano: Dott. Giuffre Editore, Podgórecki et al. (1985); Podgórecki

(1981a); Podgórecki (1981b); Podgórecki and Los (1979); Podgórecki (1973); Podgórecki (1974); Ziegert (1977).

11. Netherlands and Scandinavian studies are exceptions to that phenomenon but even there the main reference is to what happened in UK and USA, Ugelvik and Dullum (2012); Christie (1993).
12. This naivety is obvious when the scale of abusive practice is open for screening. This was not however available under the system of closed barriers. See for example: Leyton (1990) (a reprint from 1975, 1st edn).
13. Wyższe wykształcenie ma 17,5% Polaków, Informacja PAP – nauka w Polsce – 2 January 2012.
14. Prison statistics (2012) www.sw.gov.pl/pl/o-sluzbie.../**statystyka**/[*15/07/2012*].
15. Nowy wymiar polityki karnej. Upowszechnienie kar nie izolacyjnych. System probacji i sprawiedliwość naprawcza. Kancelaria Prezydenta Rzeczpospolitej Polski, Warszawa 2012.

References

M. S. Batawia (1965) 'Młodociani i Młodzi Recydywiści w Świetle 89 Badań Kryminologicznych', *Archiwum Kryminologii*, t. III: Część pierwsza.

M. S. Batawia (1931) *Wstęp do Nauki o Przestępcy: Zagadnienia Skłonności Przestępczych* (Warszawa: PWN).

M. Cavadino and J. Dignan (2007) *The Penal System: An Introduction* (London: Sage) 85–8.

M. Cavadino and J. Dignan (2006a) *Penal System: A Comparative Approach* (London: Sage) 3–39.

M. Cavadino and J. Dignan (2006) 'Penal Policy and Political Economy', *Criminology and Criminal Justice*, 6 (4): 1

N. Christie (2004) *A Suitable Amount of Crime* (London : Routledge) 7–8.

N. Christie (1993) *Crime Control as Industry* (London: Routledge).

E. Domańska (2008a) 'Badania Postkolonialne', in Leela Gandhi, Teoria Postkolonialna: Wprowadzenie Krytyczne, Translation: Jacek Serwanski (Poznan: Wydawnictwo Poznanskie) 157–65.

E. Domańska (2008b) 'Obrazy PRL w Perspektywie Postkolonialnej: Studium Przypadku', in Krzysztof Brzechczyn (ed.), *Obrazy PRLu o Konceptualizacji Realnego Socializmu w Polsce* (Poznań: UAM) 167–86.

M. Fajst (2006) Leszek Lernell, Stanisław Batawia i Warszawska Szkoła Kryminologiczna w LatachPięćdziesiątych XX Wieku "Studia Iuridica XLVI" Journal of Law of Warsaw University

M. Filar and S. Frankowski (ed.) (1982) *Prawo Karne Niektórych Państw Europy Zachodniej, Wybrane Zagadnienia* (Warszawa: Wydawnictwo Prawnicze).

D. Garland (2001) *The Culture of Control: Crime and Social Order in Contemporary Society* (Oxford: Oxford University Press).

E. Hobsbawn (2008) *On Empire: America, Wars, and Global Supremacy* (New York: The New Press) 3–13.

B. Hudson (2003) *Justice in the Risk Society* (London: Sage).

S. Lelental and P. Wierzbicki (1975) *Wykonanie Kary Pozbawienia Wolności w Europejskich Państwach Socjalistycznych* (Warszawa:Wydawnictwa Prawnicze).

M. Levay (2007) ' "Social Exclusion" A Thriving Concept in Contemporary Criminology: Social Exclusion and Crime in Central and Eastern Europe', in K. Aromaa (ed.), *Penal Policy, Justice Reform, and Social Exclusion* (Helsinki: HEUNI), 7–25.

E. Leyton (1990) *Dying Hard: The Ravages of Industrial Carnage* (Toronto : McClelland and Stewart Inc) (a reprint from 1975, 1st edn).

N. Pawłowska (2007) 'Prawo Podmiotowe Więźniów Do Powierzchni Mieszkalnej', *Państwo i Prawo*, 5: 76–89.

M. Płatek (2004) 'Punishment and the restoration of Legality In Poland', in *W kręgu kryminologiiromantycznej*, (eds) M. Płatek, M. Fajst, Warszawa, pp. 217–48

M. Płatek (1998) 'Penal Practice and Social Theory in Poland Before and After the Events of 1989', in R. P.Weiss and N.South (eds) *Comparing Prison Systems. Towards Comparative and International Penology*. Amsteldijk: Gordon and Breach Publishers., 263–89.

A. Podgórecki et al. (eds) (1985) *Social Systems and Legal Systems* (London: Crom Helm).

A. Podgórecki (1991) *A Sociological Theory of Law* (Milano: Dott A. Giuffre).

A. Podgórecki (1981a) *The Polish Burial of Marxist Ideology* (London: Poets and Painters Press).

A. Podgórecki (1981b) 'Unrecognized Father of Sociology of Law: Leon Petrażycki', *Law and Society Review*, 15: 183–202.

A. Podgórecki (1974) *Law and Society* (London: Routledge).

A. Podgórecki (1973) *Knowledge and Opinion about Law* (London: Martin Robertson).

A. Podgórecki and M. Los (1979) *Multidimensional Sociology* (London: Routledge and Keagan Paul).

J. Pratt, D. Brown, M. Brown, S. Hallsworth and W. Morrison (eds) (2005) *The New Punitiveness: Trends, Theories, Perspectives* (Portland: Willan Publishing).

A. Siemaszko (2000) *Crime and Law Enforcement in Poland on the Threshold of the 21st Century* (Warszawa: Oficyna Naukowa)...op.cit, .s. 53.

T. Ugelvik and J. Dullum (ed.) (2012) *Penal Exceptionalism? Nordic Prison Policy and Practice* (London: Routledge).

H. Valkova (2007) 'Crime and Criminal Justice Reforms in the "New Central European Countries", and the example of the Czech Republic', in K. Aromaa (ed.), *Penal Policy, Justice Reform, and Social Exclusion* (Helsinki: HEUNI) 100–19.

D.vanZylSmit and F. Dunkel (2001) *Imprisonment Today and Tomorrow: International Perspectives on Prisoners Rights and Prison Conditions* (The Hague: Kluwer Law International).

R. Walmsley (2010) 'Trends in World Prison Population', in S. Harrendorf, M. Heiskanen and S. Malby (ed.), *International Statistics on Crime and Justice* (Helsinki: HEUNI) 167.

K. A. Ziegert (1977) 'Adam Podgórecki's Sociology of Law: The Invisible Factors of the Functioning of Law Made Visible', *Law and Society Review*, 12: 151–80.

Rocznik Statystyczny (2012) *Szkoły Wyższe i ich Finanse* (Warszawa:GUS – Główny Urząd Statystyczny).

10
Soft and Harsh Penalties in Bulgaria

Philip Gounev

Penal policies have been at the heart of public debate in Bulgaria for much of the past decade. The country's criminal justice system and policies were subject to intensive outside scrutiny, both before and during the five-year period after its accession to the European Union. Inevitably, this made criminal justice and penal policies highly politicised hot topics – an area where a sense of moral panic was periodically infused by the European Commission's assessments of the country's efforts to tackle crime and corruption (see for instance Commission Report COM (2012) 411 final). The ensuing political and public pressures over the criminal justice system (and for an independent judiciary), for more 'just', that is harsher, penalties, clashed with the stark reality – the lack of vision and strategy that are necessary to transform a penal system which has changed little since the end of communism in 1989.

The issue of imprisonment, however, has remained largely outside this debate and been neglected by public or EU scrutiny. Prison was considered of marginal importance, located somewhere at the very end of the penal process, which was fraught with numerous other problems. The conditions and the rights of prisoners, on the other hand, have been examined at length in non-governmental documents (Bulgarian Helsinki Committee 2002). So have structural issues relating to the effectiveness of the judicial system and the corruption and deficiencies found in the penal system. These have been discussed at length elsewhere (CSD 2012a; Ilkova 2010; Commission Report COM 2012) 411 final; Commission Staff Working Document SWD (2012) 232 final).

This chapter will examine the functioning of the penal process focusing on the two extremes characterising it: the over-penalised (the Roma) and the under-penalised (organised criminals). The analysis presented below is based on two EU-funded policy implementation projects that were carried out over the past decade by the CSD (Center for the Study of Democracy) in Bulgaria. The first project focused on Police Racial Profiling in Bulgaria, and involved a nationally representative survey of Bulgarians and Roma, as well as semi-structured interviews with police officers and Roma communities around the country. This took place between 2005 and 2008 in a number of cities around Bulgaria (CSD 2006b). The second project was conducted between 2010 and 2012. Its main objective was to produce the first Serious and Organised Crime Threat Assessment (CSD 2012b). As part of the project the research team examined the police and prosecution tactics to combat organised crime. About 50 semi-structured interviews were carried out around the country with investigators, prosecutors, judges, NGOs, and inmates. Additional information derives from the annual crime victimisation survey[1]of the CSD, which periodically assesses the impact of criminal justice policies on crime rates (CSD 2006a: 26–32,2011b: 28–30).

Penal policies and custody

The prison system

Bulgaria's prison system is managed by the Ministry of Justice via the Chief Directorate of Implementation of Penal Sanctions. The Directorate has 27 Regional units with a Detention Facilities Sector and a Probation Sector. The prison system consists only of state-owned and managed prisons: 12 prison institutions, and 22 open and closed prison dormitories. There are two separate juvenile correctional facilities for males and females, respectively, as well as one female-only prison. The prisons are quite old, with most of them built in the 1930s. The newest prison institution is Sliven prison, dating from 1962. In the past decade there have been public discussions about the construction of new and even privately managed prisons but with little progress. In 2010 the government purchased a land plot near Sofia, which is supposed to become the sight of the next prison, with a capacity of 2,000 prisoners.

Bulgarian prisons have a total 8,740 inmate capacity, calculated on four square metres per person – over-crowding is a significant issue. The problem is more acute at the Plovdiv and Burgas facilities, which hold almost twice as many inmates as their capacity allows. The women-only and the juvenile detention facilities – in Sliven and Boytchinovtsi, respectively – are occupied at less than 50 per cent of their capacity (CSD 2011c: 42). Amnesties have been used as a tool to respond to over-crowding.Public opinion, however, has opposed them, and after a 1990 amnesty – which saw 3,800 inmates released – only a very limited amnesty was passed in 2009, when less than 200 inmates were released.

Legal framework

Imprisonment and all aspects of its implementation are regulated by a range of primary and secondary legislation: *the Penal Code, the Penal Procedure Code, the Law on Implementation of Penal Sanctions and Detention in Custody (LIPSDC), the Regulations for Application of the LIPSDC* and the rest of the instruments of secondary legislation issued in pursuance of the LIPSDC.[2] Bulgaria has ratified all relevant international legal instruments, such as the Convention concerning Forced or Compulsory Labour, the UN Convention against Torture and Other Cruel, Inhuman or Degrading Treatment or Punishment, the European Convention for the Prevention of Torture and Inhuman or Degrading Treatment or Punishment, the UN Standard Minimum Rules for the Treatment of Prisoners, the European Prison Rules.[3]

Imprisonment rates and trends

There are numerous factors that may influence imprisonment rates and the number of prisoners. Historically, Bulgaria, much like other former communist bloc countries, has followed the tradition of inflicting fairly long custodial penalties. In the early 1990s, the criminal justice system in Bulgaria experienced a period of total collapse, as the number of sentences fell around three-fold, and restarted to increase only in the late 1990s. In the meantime the demographics of the country had changed dramatically, when, due to a combination of factors, Bulgaria's population fell by around 16 per cent.

With the return of the rule of law and economic growth in the late 1990s, after a period of economic and social chaos, the past ten years have shown a growing imprisonment rate (Figure 10.1). Crime victims surveys and police statistics, instead, show a very different trend: police data show a gradual and consistent decrease in registered crimes, from 135,863 in 2001 to 114,340 in 2011, with a sharp 2009 and 2010 interlude of crime increases (most likely related to the sudden economic crisis that hit the country).

Sentences, including imprisonment, have been following a very different pattern that requires a different set of explanations. As no evaluation has been made on the nature of penal sanctions, it would be speculative to attribute changes to one single factor. For instance, with the EU accession process in April 2006 a new Penal Procedural Code (PPC) came into force. At that time, the party of Prime Minister

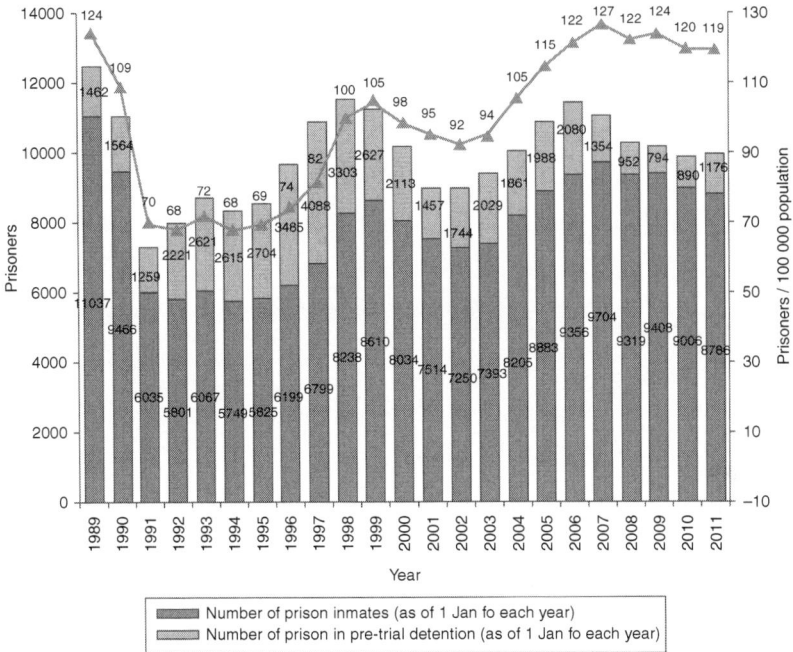

Figure 10.1 Number of inmates in prisons and pre-trial detention facilities
Source: Ministry of Justice.

Saxe-Coburg-Gotha included among its members a faction informally known as the 'lawyers' lobby', which introduced a range of procedures that favoured defendants. Following this, the number of custodial penal sanctions, as well as their average duration, was reduced.

One factor that somewhat reversed this trend, and explains the gradual increase in the average length of custodial penalties(from 10.4 months in 2009 to 11.1 months in 2011), was the pressure from the media and the European Commission for more and harsher penalties relating to organised crime and corruption (Figure 10.2). A sense of moral panic was instilled via the monitoring reports issued by the EC that called for more effective penalties. The government's unfavourable comments on specific sentences, along with the frictions between the Minister of Interior and high-level magistrates in the 2009–2012 period, attracted the attention of the EC. In its 2012 monitoring report the EC commented that such public statements by the Minister of Interior amounted to an impingement on the independence of the judiciary. This practice

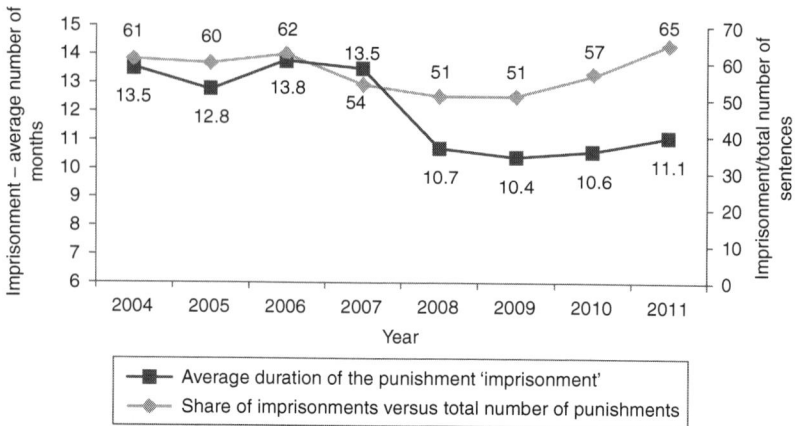

Figure 10.2   Duration and frequency of custodial sentences
Source: Ministry of Justice/National Statistical Institute.

of public commenting on sentences only followed a long-established tradition, started by the current Prime Minister in his role as head of the police, where he became well-known for frequently using the phrase 'We catch them, they [the judges] let them free'.

Preventative programmes and post-custodial measures

Measures for crime prevention, re-offending prevention, or reintegration programmes are only in their infancy in Bulgaria. They are largely considered as 'luxury' services that the underfunded prison system is not able to provide. Whenever such programmes have been implemented, they have been so for a limited period, or in limited locations. Their impact has not been assessed.

The oldest running programme is the prison employment programme. It is run by a state-owned company, called the *Prison works fund*. This company provides production services to other companies, and it is subcontracted to produce the likes of furniture, ceramics products, or mechanical parts. The inmates are also used for construction and maintenance work in and around prisons. Psychological support and harm reduction programmes are provided to drug abusers in custody and methadone is only available in some prisons.

Another programme is known as *Preparation for free life*. The main goal behind this programme is to help prisoners perform tasks they will have to face once released. The standard training package includes things such as getting personal ID cards, applying for social assistance, signing up at the local job centre. The main weakness of this programme is its slowness, as a result of which there is no support during the first month after leaving prison.

NGOs in some of the bigger cities provide support in activities, such as harm reduction programmes for drug users and HIV/AIDS prevention services. For the first time in 2012, an NGO in the town of Pazardjik was entrusted with the provision of the post-custodial services mentioned above.

Alternatives to custody

The few alternatives to custody which are available are neglected or haphazardly implemented, nor are their objectives and effects evaluated. Legislation regarding electronic monitoring as an alternative to custody was passed but never followed up with a precise implementation programme.

Probation is deemed the most advanced alternative to custody. Its implementation started on 1 January 2005 but to date has largely failed to achieve the objectives with which this kind of penal instrument is associated in Western Europe and the US. The measure is very narrowly applied – it is not used during the pre-trial period or during the adjudication phase, as it is only seen as an alternative to custody – for which a sentence is needed (see Table 10.1). Therefore, the person on probation is neither required to agree nor to cooperate. There is no pre-trial report assessing how appropriate the measure is to the offender, and the

Table 10.1   Types of penal sanctions imposed, 2007–2011

Types of penal sanctions imposed	2011	2010	2009	2008	2007
Effective custody[a]	9,676	9,164	8,891	9,463	9,726
Suspended custody	17,701	14,552	13,771	14,483	12,270
Probation	13,922	15,531	16,565	15,737	13,356
Admin. sanction (Art. 78a of Penal Code)	8,160		5,419	5,557	8,808
Other	8,860	17,012	13,975	13,660	11,759
Total sanctions	**58,330**	**56,264**	**58,631**	**58,915**	**55,934**

Life imprisonment is extremely rare – on average 10–15 cases per year.

Source: Supreme cassation prosecution office.

judge and the probation officers do not communicate after the penalty has been imposed. Judges therefore are not aware of the specifics of the probation measure. Probation is granted by local committees, consisting largely of former police officers, of whom less than ten per cent have undergone any specific training (Crime Prevention Fund IGA 2007: 39).

Community service is not considered a separate penalty, but is part of probation, and is not thoroughly regulated. The offenders are simply sent to help with any public works, irrespective of their skills, and without any marked clothing that would make them recognisable to the public. The probation service also provides training courses aimed at teaching new professional skills. These are largely inadequate, as they do not take into account the high number of illiterate offenders. Finally, probation is used as an alternative measure to other types of penalties, such as limitations on taking some types of public posts, or practicing certain professions. This narrow understanding of probation further limits its application and effectiveness.

One additional penal sanction – that has become especially relevant in the context of organised crime – is the confiscation of criminal assets. In Bulgaria there are two possibilities to deprive criminals of assets –confiscation as part of the sentence, and administrative forfeiture (carried out by specialised independent bodies). Confiscation is rarely imposed by the prosecution, as the capacity of the police or the prosecution to undertake asset-tracking and investigations is very limited. Confiscation, therefore, can only affect publicly registered assets.

Costs of incarceration

Public investment in the prison system has been very low for years. According to official figures, the subsistence cost per prisoner per year is BGN 3,000 (€1,500). However, a simple calculation – based on the known total 2011 budget for the entire penitentiary system (BGN 64 million) and the total number of prisoners – brings the average annual cost per inmate to around €3,600. By comparison, the average annual cost per inmate in the US is $31,286, but can reach as much as $60,000 in some prisons (e.g. New York) (Center on Sentencing and Corrections 2012). In the UK the Ministry of Justice estimates the cost per prisoner per year at £40,000 (*Daily Mail* 2012).

Corruption and crime in the prison system

Corruption observed throughout the criminal justice system in Bulgaria also characterises the prison system (Gounev and Bezlov 2012). This relates to two sets of issues. The first is to do with the limitation of inmates' contacts with criminals outside, with corrupt prison officers smuggling mobile phones[4] inside – including smart phones, which allow prisoners to use the internet and continue their criminal careers while in detention. The second affects the higher layers of the prison administration, including medical personnel or prison directors. The administration, for instance, may provide inmates with positive assessments regarding their conduct, thus allowing their temporary release: up to two vacation days per month, five family days per year, and 14 days of annual leave (allowed for voluntary work carried out in prison). Another loophole in the system allows individual inmates with unique skills to be allowed to work for companies that have contracts for voluntary labour within particular prisons. Organised crime and white collar criminals are known to have bribed their way into maximising their vacation time, or even spending their entire time and using their unique skills to 'work' outside the prison.

Although there are no prison gangs, drug-related crime constitutes a significant problem. A 2011 survey amongst 3,703 prisoners showed that in the preceding 12 months 21.6 per cent of inmates used some type of drug, with heroin (13.4%) and cannabis (11.8%) the most widespread. A significant number of the inmates, 23.5 per cent, admitted to heroin use prior to entering prison (http://anketi.info/images/folder/2011_national_report_bg_bg_fin2.pdf: p.20–1). This great demand for drugs, particularly heroin, is satisfied not only via different smuggling schemes, but also via corruption of prison guards who smuggle the substances in.

Punishing organised criminals

Social background of organised criminals

Assessing the penal policies regarding organised criminals in Bulgaria requires a good understanding of the socio-economic and political significance of this type of offenders in the country. The public discourse in Bulgaria is based on a much broader definition of organised crime than the one used by the police or criminologists (CSD 2007,2010: 203–31; Gounev 2011). The definition often refers to 'groups' or 'networks' involved in the provision of illicit goods (drugs, prostitution, pirated products) or in other structured criminal activities (bank card fraud, car theft).'White collar' crime, by contrast, even after the financial crisis of 2008–2009, still refers to a special category of fraudsters, rogues within otherwise law-abiding companies. 'Economic crimes', in their turn, are deemed a separate category: they escape public scrutiny, and rarely make news headlines, as instead do the spectacular raids of busted drugs trafficking or prostitution rings (CSD 2007).

These definitions and distinctions between organised and 'white collar' criminals are not persuasive. The economic elite in Bulgaria has for over two decades conducted large parts of its business in a grey zone (CSD 2011d), closely connected with markets for illicit goods and services (CSD 2011d). For example, 'legitimate' companies may produce forged products to sell on illicit markets, while also doing business with multinational corporations. In this case, are organised criminals only those who distribute such goods or also those who produce them? By the same token, are the entrepreneurs producing tobacco, alcohol, or oil products and evading excise taxes running a criminal syndicate (CSD 2012b: 36ff, 45)? If one calls VAT carrousel fraudsters 'organised criminals', how should we call the owners of big corporations in Bulgaria involved in tax fraud?

The history of organised crime in Bulgaria further complicates these definitional quandaries, as the line separating 'white collar' from 'traditional' criminals is blurred (CSD 2007; Tzvetkova 2008; Gounev 2011; Gounev and Bezlov 2012). With illegitimate practices characterising large parts of the economy,[5] it is not surprising that corruption ends up affecting the criminal justice system and influencing the development of penal policies. Corruption may target prosecutors, who can stop or mismanage investigations, or judges, who can slow down the judicial process, reduce penalties, accept improbable plea-bargain agreements, or grant early release from custody (CSD 2010: 213–8).

On a higher level, the interests of oligarchs and organised criminals have found support in a number of prominent defence lawyers. Even human rights organisations have inadvertently supported such lawyers, when, for example, campaigning for the rights of the defendants, thus indirectly impeding the prosecution and punishment of corrupt government officials or organised criminals.[6]

Organised criminals and penalty sanctions

A cursory look at the penal sanctions available in the Criminal Code leaves one with the sense that these are heavy enough to achieve the main objectives of the criminal justice system: to stop organised criminal activities for sufficiently long periods of time so that they cannot easily resume (Table 10.2).

The reality, however, could not be further removed from this sentencing menu. Two examples illustrate the actual state of affairs: penal responses

Table 10.2 Organised crime related offences and penalties

Offence	Type of crime	Imprisonment (years)	Fine
Kidnapping [Item 8 of Article 142 (2)]	Main crime	3–10	No
	Aggravated cases	7–15	No
Inducement to prostitution, procuring for molestation or copulation and providing premises for lewd and lascivious acts	Main crime	up to 3 (for inducement to prostitution / procurement)	Yes
		up to 5 (for providing premises for lewd and lascivious acts)	Yes
		1–6 (for an act committed with the aim of obtaining a benefit)	Yes
		5–15 (for inducing / forcing a person to use narcotic drugs for the purpose of prostitution)	Yes
[Item 1 of Article 155 (5)]	Aggravated cases	2–8 (inducement to prostitution / providing premises for prostitution)	Yes
		3–10 (for an act committed with the aim or obtaining a benefit)	Yes
		10–20 (for inducing or forcing another person to use narcotic drugs for the purpose of prostitution)	Yes
Trafficking in human beings [Article 159d]	Main crime	2–8 (without taking across border)	Yes
		3–12 (with taking across border)	Yes
		3–10 (for use of the victim)	Yes
	Aggravated cases	5–15	Yes
Blackmail [Item 5 of Article 213a (2)]	Main crime	1–6	Yes
	Aggravated cases	5–15	Yes
Cross-border smuggling of goods [Article 242 (1) (g)]	Main crime	Administrative violation	No
	Aggravated cases	3–10	Yes
Money laundering [Item 1 of Article 253 (3)]	Main crime	1–6	Yes
	Aggravated cases	1–8	Yes
Establishing and leading an organised crime group (Article 321)	Main crime	3–10	Yes
	Aggravated cases	5–15	Yes
Motor vehicle theft [Article 346 (6)]	Main crime	1–8	No
	Aggravated cases	3–12	No

Continued

Table 10.2   Continued

Offence	Type of crime	Imprisonment (years)	Fine
Production and distribution of narcotics [Item 1 of Article 354a (2)]	Main crime	2–8 (high-risk narcotic drugs)	Yes
		1–6 (risk narcotic drugs)	Yes
		3–12 (precursors or facilities or materials for the production of narcotic drugs)	Yes
	Aggravated cases	5–15	Yes

Source: Penal Code.

to organised car theft, and the prosecution and sentencing of leading organised/white collar crime figures and corrupt government officials. In both cases a series of loopholes in the Penal Procedural Code or the Penal Code itself brings about impunity.

Article 345a of the Penal Code[7] implies that the cloning of a vehicle should result in 'three to 10 years imprisonment', or 'up to three years imprisonment' if only the ID numbers of the vehicle are changed. Car theft brings a penalty of 'one to 8 years imprisonment' (art. 346), or one to 10 years if a ransom is asked for its restitution, if the vehicle is abandoned, or the thief is drunk or a recidivist (art. 346.2). The use of force in stealing a car, or stealing it as a part of an organised crime venture – or 'an attempt to export it outside the country, or changing the registration numbers' – carries three to 12 years imprisonment (art. 346.5). These seemingly aggressive provisions are not applied in practice, as a comparison of judicial and police statistical data shows. In 2009, for instance, 4,470 registered crimes under art. 346 and 346a resulted only in 321 court cases, of which only 19 involved three or more individuals. Unlike other countries, where 'joy-riding thefts' by juveniles are common, in Bulgaria cartheft is almost exclusively related to organised crime (Gounev 2011). Therefore, it seems that only in a very small number of cases the prosecution targets members of a criminal network.

Out of the 365 individuals sentenced in connection to the 321 cases mentioned above, only 261 received a custodial penalty, while the rest were simply fined or put on probation. The majority of the sentences were short-term: 222 were less than one year-long, 37 were between one and three years, and only two individuals were given three or more year-long penalties.[8] An analysis of the penalties for drug crimes showed very similar results: in the 2004–2009 period only 39 per cent of the cases

Table 10.3 Number and types of prosecuted high-profile cases in 2011

Crimes	Total cases investigated	Filed in court	Effective court decision
Organised Crime	39	18	14
Corruption	19	5	1
Money laundering	25	6	0
Misuse of EU funds	60	24	13
Documentary, tax and financial fraud	46	9	0
Other crimes	57	14	1

Source: Prosecutor's office of the republic of Bulgaria, 2012: 106.

resulted in convictions, while in 60 per cent of the cases the custodial sentence was less than one year (CSD 2011c: 71–4).

The second example refers to so-called high-profile cases or 'cases of special interest to the public' (Table 10.3). The 2011 data from the prosecution showed that only 12 per cent (29 out of 246) of the high-profile cases investigated resulted in a court decision. An analysis of another 17 such cases showed that only three ended up with a guilty verdict (Ilkova 2010: 6). The reasons for these outcomes include the delay of trials due to change of lawyers, the unavailability of defence lawyers, the change of judges, the lack of key witnesses (often due to threats from defendants), corruption of medical personnel to secure the release of defendants on remand, and so on.

Explaining impunity

The main factors that contribute to leniency or impunity for organised criminals are the excessive use of plea-bargain agreements and of summary judicial inquiries. The first tool was used in 28 per cent of the cases in 2011, while the second (whose principles will be explained in a moment) in 37 per cent of the cases. Both allow for a substantial reduction of sentences (Table 10.1). Both, moreover, fail to produce a preventative effect on organised criminals, who continue therefore to run their businesses.

Plea bargaining is among the provisions of the *Criminal Procedure Code* and allows to reach pre-trial arrangements. These may be agreed upon when the financial profit generated by the offence has been recovered and the defendant has renounced the examination of the case by the court.[9] The plea-bargain typically takes place only after the defence counsels have reviewed the evidence collected by the prosecution and have made sure that the prosecution has sufficient evidence to win the case. While it is understandable that defence counsels support the plea-bargain procedures, as it is in the interest of their clients, prosecutors and judges mainly use it as a tool to manage their work-load, advance their careers, or become involved in corrupt deals. Judges and prosecutors are usually overloaded with cases, and the plea-bargain agreements are seen as a useful instrument to punish offenders swiftly and avoid the typical slowness of trials.[10]Plea-bargain agreements do not affect the career prospects or the professional evaluations of magistrates – while bogged down cases do.

Summary judicial enquiries also speed up the adjudication phase. They are applicable to all types of offences[11]and may be implemented only during the trial of first instance (not during judicial appeals). When using this strategy the defendant usually confesses to the facts described in the justification of the indictment, and agrees that no evidence of these facts need to be collected. The court may then decide not to question the witnesses or experts and to pass the sentence on the basis of the evidence collected in the pre-trial proceeding. When delivering a guilty verdict, the court then imposes a sentenced reduced by one third (CSD 2012a: 116–20). In the absence of policy reviews or sentencing guidelines that help judges understand the reasons and the objectives of penalties, these instruments, supposedly meant to increase the efficiency of the criminal justice process, end up reducing it.

The two examples of how lower level and higher level organised criminals are under-penalised explains only one aspect of the penal and criminal justice policies in Bulgaria. They examine the issues largely shaped by the interests of economically powerful and politically influential players, but also benefit organised criminals who have access to defence attorneys and the resources to manipulate the criminal justice process. The next section of this chapter will look at another aspect of the penal policy process that is largely being shaped by the interests of investigators and magistrates, and affects the socially excluded part of the population.

The Roma – the over-penalised

Bulgaria has two large ethnic minority groups – the Roma and the Turks. The immigrant minorities constitute less than one per cent of the population, and are typically of higher social status (merchants from the Middle East and China) – therefore, hardly featuring in any criminal justice data. The Turkish population is mostly rural, and its crime rates are very low: while constituting around ten per cent, Turks commit only around three per cent of the recorded crimes.[12]

The treatment of Roma in the criminal justice system is the most troubling aspect of penal policies and the prison system. Roma are over-represented both in statistics about prosecutions and within the prison population. Explanations for this may be related to the following:

• For social and economic reasons Roma commit more crimes than other ethnic groups.
• Involvement in crime starts a vicious cycle that leads to greater attention towards the Roma by the police.
• As a result, a disproportionate number of Roma enters the criminal justice process, where a combination of moral panic, discriminatory attitudes, and lack of access to adequate defence further exacerbates their position.

Table 10.4   Crime suspects and homicide rate per 100,000 population[a]

		Crime suspects[b] per 100,000 population			Homicides[c] per 100,000 population			
Year	Total	Bulgarians	Roma (census)	Roma (estimated)	Total	Bulgarians	Roma (census)	Roma (estimated)
1993	802	487	7249	4733	–	–	–	–
1994	880	520	7559	4935	–	–	–	–
1997	1195	897	9411	6145	–	–	–	–
2003	1062	982	4606	3559	–	–	–	–
2006	1130	1089	4055	3093	2.77	2.91	5.46	4.16
2007	1032	1002	4653	2786	2.77	2.71	7.57	5.57
2008	1003	989	3458	2636	2.64	2.77	6.78	5.17
2009	1047	1035	3773	2876	2.39	2.3	8.37	6.38
2010	1111	1082	4530	3453	2.79	2.79	9.7	7.39
2011	957	946	3836	2923	2.44	2.56	8.61	6.56

Note:[a] The calculations are based on census data from 2001 and 2011. The Roma population is based on unpublished estimate of the actual Roma population by the Bulgarian police and a number of social surveys undertaken by the CSD, which indicate that the actual number of Roma is around 480,000.
[b] Numbers of suspects under investigation are not unique, that is individuals investigated for multiple offenses are counted multiple times. So, the figure for unique offenders is indeed lower. This means that the percentage columns are valid only if the following assumption is true: that the Roma repetitive offenders have the same rate of recidivism as the Bulgarian repetitive offenders.
[c] Homicides include only intentional homicides and attempted homicides.

Source: Ministry of Interior.

The absence of moral panic towards immigrants in Bulgaria is replaced by one against the Roma. During past decades there have been a number of occasions, especially after homicides of ethnic Bulgarians by Roma criminals, when public and media attention and ensuing riots have galvanised extremists from Roma and Bulgarian ethnic groups alike. The police response during, as well as following, such incidents has been particularly harsh, with areas around Roma neighbourhoods becoming subject to military control. Surveys conducted during the past 20 years consistently show that around 90 per cent of Bulgarians consider the Roma to be most likely to engage in criminal acts (CSD 2006b:18).

Ethnicity data in the criminal justice system, therefore, are sensitive. The Balkan wars of the 1990s and worries about spreading ethnic violence in Bulgaria, as well as the ethnic purges by the communist regime in the 1980s, make such data even more sensitive and often misleading or unreliable.[13] There are two major reasons for this:

- Figures on ethnicity and crime are not collected consistently. The analysis of individual regional police departments shows that some occasionally fail to complete the 'ethnicity' field in crime report forms. The Ministry of the Interior, on the other hand, is not eager to enforce the completion of this data, which are deemed purposeless in terms of policy making. There are no particular crime-prevention/reduction policies targeting Roma communities.
- Ethnic identity in general is not easy to pin down in Bulgaria. Some Roma speak Turkish and confess Islam – and usually have a Turkish background. Others speak Bulgarian and are Christians, and might self-identify as Bulgarians. Yet others speak different dialects of the Romani language, and may be identified as 'gypsies'. Regardless of their self-identity, society usually perceives all these groups as Roma. Therefore, the population census is not regarded as a reliable source, as many Roma self-identify either as Bulgarians or as Turks.[14]

Criminal statistics may also be misleading, as crime suspects perceive that they will be treated worse if they admit to being Roma. Even if it is obvious – from the person's language skills, skin-colour, place of residence, name, witness or victim testimonies, etc. – that the suspect's ethnicity is Roma, the police still record the self-identified ethnicity (usually Bulgarian).

Roma and the criminal justice system

The disproportionate presence of Roma in the criminal justice system inevitably prompts the question of Roma involvement in crime. In the 1990s, police statistics indicate that Roma suspects constituted between 26 per cent and 33 per cent of all suspects. Crimepeaks in 1993 and 1997 could be partially explained with the economic crisis, when tens of thousands of Roma lost their jobs and the unemployment rates in Roma communities across the country averaged over 76 per cent (81% in villages) (Tomova 1995). Following the economic and political stabilisation that started in 1998, the percentage of police-registered Roma suspects gradually subsided. The number of Roma crime suspects in the 2007–2011 period (around 12,000 per year or on average 17% of all crime suspects)remained stable and substantially inferior to the figure observed in the 1990s (see Table 10.4).

These figures, however, provide only a partial picture, as they do not account for unreported crimes or the crimes of unknown perpetrators. Thefts, for instance, for which Roma people are disproportionately sentenced,[15] are only reported in 50 per cent of the cases (CSD 2006a: 63,2011b: 49ff). The clear-up rate for property crimes is only 30 per cent, according to police statistics. Sentences for homicide, an offence which is recorded in almost 100 per cent of cases, and has a clear-up rate above 80 per cent, are two to three times higher for Roma people than for any other ethnic group (see Table 10.4 above).

Despite the large 'intake' of Roma crime suspects by the police in the criminal justice process, prosecution is selective. Cases brought to completion for ethnic Bulgarian suspects range between 14.1 and 21 per cent. For Roma people, the figure is between 22 and 38 per cent. On the other hand, arrests and detention for more than 24 hours, which are carried out under prosecutorial permission, are for Roma between two and ten times as many as those for Bulgarians. Finally, data on ethnicity of sentenced individuals have not been reported in national statistics since 2003. Only in some prison institutions are these data kept, although they are rarely made public. The latest figures available (relating to a decade or so ago) indicate that between one third and a half of the prison population in Bulgaria is Roma.[16]

Explaining Roma's disproportionate presence in the criminal justice system

Moral panic and discrimination can only partially account for the disproportionate nature of these figures. Prejudice is certainly deeply entrenched in police or magistrates attitudes, as it is society in general. But the role of discriminatory practices should not be exaggerated. While ethnic stereotypes may lead the police to paying greater attention to Roma suspects, a set of other issues come into play once the person is entangled in the criminal justice process. Even the fact that a great number of Roma cases are dropped by the prosecution, does not necessarily indicate racial prejudice by the police.

A more plausible explanation revolves around issues of professional standards and career-related factors regarding judges and prosecutors. In this respect, let us examine the criminal justice process in more detail.

Before the prosecution officially presses charges, the police carry out a preliminary investigation. Once the charges are officially made by the prosecution, the police consider the case to be 'cleared up' (CSD 2011b). Clear-up rates are the official measurements of police efficiency, to the point that they are artificially boosted by convincing suspects to admit to multiple crimes. This strategy works for two reasons. First, because the accumulation of penalties is not allowed under the current Penal Code – if a crime suspect admits to having committed 50 petty thefts or ten burglaries, s/he would still be given only one custodial sentence for the crime punished with the biggest penalty. Therefore, for instance, if suspects are arrested for burglary, the police and the prosecutor can trade with them – if they claim responsibility for ten petty thefts as well as for the offence with which they are being charged, they may receive the minimum penalty for burglary. Such deals are beneficial to all parties: clear-up rates are inflated, prosecutors show good results in their work, and suspects benefit from minimum penalties.

It should also be noted that Roma suspects are usually allocated a public defender (or legal aid). Public defence lawyers are so poorly paid[17] that they have no incentive to be involved in a trial at all, therefore they are led to cut corners and go to court unprepared. The low quality of their service explains why so many Roma people end up in prison (Analytical Creative Group 1998).

Conclusion

The above analysis sketches a picture in which it is difficult to see a comprehensive or strategic way of thinking about penal policies in the country. The impact of penal policies has never been formally evaluated or assessed. The different trends that are observed in increasing imprisonment rates or harsher penalties reflect political pressures, rather than carefully planned criminal justice policies. This has established a culture of impunity and corruption, while discrediting the criminal justice system and the courts in particular.

Impunity for organised criminals and deviant high-level officials makes Bulgaria one of the most corrupt countries in the EU (CSD 2012b: 6–8) – a country where criminal organisations deeply influence political and economic life (ibid.: 67).

By contrast, the harsh treatment of Roma people in Bulgaria's criminal justice system comes into full light when the data presented above are examined. The impact of imprisonment on criminal behaviour, particularly for first time offenders, has not been the object of study in Bulgaria, but, due to the lack of prevention and rehabilitative programmes, it can be assumed that imprisonment will contribute to the further marginalisation and criminalisation of Roma communities.

Notes

1. More information on the National Crime Survey could be found at www.csd.bg/ncs
2. Various administrative documents regulating electronic monitoring of sentenced persons, rules for the organisation and operation of the Council on Implementation of Penal Sanctions, education programmes in prison, the provision of medical services.
3. Recommendation Rec (2006) 2 of the Committee of Ministers to member states of the Council of Europe on the European Prison Rules on 11 January 2006.
4. Interviews with former inmates indicate that the prices for regular phones inside prison start at around EUR 65.
5. The largest oligarchic structure, which accumulated its initial capital through extortion racketeering and now controls some of the biggest companies in the banking, insurance, transport, and food sectors generates about 5 per cent of GDP. (Source: media interview with one of the group's founders). The penetration of the legal economy even of smaller criminal networks / groups is very high (CSD 2012c) – analysis showed that the majority of criminal groups control some type of legitimate business structure – not for the purpose of facilitating crimes, but simply as an investment and a way of laundering proceeds of crime.
6. Corruption in the judiciary is described at length in CSD 2010: 203–30.
7. State Gazette No. 67, as amended as of 29 July 2008.
8. The statistical data on conviction is based on judicial statistics published on the website of the National Statistics Institute (www.nsi.bg). The police data is drawn from the police statistics provided to the author by the Ministry of Interior.

9. In 2011, 97 per cent of the agreements were approved by the court (Prosecutor's Office of the Republic of Bulgaria 2012: 70)
10. During lengthy cases many difficulties arise, especially with witnesses who begin to forget details about their testimony.
11. The only limitation is for intentional homicide or grievous bodily injury, or where the offender was under the influence of alcohol.
12. This estimate is based on ethnic data for the 56,985 solved crimes in 2011 for which the ethnicity of the offender was registered. Some of these crimes might in fact be committed by Turkish-speaking Roma who self-identified as Turks. Therefore, the real rate might be even lower.
13. The 2002 Law on Private Data Protection allows for the collection of ethnic data, when the person gives a written permission. Such permission, though, is not necessary when at stake are the activities conducted for the by public bodies working on crimes, administrative violations, or national security cases (Art. 21.1 and Art. 21.2.5). The law also allows for such data to be collected and summarised for statistical purposes (Art. 20.2.2).
14. The 2011 census put the total number of Roma population at 345,000.
15. In 2011 66 per cent of suspects for cleared property crimes were Roma, while 39 per cent were Bulgarians.
16. A calculation taking into account the prison size indicates that the Roma are between 38 per cent and 40 per cent of all prisoners. Data for two of the biggest prisons (Sofia and Plovdiv) are not available, making a precise national average estimate difficult.
17. An average monthly salary for an average defence lawyer probably starts at 1000 Euros per month.

References

Analytical Creative Group (1998) *Analysis of Crime in Bulgaria during 1993–1997 Period: Crime of the Gypsy Ethnic Group: Short Criminological Survey* (Sofia: Center for Marketing and Social Studies).

Bezlov, T . and Gounev, P . (2005) *Crime Trends in Bulgaria: Police Statistics and Victimization Surveys* (Sofia: CSD).

Bulgarian Helsinki Committee (2002) *Bulgaria's Prisons* (Sofia: Bulgarian Helsinki Committee).

CSD (2012a) *Countering Organised Crime in Bulgaria. Study on the Legal Framework* (Sofia: CSD).

CSD (2012b) *Serious and Organised Crime Threat Assessment (2010–2011)* (Sofia: CSD).

CSD (2011a) *Crime and Punishment: Studying Justice System for Shaping Criminal Policy* (Sofia: CSD).

CSD (2011b) *Crime Trends in Bulgaria 2000–2010* (Sofia: CSD).

CSD (2011c) *Penitentiary Policy and System in the Republic of Bulgaria* (Sofia: CSD).

CSD (2011d) *The Hidden Economy in Bulgaria and the Global Economic Crisis* (Sofia: CSD).

CSD (2010) *Examining the Links between Organised Crime and Corruption* (Sofia: CSD).

CSD (2007) *Organized Crime in Bulgaria: Markets and Trends* (Sofia: CSD).

CSD (2006a) *Crime Trends in Bulgaria 2000–2005* (Sofia: CSD).

CSD (2006b) *Police Stops and Ethnic Profiling in Bulgaria* (Sofia: CSD).

Center on Sentencing and Corrections (2012) *The Price of Prisons: What Incarceration Costs Taxpayers* (New York: Vera Institute of Justice), Retrieved 21 September 2012, from http://www.vera.org/download?file=3542/ Price%2520of%2520Prisons_updated%2520version_072512.pdf.

Crime Prevention Fund IGA (2007) Independent report from implemented monitoring on the legislative and institutional establishment of the probation in Bulgaria (Pazardjik: IGA Foundation).

Daily Mail, 'Foreign prisoners cost taxpayers £430m a year…just to keep them locked up', 8 August 2012, http://www.dailymail.co.uk/news/article-2185311/ Foreign-prisoners-cost-430m-year – just-locked-up.html (accessed 20 September 2012).

European Commission (2012) Commission Report COM(2012) 411 final (2012)*Report from the Commission to the European Parliament and the Council on Progress in Bulgaria Under the Cooperation and Verification Mechanism* (Brussels: European Commission).

European Commission (2012) Commission Staff Working Document SWD(2012) 232 (2012) *BULGARIA: Technical Report accompanying the Commission Report [COM(2012) 411 final]* (Brussels: European Commission).

Gounev, P. M . (2011) *Backdoor Traders: Illicit Entrepreneurs and Legitimate Markets*, PhD thesis, The London School of Economics and Political Science (LSE).

Gounev, P . and Bezlov, T . (2012) 'Corruption and Criminal Markets', in Gounev, P. and Ruggiero, V. (eds), *Corruption and Organized Crime in Europe* (London: Routledge).

Ilkova, R. (2010) Организиранапрестъпност и корупция: ключовисъдебнидела *[Organised Crime and Corruption: Key Trials]* (Sofia: RiskMonitor Foundation).

Prosecutor ' s Office of the Republic of Bulgaria (2012) '*Annual report 2011*', from http://www.prb.bg/uploads/documents/docs_2915.pdf.

Tomova, I . (1995) *Roma in the Transition Period* (Sofia: International Center for Minority Studies).

11
Italy: Between Amnesties and Emergencies[1]

Patrizio Gonnella

In order to make sense of Italy's penal practice, it is necessary to sketch the broad political, administrative and legal framework within which its current Penal Code operates. Despite pressures for more regional autonomy, Italy remains a modern, centralised state. The penal system, therefore, is under the direct control of central government, and specifically under the Ministry of Justice, which is formally answerable to Parliament for the performance of its own Prison Department. Under the provisions of the Penal Code, courts have powers to hand out a range of punishments, from life sentences to fines, while a series of alternative treatments for offenders are also available. A historical perspective adopted in the following pages may help elucidate continuities and changes in the penal system as a whole.

The first republic: decarceration through amnesty

In the immediate post-war period, in spite of having the largest Communist Party in Western Europe, Italy came to be dominated by the Christian Democrats, who mobilised one of Europe's most reactionary state bureaucracies to begin the social and economic re-construction of the country. Given this wider priority, it was inevitable that criminal justice matters were accorded little attention. This left a number of repressive and authoritarian practices of the past in place (Galli 2004).

Since the fall of the Fascist regime, Parliament has approved numerous amnesty bills, the first dating back to 1946. In a country still deeply divided, the bill became known as the Togliatti amnesty, from the name of the Minister of Justice, who was also the Secretary of the Italian Communist Party. For over 40 years, emptying prisons became the only way of counter-balancing the inefficiency of the criminal justice system and the overcrowding of custodial institutions. Thanks to amnesties, charges and offences were deleted and sentences suspended. The option of reforming the Penal Code of 1930 – particularly repressive and authoritarian – was never considered. In this code, for instance, sexual violence was deemed an offence against 'morality' – not against women, property crime was punished very harshly, while there was a wide and wittingly vague range of 'political' crimes punishable by law. Christian Democratic pragmatism strongly felt that rules and codes could not be changed.

Governments were content with running things smoothly, without upsetting the interests of protected social groups. This was also the best way to resolve the problems associated with the relationships between politics and the economic sphere, as amnesties covered conventional as well as white collar and financial crime. Prison rules, on the other hand, maintained a fascist ideology, with retributive traits clearly prevailing. The rules dated back to 1931, and only the 1948 Constitution succeeded in bringing some amendments. For example, the very word 'punishment' was only mentioned when dealing with, and in response to, violence committed against persons in custody – which should have led to the codification of the crime of torture. But things did not go so far, as this crime is not yet codified in the Italian Penal Code. The 1948 Constitution, however, described custody as a socialisation and re-educational measure, rather than as a punitive tool: no notion of 'revenge' was to be found in the Constitution. Moreover, limits were established to custodial measures in the name of human rights, an Italian way of endorsing the principle of dignity included in the Universal Declaration of Human Rights of 1948. It has to be borne in mind that, among the Constituents – those who wrote the Italian Constitution, there were members of the anti-fascist movement who had suffered imprisonment during the Mussolini regime. These included two politicians who, in future years, were to become President of the Republic: Giuseppe Saragat and Sandro Pertini, both of whom served a sentence in Rome prison Regina Coeli.

Throughout the 1950s and 1960s the debate focused on how a specific set of prison regulations could incorporate the principles of the Constitution. The prison population was exclusively made of Italians, with a majority of people from the South, and the periodical amnesties staved off overcrowding. In 1956, ten years after the Togliatti decarceration law, there were 27,820 prisoners in Italy; that is, well under 70 per 100,000 inhabitants. Amnesty after amnesty, it is in the 1970s that the debate on reform produced some tangible outcomes. The so-called 'penitentiary law' was approved in 1975, inspired by principles of 'treatment' rather than 'punishment', in the sense that inmates were meant to be 'observed, treated, and changed'. This correctional idea of custody found favour with the Catholics, who saw correction as a synonym for redemption, but also with the Communists, who believed in re-education in a social and moral sense. Together, they held two-thirds of the places in Parliament.

The 'correctional' notion of imprisonment, in spite of its ambiguity, was destined to accompany the Italian penal system to the current time, and to degenerate into rules encouraging 'repentance' for the crimes committed and the obligation to apologise to the victims or their families.

Meanwhile, the prison population started to change, with urban proletarians now joined by radical intellectuals and members of social movements engaged in violent political conflict. Repression of these movements reached its apex in the years 1977 and 1978, with the introduction of emergency legislation in the area of police powers and police use of firearms. Many activists of the Left, and fewer of the Right, were incarcerated, creating a generation of prisoners with a clear understanding of their rights and enough strength to denounce the violent abuses they suffered – particularly in high security prison units (De Vito 2009). Prison riots followed, raising public awareness of conditions and throwing light on the hypocrisy of the 'treatment model'.

The 1980s were the years of the decline of social movements, particularly of those who had chosen armed struggle, and thousands of activists served long sentences, at times for their mere 'ideological complicity' with violent activists. The Penal Code, as highlighted above, was still characterised by fascist elements, with harsh provisions addressed at political offenders. This is when the discussion of a 'political', rather than 'juridical', solution to prison overcrowding took off, with an amnesty for political offenders being proposed from many quarters. As a result, the law on 'dissociation' was passed, which allowed offenders to distance themselves from armed struggle without having to 'grass' on their associates. In this climate, what is regarded as the most enlightened prison legislation in the country was approved. Known as the 'Gozzini law', from the name of the government minister who created it, the reform allowed all prisoners, irrespective of the offence committed, to be treated with alternative measures to custody. Of particular importance was the rule which gave access to work, in the form of day release, to 'deserving' inmates from the first day of their custodial sentence. Treatment, in this way, took place outside the prison walls, and this, combined with the amnesty of 1990, brought the prison population below 30,000, a rate of imprisonment among the lowest in Europe. This phase, however, only lasted about four years, as things were again to change.

The phases of penal intervention

It is difficult to understand the dynamics of incarceration in Italy without addressing the different aspects or phases of which penal intervention is composed. First, there is a legislative phase, which entails the statutory ruling of a minimum and maximum penalty to be inflicted for any specific offence. Second, there is a judicial phase, in which judges decide the 'quantity' of the penalty by graduating the sentence at a specific point between the statutory minimum and maximum. Finally, there is an executive phase, where prison administrations, jointly with judges supervising prison regimes, establish the 'quality' of punishment by applying a specifically identified and individualised regime. In practice, prison administrations go as far as recommending or sanctioning early release or home leave (Padovani 1990; Pavarini 1994).

Because changes in the legislative aspects of punishment are more difficult and slow to carry out, decarceration and recarceration policies were often implemented within the domain of the judicial and executive phases. For example, in periods when lenient attitudes prevailed, judges would apply the minimal penalty available for any specific offence. This process of 'reforming' the criminal justice system through judicial practice became evident and most fruitful in the mid-1980s, when institutions for young offenders were virtually emptied. This de facto abolition of custody for the under-18s was the result of judges – many of whom were women or politically progressive – applying minimal sentences sanctioned by law on the one hand, and utilising the old positivist tool called 'pardon' on the other (Ruggiero 1995; Gozzini, 1997).

Another tool at the disposal of judges for the selection of offenders and the differentiation of their treatment is provided by the three-stage trial existing in the country. The three stages entail the first trial; an appeal stage which may be mobilised by either the defendant or the public prosecutor; and, finally, a third court hearing (carried out by the Court of Cassation) where the legal correctness of the previous trials is ascertained. When a pre-established maximum time elapses between the first trial and the appeal, and between this and the final verdict of the Court of Cassation, many charges are automatically dropped (an Italian version of the Statute of Limitations). There is also a pre-established maximum remand time which varies according to the type of offence. Therefore, while awaiting the final stage of the proceedings, and when the maximum time for their specific offence elapses, defendants must be released. There is reason to believe that judges deliberately delay the subsequent hearings when faced with what they consider minor offences, while speeding up trials involving offences which raise more public outcry. On the other hand, inefficiency, rather than political sensitivity, may also explain this judicial practice, which is well exploited by white collar offenders who – through expensive, skilled defence lawyers – manage to delay proceedings to the point of systematically avoiding punishment.

The second republic: populism and the noose

After the 1990 amnesty, the penal system in Italy went through a phase of moral panic, emergency and populism. Many things happened which might explain why the prison population almost doubled in a matter of 20 years. After a number of mafia killings, notably the assassination of judges Giovanni Falcone and Paolo Borsellino, in 1992 the 'Gozzini law' was substantially repealed. Alternatives to custody became no longer available to all prisoners, while particularly harsh regimes were introduced for some types of offenders. Legislation dealt with offences deemed particularly serious and alternatives to custody were subordinated to the offenders' willingness to cooperate with investigations – namely, to accuse accomplices. Meanwhile, as shameful corruption cases came to light, many white collar offenders were arrested. Members of the new Right, led by the separatist and xenophobic Northern League, displayed nooses in Parliament, showing more than metaphorically their prospective political programme. The TV tycoon Silvio Berlusconi founded a new right-wing party, Forza Italia, and victoriously ran for Prime Minister. Judges have, ever since, tried unsuccessfully to indict him, and the justice system has experienced a definitive bifurcation, becoming tolerant with the rich and powerful, and powerful and harsh with the poor. The rule of law, in other words, came to be exclusively applied to the former. Migrants and drug users became the chosen victims of law and order campaigns launched by the Right, while the moderate Left followed suit. The variable 'safety' – and how the parties would deal with it – determined who would win the elections. Tolerance towards the powerful was complemented by harshness towards Albanians, North Africans, Roma, Romanians, squeegee merchants, the homeless and drug users. Prisons filled up quickly, with around 800 new prisoners entering the system each month as a result of new laws addressing drug use, migration and recidivism. This changed the Italian penal law to the point that it was no longer facts and offences, but lifestyles and stories, which were penalised. Consumers of light drugs were treated as hard drug dealers, while recidivists were excluded for the benefit of non-custodial measures. Migrants were heavily penalised simply for being illegally present on the Italian territory. In 2010, around 16,000 non-Italians were incarcerated as irregular migrants, because they failed to leave the country after a police injunction. As a result, in December 2010 the prison population in Italy reached the record figure of 68,000, even though a simultaneous and controversial amnesty had freed over 25,000.

After 20 years, the trend is now slowing down, and 2011 saw a slight reduction in overcrowding. At the end of that year there were 66,897 people in custody, roughly a thousand less than the previous year. Around four per cent were women, which is a constant percentage over the years. Many things happened immediately before and afterwards.

The economic and moral crisis hit Italy, but Berlusconi was less concerned with financial issues than with the charge of promoting prostitution of underage girls. After he left his position as Prime Minister, the media started discussing prison conditions and commenting on deaths in custody. In 2009 the violent death of a prisoner, Stefano Cucchi, received much attention. Everyone in Italy knows who Stefano was – thanks to activists in the area of human rights, but more so because of the courage of his family. Relatives decided to publish the photographs of Stefano's dead body, covered with wounds caused by the beating he'd suffered, while the devastated expression on his sister's face on TV triggered public outrage. This time the victim of institutional violence was not a marginalised young man, but a son of the middle classes, and this elicited some form of empathy rather than the usual indifference. Stefano Cucchi was a user of soft drugs, arrested for possession of a few grammes of hashish. Brought to the police station and then to prison, he was then returned to his parents as a corpse after seven days in detention. The press investigated and told horrendous prison stories, while – under pressure from the Associazioine Antigone and the daily paper Il Manifesto – access to prison institutions was granted to journalists and campaigners. In some cases, cameras were installed in cells so that prison conditions could be publicly monitored.

The top authorities of the state, including the President of the Republic, showed indignation at the display of prisoners sleeping on the floor even in the winter months, one on top of the other, in extremely poor sanitary conditions. In most large institutions within metropolitan areas spaces were crammed, with rooms destined for collective, recreational or educational, activities turned into dormitories. Plans to build new facilities came to a halt, due to inefficiency as well as a lack of financial resources. Therefore, the number of prison places, 45,000 in 2010, remained the same in 2011, despite the government boosting its prison building programme. When new facilities were opened, they were not fully utilised due to lack of personnel, while many institutions were shut down for lack of funds. In this context, and after the condemnation by the European Court of Human Rights of the Italian prison system, a new law was approved allowing some inmates to serve the last year and a half of their sentence outside a custodial institution, in the form of house arrest. A degree of leniency towards minor offences yielded a decline in prison admissions. What, however, caused a substantial reduction in the prison population was the ruling by the European Court of Justice of the European Union, on 28 April 2011, that the Italian authorities should abolish the law penalising irregular migrants who failed to leave the country after being identified by the police. Since then, the number of migrants in Italian institutions has decreased, although not drastically.

The overcrowding figures: an Italian anomaly?

Overcrowding in Italian penal institutions is caused by four anomalies, distinguishing the country from other European partners (Anastasia, Corleone and Zevi 2011). Although the rates of imprisonment are more or less in line with average European rates, namely, around 110 prisoners per 100,000 inhabitants, anomalies are found in the repressive apparatus and in the quality of life within prisons. Let us see where these anomalies originate.

In recent times, a key word (*spread*) – which is supposed to explain the state of the Italian economy – has become prevalent. Few know what the word means, except that it refers to the unhealthy condition of Italian state bonds – as opposed to bonds sold and bought in Germany. Being a plausible comparative entity, it is interesting to measure the Italian anomaly against the performance of Germany in the penal arena. The difference, as we shall see, is not only noticeable in the rates of interest.

The first Italian anomaly pertains to the number of non-Italians held in custody. In total, in December 2011 they accounted for 24,174 out of 66,897 prisoners – 36.1 per cent, which is ten percentage points higher than the amount in Germany. The criminalisation of unregistered migrants pushes them into illegality; even when they are employed, such migrants have little chance of obtaining a permit to stay, so they are forced to remain within the illicit or semi-illicit economy in order to survive. The high rate of incarceration is the outcome of the legislation penalising migrants, on the one hand, and of their impossibility to access the official labour market, on the other. The following are the nationalities represented, in decreasing order: Moroccans (4,895), Tunisians (3,189), Albanians (2,770), Nigerians (1,172). In respect of women, those most represented are Romanians (267) and Nigerians (174).

The situation for Romanians, many of whom are of Roma origin, is different from that of Africans. The former, of course, are part of the European Union – migration laws do not apply to them. They end up in prison due to the deficiencies of the Italian system in offering regular occupations, or because they continue a criminal career initiated in their country of origin. The African component of the prison population, both from the Maghreb and from Nigeria, is instead the result of immigration laws passed in 2002, which forced many into illegality, including potential asylum seekers.

Migration and incarceration are linked to specific offences – such as prostitution and drug distribution. Nigerian women are often incarcerated for pimping and constitute around one tenth of all women in prison. The following is another Italian anomaly, when compared to Germany. Data released on 31 December 2011 indicate that the percentage of inmates sentenced for drug-related offences is 36.9 per cent – as opposed to 15.1 per cent in Germany. This is, of course, the effect of extremely harsh legislation which neutralised timid attempts to implement harm reduction strategies at the local level. Services addressed to drug users have been reduced, with the result that many problematic users are left on the streets, where they are targeted by law enforcers. This is consistent with the demand for 'safety' originating from the media, institutions and, as a consequence, from public opinion.

The third anomaly regards the number of people on remand. In Italy above 40 per cent of prisoners is awaiting trial. Here the spread reaches a dramatic dimension, as in Germany the prison population on remand is 16.2 per cent. In brief, almost half of the people in custody in Italian institutions have not been tried or sentenced. And yet, Article 27 of the Italian Constitution affirms – in a very robust manner – that 'defendants are not deemed guilty until they have been sentenced'. The high figures of remand prisoners can be explained through a number of causes, all associated with one single factor: the police force and the judiciary, in response to pressure from public opinion, but also with the awareness that trials are excessively slow, prefer to inflict a degree of pain in advance, with the belief that the justice system will be inefficient and too lenient. The prison system, in this way, loses rehabilitative philosophy, becoming a mere container of bodies. The fact is that treatment in prison, in the form of re-education programmes, cannot start if the person to be 'treated' has not been found guilty. A remand prisoner cannot be forced to take part in rehabilitative activities. This principle is widely interpreted by prison governors as a justification to exclude these prisoners from all social programmes and to restrain them in crowded cells for 20 hours a day, pending release; which, due the statute of limitations, will almost certainly come to fruition well before the trial takes place. Hence the paradox whereby non-guilty prisoners are treated more harshly than those found guilty.

These three anomalies shape a fourth one which pertains to the rate of overcrowding. For each 100 prison places officially available, there are 148 prisoners. In Germany, there are fewer prisoners than prison places – respectively 92 and 100. Therefore, there are always some unoccupied places in each institution. Overcrowding in Italy is determined by failure to implement decriminalisation and decarceration strategies – but also by management ineptitude. Penal policies are not properly planned, and the building of new facilities is haphazard or left in the hand of corrupt developers. As a consequence, there are officially 45,000 prison places in the country, with 67,000 people to accommodate. Many (around 22,000) are kept in make-shift conditions, often sleeping on the floor without a mattress – in some cells it is hard for those occupying them to stand up at the same time. The space statutorily established to be guaranteed to inmates is calculated in a sloppy way, and the standards established by the European Committee for the Prevention of Torture – or by the very norms officially in force in Italy, are regularly ignored. Every now and then official statistics indicate the 'tolerable receptivity' of prison institutions, which miraculously is higher than the prison population. This variable appears intermittently in official discourse, although its vagueness and lack of objectivity serve mere propaganda purposes.

The socio-cultural composition of the prison population

A look at the social composition of those processed through the penal system confirms the initial assumption that the system is highly selective. Custody, for remand or sentenced prisoners, mainly targets the socially and economically disadvantaged. Among these, and considering the large dark figure of unreported crimes in big cities, custody is for the least able and least dangerous street offenders. Moreover, rules around recidivism create a situation whereby the same individuals keep entering and exiting the prison system: individuals who are victimised by a penal law which hits harshly at those who strive to make ends meet through petty illegality. In 2011 the number of people entering the prison system was 76,982; by the end of the same year the number was 66,897 (this is the picture of one single day). The figure is considerably lower than it was at the beginning of the 1990s, when on average there were around 100,000 individuals entering the system. This means that, meanwhile, the average remand period has increased, as has the overall length of sentences. This also suggests that practitioners in the criminal justice system neutralise, in their day-to-day work, the legislative provision aimed at reducing the prison population.

Statistics indicate that life imprisonment has gone up over recent years, now standing at 1,528 cases (Corleone and Anastasia 2009; Guidetti Serra 2010). Only 62 out of all lifers are non-Italian – less than five per cent, although non-Italians are 36.1 per cent of the total prison population. Foreign nationals are about 50 per cent of those sentenced to less than one year imprisonment – a total 2,733 persons. The higher the sentence, the smaller the percentage of non-nationals.

A look at those serving a relatively short remainder of their sentence reveals the malfunctioning of alternatives to custody, which should be applied exactly to this phase of the incarceration period. Bureaucratic obstacles – and the general climate of 'insecurity' – make such alternatives difficult to use as they should be by law. There are about 23,000 prisoners who have a remaining time to serve of less than three years. They are therefore eligible for completing their time outside custodial institutions. But, as has been said, few actually enjoy this 'privilege'.

The break-down of the prison population by offence committed again confirms the selectivity of the system. There are 33,647 sentenced for property crime, 27,459 for drug-related offences, 6,467 for organised criminal activity and 23,693 for violent offences. Non-nationals accused of organised criminal activity are less that one per cent, while those accused of drug-related crimes are 50 per cent of those sentenced for similar offences. The data exclude those who commit property crime to finance their drug habit. Drugs and non-nationals are at the centre of the penal question in Italy. Anti-prohibitionist legislation could contribute to emptying the prison system at a stroke and for ever.

Another indicator of selectivity is provided by the level of education of those incarcerated: only one per cent hold a university degree, while the number of illiterate prisoners, or those holding no education certificate whatsoever is four times higher. Half of the prison population does not provide any details about its level of education, while 8,000 have only completed primary school. Among Italians, southerners are still the majority; over 17,000 are younger than 30 years of age, and a very high number, around 50 per cent of the total prison population, has no work experience. In brief, the typical prisoner is a non-Italian or an Italian from the South, around 30 years of age, serving a sentence of a few years for drug-related crimes, holding a primary school certificate, and devoid of any work experience. Rehabilitation, as suggested by the enlightened Italian Constitution is, in this respect, a myth.

The map of the custodial apparatus in Italy would be incomplete without mentioning so-called 'mental institutions for criminals', where about 1,000 individuals are held. The scandal provoked by TV images showing the shocking conditions of these mental homes made the President of the Republic call for their closure. By 31 March 2013 such institutions should have been shut down and replaced by structures managed by regional and municipal authorities. The new 'homes' will be subject to a privatisation process, which is likely to expand, as we shall see, to the penal system as a whole.

Women in prison

The number of women in prison has been constant in recent years. The figure is around 2.800 – 4.2 per cent of the total prison population. Non-Italians constitute 40.4 per cent of the women incarcerated in the country, with many of Eastern European, South American and sub-Sahara African origin. This represents a specific feature of the Italian female prison population, whereas the non-Italian male prison population is mostly constituted of migrants from the Maghreb. Of course, the incarceration of these minorities reflects the hard, marginalised social conditions in which minorities live within the Italian context. While the typologies of offences committed by male North Africans are associated with masculine life styles, offences committed by females with Eastern European, South American and sub-Saharan backgrounds fall into the domain of the sex industry. A very high percentage of Eastern European women in prison is made up of former Yugoslavians and Romanians, with some prevalence of Roma people. In Roma communities it is women who bear responsibility for earning money – at times this happens through theft, which bears a strong stigma in Italian society. Approximately one out of four non-Italian female prisoners is of Roma descent while, in the penal system for minors this percentage increases to 50 per cent. A low educational level and the disadvantaged economic condition of most of them is the first cause of female detention. Five per cent of women prisoners are illiterate, only two per cent have a university degree. The percentage of completely illiterate women is three times higher than that of the prison population as a whole.

The large majority of women is behind bars for non-serious crimes. Around 40 per cent have been sentenced for drug offences, less than three per cent for organised-crime related offences. Women occupy the lower ranks in criminal organisations and 30 per cent of those in custody are serving sentences below three years. Their crimes have a deep connection with their gender and reflect a marginalised condition where petty crime is routine. Usually dependent on men, and victimised by them, the domestic violence they suffer is often the cause of their involvement in criminal street life.

There are only seven prison institutions for women in Italy, out of a total of 206. However, in 63 male prisons we find a specific wing for women only. While their relatively low numbers would suggest that forms of constructive treatment might be viable for women in custody, in fact heavy overcrowding makes treatment problematic. They are often closed in very small prison sections which are easier to manage and require fewer officers. Demands particularly associated with the female gender, whether expressing physical or psychological needs, are not appropriately addressed. These include sanitary requirements, privacy or services for children. Italian law provides for the application of alternatives to custody for women with children of a maximum of three years of age. Exceptions apply to women considered dangerous for the type of crime committed. Currently, there are around 60 children in Italian prison institutions living with their mothers – showing that 'the exception' is in fact the rule.

Treatment and entertainment

The correctional idea is at the heart of the Italian punitive model. This entails awards and penalties as a governing principle of prison life. The model has managed for the last 30 years to defuse rebellion by constantly threatening and blackmailing the prison population. The mirage of early release, subject to good conduct and cooperation with treatment programmes, has structured the system in terms of stability and manageability. In the process, prison treatment, including more or less realistic social, occupational and recreational opportunities, has become increasingly dull and bureaucratised (Ruggiero 2011). A prisoner who intends to take advantage of 'discounts' (45 days per semester) is a good inmate who has never incurred disciplinary sanctions or received negative reports regarding his/her conduct. A passive detainee, who is formally polite, is seen in a more positive light than one who has actually superseded his offending career, but displays an independent attitude in the face of the hypocrisy and pettiness characterising prison life. This custodial model tends to restrain and 'entertain' people, rather than plan for their social and occupational integration. In general, Italian penal institutions, with some notable exceptions, are places where life is spent in idleness, in a cell for 20 hours a day. Prisoners go out of their cells only for activities for which they are authorised: internal work, education, religious practices, hobbies and theatre – or to meet visitors. Every minor thing is regulated by 'application', which grants permission by the authority in charge to do whatever they think appropriate for prisoners' rehabilitation. These applications are swamped in a slow bureaucratic process where approval is discretionary, if not arbitrary.

It is unusual that written rules relating to the prison regime itself, in the respective languages of the inmates, are distributed. Often there are no common kitchens or canteens where meals can be prepared and consumed collectively; at most small camping cookers are allowed. At dawn or at night, the bars are noisily clanged in order to make sure that they have not been severed. Prisoners are never trusted, but infantilised – any form of responsibility is taken away from them. Rehabilitation activities are almost entirely left to local authorities, cooperatives and voluntary associations, and projects are poorly coordinated and haphazard. Few prisoners (less than 1,000) enjoy open regimes of incarceration – mainly drug users who accept detox programmes within the prison institution. Around 10,000 are detained in high surveillance units, where rehabilitative treatment is drastically reduced, and 600 are kept in special security prisons – mainly members of criminal organisations who are deprived of any external contact. The remaining prisoners are kept under a medium security regime. For around 67,000 prisoners there are 40,000 prison officers, about 1,000 social workers, and roughly the same number of psychologists or staff specialising in different branches of education. The daily cost of a member of staff is 80 per cent that of each prisoner, and yet prison officers, through their unions, keep claiming their numbers are insufficient.

Rights on paper and rights denied

There is a deep gap between the rights officially granted to prisoners by rules and regulations and the rights actually enjoyed by them. What is practically lacking is a 'meta right' – the right to claim one's rights

(Astarita, Gonnella and Marietti 2003). Since 1999 the Constitutional Court has highlighted several times this anomaly, remarking that prisoners are not given the opportunity to initiate legal procedures when their rights are violated. Written complaints are sent to magistrates in charge of supervising the running of institutions, but those sending them are rarely heard in person before investigations are carried out. In this way, cases end up consisting of a mere exchange of letters. Recently, a magistrate supervising the prison in Lecce ruled that a prisoner be compensated for the 'biological damage' he suffered, and for the offence to his dignity, associated with the conditions of overcrowding in which he was detained. The monetary compensation amounted to a meagre 220 euros, but the case was symbolically important. The problem is that prisoners are not allowed to report their case to civil or administrative judges, but can only relate to the magistrates in charge of prison surveillance and treatment. These are often impeded in their acts by their own senior managers within the judiciary. Moreover, in Italy a national independent organisation entrusted with the monitoring of the places and conditions of detention has never been set up. For example, there is no such an authority as a prison ombudsman.

The most important issue in custodial institutions remains the psychophysical conditions of the inmates (Clémenti 2007). This was part of the remit of the Ministry of Justice. But since 2006 – in the name of equity in the provision of health services, prisoners have access to the same health system, which is decentralised at the regional level – as ordinary citizens. However, the provision is insufficient, also because the health system is more oriented towards therapy than prevention. The sanitary and hygienic conditions in prison, particularly in large cities, would require regular monitoring and control, which do not take place. Medicaments are requested and prescribed, and mainly consist in psycho-active drugs used as control instruments, and responses to problematic conduct. Infective diseases, particularly Hepatitis C and HIV, persist and deeply affect life in prison. The general state of health among the prison population is abysmal. Illnesses which seemed to have disappeared are returning, such as TB and scabies. It takes months to arrange to see a specialist doctor or to receive surgery.

According to the official regulations governing prisons, work is a right for all inmates who have been sentenced. While in 1991 a third of prisoners had a job, today the absolute figure remains the same, but due to the growth of the prison population, the relative ratio of prisoners working has gone down to two out of five. Prisoners should earn two-thirds of the salary earned by workers in liberty for the same job, but this does not happen. Around 83 per cent of those who do work are employed by the prison administration itself, which does not provide the 'fortunate' workers with an attractive occupational record. Who would mention in their CV that they have been cooks, dish washers or cleaners in a prison institution? Moreover, among the 20 per cent who work, some do so only one hour a day – perhaps one day a week, or a month per year. In brief, prisons have been laboratories for the experimentation of what we now call the 'precariat'. Prisoners have no union representatives and can always be sacked for 'security' reasons. On the other hand, prisoners obtaining a job in the institution where they are detained can be blackmailed, as they may be asked to act as control agents. Everyone in prison needs to work, but work is normally given in exchange for some sort of cooperation with officers: the internal worker has to be prepared to turn into an internal informer.

Only around four per cent of prisoners attend professional or vocational courses, which amounts to half the percentage recorded 20 years ago. Such courses are not linked with any reasonable employment route, while the very right to education is hardly promoted and left to the discretion of governors. There is a lack of national strategy in this area, as there is a lack of understanding how education would impact on recidivism. 8,000 prisoners attended primary and secondary school in 2011, while in the whole national territory there were 18 universities who enrolled students in custody: 300 prisoners studied for a university degree and 16 got such a degree in the same year. Dropping out of courses is frequent among prisoners because they are suddenly and constantly transferred for disciplinary reasons from one institution to another – a fact that contravenes the right to education, as well as the principle of 'territoriality' of rehabilitation (that is, the right to serve a sentence in proximity of family members).

Moving prisoners around, of course, also affects the regularity of their receiving visitors, with the result that relationships are made difficult if not shattered. Finally, the right to make telephone calls excludes the use of mobile phones, and is only allowed to previously checked numbers, which makes it extremely hard for non-Italians to maintain human and social relationships when in custody.

Alternatives to custody

As in a number of European countries, the definition of alternatives to custody in Italy is very broad (Mosconi 1998). They include a wide range of dispositions and measures which can be imposed at any moment of the criminal justice process (Palma 1997). I will concentrate on two types of alternatives in operation in the country. The first type completely diverts offenders from the prison system, and their application is ruled by courts hearing specific cases. The second type relates to offenders who are already serving a sentence. These are formally ruled by judges who are in charge of prison supervision.

Conditional discharge is of the first type – the most utilised alternative to custody in Italy, and does not entail any sort of community supervision. However, if those who are given conditional discharge re-offend, they may be given both a sentence for the fresh charge and for the old offence.

A number of alternatives can also replace short sentences of up to six months: semi-detention – which implies that the convict spends at least ten hours per day in the institution, supervision orders and fines. Negotiated alternatives are applied in the judicial phase when defendants agree to 'bargain' their sentence. This procedure goes beyond the guilty plea of Anglo-Saxon courts, as it literally leads to the common establishment of the length and nature of the punishment. In these cases the sentence established by law is curtailed by the order of a third, while a life sentence can be replaced by a 30 year sentence.

A form of probation also belongs to the first type of alternative, entailing supervision by the local social services, and can be given to defendants sentenced to a maximum of three months. The measure – known as 'semilibertà' also belongs to the former type, and consists of day release allowed for work, education, or other rehabilitative activities outside the prison institution.

The second set of alternatives, as mentioned above, is applied when the executive phase of the penal process has already started. They can be granted to prisoners as forms of rehabilitative treatment to be achieved through contacts with the outside environment. Among this set of alternatives is 'liberazione anticipata', which consists of a 45-day remission for every six months spent in custody. Such alternatives, which include 'house arrest' and 'leave awards', can also be granted to offenders serving longer custodial sentences after their behaviour in custody has been 'scientifically' observed and evaluated. Leave awards can potentially be obtained by all prisoners and are meant to allow offenders some time with their family. The number of days granted to individual prisoners for leave awards must not exceed 45 days per year. Finally, conditional release is given to inmates who have shown good behaviour and are deemed reformed. It can be granted after the person has served at least 30 months, while lifers must have served 26 years.

Although the alternatives mentioned above appear to provide a degree of flexibility to the Italian penal system, rigidity has come to characterise it, due to red tape and cultural changes occurring within the magistracy. It should be noted that there are only 200 magistrates in charge of monitoring prison institutions – one for each 3,000 prisoners. Such magistrates are expected to enforce the respect of regulations by the prison administration and decide on alternatives to custody to be granted to applicants.

In 2011, more than 20,000 individuals were on house arrest, 1,832 on day release for work, while 19,229 were on probation – a total of 41,375 people enjoying alternatives to custodial measures. Looking at a snapshot of one day, the figure is halved, with 19,229 serving an alternative sentence on 31 December 2011. Non-Italians are discriminated against in this area, as their social condition in free society is not deemed conducive to their rehabilitation. Less than one per cent of those serving an alternative to custody re-offend, and in 3.15 per cent of the cases alternatives are suspended because they are regarded as ineffective. Offenders granted alternatives to imprisonment have a recidivism rate three times lower than those who serve a prison sentence. And yet, there is no debate about extending non-custodial measures and to actually offer a proper 'alternative' to prison as a system of offenders' treatment.

Violence and deaths

There are three styles for governing prison institutions in Italy. The first is adopted by governors who believe in democracy and in their mission, are usually Catholic, are not prepared to tolerate violence by officers and often denounce it. The second style belongs to prison governors who regard themselves as plain-clothes police officers and lead small gangs of guards in the use of indiscriminate violence as a disciplinary tool. The third style holds that violence is neither tolerated nor banned. Prison governors try to protect themselves from possible accusations but are not prepared to report their violent staff. The first two groups constitute, together, a minority, while the third is prevalent. Violence in prison does indeed exist. The crime of 'torture' – mentioned above – has never been codified (Gonnella and Marchesi 2006). In 2011, 186 people died in custody, of whom 66 committed suicide. These stories of personal despair have not determined some change in policy nor a revision of the role and commitment of social workers and health personnel employed in custodial institutions. Overcrowding renders prisoners invisible (Ronco, Scandurra and Torrente 2011; Ruotolo 2011).

Of course, in many cases there are legitimate doubts that the individuals who died had committed suicide or had died from natural causes.

Conclusion

Amnesties, reform on paper, and emergencies suspending reform, aptly describe the vagaries of the penal system in Italy (Gonnella and Marietti 2010). As we have seen, processes of decarceration and recarceration may be conducted by judicial decisions rather than through binding legislative measures. The general climate prevailing in the country may affect the number of the individuals punished and the nature of the punishment inflicted (Resta 2005; Ferrajoli 2007). This, however, does not seem to affect the corrupt elite ruling the country, whose criminality reproduces itself irrespective of the general climate oscillating between harshness and leniency.

Among the latest developments, the new government, led by Mario Monti, in 2012 approved a piece of legislation opening the door to private enterprise. Entrepreneurs can now build and run prison institutions and mental homes for offenders. Opposition exercised by trade unions has precluded the possibility that external surveillance and the recruitment of prison officers be also entrusted to private firms. In a country where the mafia and corruption thrive, there is a serious risk that prison institutions end up in the wrong 'private' hands. Privatisation may turn custody into yet one more sector of the illicit economy. If in the US and the UK the prison business has been appropriated by multinationals selling 'security', in Italy it may well happen that the business is grabbed by gangs of more or less legitimate entrepreneurs. Only time will be able to tell us whether the very corrupt elite within the political and business spheres – the powerful, who so easily escape punishment – will control and benefit from a prison system which seems to be exclusively addressed to the powerless.

Note

1. Translated from the Italian by Vincenzo Ruggiero.

References

Anastasia, S., Corleone, F. and Zevi, L. (2011) Il Corpo e Lo Spazio Della Pena, Rome: Ediesse Antigone, Quadrimestrale Di Critica Del Sistema Penale E Penitenziario, 4 (2–3) Diritti Reclusi (Turin: Edizioni Gruppo Abele).

Astarita, L., Gonnella, P. and Marietti, S. (eds) (2003) *Il Collasso Delle Carceri Italiane: Sotto La Lente Degli Ispettori Europei* (Rome: Sapere 2000).

Clémenti, P. (2007) 'Pensieri Dal Carcere', *Ripa di Fagnano* (Alto: Il Sirente).

Corleone, F. and Anastasia S. (eds) (2009) *Contro L'ergastolo* (Rome: Ediesse).

De Vito, C. (2009) *Camosci E Girachiavi: Storia Del Carcere in Italia* (Bari: Laterza).

Ferrajoli, L. (2007) *Principia Juris: Teoria Del Diritto E Della Democrazia* (Bari: Laterza).

Galli, G. (2004) *I Partiti Politici Italiani* (Milan: Rizzoli).

Gonnella, P. and Marchesi, A. (eds) (2006) *Onorare Gli Impegni: L'Italia E Le Norme Internazionali Contro La Tortura* (Rome: Sinnos).

Gonnella, P. and Marietti, S. (2010) *Il Carcere Spiegato Ai Ragazzi* (Rome: Il Manifesto Libri).

Gozzini, M. (1997) *La Giustizia in Galera? Una Storia Italiana* (Rome: Editori Riuniti).

Guidetti Serra, B. (2010) *Contro L'ergastolo: Il Processo Alla Banda Cavallero* (Rome: Edizioni dell'Asino).

Padovani, T. (1990) *Diritto penale* (Milan: Giuffré).

Mosconi, G. (1998) *Dentro Il Carcere, Oltre La Pena* (Padua: Cedam).

Palma, M. (ed) (1997) *Il Vaso Di Pandora: Carcere E Pena Dopo Le Riforme* (Rome: Istituto della Enciclopedia Italiana).

Pavarini, M. (1994) 'The New Penology and Politics in Crisis: The Italian case', *British Journal of Criminology*, 34: 49–61.

Resta, E. (2005) *Il Diritto Fraterno* (Bari: Laterza).

Ronco, D., Scandurra, A. and Torrente, G. (2011) *Le Prigioni Malate* (Rome: Edizioni dell'Asino).

Ruggiero, V. (1995) 'Flexibility and Intermittent Emergency in the Italian Penal System', in Ruggiero, V., Ryan, M. And Sim, J. (eds), *Western European Penal Systems: A Critical Anatomy* (London: Sage).

Ruggiero, V. (2011) *Il Delitto, La Legge, La Pena* (Turin: Edizioni Gruppo Abele).

Ruotolo, M. (2011) *Dignità e Carcere* (Naples: Editoriale Scientifica).

12
The Spanish Penal and Penitentiary System: From the Re-Socialising Objective to the Internal Governance of Prison

Mónica Aranda Ocaña and Iñaki Rivera Beiras

The penal system in transition from dictatorship to democracy

After Dictator Francisco Franco's death in 1975, the need and urgency to normalise diverse aspects of Spanish public life were intensely felt. The issues at hand included: the problems posed by the different 'nationalities' within the country, the need to enter the international arena (Carr 1988), the recognition and legalisation of political parties and unions (Bergalli 1991), renewal, depuration and regulation of the police force (Ballbé 1978; Domínguez Figueirido 1991; Muñagorri 1987; Recasens Brunet 1989,1991), the construction of a democratic judiciary (Andrés Ibáñez 1989), amnesty for political prisoners, penal and prison reforms (Bueno Arus 1978; Draper Miralles 1984; García Valdés 1977; Lurra 1978; Martí 1977; Rivera Beiras 1994).

The process of change was met with hard opposition, expressed by those social, economic or military forces that fought for a return to the past. It is important to mention, in this respect, the events that took place in Madrid in 1977 (when several labour lawyers were murdered by extreme right-wing political activists), and the continuous *coup d'etat* attempts which tried to hamper the reform programme carried out by the promoters of the 'political transition'. The most infamous among such attempts was performed in February 1981, when a group of armed military officers broke into the House of Parliament but then renounced their bellicose plan: the scene received TV broadcasting across the world. These events conditioned general elections, affected the political climate of the country, and had an impact on the philosophy of the penal policies to be adopted within the nascent democratic system.

Constitutional 'reform': principles for a penal system and the rule of law

The Spanish Constitution was promulgated in 1978, inspired by the Rule of Law. A set of principles was established guiding the criminal justice and the penal systems: principles of legality and sentencing proportionality, the abolition of capital punishment and torture, the declaration of the rehabilitative purpose of custody, supplemented by a number of elementary rights and procedural guarantees for all citizens. Penal reform was inspired by the new Constitutional principles and, in 1979, the Penitentiary Act was approved, resulting mainly from the efforts of Carlos García Valdés – at that time General Director of Penitentiary Institutions. We will return to this Act later.

Despite the important legal improvements incorporated in the 1978 Constitution, the Spanish Penal System was still based on legislation inherited from the old regime. Substantive and procedural rules reflected criminal policies designed around pre-democratic and authoritarian criteria. It is true that some new measures seemed to reflect the process of change underway – for example, the abolition of the Public Order Tribunal, the penal procedural norms introduced by the PSOE (Spanish Socialist Worker's Party), and the rules on the treatment of remand prisoners. In general, however, the spirit of renewal found immense obstacles. For instance, the jurisdiction of the National Court was kept unaltered, thus denying the constitutional principle of a natural (local) judge (Moreno Catena 1990), while its mandate was extended to deal with cases of political violence. Also, there was a procedural 'counter-reform', which extended remand periods as a result of growing public alarm fed by the political right – a counter-reform which was ratified by the same Minister of Justice who had initiated the *reform* process. All of this, which happened in 1983, may illustrate how uncertain and contradictory the whole process was. Moreover, in the background the so-called *Dictatorship Penal Code* was still in existence (it was to be repealed in 1995), which stood in open opposition to the new constitutional principles.

The slow spreading of an *'emergency culture'*

According to Bergalli (1992a), during the initial years of the democratic transition, a *new rationality* was slowly taking shape in Spain – a 'state reason' which began to replace the 'juridical reason' as the guiding rationale for judicial and penal matters. The effect of this new rationality was the creation of emergency, exceptional legislations, with the particular aim of tackling: first, terrorist violence and, then, drug traffic. Similar emergency rules were later introduced for the fight against organised crime, sexual offences and illegal migration.

The 'emergency culture' thus created, supposedly aimed at maintaining social order and defusing conflicts, might have enjoyed popular consensus, but certainly contradicted the principles of the Rule of Law and challenged the foundations of judicial and penal enlightenment on which industrial capitalism and liberalism were established. These developments did not only pertain to the penal sphere: as Spain started to enter the arena of the so-called 'First World', it had to adapt to the international climate and share with other countries the critical situation they were experiencing. Spain joined the European Union and NATO, adhered to the 'Schengen Agreements', and accepted the decisions made by the 'Trevi group'. As a consequence, the country had to create a legislative framework consistent with that of its partners – with an emphasis on emergency laws.

The 'culture of emergency' influenced all areas of public policy, affecting the provision of welfare and the enjoyment of some elementary civil rights. The growing use of punitive strategies as a response to serious socio-economic problems, therefore, contradicted the postulates of liberal judicial rationalism which, for two centuries, has advocated minimal penal intervention.

These events took place during the 1980s, when the prison system itself was in turmoil, testifying to the difficulties encountered by reform initiatives and revealing that conditions inside did not differ from those imposed by the past regime.

The triumph of the reform option

The penitentiary reform of 1979 seemed to reflect the values of the political transition to democracy. However, it did nothing to change the harsh conditions experienced by inmates under regimes which were inherited from the fascist dictatorship. The new prison legislation did not take into account the demands of prisoners themselves, who soon started a process of collective mobilisation through their own *social penitentiary movement*. This was formed of groups, associations, and organisations (involving prisoners as well as non-prisoners) who felt that, while political prisoners were being released due to the changed political situation, 'common' or 'social' prisoners were still excluded from the apparent benefits of the transition towards democracy. Their campaigns and struggles deserve to be noted in order to provide a clearer picture of those years.

After the release[1] of political prisoners, thanks to victorious campaigns for an amnesty, social prisoners started to mobilise. The anti-prison movement involved those who were excluded from the amnesty who felt that they were not being given 'a second chance'. At the end of 1976, an organisation called the 'Association of Prisoners in Struggle' – 'Coordinadora de Presos en Lucha' (COPEL) – emerged almost simultaneously with the 'Association for the Study of Prisoners' Problems' –'Asociación para el Estudio de los Problemas de los Presos' (AEPPE), the 'Association of Prisoners and Ex-Prisoners' Relatives and Friends' –'Asociación de Familiares y Amigos de los Presos y exPresos' (AFAPE), and other organisations. The main demand was a complete amnesty for social prisoners, and was only supported by the National Worker's Federation (Anarcho-Syndicalist Union) and the revolutionary left. Protest marches, university occupations, pamphlets and leaflets, newspaper editorials, the establishment of several supporting groups for prisoners' claims, constitute just some examples of these campaigns (Oriol Martí 1977).

The reform promoted by Carlos García Valdés did not address the problem of incarceration in itself, although Valdés was well aware of the demands of the prison population. In this respect, it is worth quoting the words of the Minister himself:

> it cannot be forgotten that, at that historical moment of political transition, there was a serious conflict in the sphere of penitentiary institutions, mainly produced by the inmates' progressive consciousness for their rights The amnesty granted to those sentenced for political crimes implied a form of discrimination against other types of prisoners. Indiscipline became generalised, and day after day this situation spilled over into the mass media (...). (García Valdés 1989: 253)

Reforms, counter-reforms and later emergencies

Abandoning the re-socialisation ideal

While the prison population continued to grow, innovation occurred in the architectural aspects of incarceration: 'maximum security prisons', and 'mega prisons' began to appear. The former, by emphasising strict surveillance and pure restraint of inmates, contradicted any rehabilitative purpose of custody. The latter, designed during the late period of the Popular Party (*Partido Popular*) Government, could hold as many as 2,000 inmates, marking a shift away from the use of small, more manageable, units and from open prison facilities, where re-socialising and educational activities were easier to carry out.

In terms of treatment, two things need mentioning which may describe the increased harshness of prison regimes. First, the creation of 'special files' for monitoring certain types and groups of inmates; second, disciplinary transfers and 'geographical' dispersion of other inmates. The special files (*Fichero de Internos de Especial Seguimiento – FIES*), consist of a database of information, collected without legal regulation, – about 'rebellious' or 'difficult' prisoners. The inclusion of inmates in the *files* implies a dramatic deterioration of their life conditions: constant cell-isolation, systematic requisitions and searches, prohibition of penitentiary benefits, mail censorship, frequent transfers from one penitentiary centre to another, and so on. This practice was introduced through successive modifications of Article 10 of the Penitentiary Act, which García Valdés justified as a 'bitter need' to control certain groups of inmates. The effects provoked, frequently denounced by inmate-supporting organisations,[2] include mind disorders, self-mutilation and suicide.

The second aspect of penal 'emergency' is epitomised by the 'dispersion penitentiary policy'. This is mainly an antiterrorist policy, which criminalises ETA inmates' relatives, and forces family members to travel sometimes almost 1,000 kilometres to visit the inmates. Besides this, it is important to remark that this policy lacks any kind of legislative support or clearly documented regulations, and constitutes a blatant violation of the penitentiary legislation itself. This legislation, in effect, indicates that a prison sentence must not turn into the 'social uprooting' of those serving it. It is also important to note that these measures were adopted ten years after the approval of the Penitentiary Act (exactly in 1989), thus testifying to the slow penetration of the 'culture of emergency' in penal matters in the country.

The penal code reform (1995)

During the last period of the PSOE Government, Parliamentary debate led to the approval of the new *Democracy Penal Code*, as it has been labelled. The calls for an improvement of the former Dictatorship Penal Code were then (in 1995) unanimous. The country, in other words, was governed for 20 years through a democratic system while retaining a fascist Penal Code! Although it was a weak political moment for the Government, amid important revelations around 'State terrorism', the new Penal Code was passed by the Congress of Deputies Plenary Session – on 8 November 1995 – and was put into force on May 24 of the following year.

The parliamentary discussions were very animated and the Popular Party (PP) was the only party that refused to vote in favour of the new penal code. Later on, paradoxically, this party, once in government, had to implement it. Discussions revolved around an emblematic issue, namely the 'effective execution of custodial sentences', and were triggered by moral panics and new emergencies. These included episodes of terrorism, along with particularly disturbing crimes, which led to a petition signed by over three million people asking for restrictions of penitentiary bene-fits for sexual offenders. In the background, political parties were fighting and finding compromises in view of the imminent general elections.

It cannot be denied that the new Penal Code was innovative in many respects. Among the innovations: the possibility of community work as an alternative to custody, and extended opportunities for proba-tionary measures for prisoners willing to undertake continuous cultural, educational and work activities. On the other hand, more severity was introduced for prisoners regarded as particularly dangerous, and the maximum sentence was extended to 30 years – a level never reached through the previous legislation (Muñagorri 1997).

The Act of Dangerousness and Social Rehabilitation was repealed. This allowed the imposition of pre-trial, precautionary measures on political dissidents, drug users and other 'deviants'. On the other hand, harsher innovations consisted of:

- The abolition of prison work as a partial alternative to custody.
- The introduction of exceptional regimes of incarceration, and prohi-bition of any benefits or alternatives for certain types of offenders.

The penetration of the emergency culture into penitentiary matters was testified by Article 78 of the new Penal Code, which regulated – on the basis of the assumed '*dangerousness*' of the defendant – the benefits to be eventually granted to them. The new Code, in brief, improved and expanded the use of some alternatives to custody, but imposed stricter measures on some groups of offenders. This is a typical process of bifur-cation taking place in many countries – a phenomenon inspired by 'Selective Differentiation Criteria'.

Looking at the new penalties for certain types of violent offences, the new Penal Code seemed far from being benign – rather it appeared to be characterised by a 'regressive increase of penal complexity' (ibid.). In this sense, it is legitimate to suggest that perhaps Spain missed a historical opportunity to improve or limit the use of custody. Further reform legislations reiterated this tendency.

The penitentiary regulation reform (1996)

New regulations were approved in 1996 and efforts were made to render changes consistent with the normative framework provided by the new penal Code. It should be stressed that such changes, which affect the elementary right to freedom, were and continue to be introduced without the explicit support of, or reference to, constitutional norms or specific pieces of legislation. Therefore, they contravene the principle of legality, whereby the treatment of offenders and prisoners has to abide by a set of democratically approved norms.

Among the new measures, was the normalisation of the Files of Special Monitoring Inmates (FIES), which allow prison administrations to impose long-term isolation on certain inmates. New rules were also devised to deal with the controversial issue of probation for ill prisoners. Article 92 of the new 1995 Penal Code stated that probation may be granted to those prisoners who 'according to medical reports, suffer from a serious condition or incurable disease'. With the new regulations, prisoners had to be deemed incapable of offending due to their lack of 'functional autonomy' – namely, an incapacity to look after themselves even in the most simple tasks of their daily life.

The penal, procedural and penitentiary counter-reform (2003)

New regulations in the arenas of criminal justice and penal policy were drawn up by the Government, led by the Popular Party in 2003. These included:

- An increase in the level of the maximum penalty to 40 years imprisonment, justified by the argument that 'there are certain crimes that, due to their particular seriousness, the nature of the harmed juridical good, the perpetrator's recidivism, as well as the fact that they may be committed by organised criminal gangs with the only aim of subverting the constitutional order, altering public peace, or threatening the population, require harsher juridical-penal responses'. This was a surreptitious way of re-introducing life imprisonment, which continues to be unconstitutional in Spain. At the moment of writing this chapter, proposals are being put forward to introduce a form of life imprisonment subject to regular review. In brief, a form of indeterminate, potentially infinite, sentence. Again, of course, this measure would contravene the principles of re-socialisation and rehabilitation constitutionally attributed to custody.

- Cuts in the application of penitentiary benefits, such as alternative penalties, for certain categories of crime. This runs against the principle of 'scientific individual treatment', granted in the Penitentiary Act, which indicates that prisoners should be dealt with on a personal, case-by-case basis, and forbids any consideration of crime 'categories' or 'typologies'.
- National centralisation of prison regime monitoring – which sidelines the local judges, who perform a similar function at the local level.
- Harsher criteria for the application of remand, which result in a remarkable increase in the prison population.
- Deportation of non-national offenders, with a clear violation of Constitutional principles of equity.

Prison management through 'minor norms': instructions and administrative circulars

At the end of 2011, Spain was the third European country with respect to prison overcrowding, with 142 inmates for 100 available places – just over Cyprus (150) and Serbia (146). In mid-April, 2012, there was an average overcrowding rate of 134, (18%) in Catalonia, against 127, (90%) in the rest of the country. The Figure 12.1 refers to June 2010:

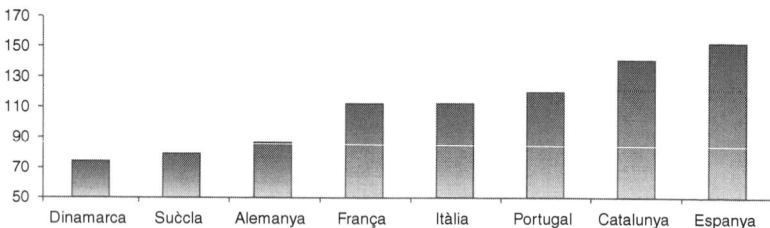

Figure 12.1 Imprisoned population per 100,000 inhabitants

Source: (http://www.gencat.cat/justicia/estadistiques_serveis_penitenciaris/1_pob.html: accessed on 22 June 2012).

The management of prison institutions in Spain transcends the official and organic legislative acts described above. In other words, it is not based on formal laws agreed upon through democratic parliamentary debate. Prisons are actually run by prison administrations, through Instructions and Circulars, which shape the daily life of inmates and modulate treatment regimes. The lists provided below, respectively relating to the State Penitentiary Administration and the Catalonian Penitentiary Administration,[3] show the precise areas in which instructions and circulars have affected prison life since the 1996 reform.

Table 12.1 General secretariat of penitentiary institutions (Spain)

Year	Number of approved Instructions	Regulated subjects
1996	3	Internal regulations and weekend arrests
1997	3	Labour issues involving prison officers
1998	5	Health problems, workload of officers and their tasks, children schools inside prisons
1999	6	Rules for internal investigations, sanitation matters, staff productivity and performance
2000	3	Nutritional aspects and the functioning of social work in prison
2001	9	Hygienic issues, juridical support to staff, syringe-change programmes, inmates' labour opportunities, visits to hospitalised inmates, personal documents of entering prisoners
2002	3	Swipe cards for officers and other staff, notification to prisoners of transfers and extradition, hospitalisation
2003	6	Assistance to inmates, health documentation and programming of activities in penitentiary centres
2004	0	
2005	11	Treatment and disciplinary measures, medical guards, inmates' labour accidents, prevention of suicides, social work in prison
2006	13	Primary health care, visits by attorneys, integration for transsexuals, notification of inspections, hygienic issues, work conditions of officers, planning and promotion of internal activities
2007	17	System of videoconferencing, participation of external organisation in internal activities, generation of Automatised Identification Systems, religious matters, inmate classification and destination, electronic mail and internet, hygienic issues, missing and deceased people, absence of leave, restraint of inmates and the use of pharmaceutical products
2008	2	Labour matters and uniforms for staff
2009	7	Service allocation to officers, centralisation of internal management, transfers to courts and hospitals, criteria for the allocation of cells
2010	5	Work conditions of staff, work by traffic offenders for the benefit of the community, security measures

Continued

Table 12.1   Continued

Year	Number of approved Instructions	Regulated subjects
2011	20	Drugs, elderly prisoners, violent sex offenders, security measures for potentially dangerous inmates, Code of conduct for officers, admission protocol at entrance, norms for closed regimes, programmes of behaviour normalisation and security measures
2012 (June)	2	Permits and leave for prisoners, acceptance of external organisations in prison activities

Source: Self-creation.

Table 12.2   General direction of penitentiary services (Catalonia)

Year	Number of penal instructions	Regulated subjects
1999	2	Juridical assistance for the Administration staff, and programmes for the evaluation of their work
2000	0	
2001	4	Acceptance of volunteers from the outside world, criteria for cell-searching
2002	1	Labour relationships in prison
2003	3	Programme for syringe exchange, day release and other permits to leave the institution, suspended sentences
2004	6	Economic support for inmates, probation, urgent transfers and problematic situations in psychiatric penitentiary units
2005	5	Religious assistance, rules for those on day release, confinement in detox centres
2006	4	Management of art workshops, language programmes, cell-phones in open-air areas
2007	0	
2008	3	Staff labour matters, control of authorised staff at the entrance, searches and control tools for inmates
2009	3	Regime for imprisoned transsexual people, inmate documentation at entrance
2010	6	Right to information, measures against sexual violence, protection for victims of violence within prison, authorised and forbidden objects, including informatics and appliance equipment
2011	2	Non-national inmates, Ethics Code for staff
2012 (June)	1	Conditional release

Source: Author.

As these lists testify, numerous aspects of prison life are regulated through administrative rather than legislative tools, and this is all the more disturbing in that such tools impinge on fundamental rights guaranteed by the Constitution. Rights are therefore eroded without the aid of a supporting law in a country which describes itself as Constitutional and Democratic.

Considering all the above, we can state that in Spain:

- Prison is becoming the criminal penalty par excellence.
- Alternative measures to custodial sentences are neglected.
- There is a need to increase investment in new prison institutions.
- Imprisonment is going to expand for different sections of the population, particularly for migrants.
- The purpose of the penal system is that of neutralising and disabling offenders through negative prevention measures, rather than constitutionally approved positive prevention (or re-socialisation).

The prison population

Finally, it is important to point out that this punitive drift has gathered momentum at time when crime rates are falling (see Figure 12.2). And

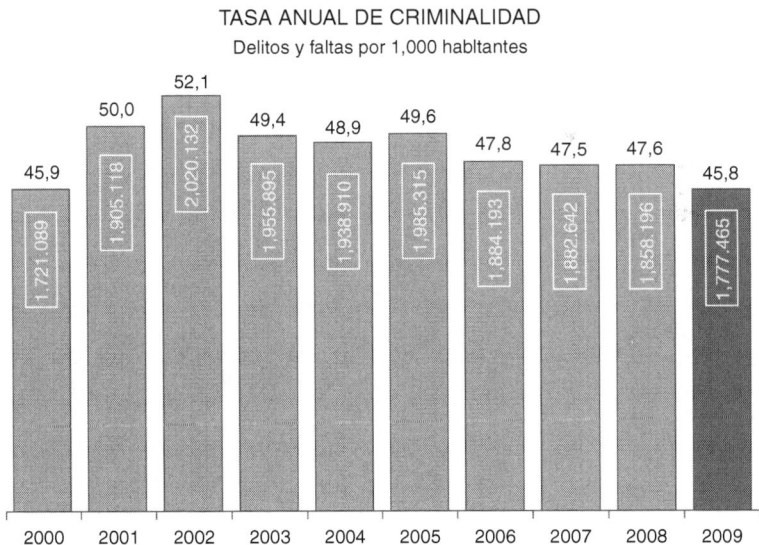

TASA ANUAL DE CRIMINALIDAD
Delitos y faltas por 1,000 habltantes

Figure 12.2 Annual crime rates

Note: Crimes and transgressions offences[4] per 1.000 inhabitants.

Source: Evolution of criminality, 2009 balance, Research Bureau of Home Security, Home Affairs.

those who suffer the pains of confinement continue to reflect Spain's traditional criminal profile, with its emphasis on property crime and drug trafficking.

According to these figures relating to the last decade, the officially recorded crime rate in Spain observes an opposite trend to that observed by the rate of incarceration. While the former continues to decline, the latter shows no sign of abating. The myth that imprisonment increases due to criminality rising is therefore exploded *(Criminality Evolution, 2011 balance,* Board for Studies of Internal Security, Ministry of the Interior).

It is time to provide a demographic breakdown of the prison population. In January 2012, there were 70,000 prisoners in Spain.

Table 12.3   Distribution of imprisoned population by sex

Gender	Total	%
Men	65,035	92,39
Women	5,357	7,61
Total	70,392	100

Source: http://www.institucionpenitenciaria.es/web/portal/documentos/estadisticas.html?r= m&adm=TES&am=2012&mm=1&tm=GENE&tm2=GENE, accessed on 2 July 2012.

The gender composition of non-nationals was as follows:

Table 12.4   Distribution of non-national imprisoned population

Gender	Total	%
Men	22,251	92,16
Women	1,893	7,84
Total	24,144	100

Source: http://www.institucionpenitenciaria.es/web/portal/documentos/estadisticas.html?r= m&adm=TES&am=2012&mm=1&tm=EXTR&tm2=GENE, accessed on 2 July 2012.

Data provided by the prison authorities indicate that the most numerous non-national groups of prisoners were, in decreasing order: Moroccan, Colombian and Romanian.

Out of the total prisoner population, 54,111 were sentenced and 11,480 were on remand.

Table 12.5   Imprisoned Population by Age Groups

Age	Men	Women	Total
From 18 to 20 years old (Sentenced)	1.023	56	1.079
From 21 to 25 years old (Sentenced)	6.118	436	6.554
From 26 to 30 years old (Sentenced)	8.393	692	9.085
From 31 to 40 years old (Sentenced)	17.537	1.379	18.916
From 41 to 60 years old (Sentenced)	15.650	1.364	17.014
Over 60 years old (Sentenced)	1.288	98	1.386
No Information (Sentenced)	73	4	77
Total	50.082	4.029	54.111

Source: http://www.institucionpenitenciaria.es/web/portal/documentos/estadisticas.html?r=
m&adm=TES&am=2012&mm=1&tm=EDAD&tm2=GENE, accessed on July 2, 2012.

The criminal typology in Spain, as it has always been in our country, is associated with property crime and drug trafficking. Recently, however, sex offences and trafficking in human beings have substantially increased.

Table 12.6   Criminal typology

	Men	Women
Homicide	3,177	210
Grievous bodily harm	2,301	131
Kidnapping and other forms of coercion	806	55
Sexual violence	2,886	61
Crimes against honour	0	0
Domestic violence	3,713	13
Child abduction and family abandonment	179	6
Property crime	18,183	1,127
Drug trafficking	12,786	2,044
Traffic offences	930	16
Forgery (falsifying of documents)	782	83
Against public administration and the treasury	170	13
Against justice administration	652	50
Public Order Offences	1,767	102
Others	885	63
Transgressions (minor offences)	128	14
No recorded crimes	134	13
Total	49,479	4,001

Source: http://www.institucionpenitenciaria.es/web/portal/documentos/estadisticas.html?r=
m&adm=TES&am=2012&mm=1&tm=TIP1&tm2=GENE, accessed on 2 July 2012.

Conclusion

The Spanish penal system, as we have described it in this chapter, shows clear violations of some elementary rights – including the right to dignity. Prison conditions are such that inmates are unable to achieve any form of development, as institutions are crammed and cells are shared (despite the official rules recognising the right to individual cells). This infringement of the rules is regularly denounced – in Spain as elsewhere – by the European Court of Human Rights, which has described it as a form of 'inhuman or degrading treatment'. Rehabilitation and other treatment activities cannot be carried out in such conditions – which are the main cause of interpersonal violence among inmates, their physical and psychological victimisation, and suicide. Discipline and control of inmates prevail over treatment programmes (as shown in Table 12.7 by the number of staff employed). Health conditions are dismal, with diseases spreading due to a lack of professional care. The situation is even more dramatic in the area of mental health, while there are still difficulties in making arrangements for the release of the terminally ill.

The economic crisis has worsened this picture, with cuts in all sectors of public provision, the abandonment of programmes for the building of new institutions, and a halt to the recruitment of staff. The Table 12.7 indicates the number of inmates between 2001 and 2010, the number of prison officers, that of other prison staff, and the staff–prisoner ratio for the same years.

Table 12.7   Number of inmates, number of prison officers, that of other prison staff, and the staff–prisoner ratio, 2001–2010

	2001	2002	2003	2004	2005	2006	2007	2008	2009	2010
Internos a diciembre	41,131	44,924	48,645	51,272	52,747	55,049	57,725	63,517	65,563	63,314
Efectivos funcionarios	17,926	18,406	18,918	19,390	19,276	19,748	20,358	21,271	22,363	23,190
Efectivos laborales	1,751	1,685	1,793	1,132	1,780	1,828	1,942	1,985	2,049	2,132
Total efectivos personal	19,677	20,091	20,711	21,122	21,056	21,676	22,300	23,256	24,432	25,322
Ratio interno/ empleado	2,9	2,24	2,35	2:43	2,5	2,55	2,59	2,73	2,68	25

Source: http://www.institucionpenitenciaria.es/web/export/sites/default/datos/descargables/publicaciones/Informe_General_2010_acc.pdf: accessed on 21 June 2012.

The declining staff–prisoner ratio, and the apparent impossibility of creating new public jobs, are met with proposals by government representatives to entrust to the private sector the surveillance and management of prison institutions (in http://politica.elpais.com/ politica/2012/06/28/actualidad/1340902553_444856.html, accessed on 3 July 2012).

What is most worrying, however, is the lack of what we might call a 'democratic culture' informing penal policies in the country. Such policies are opaque, and prisons are inaccessible to public scrutiny – closed as they are in themselves and impervious to external influence. We have noted that the actual running of prisons in the country takes place outside the legislative arena, namely through tools and ad hoc means devised by prison administrators themselves.

What is also disturbing is the fact that the growing authoritarianism of the penal system is accompanied by a serious economic crisis, and that that system ends up turning into a tough response to the problems and dissatisfaction that the crisis itself generates. The current 'culture of emergency and penal exceptionalism' brings us a bitter memory of the past – when, similarly, the penal system was energetically used against dissent and protest. In this sense, Spain seems still unable to build a genuine Social Democracy based on the Rule of Law, and before building it is already engaged in demolishing it.

Notes

1. In 1976 and 1977 several amnesty measures were approved, causing the release of political prisoners. From that moment, common prisoners, thereafter called "social" prisoners, assumed a leading role in prison reform campaigns.
2. For a deeper knowledge about this matter, consult the monograph published by *Panóptico* magazine, 2 (1996).
3. We should consider that, since 1983, the Autonomous Community of Catalonia deals in an independent fashion with penal issues.
4. Trangression means a minor penal offence which is dealt with differently from other ordinary offences.

References

Alonso de Escamilla, A. (1985) *El Juez de Vigilancia Penitenciaria* (Madrid: Ed. Civitas).

Andres Ibañez, P. (1989) 'Jueces y Administración de Justicia: un panorama de la cuestión judicial española', en R. Bergalli and E. Marí: *Historia ideológica del control social (España-Argentina, siglos XIX y XX)* (Barcelona: PPU) 323–47.

Asensio Cantisan, H. (1987) 'El Juez de Vigilancia Penitenciaria', *Revista de Estudios Penitenciarios*, 237: 9–16.

Ballbe Y Giro, M. (1978) *Las fuerzas del orden público* (Barcelona: Dopesa).

Baratta, A. (1993) Resocialización o Control Social. Por un Concepto Crítico de 'Reintegración Social' del Condenado (Universidad del Saarland: República Federal de Alemania).

Baratta, A. (1986) 'Viejas y nuevas estrategias en la legitimación del derecho pena', *Poder y Control*, 0: 77–92.

Baratta, A. (1985) 'Principi dei diritto penale minimo. Per una teoria dei deritti umani come oggetti e limiti della legge penale', *Dei delitti e delle pene*, 3: 443–74.

Bergalli, R. (1992a) 'Razones Jurídicas y Razón de Estado (en España y Latinoamérica)', Ponencia presentada a la 3ª. Sesión del IV Congreso Español de Sociología, Grupo de Trabajo no 21, *Sociología Jurídica* (Madrid: 24 a 26 de septiembre).

Bergalli, R. (1992b) 'Resocialización y Medidas Alternativas. Extravíos Conceptuales, Políticas Sinuosas y Confusiones Piadosas en las Prácticas Penitenciarias de España y Cataluña', *Ponencia Presentada en las Jornadas Sobre el Cumplimiento de las Penas* (Lérida: 1 y 2 de marzo de 1991).

Bergalli, R. (1992c) '¡Esta es la Cárcel que Tenemos...(pero no queremos)! Introducción', en I. Rivera, *Cárcel y Derechos Humanos. Un Enfoque Relativo a la Defensa de los Derechos Fundamentales de los Reclusos* (Barcelona: J. M. Bosch) 7–21.

Bergalli, R. (1991) 'Forma-Estado, Formas del Derecho y Cuestiones de la Democracia: Un Caso Para el Análisis', *Anuario de Filosofía del Derecho* (Madrid: Ministerio de Justicia) 169–90.

Bergalli, R. (1987) 'Ideología de la Resocialización-La Resocialización Como Ideología. La Situación en España', Papers d'Estudi i Formació, 1: 51–66.

Bueno Arus, F. (1988) 'La jurisprudencia del Tribunal Constitucional en materia penitenciaria', en *Poder Judicial* nº Especial III: 167–77.

Bueno Arus, F. (1985) *Lecciones de Derecho Penitenciario* (Salamanca: Universidad de Alcalá de Henares).

Bueno Arus, F. (1978) 'Las Prisiones Desde la Guerra Civil Hasta Nuestros Días: Evolución, Situación Actual y Reformas Necesarias', en *Historia 16*, Extra VII (Madrid)113–44.

Carr, R . (1988) *España (1808–1975)* (Barcelona: Ariel Ed).

Criminality Evolution, 2011 balance, Board for Studies of Internal Security, Ministry of the Interior .

De La Cuesta Arzamendi, J. L . (1987) 'Un Deber (No Obligación) y Derecho de los Privados de Libertad: El Trabajo Penitenciario', en *Papers d'Estudi i Formació*, núm E/1: 103–30.

Dominguez Figueirido, J. L . (1991) 'La Utilización de Categorías Histórico-Ideológicas en la Justificación del Sindicalismo Policial Español', en *Sociology of Penal Control Within the Framework of the Sociology of Law* (Oñati: Instituto Internacional de Sociología Jurídica) 177–94.

Draper Miralles, R. (1984) De Las Prisiones de Franco a Las Cárceles de la Democracia (Barcelona: Argos Vergara).

Faraldo Cabanas, P. (2005) 'Un Derecho Penal de Enemigos Para Los Integrantes de Organizaciones Criminales. La Ley Orgánica 7/2003, de 30 de Junio, de Medidas de Reforma Para El Cumplimiento Integro Y Efectivo de Las Penas', en I. Rivera, coord, *Política Criminal y Sistema Penal* (Barcelona: Ed. Anthropos).

Garcia Valdes, C. (1977) 'Sistema Penitenciario Español', en AA.VV.: *El preso común en España* (Madrid: Ed. La Torre) 55–68.

Garcia Valdes, C. (1989) *Derecho Penitenciario (Escritos, 1982–1989)* (Madrid: Ministerio de Justicia).

Lurra (1978) *Rebelión En Las Cárceles* (San Sebastián: Hórdago).

Mapelli Caffarena, B. (1983) Principios Fundamentales Del Sistema Penitenciario Español (Barcelona: Bosch).

Marti, O . (1977) 'La COPEL: Historia de Una Lucha Silenciada', *El Viejo Topo*, nº 13: 35–8.

Martinez Fresneda, G. (1992) 'La Reforma Nació Muerta', en *EL PAIS*, de 10 de octubre.

Moreno Catena, V. (1990) *Drecho procesal, Tomo II* (Valencia: Tirant Lo Blanch).

Muñagorri Laguia, I. (2005) 'Derecho Penal Intrecultural Y Crisis Del Principio', en *Política Criminal y Sistema Penal* ,I. Rivera, coord (Barcelona: Ed. Anthropos).

Muñagorri Laguia, I. (1997) 'Reflexiones Sobre La Pena de Prisión En El Nuevo CP de 1995: Polifuncionalidad E Incremento Regresivo de La Complejidad Penal', en J. Dobón and I. Rivera, *Secuestros Institucionales Y Derechos Humanos. La Cárcel Y El Manicomio Como Laberintos de Obediencias Fingidas* (Barcelona: M. J. Bosch).

Muñagorri Laguia, I. (1987) 'Comentario de la Ley Orgánica 2/1986 de 13 de marzo, de Fuerzas y Cuerpos de Seguridad', en *Poder y Control*, nº 1 (Barcelona: PPU) 235–46.

Muñagorri Laguia, I. (1977) *Sanción Penal Y Política Criminal* (Madrid: Ed. Reus).

Recasens Brunet, A. (1989) 'Uellas Aguas Trajeron Estos Lodos.: La Burguesía Y Los Orígenes Del Aparato Policial', en R. Bergalli and E. Marí, *Historia Ideológica Del Control Social (España-Argentina, siglos XIX y XX)* (Barcelona: PPU) 285–322.

Recasens Brunet, A. (1991) 'Enfoques Histórico-Ideológicos Sobre El Concepto de Aparato Policial', en *Sociology of Penal Control within the Framework of the Sociology of Law* (Oñati: Instituto Internacional de Sociología Jurídica) 161–75.

Rios Martin, J. C. and Cabrera Cabrera, P. J . (1998) *Mil Voces Presas* (Madrid: Publicaciones de la Universidad Pontificia Comillas).

Rios Martin, J. C. and Cabrera Cabrera, P. J . (1998) 'La Cárcel: Descripción de Una Realidad', *Cáritas, Suplemento*, nº 388 octubre.

Rios Martín, J. C. (2003) Reflexiones Sobre La Ley 7/2003: El Incremento de La Violencia Puntiva (Inédito).

Rivera Beiras, I. (2009–2010) *La cuestion carcelaria. Historia, Epistemologia, Derecho y Politica penitenciaria* (2da. Edición, Tomos I y II) (Buenos Aires: Editores del Puerto).

Rivera Beiras, I. (1998) El Problema de Los Fundamentos de La Intervención Jurídico-Penal. Las Teorías de La Pena (Barcelona: Ed. Signo).

Rivera Beiras, I. (1997) La Devaluación de Los Derechos Fundamentales de Los Reclusos. La Construcción Jurídica de Un Ciudadano de Segunda Categoría (Barcelona: J. M. Bosch).

Rivera Beiras, I. (1996) La cárcel en el sistema penal. Un análisis estructural (2ª edición revisada conforme al CP 1995 y al RP 1996) (Barcelona: M. J. Bosch).

Rivera Beiras, I. (1994) 'Cárcel Y Cultura de La Resistencia. Los Movimientos de Defensa de Los Derechos Fundamentales de Los Reclusos En Europa Occidental', en *Arguments i Propostes*, nº 3, Barcelona, 55–71.

Rivera Beiras, I. (1992) Cárcel Y Derechos Humanos. Un Enfoque Relativo a La Defensa de Los Derechos Fundamentales de Los Reclusos (Barcelona: J. M. Bosch).

Ruiz Vadillo, E. (1988) 'Algunas Consideraciones Sobre La Figura Del Juez de Vigilancia Penitenciaria. La Misión Del Fiscal Sobre Determinadas Competencias Y Sobre El Futuro de La Institución', en Fiscales de Vigilancia Penitenciaria (Madrid: Ministerio de Justicia, Centro de Estudios Judiciales) 81–112.

13

Greece: Prisons Are Bad but Necessary (and Expanding), Policies Are Necessary but Bad (and Declining)

Vassilis Karydis and Nikolaos K. Koulouris

Introduction

Prison policy and legislation since 1830, when Greece became an independent state, is described as 'whimsical' (Dimopoulos 2003), because of the successive reforms and re-arrangements, the drifting from one correctional system to another, and from one penal philosophy to another. All relevant initiatives remained incomplete and decisions were overruled because of political instability, repeated emergencies and exceptional situations (occupations by foreign forces, dictatorships, wars, civil wars, economic crises).[1] The prison system throughout the nineteenth and early twentieth centuries was characterised by dismal conditions – with institutions described as 'dirty drains' (Maurer 1835 in Courakis 2009), 'schools of crime for the young inmates and graves for the elderly' (Appert 1856,), 'earthly hells' (Dedis 1872), 'animals' hide-outs' (Parliamentary Minutes 1885).

Among the efforts to change this unacceptable situation, some important initiatives for reform were undertaken during the second and third decades of the twentieth century. Worth mentioning are measures which were aimed at broadening the sentencing framework: suspended sentences, conditional release, conversion of prison sentences into fines, 'mobile' prisons,[2] farm prisons, and so on.

During the first decades of the post-Second World War era, a period of civil war (which ended in 1949) and post-civil war 'sickly Democracy' (Nikolakopoulos 2001), slowed down the democratic process, while prisons were used to detain: political dissidents, opponents of the existing socio-economic order – or 'enemies of the nation' – and spies (communists and their democratic allies, real or supposed). The situation in terms of infrastructure and services remained at the level of the nineteenth century.

In the mid-1970s, after the collapse of the 1967 military regime, prisons regained their function as a criminal justice institution in a normal parliamentary democratic administration. Custodial institutions, though, remained the focus of academic, political and media criticism, as conditions failed to meet elementary personal and social needs of the inmates, and were deemed incompatible with basic human rights.

In the course of the last two decades, especially during the first decade of the millennium, the issue of corruption in the political and penal system has repeatedly found its way into the public debate. In July 2009, for example, the public was shocked by revelations about a criminal network in which inmates, prison officials, politicians, lawyers, police officers and others allegedly undertook a variety of illicit activities – involving murder contracts, blackmails, kidnappings and briberies. The scandal affected the prison service as a whole. The then Minister of Justice, supposedly taken by surprise, appeared to be the champion of a concerted effort to clean up the deeply rotten system – as if ignoring that the system had been rotten for a long time. Nowadays, after a long 'nothing works' period, not superseded by a 'some things do work' period, new problems emerge which transcend a crisis of legitimisation and lack of resources.

In this chapter, penal policies are presented in all their improvisation and inconsistency. An outline of the sentencing system, as well as of the structure and organisation of the Prison Service, is provided. Information about the legal framework and the living components of the system, inmates and staff, is given, with reference to the social organisation of the 'prison community'. The process of penal bifurcation and the phenomenon of penal austerity are then examined. Finally, an attempt is made to assess whether and how the situation in Greece is connected to the international penal climate – particularly to the suggestions of 'new penology'. Our main thesis is that prisons in Greece exist and function by momentum – as an end in themselves, or as a means without ends. Slightly influenced by traditional or innovative penal philosophies and cultures, they display a mixture of juxtaposing characteristics, but play a major role in the control of social problems such as, among others, illegal drug use and trafficking, and irregular migration.

The 'rhetoric' of policies

During the last 20 years or more, Greece has witnessed constant consecutive reforms of the penitentiary system, starting with the enactment of the Code of Basic Rules for the Treatment of Prisoners, in 1989, which we will consider later in the text.

At that time – especially in the 1990s, the Greek administration and society seemed at last mature enough to talk openly about the unbearable conditions in prisons, to discuss policies and human rights, as well as to link its own institutional framework with the wider European penal discourse, institutional initiatives and humanitarian commitments. In the effort to join the Eurozone and modernise society and its institutions, the administration seriously tried to construct the humane profile of a liberal European Union member state and develop the relevant rhetoric. In this context, two official documents on penal and prison reform are indicative of the reformative rhetoric and the goodwill of the country. We are referring to two reports prepared by as many Inter-parliamentary Committees and submitted to the Greek Parliament – the first in July 1994 and the second in October 2011.[3]

Both Committees were set up *ad hoc* after serious turmoil in prisons, and the examination of the relevant reports offers the opportunity to reveal, not only the content of the official public penal and prison discourse but, more importantly, also what is excluded from it. The underlying idea is that political parliamentary discourse emphasises conventional mainstream thinking of penal and prison reform, while bypassing crucial points and issues raised by critical approaches and perspectives. By directing attention to the commonplace discrepancy between 'law in books' and 'law in action', the reports obscure the fact that theory and practice are not segregated worlds, but two interacting and mutually dependent realms. Also, by inscribing the complex issue of penalty within the simplistic terms of punishment-for-crime, they ignore socio-political elements and reproduce a common-sense belief in the necessity of penal repression by an allegedly neutral state.

The 1994 report

The July 1994 Report, the first policy document of this kind ever drawn up in Greece, was subsequently (though four years later, in 1998) adopted unanimously by the then four parliamentary parties of the Greek Parliament (Socialists, Conservatives, Nationalists, Communists).

In the Introduction of the Report a multilevel crime policy is adopted, directed respectively to the legislative, the judicial and the correctional layers of the criminal justice system. A quasi 'nothing works' approach seems to have been initially adopted, whereby prison is regarded as ineffective in correctional terms and its very moral foundations are questioned. The Committee, however, goes on to suggest that a constructive use of time in custody and the separation of the inmates into categories are important pre-conditions for their social re-integration, contradicting its introductory thesis that prison does not work. Moreover, beyond the general negative picture which is given, a degree of confusion emerges in relation to penal policy models and prison aims. The Committee seems to favour the Justice Model approach while, at the same time, declaring its belief in the correctional potential of individualised sentences and the prison system itself. The report reveals criminal justice inconsistencies and arbitrariness, emphasises the lack of a coherent crime policy, denounces prison as a failure in terms of rehabilitation, and presents it as a serious threat for the human rights of the inmates. On the other hand, however, the members of the Committee unanimously agree that the effort for improvement is worthwhile because the cost will be counterbalanced by the expected benefit from crime reduction. They accept the logic of prison alternatives and community sentences and support the use of imprisonment only for those offenders who constitute a real danger to society, but fail to indicate the criteria by which dangerousness can be assessed. Finally, overcrowding is considered as the source of the many misfortunes of the prison system, in combination with serious deficiencies as regards facilities, personnel and other human and material resources.

Despite the contradictions just mentioned, the report adopts a mild liberal approach, with an important part addressing the protection of human rights, social crime prevention policies and control of prison population, advocating, among other things, decriminalisation and alternatives to custody. However, although apparently close to a reductionism stance, it would appear that such proximity is rather accidental. The report is conventional and overtly technocratic. It does not at all question the centrality of custodial institutions in the sentencing framework, nor does it consider the structural economic and social inequalities that make prisons 'continue to detain those whom penal institutions have always confined, namely the poor and dispossessed' (Sim et al. 1995: 17).

The 2011 report

This second report of another Inter-parliamentary Committee – drafted, submitted and discussed 17 years after its predecessor – was voted for by the majority of the Committee's members (Socialists, Conservatives, Nationalists, Radical Left), while this time the Communist Party dissociated itself on the grounds that the report did not take into consideration the wider socio-political context.

In the introductory note, the Head of the Committee stated that overcrowding, non-national inmates, imprisoned drug offenders, and corruption were the main causes of the problems in the Greek prison system. It is submitted that tackling these problems was certainly costly, but that the aim of re-integration should not be abandoned by the welfare state. The report was expected to initiate an open and wide discussion – particularly over its three innovative proposals: an experimental model prison, the creation of a permanent Inter-parliamentary Committee and the foundation of an independent Crime Policy Institute.

In relation to the criminal justice system, the committee suggested that it should function as a real system, with its constituent parts (police, courts, prisons) coordinating and interacting, and emphasised that offenders should be sent to prison as a punishment and *not for punishment*. However, the committee strangely expected that the decline of the welfare state would not be followed by the criminalisation of poverty and the growth of penal repression. It restated the well-known principles of exceptional, last resort use of incarceration and respect of the inmates' human rights and dignity – despite the demand for prison security and discipline. Prison conditions were related to two issues with major potential for re-integration – work and education. Both were conceived as the most proper treatment to counter serious problems and conflicts stemming from the prison subculture and the coexistence of a variety of cultures among the different ethnic groups of prisoners. The development of alternative sanctions, and the possibility of choice for a convicted person among a variety of options (community service, home detention, electronic monitoring), were also proposed.

The lack of suitable, properly built and preserved prisons was at the top of the committee's priorities, which proposed a construction programme to remedy the situation. This, however, amounted to an expansionist policy – since it suggested building more prisons when compared to those which should be abolished. Summing up, the report made clear that inmates were to be regarded as a socially excluded group, whose rights should be respected regardless of economic crises. Moreover, it was also declared that there was a need to develop a democratic culture in the administration of the prison system.

The 2011 report gave priority to a progressive liberal agenda for penal and prison reform. However, it appeared to combine both reductionist and expansionist aspects, leading to confusion about its penal philosophy and strategies. It also presented as possible and attainable a variety of mild and inclusive crime policy principles. Such principles, nevertheless, were in sharp contrast with the reality of imprisonment, as described in the report itself but also in the findings of national and international human rights bodies and monitoring authorities (e.g. the Greek Ombudsman, the Greek National Committee for Human Rights, the European Committee for the Prevention of Torture (CPT), Council of Europe Human Rights Commissioner).

To conclude, in both reports, questions about the *use of incarceration,* who should go to prison, for what reason and purpose and for how long, remained more or less unanswered or unaddressed. The prison system was presented as part of the proper solutions for social problems, while at the same time it was acknowledged that the system itself produces social harm and constitutes a burden for society. In this way, these 'policies as rhetoric' contributed to the perception of prison on the part of civil society as the turtle might perceive its shell – a burden to be carried for its own safety.

The codifications

Sentencing and sanctions in Greece

The current sentencing framework in Greece is based on the Penal Code enacted in 1950 (Law 1492/1950). With the exception of the death penalty, which has been abolished, *de facto* since 1972 and *de jure* in 1993, no substantial changes in this particular structure and penal philosophy have been put into effect throughout this more than 60-year period. Successive minor amendments have been introduced within its framework – the most important in the first half of the 1990s (1991, 1995) and in 2010, mostly under the pressure of prison population growth and a variety of prisoners' protests and riots (Bokos et al. 1992; Nikolaides 2006; Kosmatos 2010). Among the outcomes of such reforms, however, was a lengthening of sentences for certain types of offences (Cheliotis 2011; Papaioannou 2010).

Penal sanctions consist of (a) primary (main) and additional (ancillary) *penalties*, (b) *security measures* and (c) *sanctions for juveniles* (detention, educational and therapeutic measures). Sanctions for military personnel are established by special laws of the military penal code, and will not be considered in the pages that follow.

Primary or main penalties include two categories of sanctions: custody and fines. Custodial sanctions, in their turn, are of three kinds: detention (between 1 day and 1 month), imprisonment (minimum 10 days, maximum 5 years) and confinement in a penitentiary (either for life or for a period between 5 and 20 years). For habitual recidivist offenders, an indeterminate sentence of deprivation of liberty is provided, but in practice it is not imposed by courts.

Detention and imprisonment may be actually enforced or replaced under various schemes, in the form of conditional suspension of the sentence (with or without supervision) or conversion into a monetary sanction (a kind of day-fine). A converted sentence may be further converted into a community service order. Supervised suspended sentences (a probation-like scheme) and sentences converted into community service can be considered the Greek version of community sentences. It should be noted, though, that the non-custodial options are still part of the range of penal sanctions available, and that they presuppose a previously inflicted custodial sentence, which is then turned into an alternative to custody by a court (Anagnostopoulos and Magliveras 2000). According to the 2010 penal reform, courts are required to convert sentences of up to three years into non-custodial measures. In particular, sentences not exceeding one year are mandatorily converted, while for longer sentences – up to three years – courts are obliged to give reasons for refusing conversion. Conversion and suspension, in brief, act as the major filters of the contemporary Greek sentencing system, which selects and diverts from prison an important proportion of the convicted population.[4]

A special custodial sanction – detention in a young offenders' (correctional) institution – is provided for juveniles between 15 and 18 years of age. In order to impose this sentence the juvenile court has to rule that the adolescent is criminally responsible.[5] It is a sanction of last resort, imposed only if the court is of the opinion that deprivation of freedom is necessary to prevent further offending (Pitsela 2011). Except for this *special* sanction, a variety of educational and therapeutic measures are available to juvenile courts for children and adolescents between eight and 18 years old.

As Cavadino and Dignan (2007) note, sentencing[6] is the crux of the penal crisis and sentencing decisions are important contributing factors to it. They determine, along with decisions made at both pre-trial and post-sentence stage, the growth, stability or reduction of prison and probation numbers, the (in)sufficiency of resources throughout the penal system, as well as its legitimacy, in terms of potential or actual excessiveness, disparity and inconsistency. One crucial point in sentencing is the decision to impose a custodial or a non-custodial, either pecuniary or community, sanction. In a different wording, sentencing is more or less the selection of people for imprisonment. The choices made by criminal courts are affected by a variety of sometimes contradictory considerations, well known as aims of sentencing. Some of these justifications are utilitarian and consequentialist (deterrence, rehabilitation, incapacitation), while others are symbolic or restorative. Sentencing options are also dictated and shaped by political shifts, public sentiment towards crime and criminality, moral panics and stereotypes, judges' backgrounds, beliefs and attitudes – and finally by considerations of existing policy guidelines.

The inflationary use of custody determined a crisis requiring the development of diversionary measures; these can result either in fewer people being incarcerated or in time served in custody being reduced. According to Tzannetakis (2006) the prison population inflation in Greece is partially the side effect of the rise of the custody threshold from 18 months in the 1980s to (initially) two, (then) three and (later) five years of imprisonment in the 1990s and onwards. The legislative choice to introduce alternatives to long prison sentences, to expand early conditional release[7] and encourage the conversion of short-term sentences into fines or community service, caused a reaction by sentencing judges – they changed the tariffs and chose to impose longer sentences in order to make sure that those 'deserving prison' would find their place in it. Consequently, in the case of Greece, we observe a twofold tendency of penal bifurcation, which on the one hand amplifies penal control and on the other hand aims to de-escalate its repressive force. This tendency is influenced either by international trends or by deterrent considerations. On the one hand, the severity of sentences increases (penalisation) and new crimes are introduced (criminalisation) in the penal code. On the other hand, an attempt is made to expand the use of non-custodial sanctions and reduce the use of imprisonment. Penalisation and criminalisation seem to counteract reductionist prison initiatives, and also produce inflationary results, pushing courts to impose longer sentences. Sentences for certain offences – such as, drug trafficking, economic crimes, various forms of social and political violence or terrorism – have increased, as these offences are assimilated to forms of organised crime and, therefore, are harshly punished. However, laws addressing state crimes and the crimes of the powerful in general (torture, large-scale tax evasion, environmental offences and money-laundering) are rarely and reluctantly applied.

The Greek prison system and penitentiary policies

In the year 1952, a Committee was constituted and tasked with the elaboration of a new correctional legislation. The legislative Committee completed their work in 1966, and drafted a more or less authoritarian Correctional Code inspired by the rehabilitation ethos of the 1950s. The proposed draft became the first thorough penitentiary legislation in contemporary Greece – known as Emergency Law 125/1967, as the 1967 military regime accepted it without the slightest intervention. Following the re-establishment of the parliamentary democratic regime (1974), and while Greece was undergoing rapid social and political changes, which led to the election of a social democratic government (1981), the widely supported demand to replace prison legislation, and give a more liberal orientation to prison rules, resulted in a new Code of Basic Rules for the Treatment of Prisoners (Law 1851/1989). This law abandoned the positivistic treatment ideology of the 1967 Correctional Code of education and rehabilitation, replacing it with the notion of 'social re-integration'. During the preparatory stages, a disproportionately great amount of energy was spent in endless discussions and arguments about means, ends and philosophy of the execution of sentences, leaving untouched the daily routines and the deteriorating conditions of prison life. Moreover, many aspects of the law could not be implemented due to a lack of recourses – as was quickly realised.

Under these circumstances, a few months after the enactment of the 1989 law, the Ministry of Justice initiated the drafting of a new Correctional Code, which in 1999 was completed and currently constitutes the legal text ruling prisons and the treatment of inmates (Law 2776/1999). In this law, all utilitarian aims of the previous penitentiary legislation were abandoned, and priority was given to the respect of inmates' human rights, as – according to the law – the restriction of personal liberty of movement in a particular place for a judicially predetermined period of time is the *only* right inmates are deprived of. It is a piece of legislation with no declaration of any official aim for the treatment of inmates, putting legality and transparency as an end in itself at the top of its priorities. According to this, it is neither acceptable – nor allowed – for the prison service to interfere with or affect inmates' personality against their will.

Pursuant to the 1999 Correctional Code, in 2003 and 2005 two Ministerial Decrees were ratified containing the Regulations for the internal operation of general custodial institutions for adults (2003) and the special custodial institutions for juveniles (2005), respectively. These Regulations restrict prisoners' rights, re-define some of these rights, and (re)introduce utilitarianism into the legal framework. The Regulations stress the necessity for a fair trial for remand prisoners and indicate that custody is aimed at preparing inmates for a law-abiding lifestyle. According to both Ministerial Decrees, all detainees shall cooperate, only *if they so wish*, in the design of constructive treatment activities (education, work, vocational training, therapy, etc) so as to limit the further degradation of their legal status and the aggravation of the position of their dependants. In this way, the Regulations somehow bridge the gap between the neutral, non-interventionist approach of the 1999 Code, and international prison rules – especially the 2006 European Prison Rules of the Council of Europe (Koulouris 2009).

The custodial institutions

In October 2012 there were in Greece 34 custodial institutions (28 in 1998, 27 in 1988, 28 in 1979). These are spread across the national territory and operate under the control of a central governmental authority – the Ministry of Justice, Transparency and Human Rights. All prisons are run by regional authorities and their supervision is performed by a central administrative body, the General Directorate for Correctional Policy (Table 13.1). A Special Secretariat for prison security issues was established in 2006 and recently transformed into a General Secretariat for Crime Policy. Public prosecutors are normally assigned to prisons as interim judges for 'the execution of sentences', and are entrusted with supervising the observance of prison rules and regulations and, in general, the legal appropriateness of the inmates' treatment. Prisons are administrative units, headed by directors who are accountable to

Table 13.1 Imprisonment rate per 100,000 inhabitants (based on daily prison population counts, dates of reference vary by year)

1980	1988	1990	1992	1998	1999	2001	2004	2006	2007	2009	2011	year
36.6	44	49.2	61	68	71	79	82	96	99	104	111	Inmates

Source: Various sources based on data published by the Ministry of Justice. Elaboration by authors.

Table 13.2 Total number of inmates (daily prison population counts, dates of reference vary by year)

1980	1990	1992	1995	1998	2001	2004	2007	2008	2009	2012	Year
3,016	4,582	6,252	5,887	7,129	8,343	8,760	11,120	12,192	11,736	12,586	Inmates

Source: Various sources, as referred to above, based on data published by the ministry of justice. Elaboration by authors.

the Ministry of Justice. In five prisons there are also social work departments, while in the four agricultural prisons there are technical (farm) departments. Finally, in the one institution for drug-addicted inmates there is a therapeutic programme department.

According to the Greek Prison Law, 'custodial institutions' (as prisons have been renamed) are distinguished into General, Special, and Therapeutic. General Custodial Institutions are further classified into General Custodial Institutions type A – for inmates awaiting trial and for convicted inmates who serve short-term prison sentences, type B – for inmates convicted to long-term prison sentences, including lifers, and type C[8] – for people convicted to more than ten years. The latter, including lifers, are considered particularly dangerous and are dealt with under particular regimes of detention. Special custodial institutions include farm (agricultural) units, the central open productive unit (bakery, called KAYF), juvenile institutions and semi-liberty centres (never actually established, except one in a female facility). Therapeutic institutions are distinguished between general and mental hospitals and drug detoxification centres. In juvenile institutions (two closed and one agricultural), at times young adults are also kept (until they reach the age of 21, and in exceptional cases, exclusively for educational reasons, until their 25th year of age).

The total operating capacity of all these prisons, which is rising due to a continuously revised construction programme,[9] exceeds 9,000 places, while the number of inmates reaches 13,000 (figures for 2012). In the recent past, the lack of prison places was much more acute, and the country faced a serious custodial inflation problem – with overcrowding among the worst in Europe (Tzannetakis 2006).

Implementation of policies and practices

Inmates

The prison population in Greece has undergone substantial change, in both quantitative and qualitative terms. The imprisonment rate, calculated on *daily* counts, was among the lowest in Europe in the 1980s, but in the 1990s it followed a generally steady upward trend, climbing to a peak in the first years of the twenty-first century.

These figures place Greece in the group of Western European countries occupying the middle of the punitiveness ladder (Spinellis et al. 1996; Spinellis and Spinellis 1999; Tzannetakis 2006; International Centre for Prison Studies, http://www.prisonstudies.org/info/worldbrief/). In absolute terms, when the *daily* prison population is considered, a figure quadruple that of 30 years ago is observed.

This is not, however, an accurate picture, as evidence suggests that things may be worse. Cheliotis (2011) sums up his account based on *annual* caseloads of prisoners and *annual* admissions to prisons, suggesting that they show a much higher rate of imprisonment – more than 160 inmates per 100,000 inhabitants for the year 2006 – than what is commonly referred to. The same data are used by Papaioannou (2010), whose conclusions support Cheliotis' research findings.

Among the contributing factors to the increase in the prison population is the hardening of sentencing policies and practices, especially associated with the 'war' against drugs and organised crime. Legislation passed in the early years of the 2000s epitomises a 'tough on crime' policy, with judges competing in penal austerity and harshness to prove their integrity under the shadow of a major corruption scandal at that time (Karydis 2010). This is clearly reflected in prisoner numbers: inmates serving long-term and life imprisonment for drug-related offences have increased, while remand prisoners form a significant part of the total number of inmates (a quarter to one third, despite the fact that remand custody should be used as a last resort). Finally, the practice of keeping in incarceration irregular immigrants, awaiting deportation after serving a sentence (Law 2721/1999), constitutes an additional burden for the prison administration.

Official prison statistics published annually by the [former] National Statistical Service of Greece [ESYE] – recently re-established as Hellenic Statistical Authority [ELSTAT] (http://www.statistics.gr/portal/page/portal/ESYE) – show that the prison population is male (93.3% of the convicted inmates in 1996, 93.4% in 2006), young (65.5% of the convicted inmates in 1996 and 65.3% in 2006 under 40 years old), unmarried (47% of convicts in 1996, 49.3% in 2006) and of low educational level (only 40% in 1996 having attended school for more than the obligatory, nine-year education period; only 24.6% in 2006 having completed secondary education).

Recent changes regarding the ethnic composition of inmates are striking. Within a period of 12 years, non-nationals increased from one quarter to more than one half of the total prison population (Courakis 2009; Papaioannou 2010; Cheliotis 2011). Research conducted in the big Korydallos prison of Athens in 2005 showed the presence of an extremely varied prison population – in terms of ethno-cultural identity, age and penal status – living in conditions of extreme overcrowding (2,078 persons in establishments with 700 certified accommodation places). The social profile of non-nationals (from 73 different countries) differed systematically from that of Greek national prisoners: the former were on the average younger – being by a huge majority manual workers, had comparatively limited family ties and social support, and less economic means than Greeks. Almost half of them were serving sentences or awaiting trial for drug dealing or trafficking. Non-nationals on remand were significantly more numerous than nationals. Important differences were also observed among non-nationals themselves, based on country of origin and cultural background. Finally, non-nationals were less likely to be granted prison leave and other benefits (Aloskofis 2009: 39ff.). A research update (October 2012) confirmed the 2005 findings, showing a substantial further increase of non-national inmates who are now even younger, the majority of them Muslims, and detained mainly for drug legislation violations, robberies and theft (Aloskofis 2012).

In general, the social characteristics of the inmate population have not changed substantially over recent decades, although recently a small – but not entirely negligible – section of that population is formed of people from the middle and upper classes. As for the type of offence committed, while in the 1980s inmates serving sentences for drug dealing represented ten per cent, in 2005–2006 they approached a third of the total number of convicts (30%–31%). Convicts for property crimes decreased from 34 per cent in 1985 to 25 per cent in 2006. A category not appearing at all in the statistics during the 1980s (non-nationals entering the country illegally) reached 11–14 per cent of the sentenced inmate population in 2005 and 2006. In brief, the general picture seems to indicate that a very significant proportion of those entering a prison institution is composed of violent offenders competing in illegal networks, as well as persons with serious mental health problems and/ or with substance abuse life histories.

Prison staff

The great majority of the personnel currently staffing prisons are not properly trained to perform such demanding work (Vidali et al. 2011). Officers limit their contacts with prisoners to daily routine and tasks, they refer them to older colleagues, social workers, administrators or doctors, and observe inmates from a distance. They also monitor prisoners'

movements, conduct searches and write reports – as well as operate security devices and communication equipments (Nikolaou 2009).

Only in 1973 were social workers hired for the first time to offer their
services in prison. Then, it took more than 25 years for the first sociologists
to appear on prison personnel lists. In the year 2000, a group of specialists (sociologists, psychologists, social workers and one psychiatrist) were
appointed to staff the first detoxification prison unit, in Eleonas, Theves.
In the same year one sociologist and one criminologist were also appointed
to cover two vacant posts in Korydallos (Athens) prison. In 2007, more
than 20 psychologists were added to the small number of specialists.
The general picture, however, remains relatively constant: 75 per cent of
the total number of staff is formed by prison officers (excluding officers
engaged in external surveillance). From the 1980s onwards, numbers show
that the ratio between inmates and staff is slowly improving, especially as
regards custodial staff, but in general, the picture remains disheartening
(Lambropoulou 2000). Problems of inappropriate training for staff persist,
as do poor working conditions, lack of guidance and minimal career
expectations in a more and more demanding working environment,
where not only locking-up duties, but also supervisory and technical skills
are necessary. The Federation of Correctional Personnel Unions notes that
the prison service is working in isolation, without other criminal justice
agencies and community partners giving a helping hand. Moreover, public
distrust and a common belief, strengthened by politicians' statements after
serious events in prisons that corruption is spread throughout all the layers
of the personnel, complete an image of the prison service as degraded
(Panoussis 2007). In these circumstances, it does not come as a surprise
that the Council of Europe Committee for the Prevention of Torture and
Inhuman or Degrading Treatment or Punishment (CPT), according to its
public statement concerning Greece (15 March 2011)

> has observed a steady deterioration in the living conditions and treat-
> ment of prisoners over the past decade. The Committee has identified
> a number of fundamental structural issues which serve to undermine
> attempts to remedy this state of affairs. They include the lack of a
> strategic plan to manage prisons, which are complex institutions, the
> absence of an effective system of reporting and supervision, and inad-
> equate management of the staff. (http://www.cpt.coe.int/documents/
> grc/2011–10-inf-eng.htm)

Law enforcement selectivity: attitudes and practices

We have already mentioned that in recent years more than half of the total
prison population consists of alien inmates, overwhelmingly coming from

non-European Union member states. The question arising is whether this percentage really reflects the involvement of immigrants in (serious) crime. To address this issue, we must first consider the official indices of criminality, notwithstanding the well-known deficiencies regarding the reliability of criminal statistics (Maguire 2007; Coleman and Moynihan 1996).

If we examine the rates for street crime, including murder and robbery (as well as other predatory crimes, such as theft and burglary), we find a substantial overrepresentation of foreign offenders. For example, according to Police Statistics for the year 2011, among offenders known to the police, foreigners constituted 41.3 per cent for homicide, 54 per cent for robberies, 43.8 per cent for theft and burglaries, while their percentage in the general population is approximately ten per cent. During the period between 2000 and 2006, foreigners accounted for 43 per cent of known homicide offenders and over 70 per cent of them were Albanians (constituting about 50% of the total immigrant population). During the same period, foreigners accounted for 40 per cent of known robbery offenders, with Albanians and Romanians being the most prevalent among them. Other research data show that, during the first decade of the 2000s the disproportionate participation of non-national offenders in particular forms of conventional criminality – such as murder, rape, robbery, theft and burglary – is still growing (Zarafonitou 2011).

In relation to the above, certain qualifications must be made. For example, in the case of murder (where the clear-up rate is as high as 85%), we must consider the age and gender factor. According to the 2001 Census, about 60 per cent of the (largely male) immigrant community belongs to the productive 20–44 age groups, while the corresponding percentage of the Greek national population (in which the gender distribution is equal) is approximately 40 per cent. The significance of these data becomes clear when we consider that over 90 per cent of murders, robberies and rapes is committed by males between 20 and 40 years of age. In relation to predatory crimes, we should bear in mind that the clear-up rate is particularly low: 35 per cent for robberies and approximately ten per cent for theft and burglary (Karydis 2011). This brings us to the widely acknowledged fact that the focus of police activities on certain groups of the population, certain areas of the city or certain categories of crime, lead to the disclosure of more hidden crime in those specific areas and categories; thus, differential policing affects crime statistics, acting as a self-fulfilling prophecy (Cook and Hudson 1993; Karydis 1998). Undoubtedly, the immigrant community in Greece lives under constant and heavy policing. Research shows that the immigrants are 15 times more likely than Greek nationals to be brought, proactively and preventively, to a police station (Papantoniou et al. 1998), not taking into account the large military-type operations to apprehend irregular immigrants. Indicatively, according to the data of the General Police Directorate of Attica, during the week two–eight June 2012, 70 per cent of the persons stopped in the street in the central area of Athens, and 85 per cent of those brought to a police station, were non-nationals. A similar picture emerges from data on police activities during the previous weeks.

The judicial treatment of the offenders

Another factor contributing to the overrepresentation of non-nationals in the prison population is the length of sentences imposed on them, when compared to the sentences passed on Greek defendants for similar offences. Research conducted by Karydis (2010) into convictions for drug offences (trafficking) at the Felonies Court of Athens, in the period 2004 to 2006, found the penal treatment of offenders in similar cases to be extremely differentiated on the basis of ethnicity. The sample studied consisted of 767 convicted offenders – of whom 385 were Greeks (50.2%) and 382 were non-nationals (49.8%). In the 29 cases where life sentences were imposed, 24 of the offenders were foreigners. Where similar drug offences were compared – relating to the type and amounts of drugs involved – it was found that sentences imposed upon non-nationals were consistently higher (almost double) than those inflicted on Greeks. Apart from the obvious judicial bias against immigrant defendants, other factors also militated against them – poor knowledge of the language, poor legal representation, an inability to draw on 'reliable' witnesses for their defence, and so on.

Criminality, insecurity and penalty: trends and interactions

Crime trends, depicted in the media with exaggerated overtones that cause insecurity and fear, have a serious impact on state and public punitiveness (Panoussis 2011; Vidali 2012; Cheliotis and Xenakis 2011; Zarafonitou 2008; Zarafonitou 2011). According to Lazos (2012), the increase or decrease in crime-talk is inexorably bound to serious issues – for example, which types of crimes raise more concern and how they should be dealt with. The author criticises mainstream approaches which are selective, biased, and manipulative, as they feed conventional knowledge, presenting crime problems as the exclusive domain of socially dangerous classes who disturb or threaten public peace and order.

Recent official data show a considerable change not so much in quantitative as in qualitative terms: 'Reported street crime (drug trafficking, thefts and robberies) increased in certain urban areas where structural changes altered the profile of the population and the composition of the labour force and markets', (while) 'white collar and state corporate crimes became a normal practice in the relationship between the State, political parties and the private sector' (Vidali 2012: 163–5). Eurostat

Table 13.3 Crimes recorded by the police in Greece 2002–2008 (figures include penal code offences)

	2002	2003	2004	2005	2006	2007	2008
Total	441,138	441,839	405,627	455,952	463,750	423,422	417,391
Homicide	108	122	109	127	109	115	118
Violent crime	7,507	10,140	10,145	10,271	10,427	10,851	11,220
Robbery	2,131	2,320	2,400	2,383	2,598	2,845	3,097
Domestic burglary	31,805	31,181	26,489	30,207	32, 407	37,917	44,150
Motor vehicle theft	5,385	5,865	5,568	5,860	6,799	7,494	7,834
Drug trafficking	10,001	10,556	7,761	8,393	8,152	7,959	9,852

Source: c. Tavares and g. Thomas, population and social conditions, Eurostat statistics in focus 2010, 58/2010, European Union. Data selected by authors.

Note: Index (base year 2005 = 100) 2006: 102, 2007: 93, 2008: 92.

data show an increase of 26.8 per cent during the period 1995–2008, mainly attributed to drug trafficking (+236%) and robberies (+93%), or generally to property crimes (Zarafonitou 2011; Courakis 2005). In another study, the findings show

> a significant, but modest increase (27%) in the number of recorded crimes over a 20-year period ending in 1999, with a complex pattern of ups and downs over the intervening period, although the rate of recorded crime per person has increased only slightly [...] Crimes that have substantially increased in number are thefts, robberies and homicides, as well as serious and violent offences involving drugs, arms, trafficking in women, and counterfeiting. (Lambropoulou 2005: 217–20)

Police sources remarked that in 2011, in comparison to the previous year, there were variations in the frequency of specific recorded offences, with an increase for some and a decrease for others. These opposite trends were attributed to local and regional conditions and characteristics, while the increase consisted of 'crimes of survival' – petty property offences causing small loss or damage (Greek Police Headquarters Press Release, 11 March 2012). It is also important to note that, despite the sometimes large increase in specific crimes (thefts, robberies, drugs), police data show that increases are not even and continuous, that in some categories a decline

Table 13.4 General statistical table for inmates and sentences 2003–2012 (daily counts – reference date 1 January)

no year	2003	2004	2005	2006	2007	2008	2009	2010	2011	2012 Remarks (added)
1 Total number of detainees	8418	8726	8722	9964	10370	11645	11736	11364	12349	12479 (serious increase)
2 Number of pretrial detainees	2084	2570	2481	3104	3065	3045	3218	3541	4050	4254 (serious increase)
3 Number of foreign detainees	3858	3708	3704	4281	4695	5622	6078	6307	7210	7887 (more than double)
4 Number of female detainees	394	506	594	592	582	559	695	554	577	562 (serious increase)
5 Number of juvenile detainees	449	543	445	420	376	446	520	510	568	587 (serious increase)
6 Number of detainees for drug legislation violations	3386	3562	3465	4346	4640	4912	4937	4345	4303	4136 (increase)
7 Number of detainees sentenced to death	2	1	1	1	-	-	-	-	-	-
8 Number of detainees sentenced to life imprisonment	599	618	594	654	715	776	742	823	807	977 (serious increase)

9 Number of detainees sentenced to temporary confinement										
a) 5–10 years	1767	1642	1552	2000	2300	2720	2737	2594	2385	2511
b) 10–15 years	1214	1139	1220	1171	1333	1549	1671	1564	1584	1665
c) 15 years and more	944	898	989	1003	1041	1108	1109	1090	1173	(serious increase) 3100
10 Number of detainees sentenced to imprisonment										
a) Up to 6 months	211	249	359	223	125	316	182	260	261	290
b) 6 months – 1 year	271	313	300	287	257	301	254	229	222	252
c) 1–2 years	270	303	300	355	306	453	309	288	253	260 (stability or decline)
d) 2–5 years	842	854	839	1063	1102	1303	1310	765	701	727
11 Detainees for private debts	17	30	27	24	23	4	66	43	29	36
12 Guest detainees [for pending deportation procedures]	122	66	40	35	63	44	92	116	237	121

Source: Ministry of Justice, transparency and human rights http://www.ministryofjustice.gr (elaboration by authors).

is observed and that in some of the traditionally recorded categories of crimes (i.e. homicide, smuggling) crime rates follow a downward trend.

Eurostat and other data give a rather different picture: a decrease in serious crime in 2007 and 2008 in comparison to 2006 (peak), with 2005 taken as the base year. Total serious criminality in these years has also declined in comparison to the period 2002–2003, although specific, traditional criminal offences show an upward trend.

However, during all this period, as was also the case in the previous few years, a continuous rise in the prison population is observed, as shown in the Table 13.4 below.

The upward trend in some categories of police-recorded serious crime is concomitant with a substantial downward trend in convictions in the 1980s, the 1990s and the 2000s (Lambropoulou 2005; Cheliotis 2011). In any case, it does not correspond to the increase in the caseload of convicted and remand prisoners (a 65.6% increase from 1980 to 2006 in absolute numbers, and 43.2% as a rate per 100,000 inhabitants – see Cheliotis and Xenakis 2011). Despite the use of conversion and suspension of custodial sentences on the one hand, and conditional release on the other, the prison population is increasing, with both sentenced and remand inmates staying for longer periods in jail. In Greece the average stay in prison is the longest in the EU: between 1990 and 2006, a 'meteoric' rise was observed in the average time served by convicted inmates, from 5.1 months to 6.1 years.

Concluding remarks

Current criminality trends in Greece reflect the globalisation of the economy and the loss of a *gemeinschaft* type of society. These have brought more anonymity and heterogeneity, urbanisation and alienation, individualism and distrust – shaping in many respects the crime scene (Lambropoulou 2005; Spinellis and Spinellis 1999). Greece has been transformed into a host country for masses of migrants (Karydis 2011; Zarafonitou 2011) who are perceived as a threat to public order (Papanicolaou 2011). The market economy Greek-style has collapsed; some major institutions, in the context of a huge public debt and the Eurozone crisis, are increasingly de-legitimised; austerity/recession measures are demolishing the already weak welfare state, causing poverty and unemployment; finally, the lower middle classes face the 'fear of falling' – and its realisation (Young 2007). Crime is shaped and bred by these developments (Vidali 2012).

The rise of the prison population is the result of increased punitiveness on the part of the judiciary (coinciding with the application of more conservative penal policies), which relies on tougher legislations and greater use of custody in response to an increasingly anxious and punitive public opinion. Prison statistics and crime statistics are not clearly correlated: the former are determined by a growing number of longer sentences imposed on offenders, as well as a kind of 'recycling' into the penal system of a significant socially marginalised penal population.

As Koulouris (2009a) has noted, the international climate encourages both authoritarian and liberal penal policies. On one hand, there is a proliferation of zero tolerance, penal austerity, mass imprisonment, maximum security prisons, inhuman and degrading conditions in custody. On the other hand, efforts are being made to control the rise of the prison population, humanise conditions, respect prisoners' rights, make imprisonment meaningful, and expand the use of alternatives to custody. Penal policies in Greece reflect this contradictory international climate, in particular favouring more use of imprisonment and further restrictions on inmates' fundamental rights – while claiming the exact opposite.

Notes

1. For a full account of the prison history in Greece see Courakis 2009: 212–2, 236–51, 284–336 and Dimopoulos 2003: 610–731.
2. An early variant of community service, with convicted inmates working in shifts in various areas of the country for public works (mainly road construction). Inmates were also offered productive work for the reforestation of hills in the Athens area (1919–1920).
3. The Committee concerned was the Inter-Parliamentary Committee for the Examination of the penitentiary System of the country and the inmates' living conditions
4. For a detailed description of the currently (October 2012) existing non-custodial sentencing framework in Greece see http://www.euprobationproject.eu/national_detail.php?c=EL
5. For age groups and criminal responsibility see Pitsela 2011: 511–2.
6. Sentencing is meant as the judicial treatment of offenders at the point of choosing the individual penal measure which is decided to be imposed by the court and enforced by implementation authorities (prison and probation administration). It is one of the processes operating within the criminal justice system, which affects the use of penal sanctions, and, from this point of view, is an indicator or determinant of its punitiveness. Moreover, it reveals and is related to the scale of penal sanctions.
7. For a detailed presentation of legislative reforms and the use of parole see Cheliotis 2011: 571ff.

8. Established by L. 3772/2009.
9. Initially, at the beginning of the twenty-first century, it was planned that 20 new prisons would be built (2002). A few years later only six prisons under construction appeared in the Ministry of Justice building programme (2005) while, more recently, the number of new establishments referred to in the prison construction programme was seven (2006–2007). After the millennium six new prisons (Eleonas Detoxification Centre, Malandrino, Domokos, Trikala, Grevena and Eleonas Womens' Prison) have come into operation. For all these see Spinellis 2003: 1243ff.; Koulouris 2009: 14.

References

Aloskofis W. (2009) 'Inmates Social and Penal Status in Korydallos Prison: Differences between Greek Nationals and Foreigners', in Koulouris N. (ed.), *On Standby. Korydallos Prison. Function, Condition and Inmates Treatment* (Athens-Komotini: A.N. Sakkoulas Publ) 39–109 (in Greek).

Aloskofis W. (2012) 'Korydallos Custodial Institution Inmates Social Characteristics and Penal Status', *Statistical Data, Korydallos Custodial Institution* (Athens: Department of Justice) (in Greek).

Anagnostopoulos I. G. and Magliveras K. D. (2000) *Criminal Law in Greece* (The Hague, London, Boston/Athens: Kluwer Law International/Sakkoulas).

Bokos V., Koulouris N., Stathoulopoulou E., Tsironis G., Vidali S. and Zaphiropoulou E. (1992) 'Prisoner's Struggle, Governmental Manoeuvres and Social Inertia in the 90s: The Neutralization of Abolitionist Tendencies and the Intervention of Criminologists (The Greek case)', in *Chronicles of the Laboratory for Criminology and Forensic Psychiatry Democritus University of Thrace*, 5: 133–45.

Cavadino M. and Dignan J. (2007) *The Penal System: An Introduction* (London: Sage).

Cheliotis L. (2011) 'Prisons and Parole', in Cheliotis L. and Xenakis S. (eds), *Crime and Punishment in Contemporary Greece: International Comparative Perspectives* (Oxford: Peter Lang) 557–91.

Cheliotis L. and Xenakis S. (2011) 'Crime, Fear of Crime and Punitiveness', in Cheliotis L. and Xenakis S. (eds), *Crime and Punishment in Contemporary Greece. International Comparative Perspectives* (Oxford: Peter Lang) 1–43.

Coleman C. and Moynihan J. (1996) *Understanding Crime Data* (Buckingham: Open University Press).

Cook D. and Hudson B. (1993) 'Racism and Criminology: Concepts and Controversies', in D. Cook and B. Hudson (eds), *Racism and Criminology* (London: Sage) 1–27.

Courakis N.E. (2005) 'Crime in Greece Today', in Courakis N.E., *Criminological Horizons* (Athens-Komotini: A.N. Sakkoulas Publ) 3–17 (in Greek).

Courakis N.E. [contribution Koulouris N.] (2009) *Penal Repression Between Past and Future* (Athens-Thessaloniki: Sakkoula) (in Greek).

Dimopoulos Ch. (2003) *Prison. Historical and Architectural Approach* (Athens-Komotini: A.N. Sakkoulas Publ) (in Greek).

Karydis V. (1998) 'Criminality or Criminalization of Migrants in Greece? An Attempt at Synthesis', in Ruggiero V., South N. and Taylor I. (eds), *The New European Criminology* (London: Routledge) 350–67.

Karydis V. (2010) *Visions of Social Control in Greece. Moral Panics, Criminal Justice* (Athens-Komotini: A.N. Sakkoulas Publ) (in Greek).

Karydis V. (2011) 'Immigration and Crime', in Cheliotis L. and Xenakis S. (eds), *Visions of Social Control in Greece. Moral Panics, Criminal Justice* (Athens-Komotini: A.N. Sakkoulas Publ) 87–109.

Kosmatos K. (2010) 'Recent Revolts in Greek Prisons. Prisoners Demands and the Response of the Ministry of Justice', in Pitsela A. (ed.), *Criminology: Searching for Answers. Essays in Honour of Professor Stergios Alexiadis, Aristotle University of Thessaloniki* (Sakkoula: Athens-Thessaloniki) 500–15 (in Greek).

Koulouris N. (2009) *The Social (Re)integration of Prison* (Athens: Nomiki Vivliothiki) (in Greek).

Koulouris N. (2009a) 'Painless Containment of Inert Human Beings: A Mission for the Greek Prisons?', in Koulouris N. (ed.), *On standby. Korydallos Prison. Function, Condition and Inmates Treatment* (Athens-Komotini: A.N. Sakkoulas Publ) 11–37 (in Greek).

Lambropoulou E. (2000) 'The "End" of Correctional Policy and the Management of the Correctional Problem', in Courakis N.E. (ed.), *Criminal Policy II* (Athens-Komotini: A.N. Sakkoulas Publ) 163–86 (in Greek).

Lambropoulou, E . (2005) 'Crime, Criminal Justice and Criminology in Greece', *European Journal of Criminology*, 2 (2): 211–47.

Lazos G. (2012) 'The Rise in Criminality in Contemporary Greece', Thesis, 5 (120): 125–42 (in Greek).

Maguire M. (2007) 'Crime Data and Statistics', in Maguire M., Morgan R. and Reiner R. (eds), *The Oxford Handbook of Criminology* (Oxford: Oxford University Press) 241–301.

Nikolaides A. (2006) 'Mass Media and Prison: The November 1995 Korydallos Prison Revolt Case', in Koukoutsaki A. (ed.), *Images of Prison* (Athens: Patakis) 261–303 (in Greek).

Nikolakopoulos E. (2001) *The Sickly Democracy. Parties and Elections 1946–1967* (Athens: Patakis) (in Greek).

Nikolaou C. (2009) 'The "Least Successful" Citizen', in Koulouris N. (ed.), *The Sickly Democracy. Parties and Elections 1946–1967* (Athens: Patakis) 111–96.

Panoussis G. (2011) 'Media, Crime and Criminal Justice', in Cheliotis L. and Xenakis S. (eds), *Crime and Punishment in Contemporary Greece: International Comparative Perspectives* (Oxford: Peter Lang) 65–75.

Panoussis G. (2007) 'Corruption in Prisons', in Panoussis G., *Crime-producing and Crime-produced Risks* (Athens: Nomiki Vivliothiki) 347–82 (in Greek).

Papaioannou D. (2010) 'The Changes to the System of Penal Repression during 1985–2005', *Criminal Justice and Criminology*, 1: 20–3 (in Greek)

Papanicolaou G. (2011) *Transnational Policing and Sex Trafficking in Southeast Europe: Policing the Imperialist Chain* (Houndmills: Palgrave Macmillan).

Papantoniou A., Frangouli M. and Kalavanou A. (1998) *Illegal Migration and the Problem of Crime*, Research Report, CHER Project.

Pitsela A. (2011) 'Youth Justice and Probation', in Cheliotis L. and Xenakis S. (eds), *Crime and Punishment in Contemporary Greece: International Comparative Perspectives* (Oxford: Peter Lang) 505–27.

Sim J., Ruggiero V. and Ryan M. (1995) 'Punishment in Europe: Perceptions and Commonalities', in Ruggiero V., Ryan M. and Sim J. (eds), *Western European Penal Systems: A Critical Anatomy* (London: Sage) 1–23.

Spinellis C. D. (2003) 'Custodial Institutions in Greece', in Manganas A. (ed.), *Essays in Honour of Alice Yotopoulos-Marangopoulos*, (Athens/Bruxelles: Nomiki Vivliothiki / Bruylant) 1243–71 (in Greek).

Spinellis C. D., Angelopoulou K. and Koulouris N. (1996) 'Foreign Detainees in Greek Prisons: A New Challenge to the Guardians of Human Rights', in Matthews R. and Francis P. (eds), *Prisons 2000: An International Perspective on the Current State and Future of Imprisonment* (Houndmills: Macmillan Press) 163–78.

Spinellis D. and Spinellis C. D. (1999) *Criminal Justice Systems in Europe and North America* (Helsinki: European Institute for Crime Prevention and Control).

Tzannetakis T. (2006) 'Pathology of the current sanctions system of the Penal Code: Thoughts and proposals for its radical revision in the context of the draft for the new Penal Code', *Poinika Chronika*, 5 (46): 590–4 (in Greek).

Vidali S. (2012) 'Social Crime Prevention in Greece', in P. Hebberecht and E. Baillergeau (eds), *Social Crime Prevention in Late Modern Europe: A Comparative Perspective* (Brussels: Brussels University Press) 151–80.

Vidali S., Koulouris N., Gasparinatou M. and Konstantinou A. (2011) Greece, FREE Survey, Fundamental Rights Education in Europe, www.thefreeproject.com.

Young J. (2007) *The Vertigo of Late Modernity* (London: Sage).

Zarafonitou Ch. (2008) *Punitiveness: Modern Trends, Dimensions and Criminological Problematic* (Athens: Nomiki Vivliothiki) (in Greek).

Zarafonitou Ch. (2011) 'Fear of Crime in Contemporary Greece', *Criminology, Special Issue Fear of Crime: A Comparative Approach in the European Context*, 34: 50–63.

14
Conclusion

Vincenzo Ruggiero

There are some commonalities and divergences in the penal systems of the countries examined in this volume, and attempts to explicate both are fraught with difficulties.

Universal explanations, of course, are often presumptuous, as they presume to convey comprehensive knowledge while claiming to result from neutral, objective, analytical efforts. Therefore, if attempts to draw comparisons and general analyses of phenomena are less 'culture-free' than they purport to be (Nelken 2010), one had better clarify in what way they are, instead, 'culture-bound'. Abandoning the pretence of neutrality, national contexts might be invoked which explain differences, in our case, in penal policies. On the other hand, those who feel that their own national background fails to provide them with a distinct sense of identity have, perhaps, only one viable option: appealing to a set of principles which constitute a 'culture', a non-neutral orientation determining how they perceive and interpret social phenomena. The following is my own set of principles, making the considerations below 'biased' and 'culture-bound'.

In the choice of penal policies the principle of consequentialism is essential. This principle posits that human practices are just when they yield actual or expected consequences, thus making a measurable contribution to a precisely identifiable good (Michael 1992; Duff 2001). From this perspective, punishment as a human action is expected to produce good and reduce evil, and – as in classical utilitarianism – is aimed at increasing happiness while diminishing grief. The most obvious social good, for our purposes, is the prevention of criminal activity, the reduction of the actual harm caused by it and any actual or perceived fear associated with it. A related good is satisfaction for the victims – reparation of the damage inflicted and reassurance to society as a whole that the amount of harm produced will consequently decline.

This principle is also defined as 'opposition and incongruity', being opposed to, and incongruous with, retributive philosophies. These indicate that offenders are punished because they offend, not in an attempt to improve them (Kant); that they have a right to be punished, because by inflicting penalties we honour them as rational human beings (Hegel); and that punishment stems from the impossibility of disposing of our instincts of vengeance (Durkheim 1982). Such philosophies presuppose perfect societies, where offenders, by breaking the law, gain unfair advantage over law-abiding individuals. Hence, the requirement that they pay a debt to society (Ruggiero 2010). Considering that the large majority of conventional offenders are economically and politically excluded, the question could be posed what that debt is for.

The manifest and latent functions of social acts constitute the dual focus of sociological enquiry (Merton 1968). The second principle inspiring the analysis below is associated with the awareness of this duality. More specifically, it is a principle forged by scepticism towards the official, manifest effects of punishment – deterrence, rehabilitation and incapacitation – and shaped, rather, by an understanding of its latent functions – the manufacture and enhancement of criminal careers and the deliberate inflicting of pain.

Third, there is a principle of parsimony, stemming from the awareness of the dysfunctional nature of punishment. Fourth, there is the principle of collective responsibility, implying that crime – but also poverty and exclusion – are not the result of individual, rational, choice, but of social arrangements involving the collectivity as a whole. Finally, there is an analytical principle suggesting that only by collective, social dynamics may we achieve an appreciation of the harm caused by conventional crime – as compared to that caused by the crimes of the elite.

Adherence to this set of principles, and rejections of others, may provide a more illuminating framework than national context or identity for the analysis that follows.

Strong with the weak and weak with the strong

There are some uniform modalities in the treatment of migrants, nonnationals and ethnic minorities in the countries examined. The harsher punishments inflicted on these groups reveal a process of penal differentiation which has been occurring for decades in most developed countries. Migrants and minorities committing offences are more likely to be reported by victims and witnesses, they are more speedily charged and, when tried, more routinely, and more harshly, penalised. Similar uniformity, however, is found in the lack of penal responses against crimes committed by relatively powerful individuals and groups, referred to below with the comprehensive description of white collar offenders. Such commonalities need some qualification.

It has become by now a common practice to punish individuals who belong to specific groups because of an actuarial calculus indicating them as more likely to offend and re-offend. What is penalised, in most circumstances, is not their actual illegitimate conduct, but their social condition – which is deemed conducive to crime. In contexts in which the labour market offers scarce opportunities to migrants, penalties may be heavier due to the low expectations relating to their current and future participation in the productive process. In such cases, it is their 'indolence' and lack of participation in consumers' markets that are punished, inactivity being perceived as prone to the adoption of unpredictable conducts, and punishment being deemed an exclusionary measure from a crowded labour market. This preventative punishment, in brief, is aimed at preventing less crime than law-abiding behaviour which would come with work. We can assume, by contrast, that in countries where peripheral areas of employment are still available, punishment, whether more lenient or otherwise, will take on an 'educational' function: training the punished to accept peripheral jobs.

Turning to white collar crime, perception rather than its actual incidence plays a crucial role. Here, the similarity mentioned above is accompanied by diversity. In some national contexts this type of criminality is not only widespread, but also disturbingly visible, ostentatious, and – where it is no longer seen as repellent – signals its full assimilation into the national culture. In such contexts, a form of silent, complicit, legitimacy is granted. Here, white collar offenders display their illicit acts as 'propaganda deeds', a phrase belonging to the vocabulary of social movement theory, and they act indeed as a social movement, addressing messages to the general public with the intent of finding followers. In brief, those who offend try to persuade all to do the same. Imitation, in this sense, creates illicit conduct which snowballs from the elite down to the ordinary interactions of daily life. In such contexts, although the remark can be made that it is the judiciary which, through its independence, exposes white collar offenders and reveals the social harm they cause, the public spectacle of investigations and prosecutions seems to have little deterrent effect. On the contrary, it may act as an incitement to imitate.

In other contexts, where the judiciary is relatively more controlled by the executive, white collar illegality may be more difficult to detect and be exposed, or may just escape definitions of illegality, as the elite enjoys undeserved trust and is statutorily protected by secrecy. Here, a firewall of complicity, based on class origin, wealth and life style, does not allow extraneous groups to enter elitist circles, so that illegal conduct is, in a sense, monopolised by restricted enclaves who are reluctant to share proceedings with others.

Flexible bifurcation

More than an overall expansion of the penal state, which is perhaps happening in some countries, what is most noticeable is a discriminatory process, commonly described as *bifurcation*. This entails not only, as remarked above, leniency for the powerful and harshness for the powerless, but also separate treatment for distinct categories of offences. The situation, of course, varies according to the perception in the different countries of what constitutes major threats to social order and the reproduction of the status quo. Perceptions, on the other hand, are partly the result of media power, moral enterprise and anxiety brooding, all elements which end up drawing league tables of dangerousness, designating preventive priorities and correspondent degrees of stigmatisation and punishment. In this situation, the dangerousness of crime is no longer associated with the uncanny power of hidden offenders, but with the overt power of morality and anxiety entrepreneurs. Perhaps it is for this reason that paedophiles are seen as a major threat in one country and serial killers in others – drug traffickers here, rapists there. Serious crime, in this way, corresponds to the seriousness with which media agents and moral entrepreneurs take their job. In all instances, however, anxiety associated with economic, political and 'spiritual' difficulties is translated into fear of the other, and the other, whether actually dangerous or not, is subjected to differentiated penal treatment.

Notwithstanding these differences, we can observe in this respect some similarities. In most of the countries examined, the process of bifurcation sees some minor offenders being treated with relative leniency, often in open rehabilitative institutions, or through community penalties. Meanwhile, a core of serious or repeat offenders seems to bear the brunt of the penal system and the harshness of its punishments. Principles of social defence are applied against offenders perceived in specific national contexts as particularly dangerous, who are regarded as impervious to rehabilitation and must therefore be merely neutralised and incapacitated. But does this trend suggest that there is a gradual withering away of the penal system – or even a 'civilising' process affecting it – whereby only residual types of offenders are penalised? Two brief answers can be provided to this question.

The analysis of penal evolution may lead us to conclude that punishment is becoming less and less severe. This alleged decline of punitive harshness can be explained with the corresponding softening of mores taking place in societies, which are increasingly horrified by violence, and where cruelty elicits a growing sense of repugnance. This explanation, however, may be reversed. The more odious certain acts appear to us, the more we may feel legitimised to inflict pain on those who perform them (Durkhein 1982). In other words, our more developed altruism finds the idea of making others suffer repugnant – for the very same reason the crimes which inflict suffering will seem to us just as, or even more, abominable. Consequently, we will be tempted to react with harsher penalties.

Of course, there is a difference between gruesome public executions and incarceration, between suffocating reclusion and custody in a single room, with cold and hot water and a TV set. But does this indicate an objective reduction of the pain caused by imprisonment?

> I just do not know. Each form would have to be evaluated according to its own time, by those receiving the pain, in the framework of their usual life and other people's life, and in the light of what they saw as their sins. I do not see how a scale could be established. (Christie 1982: 9)

Law texts establish when punishments have to be inflicted, while judges decide how long they should last; neither examines their effects on bodies and minds – the suffering produced, how it feels. The belief in slow progressive humanisation accounts for the lack of this type of information (Hulsman 1986). Criticising the humanisation thesis, we may find the assessment of the qualitative aspects of punishment difficult. It is true that the application of the death penalty has been greatly reduced in recent centuries, and in normal times has been abolished in many countries. The same can be said of many forms of corporal punishment. It may also be true that some progress has been made in improving the regime in prison systems. Caution, nevertheless, is advisable when judging qualitative amelioration and humanisation. The amount of suffering incorporated in legal penalties cannot be measured on a scale of absolute values, because that amount consists of the difference between normal living conditions and the conditions experienced by those who are penalised. Because the prison system 'has always drawn its clientele mainly from the most disadvantaged sections of the population', conditions in prison will reflect the lowest standard of living experienced by this social sector. Now, as 'the living standards of those same sections have in Europe improved considerably in recent years', improvements inside prisons do not appear to have kept pace. The conclusion is that 'if this supposition is correct, then the degree of suffering from the penal sanction has in a sense increased' (ibid.: 64–5).

Returning to the issue of bifurcation, questions should be raised about how the lenient and harsh ends of the penal system are intimately connected. Particularly harsh punishment may represent a major tendency towards hard-core institutions performing pure 'legalised abduction', on the one hand, and institutions geared to community treatment, on the other. Bifurcation, however, may be only apparent, as the very same prisoners might experience both harsh and lenient punishment depending on their 'behavioural career' as prisoners. In this sense, bifurcation may not describe a characteristic trait of the prison system vis-à-vis two different types of offenders, but rather a dual possibility faced by all offenders. We are faced with a form of flexible bifurcation.

According to related critical analyses, it is inappropriate to draw a neat line between harshness and leniency, with the first characterising punishment for serious offenders and the second treatment of 'ordinary' offenders. Trends observed in many European countries indicate that the latter are met with increasing degrees of severity, even though they are punished in the 'community'. Disciplinary aspects – and the emphasis on surveillance – are becoming inescapable traits of 'alternative' penalties, to the point that the very survival of non-custodial alternatives could be put in danger if these traits were to disappear (Ruggiero et al. 1995).

The costs of injustice

In different parts of this volume hypotheses have been formulated around the nature and intensity of the penal system in relation to the different socio-economic arrangements prevailing in a specific context. Previous discussions on this topic have revolved around the particular punitiveness of systems in which neo-liberalism is prevalent as a philosophy, as well as a practical modality of governing conflict. Conversely, suggestions have been made that in contexts where models of coordinated, controlled economy prevail, and welfare performs an inclusive role, penal policies display a more lenient nature (Cavadino and Dignan 2006). These macro-economic analyses, related to penal systems, may lead to general conclusions which, while emphasising structural forces, do not take into account the 'variations in the institutional framework through which those forces are mediated' (Lacey 2008: 50). Also, they seem to assume that crime rates are the same in the countries analysed, offering no explanation of how more lenient systems, resulting from more participatory economic models, affect crime prevention rather than just responses to it (Nelken 2010). While these aspects deserve further analytical efforts, in an ideal agenda for future work the following might also find a place.

Welfare economies, as well as unfettered free market economies, need robust consensus and strong elites in order to deliver their doses of rewards and penalties. It is not easy to quantify the amount of support and contempt provided by citizens to the dominant groups in the political and the economic sphere, although we could hypothesise that these play a role in legitimising harsh or lenient penal systems. In a simple scheme of interpretation, we might suggest that 'strong' elites manage to penalise minor offenders thanks to the ideological support they enjoy among those who, while sharing the social conditions of offenders, manage not to offend. A form of competition among the disadvantaged may therefore determine the quantity and quality of punishment suffered by the losers. Criminals become unfair competitors, not of the rich but of the poor. Strong elites include the groups described above – who manage to hide their deviancy through class isolation, secrecy, and cultural and social barriers of different varieties. Where such elites rule, wealth polarisation is wider, success is highly rewarded and failure highly stigmatised. Income differences, in brief, determine the degree of coercion applicable to a society in order for those differences to be maintained.

Weak elites include political and economic agents, who are regularly exposed for their illegality and corrupt practices. Such elites may show a relatively lenient attitude towards the deviance of others, as a way of seeking support and complicity for their own. Mutual tolerance, rather than consensus, in this case, may determine the quantity and intensity of penal measures.

It could be suggested that even the costs of the penal system are linked to the type of elite – and the degree of wealth polarisation – in specific national contexts. Reform campaigners – basing their arguments on the 'costs' of imprisonment – appear to neglect that the elite to which they address their demands embraces a system of waste: where wealth is squandered, dilapidated and the elite itself is prone to destroy what it creates. This practice, as Bataille (1967) would remark, is a characteristic of ruling groups, disingenuously displaying a lack of interest in their riches while reproducing the conditions to acquire growing quantities of them. 'Waste' is a good investment if it sustains a penal system that defends privilege, and cannot be measured with the conventional rational calculus applied to common mathematical operations. The 'costs' of penal systems, in other words, have to be measured through the degree of income differences they are supposed to maintain or exacerbate. Where wealth polarisation is higher the costs of reproducing it through penal measures are consequently higher, nor will rational argumentations of a mathematical or monetary nature be heeded. These 'costs', therefore, are not those required for the prevention or punishment of crime, but for the reproduction of social injustice.

Extra-legem institutions

All organisations have official aims, on the one hand, and operative aims, on the other. Prisons *qua* organisations, and penal systems in general, pursue official, imaginary goals, such as re-integration, although re-integrative programmes have no objective possibility of being implemented. Practitioners working in such organisations may be convinced that they cannot do what their official mission indicates, but have to act as if they can (Carlen 2008). Prisons, in particular, can be identified as 'mock bureaucracies', which grow more powerful exactly because they disrespect their own official principles and mission. The official rhetoric presents them as essentially benevolent and accountable, while the grim and violent reality of their everyday functioning is lost among a number of imaginary elements. These are built on the fallacy that more prisons equals less conventional crime, that custody delivers redemption and rehabilitation, and that prison staff and fellow professionals believe in their mission to alter offenders' behaviour (Sim 2008). These imaginary elements, however, are constructed within a normative void which locates prisons in a typical extra-legem territory. These institutions seem to be impervious to change, and radical, as well as mild, changes in the political and legislative spheres are denied access beyond their walls. They possess their own 'operative legality' – made by internal rules, administrative decisions and discretionary provisions. Based on 'blank norms', the management of prison institutions is exempt from respecting legal frameworks and official guidelines. Derogation from general legal principles is regarded as indispensable, as prisons are deemed to be responding to constant emergencies and unpredictable crisis situations stemming during the course of their routine existence. Securing internal order, in brief, is the only concern – even if the maintenance of order requires acting outside or against the law (Wacquant 2012). The process of incarceration, in other words, supplements the illegal choice presumably embraced by prisoners with its own illegality, thus creating an intelligible cultural continuity between the realm of crime and that of punishment. Prisons, in brief, perpetuate the cognitive structure of offenders prior to imprisonment, so they are more than likely to re-offend after being released (Hockey 2012).

The chapters composing this book have highlighted the existence of unofficial punitive wings, the gap between officially granted rights and the rights actually enjoyed by prisoners, forms of bureaucratic coercion affecting regimes and treatment, overcrowding beyond legally acceptable limits, privileges and punitive measures applied outside a recognisable legal framework: in sum, a distant universe which reproduces itself despite, or perhaps because of, its illegality, lack of transparency and dysfunctional nature.

References

Bataille, G. (1967) *La part maudite* (Paris: Editions de Minuit).

Carlen, P. (ed.) (2008) *Imaginary Penalities* (Cullompton, Devon: Willan).

Cavadino, M . and Dignan, J . (2006) *Penal Systems: A Comparative Approach* (London: Sage).

Christie, N. (1982) *Limits to Pain* (Oxford: Martin Robertson).

Duff, R.A . (2001) *Punishment, Communication and Community* (Oxford: Oxford University Press).

Durkheim, E. (1982) 'Two Laws of Penal Evolution', in Gane, M. (ed.), *The Radical Sociology of Durkheim and Mauss* (London and New York: Routledge).

Hockey, D. (2012) 'Analytical Reflections on Time in Custody', *The Howard Journal of Criminal Justice*, 51 (1): 67–78.

Hulsman, L. (1986) 'Critical Criminology and the Concept of Crime', *Contemporary Crises*, 10 (1): 63–80.

Lacey, N. (2008) *The Prisoners' Dilemma: Political Economy and Punishment in Contemporary Democracies* (Cambridge: Cambridge University Press).

Merton, R. (1968) *Social Theory and Social Structure* (New York: The New Press).

Michael, M.A . (1992) 'Utilitarianism and Retributivism: What's the Difference?', *American Philosophical Quarterly*, 29: 173–82.

Nelken, D. (2010) *Comparative Criminal Justice* (London: Sage).

Ruggiero, V. (2010) *Penal Abolitionism* (Oxford: Oxford University Press).

Ruggiero, V., Ryan, M. and Sim, J . (eds) (1995) *Western European Penal Systems: A Critical Anatomy* (London: Sage).
Sim, J. (2008) 'Pain and Punishment: The Real and the Imaginary in Penal Institutions', in Carlen, P. (ed.), *Imaginary Penalities* (Cullompton, Devon: Willan).
Wacquant, L. (2012) 'The Prison is an Outlaw Institution', *The Howard Journal of Criminal Justice*, 52 (1): 1–15.

Index

Albrecht, H.-J., 146
alcohol programmes, 38
alternatives to custody, 261
  Bulgaria, 211–12
  France, 111–14
  Germany, 142–3, 144–5
  Greece, 271
  Ireland, 91–3
  Italy, 235, 240–2
  Netherlands, 17–19
  Poland, 185
  Russia, 165–6, 168–70
  Sweden, 37
anger-management programmes, 169
Anti-Social Behavior Order (ASBO),
  59, 62, 71, 80n11
anti-social behaviour, 59, 60, 62
anti-social families, 70
anti-terrorist legislation, 58–9, 66
assault, 118

bail, 64, 88–9, 91, 101
Beckett, Katherine, 26
Berlusconi, Silvio, 230, 231
bifurcation, 21, 46, 145, 230, 250,
  266, 272, 292–4
Black, Asian, and Minority Ethnic
  (BME) groups, 66
Bonnemaison, 119–20
Boone, Miranda, 15, 16
Boutellier, Hans, 26
broken society, 70
broken windows, 25
Bulgaria, 16
  alternatives to custody, 211–12
  corruption in, 212–13
  costs of incarceration, 212
  imprisonment rates, 208–10
  legal framework, 208
  organised crime, 213–18
  penal system, 206–25
  post-custodial measures, 210–11
  preventative programmes, 210–11

prisons, 207–8, 212–13
Roma, 219–22
burglary, 88, 116, 119, 121,
  222, 278
Buruma, Ybo, 16

California, 2
Cameron, David, 70, 75, 76
capitalist societies, 2–3
capital punishment, see death penalty
Catholic Church, 94–5
Cavadino, Michael, 2–4, 21, 132, 136,
  199, 271
charitable organisations, 95
Chechnya, 171, 176
children, 67–8, 91, 107, 173, 174, 271
citizens, safety of, 114–19
civilisation process, 42
civil rights, 146, 148, 247
cognitive behavioural therapy, 169
Cohen, Stanley, 27
collateral sentencing, 27
communism, 197–9
community organisations, 94–5
community policing model, 122
community safety, 25
community service, 17–19, 61, 91–2,
  112, 113, 143, 212, 271
comparative approach, to penal
  systems, 2–5
conditional release, 23, 143, 146, 241
consequentialism, 289–90
continental law system, 166
coordinated market economy, 137–8
Coornhert Liga, 15
corporal punishment, 293
corporatist states, 2, 132, 137–8
corruption, 212–13, 243, 266
court system
  Germany, 137
  Italy, 229–30
  Russia, 166
Crime and Disorder Act (UK), 59

crime prevention, 24–7, 210–11
  see also deterrence
  France, 120–2
  Netherlands, 24–7
crime rates, 74
crime statistics
  England and Wales, 74
  Greece, 279–84
  Poland, 195
  Spain, 259
crime victims, 43–4, 50, 143
criminalisation, 11, 28, 42, 47, 49,
    124, 139–42, 145, 149, 173, 223,
    232–3, 269, 272
criminal proceedings, Germany,
    140–2
criminals, 51–2
criminological research, 105
criminology, 196, 203n10
cross-country comparisons, 126, 199,
    289–97
Crouch, C., 76–7, 79
Cuchhi, Stefano, 231
curfews, 62

death penalty, 33, 62, 74, 119, 176,
    192, 270, 293
deaths in custody, 65
decriminalisation, 41, 42, 47, 142,
    145, 268
de-penalisation, 41
Detention and Training Order, 70
deterrence, 46, 53n12, 135, 158,
    272, 290
detoxification centres, 145
Dignan, James, 2–4, 21, 132, 136,
    199, 271
disadvantaged groups, 75, 140, 149,
    150n4
  see also ethnic minorities;
    immigrants/immigration
domestic violence, 194
Downes, David, 12–13, 14, 21, 29
DPP v. Murray, 98–9
drug issues, 2, 44
drug offences, 35–7, 118, 123, 145,
    193–4, 213, 233, 260, 280
drug programmes, 38
drug users, 2, 20, 148–9, 169, 230

drunk driving, 192–3
Dutch League for Penal Reform, 15

economic crimes, 40, 47, 213
economic crisis, 101, 161, 208, 221,
    261265, 269
education, 134–5, 200, 235–6, 240
electronic monitoring, 17, 19, 22, 62,
    92, 112, 143, 146, 170
elites, 75, 295–6
emergency culture, 246–7, 250
Engbersen, Godfried, 26
England and Wales
  crime rates, 74
  influence of private sector in, 71–4
  penal policy, 74–9
  penal system in, 58–85
  prison conditions in, 64–5
  prison population, 58–64
  prison system, 60–4, 71–4
  punitive pressures in, 74–8
  social composition of prisoners in,
    58–9
  targeting of marginalized in, 65–71
Esping-Andersen, G., 132
ethnic minorities, 19–20, 66, 170–2,
    219–22, 276–7, 278–9
European Commission for the
    Efficiency of Justice (CEPEJ), 125
European Convention on Human
    Rights (ECHR), 187
European Court of Human Rights
    (ECHR), 177
European Crime Survey, 74
European Union, 16
evidence-based practice, 13
exclusive policies, 26, 28
extra-legal institutions, 296–7

family, 3, 70
female prisoners, 68–70, 91, 97, 149,
    164, 166–8, 236–7
Files of Special Monitoring Inmates
    (FIES), 251
financial crime, 98–9, 108, 116, 227
  see also economic crimes
fines, 19, 33, 61, 92, 102, 105,
    112–13, 142, 166, 185, 186, 191,
    226, 241, 271

Finland, 195
Forced Return, 16
foreign nationals, 66, 140, 141,
    232–3, 260, 276–9
    see also immigrants/immigration
France
    alternatives to custody, 111–14
    detention rate, 113
    penal policy, 119–23
    penal system, 111–31
    politics, 119–21, 123–5
    public order and safety, 114–19
    sentencing policies, 123–4
    types of offences in, 114–19
    types of sanctions in, 111–14
Franco, Francisco, 245

G4S, 94
gangland crime, 100–1
    see also organised crime
Garland, David, 4, 10
gay, lesbian, bisexual and transgender
    (LGBT) people, 69
gentrification, 26
Germany
    alternatives to custody, 142–5
    court system, 137
    crime statistics, 134, 135, 139–40
    incarceration rate, 144
    institutional context, 136–9
    juvenile justice, 133–6
    law enforcement, 139–42
    penal system, 132–56
    prison population, 140–2
    prisons, 143–9
    privatisation in, 146
    professional practice, 136–9
    punitive tendencies in, 149–50
    social composition of prisoners in,
        141–2
    social policies, 137–8
globalisation, 6, 12
Greece
    alternatives to custody, 271
    crime trends, 279–84
    law enforcement, 278–9
    penal policy, 267–70
    penal reform in, 265, 270
    penal system, 265–86

    pentitentiary policies, 273–5
    politics, 265–4
    prison population, 273–7, 281, 284
    prisons, 269, 273–5
    prison staff, 277–8
    sentencing policies, 270–2
    social composition of prisoners in,
        276–7
    types of offences in, 279–84
Gulags, 158, 159, 160, 162, 166–7,
    170, 197

hate crimes, 171
Henderson, T. N.-Y., 106
Herbert, Steve, 26
homicide, 18, 88, 115, 118, 173–4,
    193, 219–21, 224n11, 279, 281
house arrest, 241, 242
humanisation thesis, 293
human rights, 50, 64, 148, 158, 159,
    173, 175–6, 187, 260
human trafficking, 260

immigrants/immigration, 16, 44–5,
    67, 77, 89, 99, 122, 140, 171–2,
    230, 231, 232–3, 278–9, 290–1
imprisonment rates, 2–4, 195
    Bulgaria, 208–10
    Germany, 144
    Greece, 274–5, 282–3
    Netherlands, 14–17
    Russia, 162
    Spain, 258
    Sweden, 33–4, 37, 41–3
impunity, 217–18
inclusive policies, 26, 28
Indeterminate Sentences for Public
    Protection (IPPs), 62
indeterminate sentencing, 62, 251–2
insecurity, 10–11, 25, 235
institutional detention, in
    Ireland, 107
intellectual freedom, 197–8
International Crime Victimisation
    Survey (ICVS), 74
Ireland
    accountability deficits in, 104–5
    advocacy groups, 95–7
    alternatives to custody, 91–3

Ireland – *continued*
  immigration to, 99
  moral panics, 99–101
  penal policy, 86–90, 101–8
  penal system in, 86–110
  politics, 100–1, 105–7
  post-custodial measures, 93
  prison population, 86–90, 97–9, 107
  prisons, 90–1, 103–5
  private sector involvement, 93–5
  social composition of prisoners in,
    87–9, 97–9
  types of offences in, 88
Islamophobia, 11
Italy
  alternatives to custody, 235, 240–2
  female prisoners in, 236–7
  penal system, 226–44
  phases of penal intervention,
    229–30
  populism, 230–2
  prison population, 227–8, 230
  prisons, 232–4, 237–8, 242
  privatisation in, 243
  rights of prisoners in, 238–40
  second republic, 230–2
  social composition of prisoners in,
    234–6

judicial activism, 124
juvenile delinquency, 132
juvenile justice, 133–6, 166, 173
juveniles, 67–8, 91, 107, 141, 164,
    174, 271

Khodorkovsky, Mikhael, 177
Konovalov, Alexander, 160

labour markets, 4, 6, 291
Lacey, Nicola, 3–5, 7n1, 137–8
law enforcement
  France, 117, 122–3, 125
  Germany, 139–42
  Greece, 278–9
  Netherlands, 15–16
  Russia, 166
leave awards, 241
liberal market economy, 137–8
liberal states, 2, 3

life imprisonment, 36–7, 88, 235,
    251–2
  mandatory, 62
Loader, L., 6–7

MacBride, Maud Gonne, 95–6
mandatory life sentences, 62
mandatory minimum sentencing,
    62, 166
marginalized populations, 65–71,
    136, 139, 149, 170–2, 219–22
market economy, 137–8
maximum security prisons, 248–9
McAuley, M., 166, 173–4
media, 43
mediation, 143
mega prisons, 248–9
mentally ill, 14, 28, 236
migrants, *see* immigrants/
    immigration
Mills, H., 4
minimum sentencing, 62, 145–6
minorities, 11, 66, 149, 171–2,
    219–22
Moerings, Martin, 15, 16
monitoring orders, 93
Monti, Mario, 243
moral panics, 99–101, 209, 230
Morgan, Rod, 73
Mubarek, Zahid, 65
multiculturalism, 11
murders, *see* homicide
Muslims, 11, 28, 58–9

national contexts, 5
National Offender Management
    Service (NOMS), 73
national security policy, 123
Neighbourhood Justice, 26
neoliberalism, 2, 3, 6, 75, 76, 78, 79,
    137, 199
neo-rehabilitative penal system, 73–4
Netherlands, 2, 9–32
  alternatives to custody, 17–19
  changes in, 9
  collateral sentencing, 27
  conditional release, 23
  crime, 10–11, 13
  penal policy in, 12–15

penal regimes in, 21–2
political context, 10–12
politics in, 12–15
post-custodial measures, 22–3
preventative programmes, 24–7
prison population, 14–17, 27–8
private sector involvement, 23–4
social composition of prisoners in,
    19–21
social context, 10–12
New Labour, 59, 70, 73, 75–6
non-custodial sanctions, 17–19, 37,
    61, 62, 91–3, 111–14, 141, 142–5,
    165–6, 168–70, 185, 211–12,
    240–2, 271
nuisance offences, 59

O'Donnell, I., 100, 105, 106
opportunity-oriented model, 147
organised crime, 100–1, 174, 212,
    213–18, 243, 266
O'Sullivan, E., 100
Others, 6, 11

pardons, 16, 37, 93, 229
parental responsibility, 70
parole, 13–14, 23, 34, 37–41, 62, 63
parsimony, 290
penal systems
    see also specific countries
    common sense approach to, 1–2
    comparative approach to, 2–5
    cross-country comparisons, 289–97
    interpretations of, 6–7
    national contexts, 5
    typologies of, 132–3, 199
penal-welfare complex, 26–7
penitentiary law, 228
Peyrefitte, Alain, 119
plea bargaining, 217–18
Poland
    alternatives to custody, 185
    crime statistics, 195
    criminal justice in, 192–5
    democratic transition in, 183–6
    imprisonment rates, 195
    intellectual freedom in, 197–8
    penal reform in, 185–6
    penal system, 183–204

prison population, 194–5
prisons, 186–91
types of offences in, 193–4
unemployment min, 200
political economy, 2–3
political prisoners, 245, 247–8, 266
politics
    France, 119–20, 121, 123, 124–5
    Greece, 265–4
    Ireland, 100–1, 105–7
    Netherlands, 10–15
    of punishment, 2
    Russia, 157–8
    Spain, 249–50
    Sweden, 41–2, 45–6
poor, 51–2, 59, 71, 75, 77, 97–8, 173
populism, 230–2
Portalaoise Prisoners' Union, 96
post-custodial measures, 210–11
    Ireland, 93
    Netherlands, 22–3
    Russia, 165–6
pre-crime behaviour, 25, 27
pre-deportation detention, 144, 148,
    150n3
preventative programmes, 24–7,
    210–11
    see also deterrence
preventive detention, 150n1
prisoners
    see also prison population
    disadvantaged groups, 69–71, 75,
        140, 149
    ethnic minorities, 19–20, 66,
        170–2, 219–22, 276–9
    female, 68–9, 70, 91, 97, 149, 164,
        166–8, 236–7
    foreign nationals, 66, 140, 141,
        232–3, 260, 276–9
    immigrants, 16, 44–5, 67, 77, 89,
        99, 122, 140, 171–2, 230–3,
        278–9, 290–1
    juveniles, 67–8, 91, 271
    political, 247–8, 266
    rehabilitation of, 147, 150, 167
    rights of, 148, 173, 176, 238–40,
        273–4
    work by, 239–40
prison population

prison population – *continued*
England and Wales, 58–64
Germany, 140, 141–2, 147–9
Greece, 273–7, 285
health conditions of, 148–9 Sweden
Ireland, 86–90, 97–9, 107
Italy, 227–8, 230, 234–6
LGBT people, 69
Netherlands, 14–17, 19–21, 27–8
Poland, 194–5
Russia, 162, 164, 166–8
social composition of, 19–21,
        40–1, 58–9, 87–9, 97–9, 141–2,
        234–6, 274–7
Spain, 252–60
Sweden, 40–1, 42
UK, 4
prisons, 296–7
alternatives to. *see* alternatives to
        custody
Bulgaria, 207–8, 212–13
conditions in, 103–4, 147–8, 161,
        187–91, 237–40, 260, 269, 278,
        293–4
costs of, 212
crime in, 212–13
England and Wales, 60–5, 71–4
Germany, 143–9
Greece, 269, 273–5
Ireland, 90–1, 103–5
Italy, 232–4, 237–8, 242
overcrowding, 65, 72, 92, 103–4,
        112, 113, 161, 187, 190, 202,
        227, 228, 231, 232–4, 242, 252,
        260
Poland, 186–91
privatisation of, 23–4, 71–4, 77–8,
        93–5, 146, 243
Russia, 161, 164
Spain, 248–9, 252–60
Sweden, 37–8
U.S., 2
violence and deaths in, 104, 242–3
working, 77
Prisons Act (Ireland), 94
prison staff, 277–8
Prison Study Group, 96
private security services, 121
privatisation

Germany, 146
Ireland, 93–5
Italy, 243
Netherlands, 23–4
United Kingdom, 71–4, 77–8
probation, 17, 23, 91–2, 112, 142–3,
        166, 169, 170, 185, 211–12, 241
property offences, 116–19, 145,
        194, 260
prostitution, 233
protection of persons order, 93
psychiatric hospitals, 145
public criminology, 6–7
public order, 114–19, 127
public-private partnerships, 24, 25
public prosecutors, 125, 127
Punishment Orders, 16–17
punitive city, 27
Pussy Riot, 157–8
Putin, Vladimir, 157–8, 170, 172

racial profiling, 140
racism, 7, 170–1
Radzinowicz, L., 7n2
rape, 118
Recidivism Assessment Scales
        (RISc), 20
recidivism rates, 13, 18, 19, 20, 21,
        23, 38–9, 47, 48, 70, 74, 77, 112,
        133–5, 146, 149, 150, 231, 234–5,
        251, 271
rehabilitation, 72, 73, 106, 144, 147,
        150, 167, 190, 234, 236, 241, 260
repeat offenders, 166
restorative justice, 26
retribution, 290
Riot Grrrl bands, 157–8, 179n1
robbery, 118, 277–9, 280
Roberts, 4
Roma community, 100, 194, 219–22,
        233
rule of law, 246, 261
Rumania, 16
Russia
alternatives to custody, 165–6,
        168–70
crime statistics, 173–4
imprisonment rates, 162, 164
minorities in, 170–2

penal policy, 175–7
penal reform in, 159–62, 175–7
penal system, 157–82
political culture, 157–8
post-custodial measures, 165–6
prisoners, 166–8
prison population, 162–5
prisons, 161, 164
sentencing policies, 158–9, 166
socio-economic context, 170–4
types of penal facilities in, 162–4
women prisoners in, 166–8
Russian Orthodox Church, 165
Rutte, Marc, 24
Ryan, Mick, 7b3, 58, 96

safety crimes, 71
safety of citizens, 114–19
Schengen Agreements, 247
Schinkel, Willem, 27
security assemblage, 25
semi-detention, 241
sentencing policies
   England and Wales, 62
   France, 111–14, 123–4
   Greece, 270–2
   Ireland, 89–90
   Russia, 158–9, 166
   Spain, 251–2
   Sweden, 35–7
serfdom, 199
sexism, 7
sexual offenses, 35–7, 61, 91, 93, 136,
   145, 146, 150, 194, 260
Shatter, Alan, 102
Sim, Joe, 58
Single Community Order, 62
slavery, 199
social context, 10–12, 170–4
social crime prevention, 120–1
social democratic states, 2, 3
social mediation workers, 122
social movements, 6–7
social penitentiary movement, 247–8
social policies, 6
social renewal, 26
social workers, 278
socio-economic context, 294–6
Solidarity, 183–4, 200–1

solitary confinement, 65
Soviet Union, 157, 160, 196–7
   see also Russia
Spain
   alternatives to custody, 261
   constitutional reform, 246
   democratic transition in, 245–6
   emergency culture, 250
   emergency culture in, 246–7
   penal reform in, 247–52
   penal system, 245–52
   politics, 249–50
   prison population, 252–60
   prisons, 248–9, 252–60
   sentencing policies, 251–2
   types of offences in, 259
Sparks, 6–7
street crime, 25, 71, 75, 278, 280
surveillance, 122–3
Suspended Sentence Order, 62
suspended sentences, 63, 112, 146,
   185, 265, 271
Sweden, 33–57
   alternatives to custody, 37
   crime victims in, 43–4
   drug issue in, 44
   immigrants in, 44–5
   imprisonment trends in, 33–4, 37,
      41–3
   media in, 43
   parole in, 37–41
   penal policy, 41–52
   politics, 41–2, 45–6
   sentencing policies in, 35–7
   social composition of prisoners in,
      40–1
   treatment programmes in, 37–41

targeted governance, 150
terrorism, 11, 14, 21–2, 66, 119
theft, 118, 119
Tonry, M. H., 74
traffic offences, 113
transcarceration, 16
Traveller community, 99
treatment programmes, 37–41
12-step programmes, 38

underemployment, 6

unemployment, 6, 20, 73, 97, 200
United Kingdom
    see also England and Wales
    penal system, 58–80
    prison population, 4
    private sector involvement in,
        71–4, 77–8
United Nations Committee for
    the Elimination of Racial
    Discrimination
    (UNCERD), 170
United States, prison system in, 2
urban policy, 122–3

Valdés, Carlos García, 248
van de Bunt, Henk, 26
van der Laan, Peter, 17–18
van der Leun, Joanne, 12
van der Woude, Maartje, 12
van Gogh, Theo, 11
van Swaaningen, René, 12–13, 26
Verhagen, Jos, 20
victimless crime, 118, 123
victim-offender mediation, 143
violence, in prisons, 104, 232–3
violent offences, 35–7, 51, 61,
    115–16, 118, 136, 145, 146, 150,
    171, 173–4, 250–1

voluntary organisations, Ireland,
    94–5
von Liszt, Franz, 135

Wales, *see* England and Wales
wealth disparities, 295–6
welfare sanction, 59, 70–1, 76
welfare state, 5, 7n2, 26, 106, 132,
    138, 200, 269, 284, 295
white collar crime, 98–9, 108, 227,
    291–2
    see also economic crimes
Winterdyke, 132
women, 20–1, 68–9, 70, 91, 97, 107,
    140, 141, 149, 164, 166–8, 172–3,
    236–7
Women Prisoners Defence League,
    95–6
working prisons, 77
Working Prisons Programme, 73

xenophobia, 230

youth, 67–8, 136, 140, 141, 173, 174
youth correction facilities, 271
Youth Rehabilition Order, 80n10

zero-tolerance policing, 25

Printed in Great Britain
by Amazon